European Weapons and Warfare
1618 - 1648

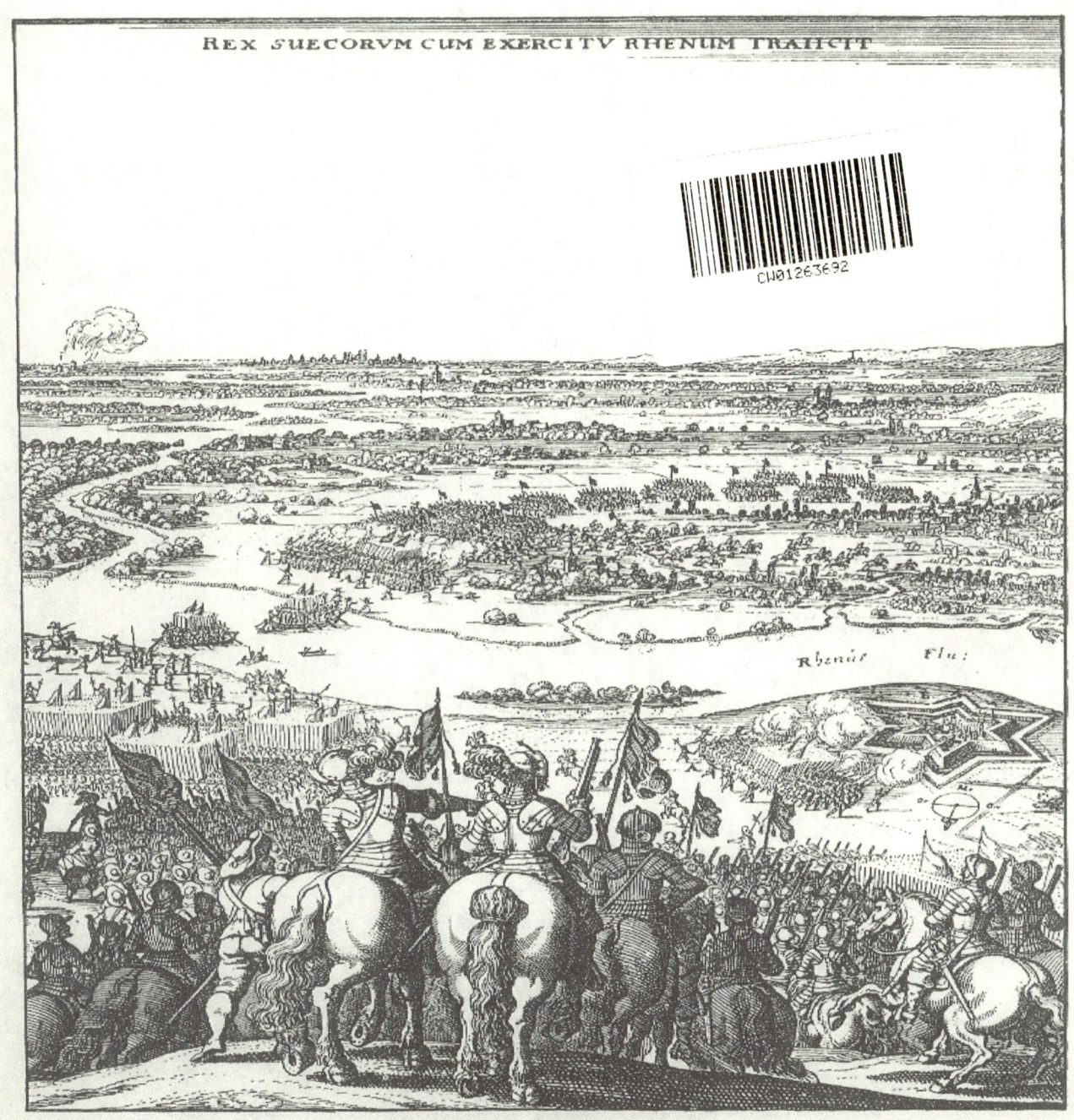

REX SUECORVM CUM EXERCITV RHENUM TRAIICIT

Rhenus   Flu:

CW01263692

By
Eduard Wagner

Eduard Wagner

Winged Hussar Publishing edition edited by Vincent W. Rospond
ISBN 978-0-9889532-5-3
Library of Congress Control Number 2014953326
Point Pleasant, NJ
Cover design by Mark Owen. Cover Art by Peter Dennis (courtesy of Warlord Games Ltd)

For more information on Winged Hussar Publishing, LLC Visit us at:
https://www.Wingedhussarpublishing.com
Follow our news at:
Twitter: WingHusPubLLC
Facebook at Winged Hussar Publishing LLC

To John, because he kept asking me for this book

Contents

CHRONICLE OF THE THIRTY YEARS' WAR
BOHEMIAN WAR 1618-1620

1618, May 23 – Insurrection of Bohemian Estates, government passing into the hands of 30 Directors.

1618, August – Imperial troops commanded by Bucquoy and Dampierre invading Bohemia to suppress the insurrection.

1618, November 21 – Gen. Ernst von Mansfeld in the pay of the Bohemian Estates taking Pilsen (Western Bohemia).

1619, March 20 – Death of Emperor Matthias, the vacant throne occupied by Ferdinand II.

1619, May – Czech Estates' troops under the command of gen. Thurn entering Moravia.

1619, June – Czech Estates' troops commanded by Thurn at Vienna.

1619, June 16 – Mansfeld defeated by Bucquoy at Zablat (Southern Bohemia).

1619, July 5 – Dampierre defeated by the Moravian Estates at Dolní Věstonice (Southern Moravia).

1619, August 26 – Elector Frederick V of the Palatinate elected Czech King.

1619, October 8 – Maximilian of Bavaria reaching an agreement with Ferdinand II to join the fight against the Estates' insurrection.

1619, November – December- Czech Estates' army under Thurn again at Vienna.

1620, September – Joint offensive of the Imperial and Catholic League armies (under the command of Maximilian of Bavaria and Johann Tserclaes von Tilly) against the Estates. The troops of the Estates retreating into Bohemia.

1620, November 8 – The Estates and their troops defeated at their White Mountain near Prague, Frederick of the Palatinate fleeing from Bohemia.

1621, June 21- 21 representatives of the Estates beheaded in Prague.

PALATINE WAR 1621-1623

1621, July 28 – John George of Krnov defeating the Imperials at Neutitschein (Moravia) and proceeding with his troops to Upper Hungary to join Gabor Bethlen of Transylvania.

1622, January – Conclusion of the so-called Pressburg Peace between Gabor Bethlen and Ferdinand II.

1622, April 27 – Mandfeld in the pay of Frederick V of the Palatinate defeating Tilly at Wiesloch (Baden-Heidelberg).

1622, May 6 – Tilly defeating the Protestant Estates' army (George Frederick of Baden-Durlach) at Wimpfen (Hesse).

1622, June 20 – Tilly defeating the Protestant Estates (Christian of Brunswick) at Höchst (near Mainz). 1623, August 6 – Tilly invading the northwestern part of the Empire and defeating the Protestant Estates (Christian of Brunswick) at Stadtlohn (Prussia).

DANISH WAR 1625-1629

1625, July 25- To become independent of Bavaria's support the Emperor decided to raise an army of his own with Wallenstein at Dessau (Duchy of Anhalt).

1625, August 27 – Tilly and Wallenstein defeating the Danish army of King Christian IV of Denmark at Lutter am Barenberg.

1626, December 23 – Ferdinand II concluding a new peace agreement with Gabor Bethlen to free his forces for campaigns in the north.

1627, September I – Wallenstein and Tilly joining their forces against the peasants revolting at Lauenburg (Pomerania).

1627, November – Wallenstein's army gaining control of Lower Pomerania and Rügen Island.

1628, May 23 – Wallenstein's laying siege of Stralsund (Mecklenburg)

1628, August 3 – Having not succeeded in securing the support of Tilly's troops, Wallenstein's army lays off the siege of Stralsund.

1628m September 2 – Part of Wallenstein's army defeating the Danes (Christian IV) at Wollgast (Baltic Coast).

1629, March 6 – Ferdinand II issuing his Edict of Restituion ordering that all ecclesiastical property confiscated after the Peace of Augsburg (1555) be returned to the Catholic Church.

1629, May 22 – Peace concluded between Ferdinand II and Christian IV

1630 – Catholic Electors meeting at Electoral Diet at Regensburg; at the instigation of the Electors, especially Maximilian of Bavaria, Ferdinand II stripping Wallenstein of his post of Supreme Commander (August 13, 1630).

SWEDISH WAR 1630-1635

1630, June 24 – The Swedish army (Gustavus Adolphus) landing in Pomerania.

1631, May 20 – Tilly took one of the centers of Protestantism, Magdeburg, his troops massacring the population and razing a greater part of the houses by fire.

1631, September 17 – The Swedish troops Gustavus Adolphus) and the Saxons (Hans Georg von Arnim) beating Tilly at Breitenfeld near Leipzig.

1631, November 15 – The Saxons (Arnim) invading Bohemia and occupying Prague.

1631, December – Wallenstein accepting the Emperor's offer to raise a new strong army for him.

1632, beginning of the year – The Swedes (Gustavus Adolpus) gradually gaining control of the southwestern part of the empire.

1632, April 4-14 – Battle between the Swedes (Gustavus Adolphus) and Tilly's troops, with the Swedes effecting a forced crossing of the river Lech near Rain.

1632, - The Swedes under Gustavus taking Augusburg and returning to the central regions of the Empire.

1632, May – Wallenstein's new army driving the Saxons (Arnim) from Bohemia.

1632, September 3 – The Swedish army (Gustavus Aldolphus) assaulting futilely Wallenstein's army protected by their field fortification at the Zirndorf Castle near Nuremberg.

1632, November 16 – Gustavus dying in action in the relatively indecisive Battle of Lützen, with the Supreme Command passing into the hands of Bernhard of Saxe-Weimar.

1633, October 20 – Wallenstein defeating the Swedes (Thurn) at Steinau a.d. Oder (Silesia).

1633, November 14 – The Swedish troops (Bernhard of Saxe-Weimar) gaining the free city of Regensburg and some other towns in the southwestern part of the Empire.

1633 – Wallenstein negotiating secretly with representatives of the anti-Imperial coalition.

1634, January 24 – Wallenstein stripped of his supreme command by secret order of Ferdinand II and replaced by Ferdinand III.

1634, February 25- Wallenstein and part of his entourage murdered in Eger (Western Bohemia).

1634, May 13 – The Emperor's defeat at Liegnitz causing the subsequent loss of Prussian Silesia.

1634, September 6 – The Imperials (Ferdinand III and Gallas) together with the Bavarians (Johann von Werth) defeating the Swedes (Hornand Bernhard of Saxe-Weimar) at Nördlingen (Bavaria).

1635, May 30 – The Peace of Prague concluded between the Emperor and the Elector of Saxony

FRENCH AND SWEDISH WAR 1635-1648

1635, April 28 – A French-Swedish alliance concluded with Richelieu acting as a mediator in the Truce of Stuhmdorf which extended the truce between the Swedes and the Poles allowing the Swedes to concentrate their troops for military campaigns in Germany.

1635, November 1 – Swedish army victorious at Dömitz (Mecklenburg).

1636, October 4 – The Swedish troops under command of Johan Banér beating the Imperial and Saxonian armies (Melchio von Hatzfeld) at Wittstock (Prussia).

1636 – Banér attempting to take Prague.

1637 – Death of Ferdinand II and succession of his son Ferdinand III.

1638, February 20 – Bernhard of Saxe-Weimar in French pay defeating the Imperials at Rheinfelden near Basle.

1640- The Imperial Diet in session at Regensburg.

1641 – The Diet at Regensburg dissolved due to the rapid advance of the Swedish troops (Banér) to Regensburg.

1642 – The Swedes under the command of Lennart Torstensson invading Bohemia and Moravia.

1642, June 6 – Torstensson beating Ottavio Piccolomini at Schweidnitz (Prussian Silesia).

1642, November 2 – The Swedes under Torstensson leaving Bohemia and advancing into Saxonia, beating the Imperials (Archduke Leopold Wilhelm and Piccolomini) at Breitenfeld near Leipzig.

1642- French troops entering the central European theatre to support the Swedish armies.

1643 – The Danes re-entering the war, this time as allies of the Emperor (Swedish-Danish War).

1643, May 5 – The French armies (Mercy) defeated by the Imperials (Werth) at Tuttlingen (Baden-Württemberg).

1645, February 23 – Torstensson's troops beating the Imperial (Götz) at Jankau (Southern Bohemia).

1645, August 3 – The French under the command of Prince de Condé defeating the Bavarian army at Allerheim (Bavaria).

1645, August 23 – The Peace of Brösembro between the Danes and the Swedes allowing the latter to free their hands for the final sweep-up operations.

1646 – The Swedes and the French in Bavaria.

1647 – Maximilian of Bavaria forced to conclude peace with Sweden and France.

1647, June – The Swedes under Wrangel taking Eger (Western Bohemia)

1647, August 25 – Further advancement of the Swedish troops checked by the Imperials (Götz) at Triebl (Western Bohemia).

1648, May 16 – Victory of the joint French-Swedish armies (Turenne and Wrangel) over the Bavarians and the Imperials at Augsburg.

1648, July-October – The Swedes (Königsmark and Wittenberg) at Prague.

1648, October 24 – Conclusion of peace negotiations started back in 1645. Peace between Ferdinand III and France concluded in Münster and with Sweden in Osnabrück.

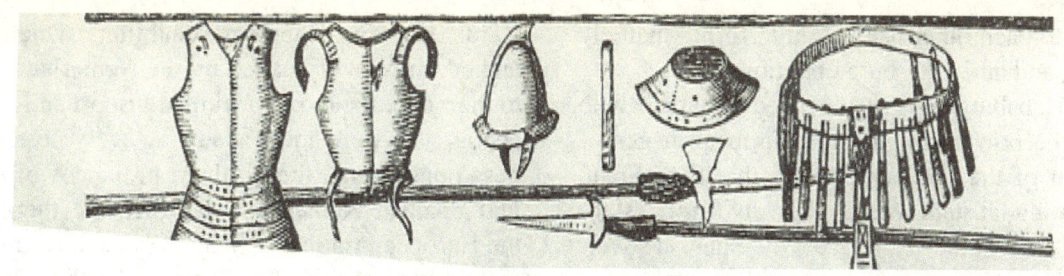

INTRODUCTION

The struggle for power in Europe and overseas during the 16th and the first half of the 17th centuries encompassed the entire European continent. At stake were the classic political and power interests, and the question of whether Church or state should exercise dominant power. Fierce struggles were waged over the control of sea routes and world markets. New colonial empires were being created and the period was characterized by the growth of new states striving to gain greater living space for their far-reaching business and trade activities.

The period ranks among the most distinctive historical eras. The old society was rapidly losing a great number of its traits and new phenomena characteristic of a new age in the development of human society began to assume importance.

Great centralistic absolutist feudal monarchies were being created and consolidated. On the one hand they were fighting desperately with those who advocated the ancient privileges of the estates, but on the other hand they viewed belligerently the new type of state that was just being born, the republic, which was being established at the time in the United Provinces of the Netherlands.

The surviving guild system was gradually being replaced with more progressive and often state-sponsored manufacturing organizations that could match better the need for a rapid increase in production and at the same time were better suited to the newly asserted economic policy of mercantilism. In connection with the development of trade with the new colonies overseas, the importance of the Mediterranean trade market and of the German Hanseatic cities was gradually vanishing, while new trade and finance centers were being established on the North Sea coast with the cities of the northern Dutch provinces coming rapidly to the fore. Great political power was also being concentrated in the hands of the newly established trade companies, e.g. the East India Company.

As a result of all these changes new European powers entered the battlefield to fight for the control of the European and world markets. On the ideological plane the struggle took the form of a clash between the ideas of the Catholic faith representing the efforts to establish the centralist absolutist monarchies, and the intellectual world of the Protestants – both of the Lutheran and the Calvinist denominations – who fought to defend the privileges of the estates against the encroaching oppression by the absolutist elements of society.

The struggle that the new had to wage against the old was expressed in a series of wars, armed conflicts, revolutions, and uprisings. For the sovereigns and other representatives of state power it was an era of diplomacy extending far beyond the limits of the European continent. It was an era of political coalitions and military treaties, the sovereigns enforcing their interests through the leverage of huge mercenary armies which had just begun to be of great importance than the surviving land reserves of the estates.

Yet the duty to support these great armies had to be borne by the common populace. The ever increasing volume and number of levies and taxes together with the increasing infringements of personal freedom led to many popular uprisings and armed revolts. The grave situation of the people was even further aggravated by the havoc played by the mercenary troops who took to plunder, looting towns and villages whenever their pay was delayed.

At the turn of the 16th and 17th centuries internal conditions in individual European countries as well as their mutual relations further deteriorated. Thus the seed of a great power conflict was sown that was to be reaped later during the first half of the 17th century.

The origins of this conflict that was to ravish the entire European continent can be traced as far back as the very beginning of the 16th century when two political blocs hostile to each other had begun to form – namely the Habsburg and anti-Habsburg coalitions.

The Habsburg bloc was headed by Spain who had entered the power struggle for European hegemony at the turn of the 16th century. By that time Spain was already a feudal state with a relatively firmly established central state authority. In 1519 the Spanish sovereign Charles V had become the German Emperor and in 1530 the Holy Roman Emperor, and with this extension of her power, Spain reached the height of her bloom in the period between 1530 and 1556. The basis for this great increase in Spanish political activity was the influx of silver from her overseas colonies that filled the state treasury. The Spanish mercenary army with its well trained and well armed infantry as its most essential service was at the time the best and strongest army in Europe. Although Spanish political ambitions later proved to be beyond the means of the state treasury, Spain remained the leader of the Habsburg coalition until the outbreak of the Thirty Years' War.

The interests of the other major member of this coalition, the Habsburg monarchy of Central Europe, were concentrated throughout the entire 16th and early 17th century on three different struggles: against the Ottoman Empire, against the internal opposition of the estates, and after the sovereign of the Habsburg monarchy, Ferdinand I, had become the Holy Roman Emperor in 1556, against the Protestant estates of the individual German states as well.

An important ally of the coalition, especially after the beginning of the 17th century, was Maximilian I, Duke of Bavaria, although his particular reason for joining the coalition was an attempt to use the current political situation to strengthen his own power at the cost of the Habsburg. In the east the Spanish and Austrian Habsburg depended on Lithuania and Poland, whom they had assisted with money and troops in their intervention against Russia.

The most important rival of the Habsburgs, especially the Spanish branch, was France. She wanted to enlarge her territory at the expense of the Spaniards, pushing the borders down to the Pyrenees in the southwest and up to the Rhine in the north-east. However France remained excluded from European politics for a long time because of immense internal problems stemming from the conflict between the Catholics and the Huguenots.

From the second half of the 16th century onwards the anti-Habsburg coalition, which always lacked unity, was headed by the Netherlands. Owing to their command of maritime transport and their merchants who were adept at seizing every possible business opportunity, the northern provinces of the original Spanish Netherlands had become the centre of the European trade and finance system. And since the mercantile system of the Spanish Habsburg monarchy had become an obstacle to further development of manufacture and trade in these provinces, isolated actions by frustrated tradesmen in the area finally grew into an open uprising of all classes against the feudal oppression by the Habsburg. This armed uprising is generally known as the Dutch Bourgeois Revolution (1566-1609).

The military campaigns of this conflict, in which an outstanding role had been played by the great Dutch military reformer Maurice of Orange, provided a great impetus for the future development of the military arts, especially in the field of ordnance improvement and troop organization and enlistment. Further improvement of tactics and greater co-operation between the individual services originated in this period and greatly influenced the further development of the military arts throughout the world.

During the struggle of the northern Dutch provinces against Spain, England sided with the anti-Habsburg coalition in an attempt to prevent the north German coast from being occupied by the Spanish Habsburgs. Their motive in this was that such an action on the part of Spain might endanger the development of English overseas trade.

Under the influence of the Dutch revolution the German Protestant states formed another anti-Habsburg coalition during this period.

In 1608 the so-called Union was set up uniting the dukes of the southern and western German states, and headed by the Calvinist oriented Frederick, Elector of the Palatinate. However, the Elector of Saxony did not join in. on the initiative of Maximilian, Duke of Bavaria, the Catholic estates formed the Catholic League in 1609 as a countermeasure against the Union. An experienced mercenary army general, Tilly, was placed in the supreme command of the League armies. Thus at the beginning of the 17th century, Germany became the main focus of a war crisis affecting most of Europe. It became clear that the age-old struggle of the two main rival forces, aggravated further by sharp international conflicts, had finally come to a head-on clash.

At the same time a fierce contest for the hegemony of the Baltic area had been waged for some time preciously. The struggle had opened in 1557 with the so-called Livonian Wars, with Russia attempting to gain access to the Baltic Sea. Owing to the united intervention of Denmark Lithuania, Poland, and Sweden the Livonian Wars had grown into a long drawn out armed conflict ending with the dismemberment of the Livonian territory but with no single party gaining the desired hegemony. Once Russia had been pushed back into the interior, the long years of struggle for the control of the Baltic coast ended in a war between the former allies, the Swedish-Polish War (1621-1629). Sweden emerged victorious and was by then recognized as the strongest country of the Baltic area. To a great extent this was the work of the Swedish king Gustavus II Adolphus Vasa who personally built up a mighty, well trained and well armed army. The wars also saw the blossoming of the military arts of the Swedish troops who after 1630 became one of the decisive factors of the European armed power struggle, the Thirty Years' War.

The War was the culmination of the prolonged political crisis that had seized the whole of Europe, and was a contributing factor in the collapse of the feudal system, a process that had been started by the Dutch bourgeois revolution.

The War opened with the revolt of the Czech estates against the Habsburgs in 1618-1620, the outcome of the long conflict between the Czech estate opposition and the court claque of the Catholic nobility who were supporting the Habsburg policy. However, the revolt of the Czech estates was doomed to fail since it remained isolated and idi not transform into a popular anti-Habsburg movement. Thus the Catholic League armies were able to defeat the mercenaries in the pay of the estates at the Battle of White Mountain in 1620.

Once the Czech estates had been defeated, the military action moved to southern Germany, especially into the Upper Rhineland and the Palatinate. Thus period of the Thirty Years' War became to be known as the Palatine War (1621-1623) and ended with the occupation of both the Palatinates (Upper and Rhenish) by Spanish and Bavarian troops. Just as the rising of the Czech estates before it, the Palatine War did not grow into an all-European conflict, although it

changed the balance of power in Germany. Then at the end of 1625 a new anti-Habsburg coalition was formed. It was led by the Danish king Christian IV who invaded the north-western corner of Germany and thus opened yet another stage of the Thirty Years' War called the Danish War (1625-1629). However, the German protestant dukes whose support Christian had been banking on did not come forth and so the Danish troops were in the end defeated by the Bavarian army of General Tilly and the Imperial army of Albrecht of Wallenstein. After the defeat of his troops at Lutter in 1626 the Danish king was forced to retreat back into his own territory. The Bavarian and Imperial troops remained lying close to the Baltic Sea coast to prevent the expected Swedish invasion of German territory.

It was characteristic of the period that mercenary military activities were gradually growing from mere military craft into real military enterprise. The greatest military entrepreneur of the period was the Imperial General Albrecht Wenzel Eusebius of Wallenstein, a Czech nobleman by birth, whose troops controlled Mecklenburg, Schleswig, Holstein and Jutland and partially also Brandenburg and Pomerania in the late 1620s. However, in 1630 at the insistence of the Imperial estates Wallenstein was dismissed from the Imperial services and his army was disbanded.

This move unintentionally cleared the field for Sweden's entry into the Thirty Years' War. Once Sweden had become involved in military campaigns, another stage of the War started, known as the Swedish War (1630-1635). This was characterized by military and political activity of the Swedes within the camp of the Habsburgs' adversaries. The French and Russian diplomatic and financial assistance enabled the economically strong Swedish state to engage in a victorious campaign, sweeping through the entire German territory and scoring several great victories, e.g. at Breitenfeld in 1631, and Lützen in 1632. Although the Swedes were defeated at Nordlingen in 1634, they still remained an important military factor in the European theatre of war.

The last period of the Thirty Years' War started when France entered the War as one of the important European powers, with her strong armies commanded by Prince Condé and Turenne. This fourth and last stage of the Thirty Years' War is known as the French and Swedish War (1635-1648). The Franco-Swedish alliance concluded in 1635 became the cornerstone of the anti-Habsburg coalition camp. At the same time

France became also an ally of the Dutch in their struggle against Spain. Richelieu, the first minister to the French king, arranged the extension of the truce between the Swedes and the Poles and thus helped the Swedish army to disengage and subsequently to stage military action in German. At the beginning the French were fighting the Spaniards close to French territory but after 1638 when France had declared war against Ferdinand III, and especially after the death of Bernhard of Saxe-Weimar who had become the head of the anti-Habsburg coalition on Gustavus II's death, she waged campaigns also in south-western Germany.

However, although the conflict had become even deeper, the end of the war was nowhere in sight. It dragged on, but military actions were being gradually curtailed and the main reason for operations of huge armies was nothing but looting. Poor supply system force the troops to be constantly on the move, constantly entering new areas. The increasing economic exhaustion of both sides and fear of social unrest led finally to discussions on suspension of hostilities. By the time the so-called Peace of Westphalia had been concluded in 1648, all hopes for unification of Germany were gone, although the Habsburg plans for supremacy in Europe also collapsed totally.

This was the end of the war that had lasted thirty years and had been started with a single aim: to gain hegemony in Central Europe. Greatest gains gad been won by France and Sweden who-especially the former—became the most important factors in post-war politics. On the other hand the Peace of Westphalia enabled the Habsburg to shape their Australian, Czech, and Hungarian lands into a strict absolutist state.

The Thirty Years' War had inflicted enormous economic loss on all belligerent countries and the lands that had had to provide supplies for the troops. The population had dropped, trade connections had been disrupted, crafts crippled and the countryside devastated by the never-ending passage of troops.

The experience gained from the war led to some fundamental changes in the internal political situation of European countries. Centralization in the absolutist monarchies became even more severe and mercenary armies firmly subjected to the state. The new social class, the bourgeoisie, was slowly penetrating political life. A new era in the history of mankind started, an epoch that had been opened with the English Revolution of 1640-1660. But that is already the next chapter of world history.

Troop Hiring System

Whenever a sovereign of the 16th and early 17th centuries intended to wage a campaign he hired either directly or through a go-between on entrepreneur who took responsibility for raising, arming and supplying an army. The entrepreneur was paid for services and rendered. Albrecht Wenzel Eusebius of Wallenstein (1583 – 1634) was contracted through Count Questenberg to mount military operations on behalf of the Emperor Ferdinand II (1578 – 1637) in the Thirty Years' War. However, the function of the sovereign as well as of the supreme war lord were sometimes united in one person, as in the case of the Swedish King Gustavus II Adolphus (1594 – 1632).

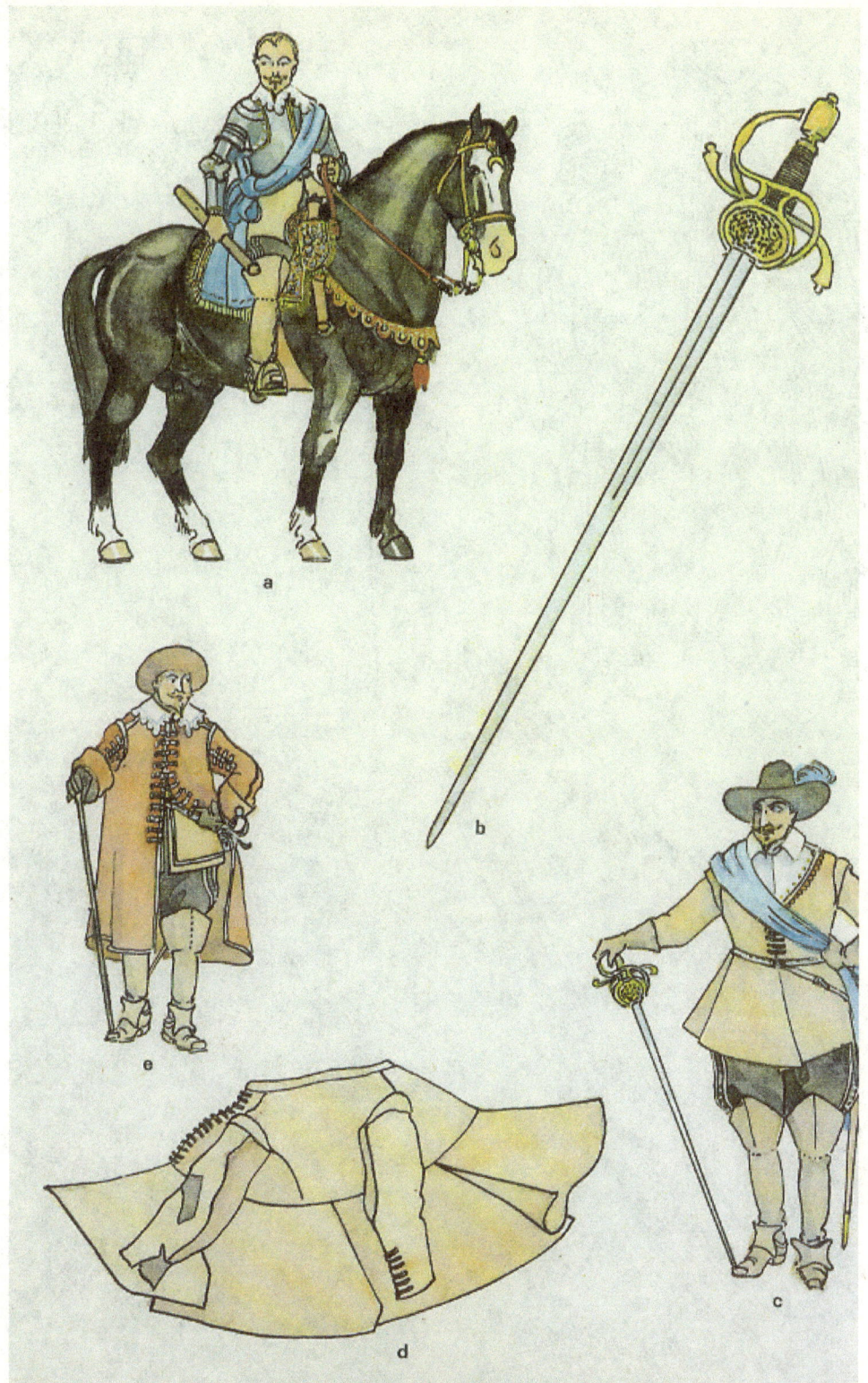

King Gustavus II Adolphus of Sweden
a) In half-armor mounted b) Gustavus' rapier c) Clothing worn by Gustavus at the Battle of Lützen, 1632 d) Gustavus' buff coat

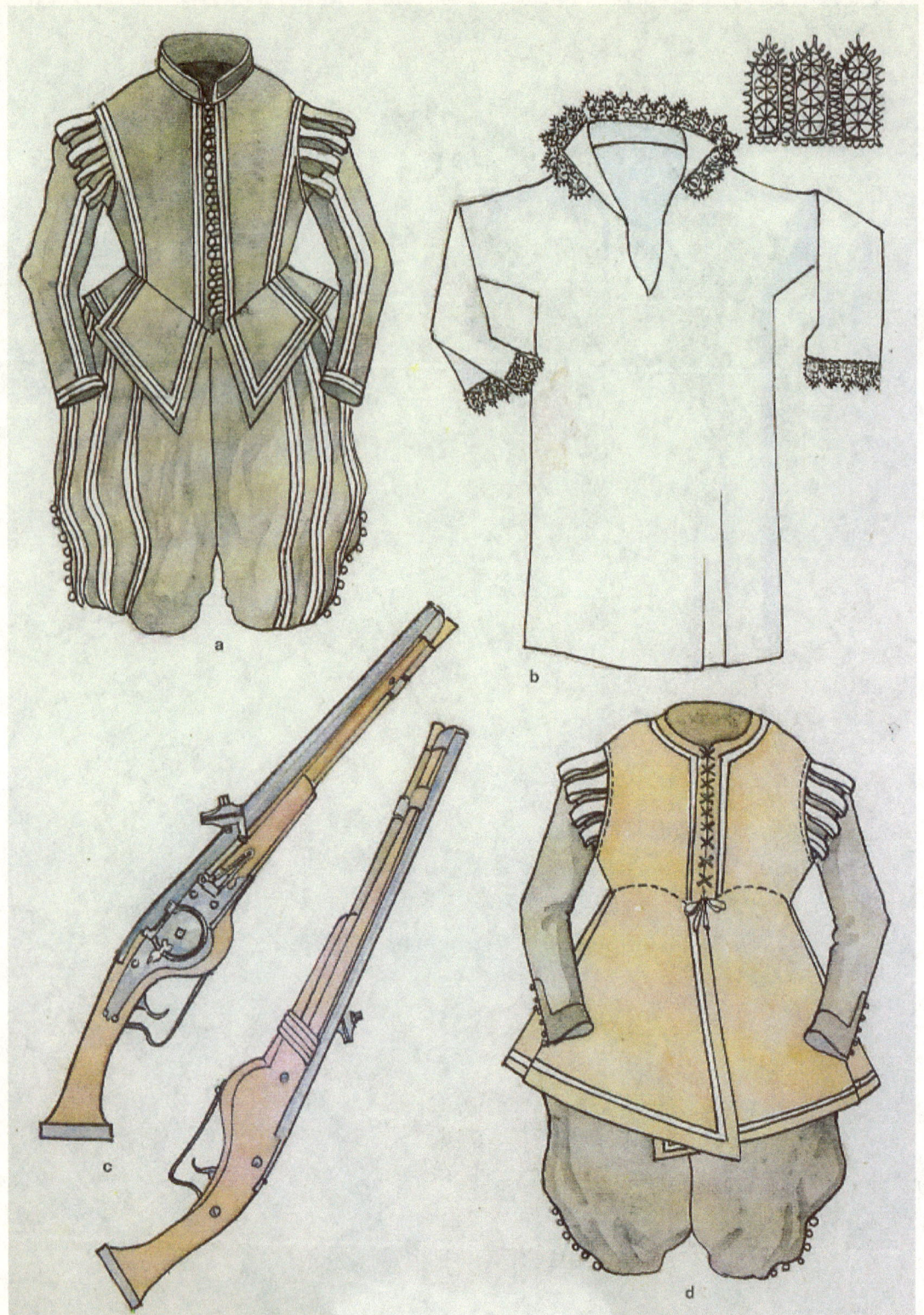

Dress of Gustavus II
a)One of the King's uniforms 1627 b) The King's shirt c) The King's wheel lock pistols d) The King's Battle dress

Gustavus II's favourite horse. The saddle was presented to the King by the Queen as a New Year's gift.

*Albrecht Wenzel Eusebius of Wallenstein, Duke of Mecklenburg, Friedland, Sagan
and Glogau (1583 – 1634), the Imperial Generalissimo of the Thirty Years' War*

Ottavio Piccolomini (1599 – 1656), a Hapsburg general of the Thirty Year's War

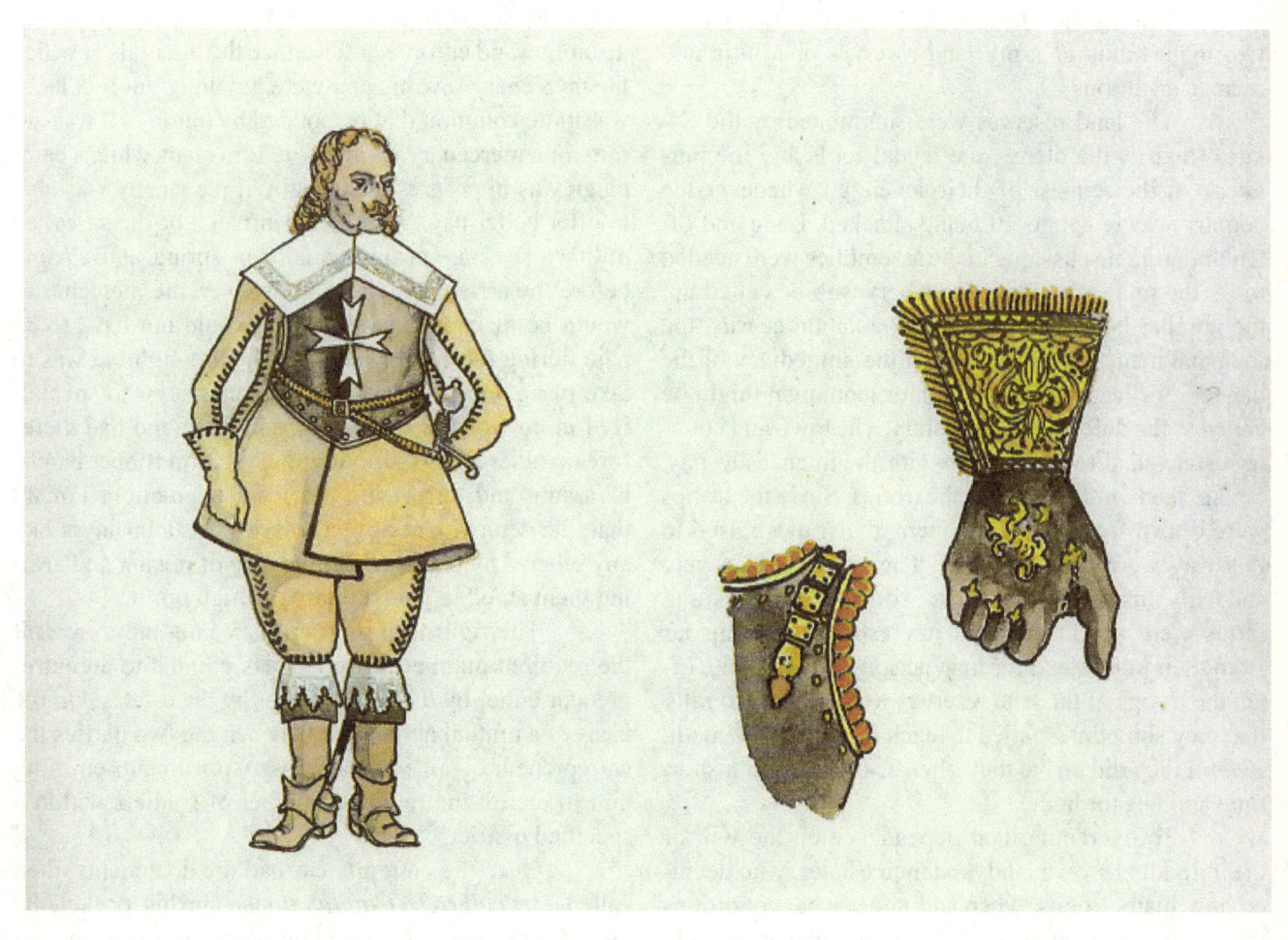

Bartolomeo Marradas (1560 – 1638), another Habsburg general of the period

CHARACTER OF THE ARMY

During the 16th and 17th centuries there were two main kinds of army land reserves or militia and mercenary troops.

The land reserves were summoned by the Estates (that is, the clergy, the feudal lords and the burghers) at the request of their sovereign whenever the country was in danger of being attacked. Long and often dragging discussions in the assemblies were needed to fix the total strength of the reserves to be called up, the number being based on the population census, the financial means available and on the immediacy of the danger. For instance, every fifth or tenth man might be called to the defense of the country. The town and country estates had to come forth with the finances to pay, clothe, feed, outfit, and arm the troops. Since the troops were drawn from the commoners, the armies raised in this way were poorly trained. The soldiers who were suddenly uprooted from their workshops, trades and farms were not in the least interested in fighting far from their homes and for long periods at that. Quite often the troops of the land reserves were so slow to rally that they sometimes failed to reach the battlefield at all. Even if they did arrive they often scattered after a short time and left for home.

To overcome their dependence on the will of the individual crown lands and their estates, who decided how many troops, when and under what conditions would be made available, sovereigns began to rely more and more on the other type of army then common, that is, the mercenaries. From then on, the only thing required of the estates was to provide the money for the hire of the troops. The estates were relatively happy with the solution, since the planned military campaigns did not interfere much with farming and did not disturb crafts and trade since there was no drain on the skilled labor force. So the recruitment of mercenaries began to be the decisive factor in raising any army although the system of land reserves remained in effect in many European countries even in later periods.

The core of the mercenary armies consisted of people who had been stripped of other means of earning their living by the evergrowing destitution and impoverishment of the common folk. Most mercenary armies swelled their ranks with complements of various dé-classé elements of many different nationalities, to which the national interests of the country they were serving were totally foreign. Understandably, these armies lacked discipline. Needless to say, severe corporal punishments had to be adopted to preserve a semblance of discipline and enforce order. Since the intervals at which the mercenary saw his pay were anything but regular, it was quite common that responded by mutiny. It was not rare for a mercenary company to turn coats while a campaign was in progress, especially if the enemy was able to offer better pay. When the campaign or the so-called military season, starting usually in spring and closing before the arrival of winter, were over, the mercenaries would be disbanded as that they would not have to be paid during the coming season when no fighting was to take place. Once disbanded, mercenaries, who specialized in no work or trade except fighting and had therefore no other means of living; would form robber bands, harassing and terrorizing the local population. For all that, the deployment of mercenaries was a business like any other. Any entrepreneur capable of raising and arming them stood to gain a relatively high profit.

The right to raise a military unit and to recruit the required number of troops was granted to an entrepreneur either by the sovereign or by the estates. On the basis of a mutual agreement between the two parties the entrepreneur obtained the necessary documents entitling him to recruit the required number of soldiers within a specified district.

Once the entrepreneur had the documents, then called, *Articelbriefe Capitulationen*, in his pocket, he picked a capable officer and entrusted him with the actual recruitment. Accompanied by a band of musicians, the officer would then criss-cross the district, making it publicly known that troops were being recruited for the services of such and such sovereign or entrepreneur or for this or that campaign. At recruitment time the amount of pay was also announced, usually fluctuating within a certain range, the exact pay depending on the recruit's arms equipment and combat experience. The length of the service was contracted either for six-months or, more often, for one military season.

Those who were interested in serving as mercenary troopers simply notified the scribe who was making out the muster roll of the troop and gave him their names, surnames, and residence. Supplying a false name or other incorrect data was an offence punishable by death.

When enough troopers had been enlisted, the recruiting officer presented the fresh troop to its proprietor and the men were informed of their duties and the punishments for breaching discipline. The following lines paraphrasing an early 17th century code give an idea what was demanded of the trooper as regards his conduct.

'A soldier who should accept monies upon recruitment and then defect, shall be punished by death.

In a castle, town or any such fort captured, the proprietor of the unit or the supreme commander of the forces that had taken the fort is entitled to all artillery pieces, gun powder and captured victuals. All other things belong to that who seized them first.

Anybody who should attempt to take another's war booty shall be punished.

Taking revenge on another either for foul words or debt is forbidden under pain of death.

No malice shall be borne among soldiers, especially between infantry and cavalry, or the offender shall be severely chastised.

Death shall be the lot of those who should kill others or incite mutiny. Should anybody be assaulted and should the felon continue in his deed in defiance to warning, the attacked party may kill the assailant and go free.

No one shall incite riot or provoke panic among the troop.

Anyone intending to commit treason shall be immediately reported.

Under pain of death no one shall leave his encampment. No one shall converse with the enemy without consent of the high command of his troop.

It is expressly forbidden to fire arms willfully, especially in villages or at night. The offender shall be punished by death.

He who should kill anybody intending to desert from battle shall go unpunished and will be rewarded.

When marching through own territory no one shall wantonly appropriate anything from the local folk and everybody is bound to pay for all victuals furnished or services rendered.

After a battle is won no one shall plunder before issued permission.

When alarm is sounded everyone must hurry to his company or he shall be punished.

If the soldiers who had been familiarized with the conduct code at the mustering, that is, at the time when their roster was made, could not remember these articles, they had the right to read them again to refresh their memory. The code was kept either with the commander or some appointed deputy.

The proprietor of a troop which at first had been a mere band of *landsknechts*, later a battalion or even a regiment, had absolute power over his men. He appointed the officers, received the hire monies from the sovereign or the estates and paid them out. At paytime many a mercenary met with gross injustice. Quite often the pay was late and it was common practice to hand it out only after a battle was over, so that the commander might pocket the share of those who had been killed. Commanders also often fixed the muster rolls to show higher number of men than the actual strength of the unit.

From his pay the mercenary had to purchase his food and parts of his armament and kit; cavalrymen had to stretch their pay to cover their mounts' fodder.

The troops were usually trailed by a band of women, children, tarts, and camp follower, which considerably slowed their marching speed. An infantry troop of 5,000 men would be followed by as many as 2,000 women, and children. The women took care of the soldiers' washing and trundled parts of their baggage.

At the beginning of the 16th century mercenaries were recruited only in battalion strengths, but in the course of the century and especially in its latter half larger regimental units were already being assembled. As were the mercenary battalions and companies before them, the regiments were independent units whose internal structure was as a rule devised by their commanders. During the 16th century the growing specialization of mercenary trips was shown by the gradual disappearance of the old, general term for mercenaries—*landsknechts* – and the emergence of new terms: infantry, cavalry and artillery. By the turn of the 17th century the basic military unit was already generally formed by a regiment of 10 regular battalions. Several regiments, each headed by a colonel, were grouped into a battle array called the battalion. During military campaigns the regiments were subordinated to a supreme command. At the end of the 16th and beginning of the 17th centuries this large military formation had in its head a commander with the rank of general.

Although the practice of disbanding the mercenary units at the end of the military season before inter approached was still quite common, some regiments were sometimes kept in standing service. For instance it was customary for the Habsburg army to keep two or three regiments in arms to defend the forts lying at the frontier between the Habsburg and Turkish territories.

In the past, the sovereign himself had always decided questions such as the number of regiments left in standing service of disbanded, the number of newly-mustered regiments and their outfitting, financial backing and military objectives. He had of course an advisory body, the war council, at his disposal but its composition and importance greatly differed at different times. In the later 16th century the war councils of the individual European countries still had no great importance. However, by the time of the outbreak of the Thirty Years' War they had become one of the most important arms of the state power, deciding often not only purely military affairs but also matters concerning policy and finance.

By the beginning of the 17th century other important changes in the character of the military had taken place. These changes had been triggered by a whole set of contemporary political events, especially the Dutch revolution and the outbreak of the struggle between the European powers to gain influence on the central European affairs.

In this period of almost incessant warfare strong mercenary armies were formed by great military entrepreneurs such as Dampierre, Bucquoy, Mansfeld, Tilly and later Wallenstein.

The total military strength of the individual state formations had considerably increased. In the time of Phillip II of Spain an army of a mere 40,000 had been enough to dominate Europe by the time of the reign of Louis XIV the strength of France's army was already 400,000 men. Within one century the Brandenburg army grew from 900 to 80,000 troops. The armies were growing in proportion to the increasing strategic and economic power of the individual states. In the struggle for hegemony in Central Europe those states that did not want to stay apart from the power game were force to maintain strong forces. In order not to weaken them temporarily, the majority of the mercenary troops were no longer disbanded for winter. This was of course a heavy burden on the budget and from the beginning of the 17th century the military expenditure of European states grew constantly. The Swedish king Gustavus II Adolphus regularly spent more than half of his annual budget on military affairs. The need to keep the armies supplied with food and arms provided the impetus to efforts to increase the output of farming and weapons manufacturing. The result was that military affairs began to be interlocked with the national economy to an unprecedented extent.

A classic example of a military entrepreneur whose activities enveloped both military and economic interests was Albrecht Wenzel Eusebius of Wallenstein subordinated most of the economic enterprises within his extensive estates to the needs of his army. The agricultural areas had become the food-growing base; his manufactories produced ammunition and uniforms for his troops. At the beginning o the Thirty Years' Wars, Wallenstein, then merely the colonel of one Moravian regiment, had become wealthy thanks to the shady financial operations in which he had been involved after the defeat of the Czech Estates in 1620. This gave him the means to raise at his own expense a great mercenary army which would assert and protect the aims of the Imperial policy. At that Wallenstein required from the emperor the recruitment patents and right to nominate the colonels and other officers of his regiments. Once the emperor conceded, Wallenstein selected his regimental colonels from experienced veterans and gave each 10 patents entitling him to recruit 10 battalions of troops. The nominated colonels in turn selected their own officers and entrusted them with the raising of the battalions. In practice this meant that the top ranks in the mercenary armies no longer had to be assigned to men of noble birth but that the responsibility could be given to experienced soldiers and organizers. Wallenstein's system of troop-raising remained basically unchanged until the 18th century.

Another important change was that the overwhelming majority of regiments were kept on constant active service even if the regimental commander, the colonel, was killed in battle. In such cases a new colonel was nominated to head the regiment, taking it over with all his predecessor's right and obligations.

A colonel might sometimes have had two or even three regiments raised at his expense although taking personal command of only one, the others being entrusted to his hand-picked deputies. But the system of multi-proprietorship of regiments created confusion in the organizational structure of the army and Ferdinand II decreed that his commander should have more than one regiment. Later Ferdinand, III ordered that anybody who did not personally take part

a)Wolfgang Adam, Count of Pappenheim (1605 – 1647), a general of the Hapsburg army of the period. b) Detail of the bandolier decoration and of the pattern on the fabric. c) Early 17th-century order badge of the order of the Golden Fleece, an Austrian and Spanish order founded by Philip (III) the Good, Duke of Burgundy in 1430

Dress of higher ranking officers, early 17th century

Dress of higher officers, early 17th century

Coat styles, early 17th century

Military Salute

As a rule, a junior or inferior always removed his hat in the presence of a superior a/e) Salute
to the commander-in-chief b)Salute and report to the commander-in-chief c) Junior being
issued an order d) Peasant standing humbly in front of a musketeer sentinel

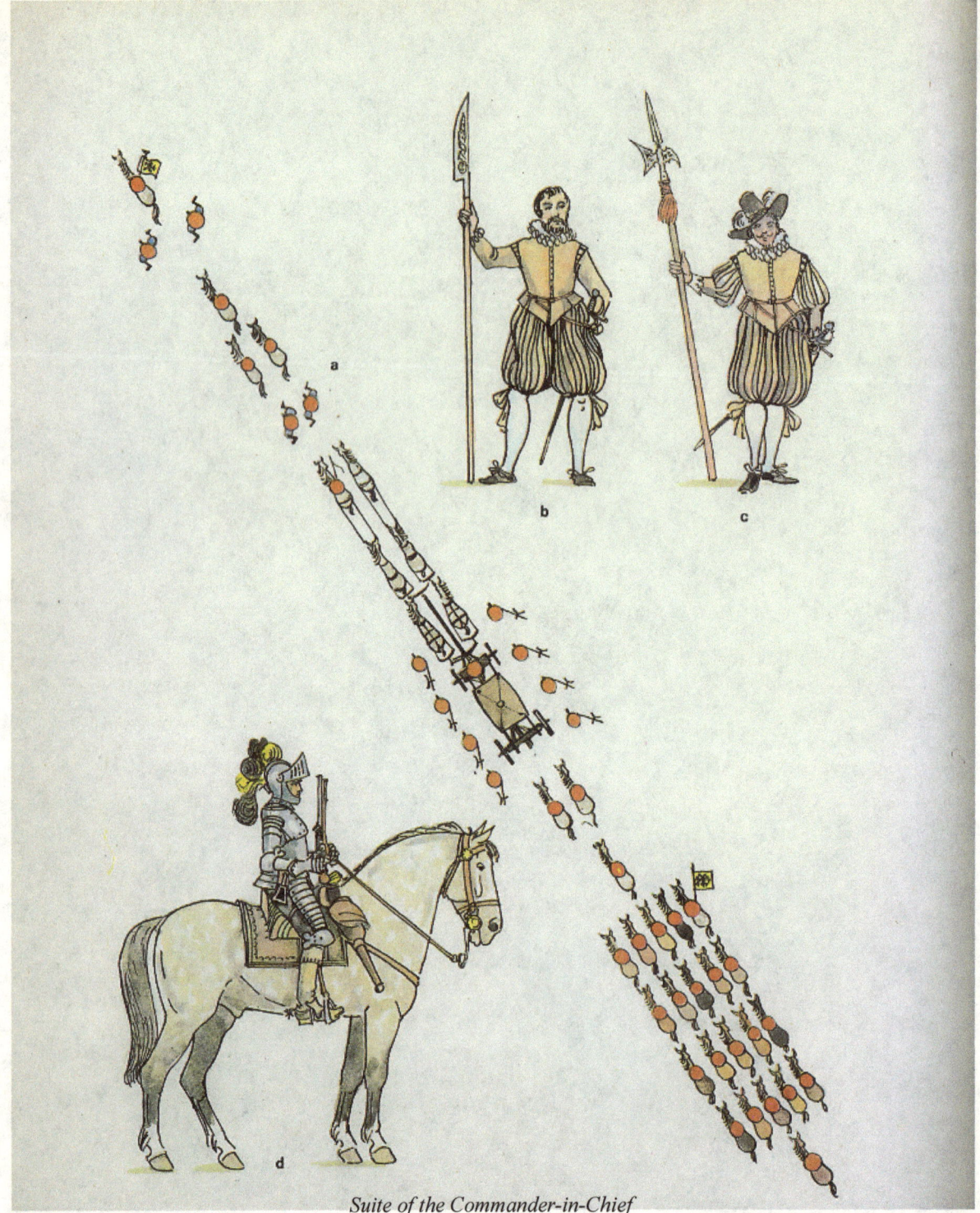

Suite of the Commander-in-Chief

a) Suite of the Supreme Commander driving a coach. Formation: A mounted bugler mounted as an outrider, then two foot runners followed by three riders and another two foot runners. After them came a coach of six flanked by four body guards on each side. The coach is trailed by two followed by the accompanying guards' troop of twenty riders preceded by the group commander. The deputy commander brings up the rear. b) Halberd-armed personal guard of the Hapsburg monarch. c) Member of the Swiss household guards of King Louis XIII of France. d) Cuirassier presenting his pistol at a ceremonial occasion.

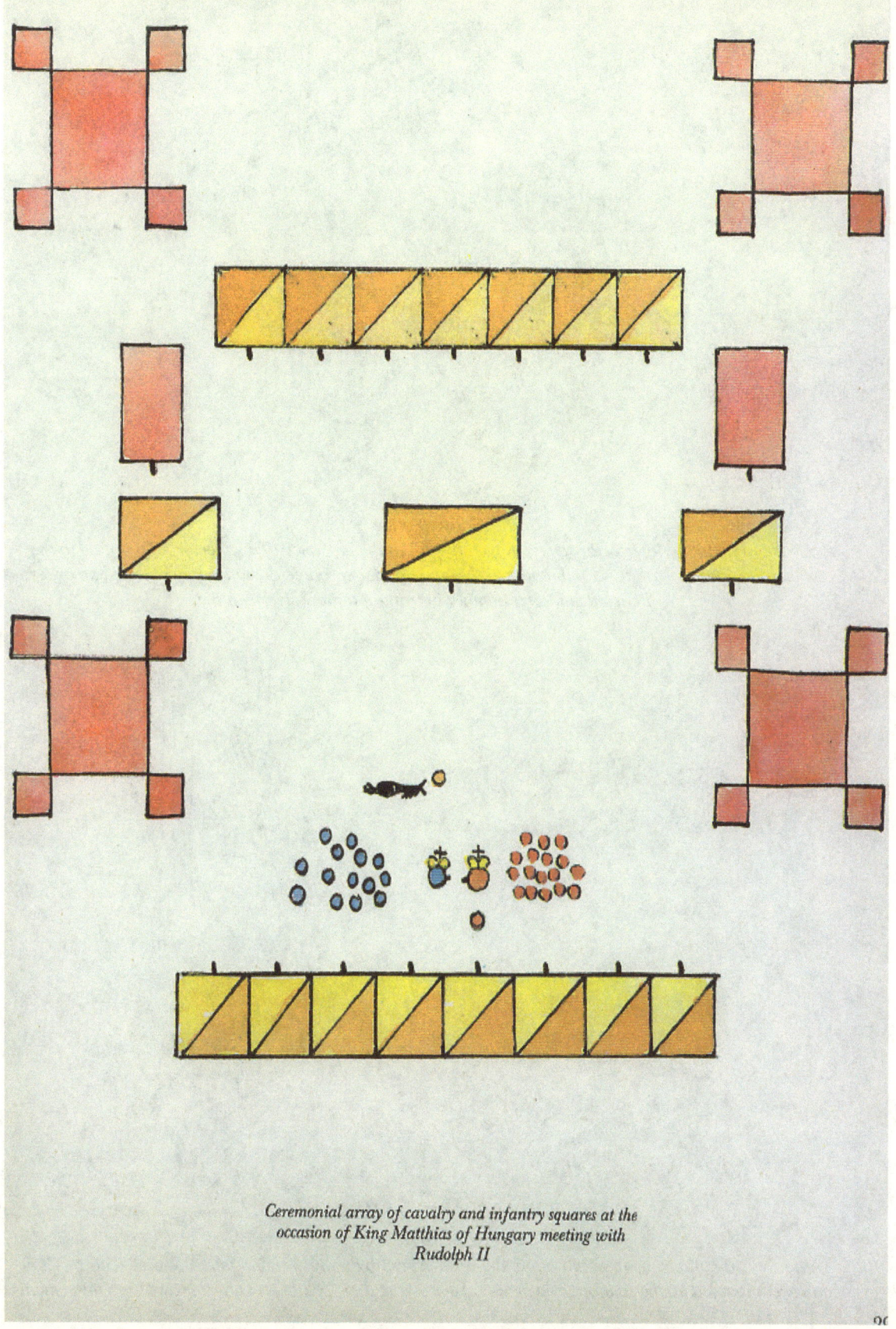

Ceremonial array of cavalry and infantry squares at the occasion of King Matthias of Hungary meeting with Rudolph II

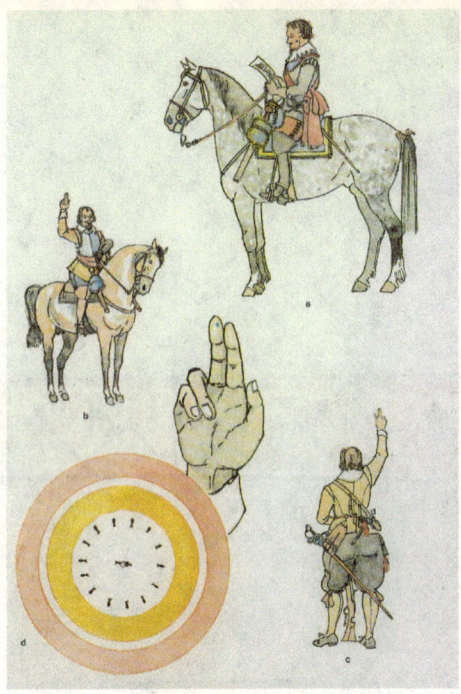

Military Salute

As a rule, a junior or inferior always removed his hat in the presence of a superior a/e) Salute to the commander-in-chief b)Salute and report to the commander-in-chief c) Junior being issued an order d) Peasant standing humbly in front of a musketeer sentinel

Courts-martial

a) Riding a donkey; the punishment could be made more severe by tying weights to the felon's feet. b) Condemned man accompanied up the scaffold by a priest. c) Throwing dice for life. d) Deserter awaiting judgement

Military capital punishment
Beheading with a sword was regarded as the most honourable kind of execution and it was usually the privilege of noblemen and officers.

a) Condemned man's shirt collar being adjusted prior to the execution. b) Apart from the condemned man and the Lord Executioner, there are several other people to act as witnesses who were present on the scaffolding. c) Execution without scaffold. Behind the priest is a Provost Marshal, the highest army authority on matters of discipline and order enforcement.

d) Execution block with axe, a type used in early 17th-century England. e) Condemned man led to his end.

in the campaign was not allowed to command a regiment. Thus a number of former regimental commanders, among them for instance General Hanibal Gonzaga who had been in command of the garrison in Vienna, had to hand their regiments over to other officers. The new commander, however, usually had close administrative and financial ties with the former proprietor.

Wallenstein also introduced new officer ranks. The term general had been already more or less accepted for the commander of a group of regiments. Newly introduced was the rank of *generalissimo*, the supreme commander of a huge army. Since the regiments had ceased to be independent operational units and their colonels no longer the sole lords of their troops, all power was now concentrated in the *generalissimo*'s hands. Gradually the notion of the army as a unit of military force began to be accepted, the *generalissimo* nominating not only the colonels of individual regiments but also the generals who commanded groups of regiments.

The Swedish armies of the 17th century introduced several other important developments in military

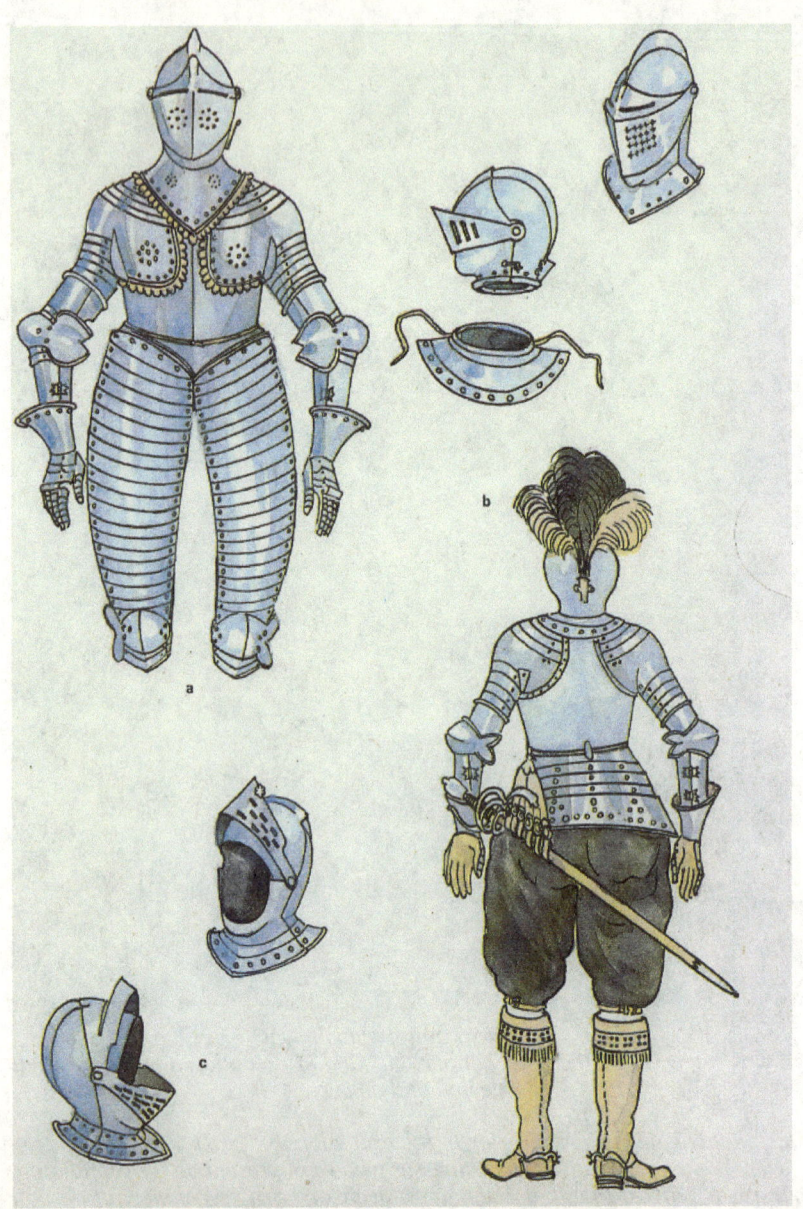

Cuirassier plate armor, early 17th century
a) Front b) Back c) Various cuirassier helmets and gorgets

art and organization.

In its struggle against Denmark, Norway, Poland and Russia for control of the Baltic coast, Sweden had grown to be a militarily strong nation. In contrast to the European practice of the time, the Swedish army obtained most of its manpower by regular conscription. Only a small proportion of the troops were mercenaries. Not even the strong influx of mercenaries into its ranks at the time when Sweden was waging campaigns in Central Europe after 1630 could much change the system. By adopting conscription, Sweden was able to build up a national army backed mainly by its own population. Understanding discipline in this type of army was much better than in the rank-and-file mercenary units of other European states.

Sweden had abundant financial means for the up-keep of its army in the form of revenues from its exports of copper, iron, and tin. Sweden's income from the export of cast-iron-artillery barrels had also been increasing considerably, the export quota of gun barrels having grown from 22 to 1,000 tons annually in 1626-46. This was also a boom period for Swedish shipbuilding.

The ordinance of the Swedish army was in the line with the tactical concepts of Gustavus II Adolphus. Muskets became the main ordinance of the infantry troops and the number of musketeers in relation to pikemen increased. The drill order technique was considerably simplified and the introduction of paper cartridges containing both ball and charge greatly speeded the rapidity of fire.

Swedish cavalrymen's combat tactics differed from the caracole common elsewhere in Europe at the outbreak of the Thirty Years War. Their main weapon was the backsword; pistols were used only in the first phase of a charge and in skirmishes. The cavalry had thus been given back its main task, to be a strong shock force.

Gustavus Adolphus was the first among the supreme war lords to realize the potential advantages of field artillery and under his command artillery became the third important army service. In elaborating the concept of field artillery deployment Gustavus was greatly assisted by the work of a Swedish artillery commander, General Torstenson.

The Swedish army had also at its disposal a strong corps of engineers who were mainly recruited from civilian experts and called up for field duty whenever required.

The tactics of Gustavus's army were based on strong discipline, good firing drill and well-rehearsed maneuvers of foot formations, the Swedish officer corps drilling their troops in the latter two throughout the entire year.

All troops were clothed in regulation uniforms. Although military uniform dress had not been unknown, the Swedish were the first to use uniforms and rank insignia on a mass scale. The Swedish troops' uniforms, made of good quality cloth for rough weather, contributed much to their discipline and morale.

In the course of the wars waged against the Huguenots, France had also succeeded in building an army that was strong and modern according to standards of the period. It was an army fully subordinated to the state. Such outstanding soldiers as Le Tellier, Prince Condé and Turenne contributed to the modernization of the French army. When the Peace of Westphalia of 1648 was concluded, the French army had already become the mightiest military power in Central Europe as well as a model for army reorganization of most other European nations.

Using the cuirassier lance in combat
a) Holding the lance prior to combat b) Tilting the lance down c) Lance ready for charge d) How individual cuirassier ranks brought their lance down to charge. When the charge started, the 7th and 8th ranks still held their lances upright, while the 3rd to 6th ranks were bringing theirs down gradually and the 1st and 2nd ranks were already charging towards the enemy

CAVALRY

In the early 17th century there were two kinds of regular cavalry troops, the cuirassiers and the arquebusiers.

The cuirassier was protected from his head down to knee level with plate armor. His arms were covered with pauldrons, couters and vambraces and his hands were gloved with gauntlets. His thighs were fully protected with tasses. The breastplate was designed to withstand not only a pistol shot but also a ball fired from the more powerful musket. The cuirassier wore high, leather riding-boots with spurs and wore a sword by his side, often a backsword designed as a piercing as well as slashing weapon. The cuirassiers were divided into two subgroups according to their ordnance. The first kind was armed with two wheellock pistols carried in holsters fastened to the front sides of the saddle. The other group also had heavy cavalry-type lances, although the lance had already begun to disappear from heavy cavalry ordnance by the beginning of the 17th century and cuirassiers generally used pistols in combat, or if necessary, swords or backsword. Long lancers of lighter weight survived only in some irregular cavalry units of certain Eastern European nationalities.

The arquebusiers or harquebusiers, called sometimes also carabiniers, wore only the breastplate and the morion helmet. Their ordnance was limited to a short wheellock hand-gun or arquebus and one or two pistols. Like the cuirassiers, they also had a side weapon. The arquebus was carried slung from the bandolier by means of a snaphook and the pistols were in holsters like those of the cuirassiers.

As a rule, these two types of cavalry troops – the cuirassiers and the arquebusiers – fought mounted, using mainly their dire arms, the arquebus and pistol, in combat.

A third type of troops, the dragoons, also rode horses but their mounts served only to carry them to the battlefield. In the early 17th century the dragoons' tactical task was similar to that of the regular infantry and therefore the dragoons were not ranked among the regular cavalry.

The organizational unit of cavalry was the regiment. The Imperial army regiments of the early 17th century and the Thirty Years War period had 500 to 1,000 riders. The regiment was further divided into companies. In wartime, however, regiments rarely had their full strength and a unit of 600 to 700 men could be regarded as a strong regiment. Some early 17th century regiments were down to a mere 200 to 300 riders.

A cavalry regiment was commanded by a colonel or, if he had raised the troops himself, a colonel proprietor.

The regimental commander's staff was composed of the following officers: lieutenant-colonel, sergeant-major, quartermaster, judge advocate, chaplain, adjutant, wagonmaster, purveyor, drum-major (only in cuirassier and arquebusier regiments), provost and executioner with his mates.

The organization of companies followed these lines. First came the officer ranks listed on the first page of the company roll (these grades therefore being called prima-plana). They were: one rittmeister (captain), one lieutenant, one sergeant, one cornet (ensign with the dragoon units), one forager (quartermaster), one mustermaster, one surgeon, one or two buglers (or, with the dragoons, drummers), two or three corporals, one farrier, and one armorer (armor-smith in charge of repairs of armor). The ranks were formed by 80 to 90 riders.

Each company has its ensign, called a guidon, which was a small triangular flag attached to a lance and carried by the company cornet.

The tactical cavalry unit was the squadron, a large array composed of several companies. At the beginning of the 17th century the terms squadron and company often overlapped, the results being that regiments were divided directly into squadrons which became an independent unit in a tactical as well as organizational sense.

The following survey gives an idea of the number of regiments of individual cavalry types in the Imperial army during the Thirty Years War.

Arquebusiers 1634 20 regiments
Cuirassiers   1642 61 regiments
Dragoons   1636 19 regiments

(at the beginning of 1623 the Imperial army had at its disposal only 1 dragoon regiment)

The strongest irregular cavalry forces raised in the Eastern regions were regiments composed of Croatians who had, however, an organizational structure quite different from the regular cavalry. In 1637 the Imperial army employed 19 Croatian regiments although as recently as 1625 there had been only one regiment of this type.

As we have said before, the dragoons were a special kind of troop who ranked somewhere between cavalry and infantry. They were actually infantry transported on horseback; their training did not fundamentally differ from that of the regular infantry troops. Their organization was also quite similar to the regimental structure of the infantry. About half of the dragoon troops of the early 17th century were armed with muskets. The rest were mounted pikemen using the typical infantry pike of the period, slightly modified to facilitate carrying on horseback.

The main task of the dragoon troops was foot combat, although a dragoon musketeer had to learn to fire his weapon from horseback. Authors of the period, writing on the problems of combat training and deployment, considered the dragoons to be a very useful service. Since these troops rode to the battlefield, they were able to keep the pace with the regular cavalry columns. When attacked by enemy cavalry formation with musket fire, especially if charged from the flanks. Forming the centre of a cavalry formation, dragoons could provide a very effective defense, since their long thrusting lances offered cover to musketeer and cavalry detachments behind and could protect them from a direct charge by enemy cavalry. The dragoons were used for both day and night combat, for assaulting smaller remote forts, for blowing up the enemy for gate with a powder charge or for surprise attacks of enemy encampments. Their main weapon was the dragoon musket which was quite similar to the regulation infantry musket, the only difference being a slight modification allowing the musket to be carried on horseback. Later the dragoon musket was made slightly lighter than the infantry musket, both types having a matchlock. The dragoons usually had no pistols.

The dragoon did not require such a good horse as the cavalryman, and if it came to worst, his horse could be abandoned with no great financial loss. When the dragoon dismounted to fight on foot, he threw the reins of his horse over the neck of his neighbor's mount. In this way a long line of linked horses was formed, which was usually left guarded by a few veterans. If the day was lost, a dragoon might have great difficulty in regaining his horse since it could well be somewhere in the middle of a line. This explains why dragoons' horses were so often abandoned on the battlefield.

If the dragoons were ordered either to build or wreck some field fortifications, they would be issued at least with the basic sapping tools, that is, hoes and shovels.

The Thirty Years' War gives testimony to the evergrowing number of dragoon regiments. Their numbers increased especially after the reforms introduced by the Swedish King Gustavus II Adolphus, who transformed the dragoons into a kind of troop approaching the regular cavalry in character. After these reforms had been introduced in other European armies as well, the dragoons gradually began to replace the cavalry arquebusiers, so that by the end of the Thirty Years' War the cavalry branch of the services consisted only of cuirassiers and dragoons.

All types of cavalry had to undergo a very thorough training before being sent to battle. First came the basic training in proper mounting and dismounting. Then the rider had to learn how to control his horse at carious gaits and to negotiate natural obstacles. The entire training aimed at the closest possible co-ordination between the rider and his horse.

Other areas of training were oriented as teaching the trooper to master the basic cavalry weapons, that is, any of the cutting side weapons, the pistols, arquebus or musket. Handling the weapons was not easy. For instance when a rider wanted to draw his side weapon from the scabbard, he could not grasp the latter with his left hand as did the infantryman, since the left hand was holding the reins. While rising, he had to reach for the hilt with his right hand crossing over the left because if he attempted to draw the weapon between the left and his body, he was in danger of cutting himself. Pistols were drawn from holsters with the hand turned towards the back. This applied both to the right and left holster, actually there was no other way to draw since the pistols usually had very long barrels. That is why early 17th –century pistols were carried in the saddle holsters with the trigger facing to the front.

In peacetime, cavalry training in weapon handling was done on specially-built field training grounds with marked tracks and designated stations where the novice rider was to load, fire at targets or put his pistol away. At the other stations he was expected to draw his sword or sabre and slash or pierce a manikin, then putting his side weapon away at the end. The shooting targets were usually placed either in the height of the rider's head, others in the level of the horse's breast, still others low above the ground.

Various tournament or riding games, for instance tilting at a ring, were part of the training programme. Another riding game, which had originated in Arabia and Caucasia, was the so-called Quintana. At full trot or gallop the rider was to thrust his lance into a shield held by a pivoted stuffed manikin. On impact, the manikin started spinning quickly, the centrifugal force raising a long sand-filled bag suspended from a plank fixed to the manikin. If the rider was not quick enough to escape, he was hit by the bag.

When basic training in mastering horse and weapons was complete, cavalry trainees were taught to fall into squadrons and other combat formations as well as to master combat tactics.

The most common combat formation of the earth 17th century was the caracole which could be employed in two ways. According to the first method, the first rank of the cavalry formation charged frontally against the enemy, the riders firing their weapons at a distance of 30 to 50 paces. Turning their horses to make a file, they returned to the rear and became the last rank. Thus they cleared the way for the following rank who similarly charged, fired at the enemy and then rejoined at the rear. In this way the first rank was always attacking while the other ranks were loading and waiting their turn to charge.

The second method was the charge of a single file. When the riders had the enemy on their right, they fired and, making a big circle, the entire file then returned to its original position in the formation, reloading on the way.

Cavalry horses had to be thoroughly trained not o fear the turmoil of battle, and to behave in such a way as to enable their riders to concentrate fully on their main task. Thus, horses were schooled to stop, back, charge forward, follow circles and serpentines and to step and jump aside in both directions. The last was a necessary maneuver for combat formation grouping. Horses also had to learn to negotiate terrain obstacles and to jump ditches, bars, hurdles, hedges, fires as well as barrels. They had to be able to cross both dry and water moats and learn not to fear the swinging and swaying of the footbridge when crossing a stream. It was characteristic of the period that horses were rained to attack enemy soldiers and their mounts on their own. When cavalry troops started to rely mainly on firearms such as the pistol carbine or muskets, the horse had to be schooled not to be scared of his rider's fire, since the muzzle was not far from the horse's head.

For each type of cavalry suitable horses had to be selected to match the function of the troops. Cuirassiers required strong, tall and easily controlled horses which would not become jumpy or be easily scared and which would react to the slightest shin pressure and the softest motion of the reins. A cavalry horse needed an especially good saddle, so as to give the rider a firm posture and at the same time not chafe the animal. Whenever a contagious disease broke amongst the cavalry horses, the greatest care was taken to ensure cleanliness of the stables and watering vessels.

But in spite of all the advantages of cavalry, in the course of the 17th century the service lost priority in West European armies, and the European theatres of war came to be dominated by the infantry.

Dragoons – mounted infantry
a) Dragoon musketeer b) Dragoon pikeman

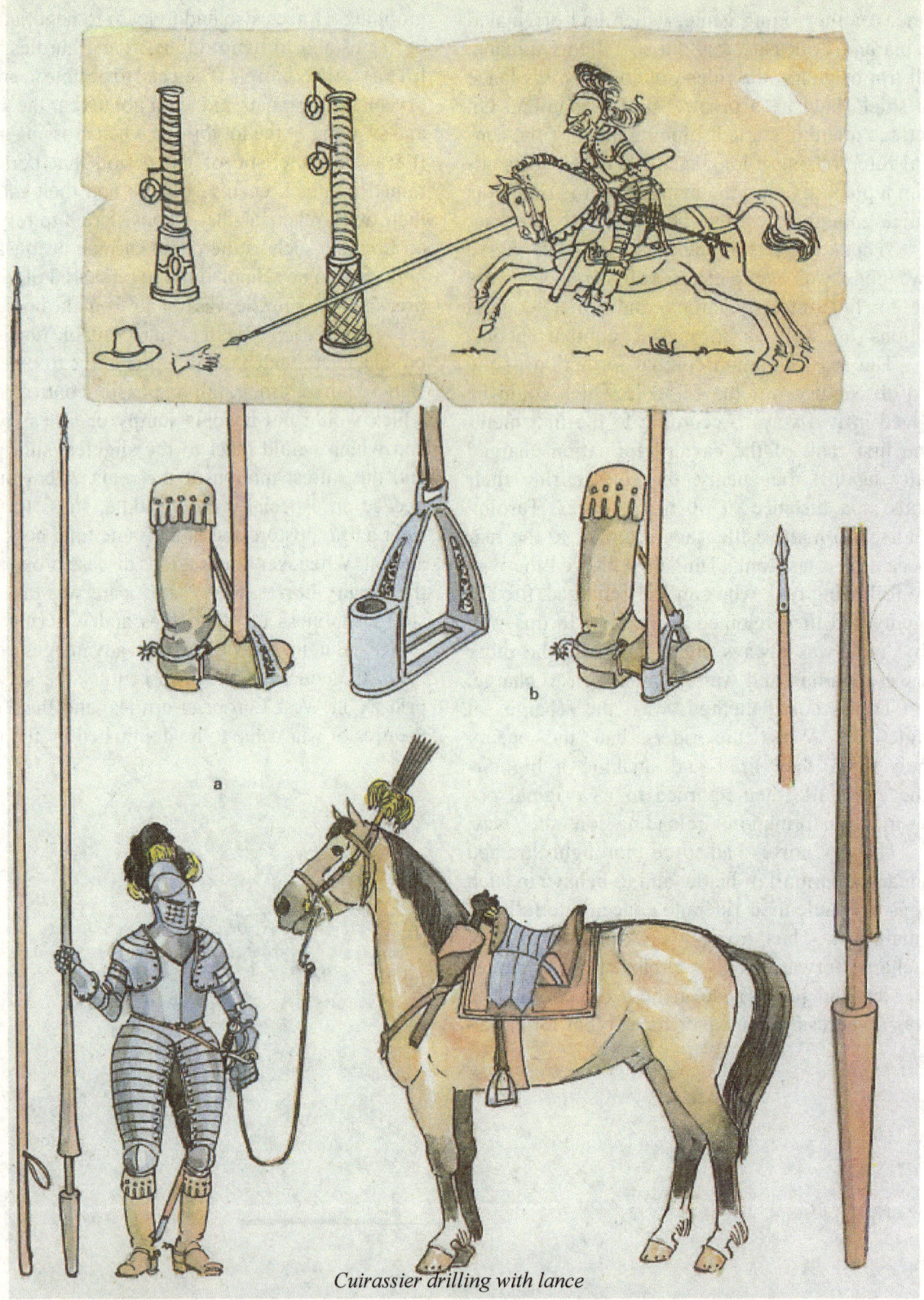

Cuirassier drilling with lance

a) Lance size compared with the size of the cuirassier and the horse b) Lance butt end was supported either in the stirrup bucket or rested on the boot instep next to the stirrup arch.

Pistols, the typical Thirty Years' War cuirassier ordinance a) Typical pistol grip   b)
Pistol training   c) Pistol types   d) Pistols were slung in holsters with attached shot
bag, winding key or spanner and powderhorn   e) Detail wheellock winding spanner

Arquebusiers
Examples of this branch of light cavalry in the Thirty Years' War period

Using the main arquebusier weapon, a short wheellock carbine a) Leather hanger with shot bag and powderhorn b) Arquebusier with his carbine after firing c) Loading d) Arquebus in bandolier

Light cavalrymen types, with partial plate armor and typical cavalry helmets

*Dragon and his kit a) Dismounted b) a matchlock musket, the main dragoon ordnance with kit
c) Carrying matchlock musket and kit d) Mounted dragoon. During the Thirty Years' War the
original bandolier with powder receptacles was replaced with a bag and paper cartridges.*

Dragoon Pikeman

*At the outbreak of the Thirty Years' War some dragoons were
still armed with pikes. a) Pikes suspension prior to combat
b) Dragoon holding pike d) Morion type helmet c) Pike types*

Polish cavalry
a) Nobleman of the Lisowski regiment   b) Polish cossack

a) Mounted Polish Hetman with buzdigan mace   b) Polish nobleman, early 17th century c) Buzdigan mace and saddle

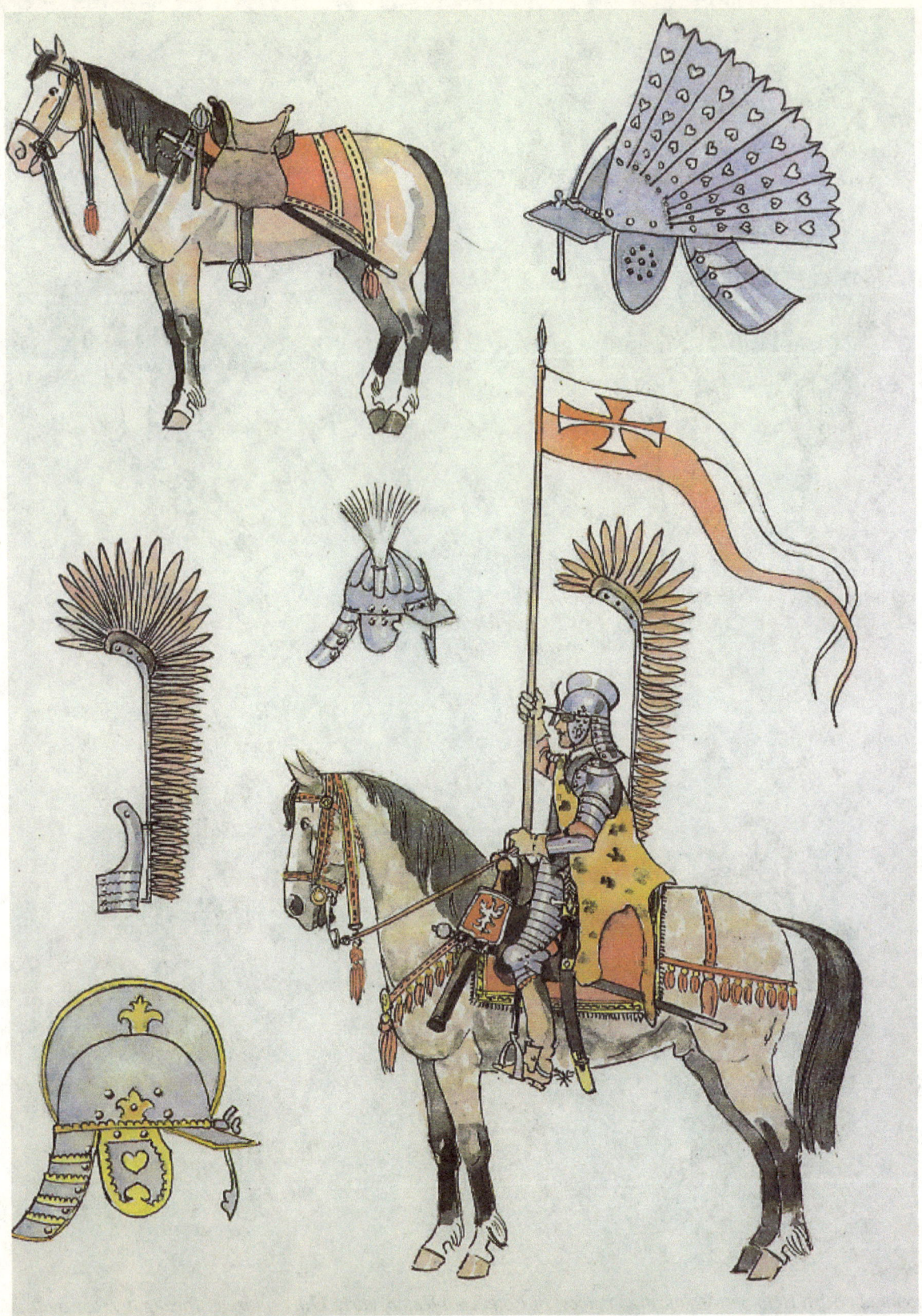

Polish heavy cavalry: the Polish Hussar and his equipment

a)Polish cavalrymen, early 17th century b) Members of the mounted Lisowski regiment

Polish cavalrymen, early 17th century

Hungarian noblemen, late 16th and early 17th centuries

Saddles and stirrups from the 17th century

Hungarian cavalrymen, early 17th century a) Hungarian Hyduk b) Gypsy farrier with the tools of his trade c) Hungarian hussar with a raven feather on his hat d) Hungarian rider

Croatian cavalrymen types, early 17th century

Early 17th century Turkish soldier types

Early 17th century Turkish soldier types
a) Turkish banner b) High Turkish official c) Fully armed janissary and a janissary hat
d)Turkish helmet early 17th century

Turkish riders, early 17th century

Turkish cavalrymen

Cavalry Standard
a) Salute with standard dipped towards the reviewing dignitary b)In combat, the butt of the staff rested in the stirrup bucket and the staff was strapped to the cornet's arm c) Cornet with standard d) Type of cavalry guidon with an emblem found commonly on the Austrian cavalry colors of the 17th and 18th centuries

Dragon ensigns and drummers
Dragoons, who were nothing more than mounted infantry retained some features characteristic of infantry, e.g. infantry flags and drums instead of cavalry standards and bugles

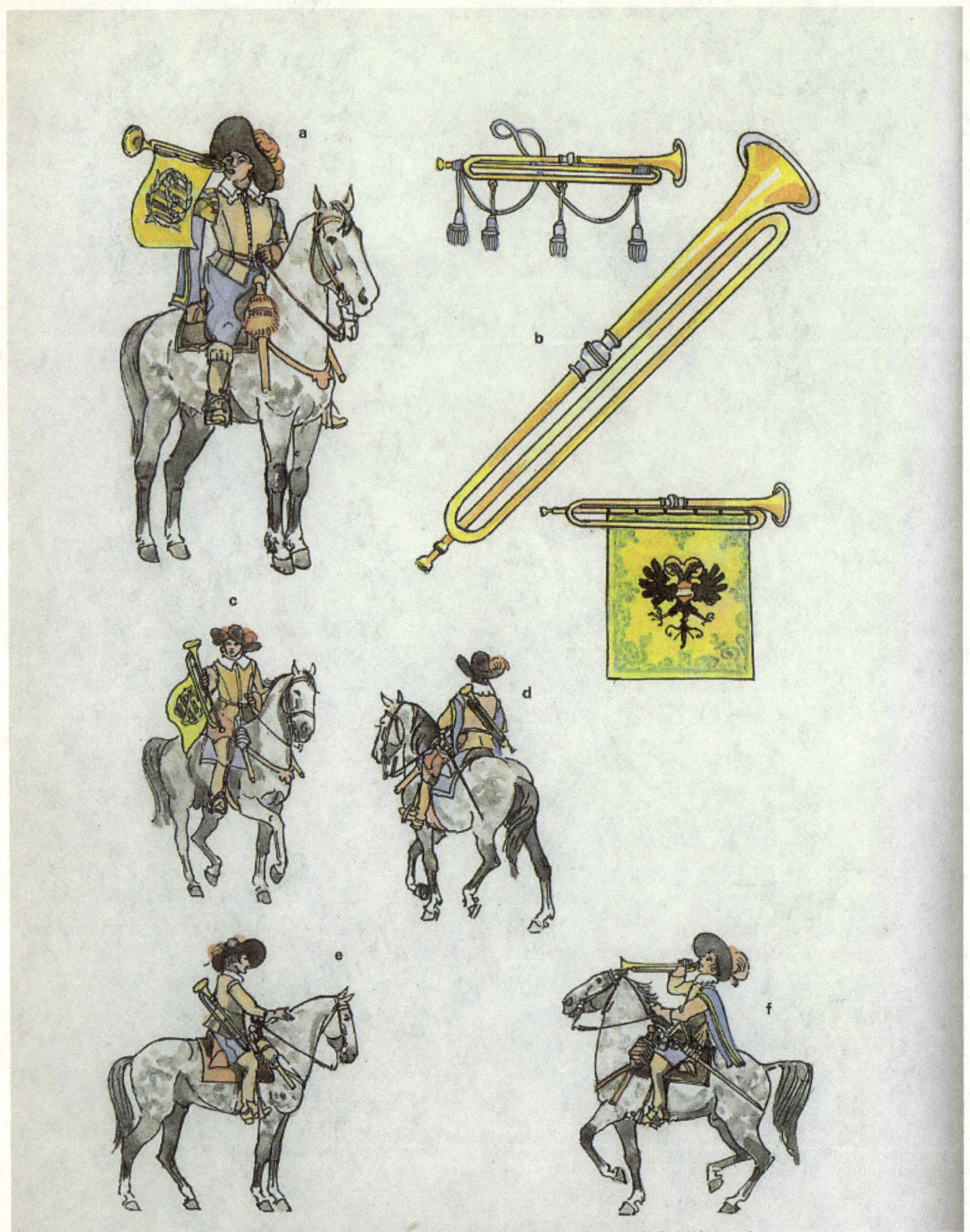

Cavalry especially the heavy type used bugles on the battlefield for orders
a) Bugler with instrument turned slightly to the right to protect it against the horse jerking his
head slightly b) Bugle with pennon c) Another way of holding the bugle d, e) Bugler carrying the
instrument on his back and side f) One way of holding the bugle while riding

Cavalry kettledrums
These types of drums were used by cavalry regiments a) Turkish-type kettledrum b) small kettledrum used for horseback c) Pair of horseback kettledrums with a strap by means of which the drums could be suspended from the horse's neck and attached firmly to the saddle. d,e) Kettledrums transported on horseback

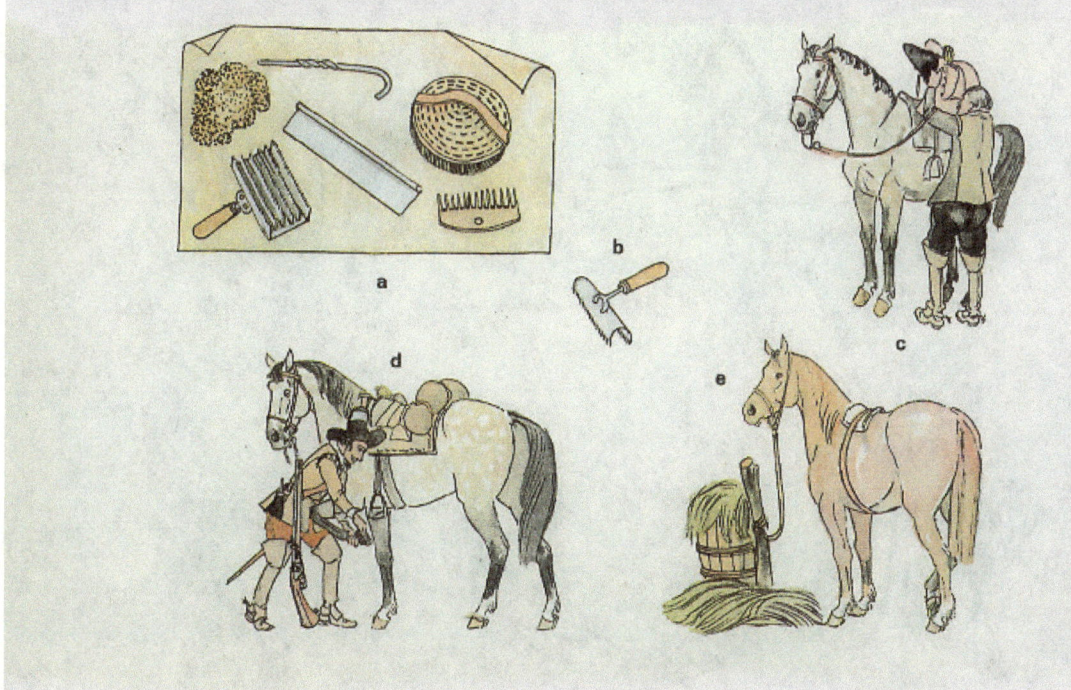

Horse grooming
a) Grooming gear laid out on a rag: washing sponge, hoof pick, body brush, currycomb, comb, sweat scrapper b) Currycomb, 16th century c) Horse saddling; the horse wears a saddle blanket under the saddle d) Picking out the near front hoof e) Dressing saddle sore on the withers

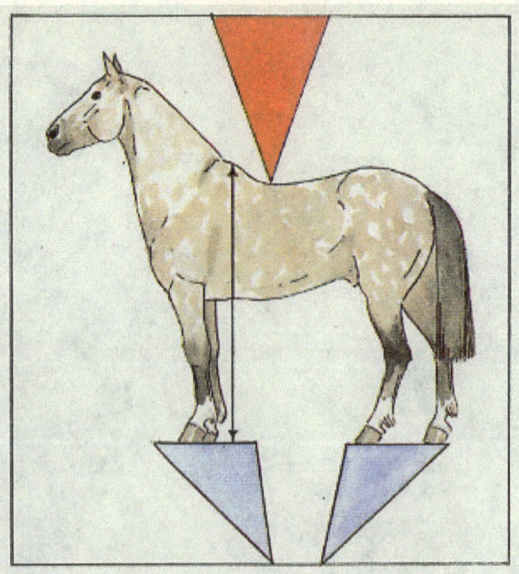

Statistics for a typical cavalry mount
Daily food: 4-5 kg. oats, 5-7 kg hay Water: 15-40 lt. daily Bedding: 1.5 – 2 kg straw Time for feeding:
1 hour

Time needed for shoeing: 1.5 hours (four shoes lasted about 6-8 weeks), Height: About 16 hands,
Weight: 450-550 kg, Weight carried: about 140 – 150 kg or more

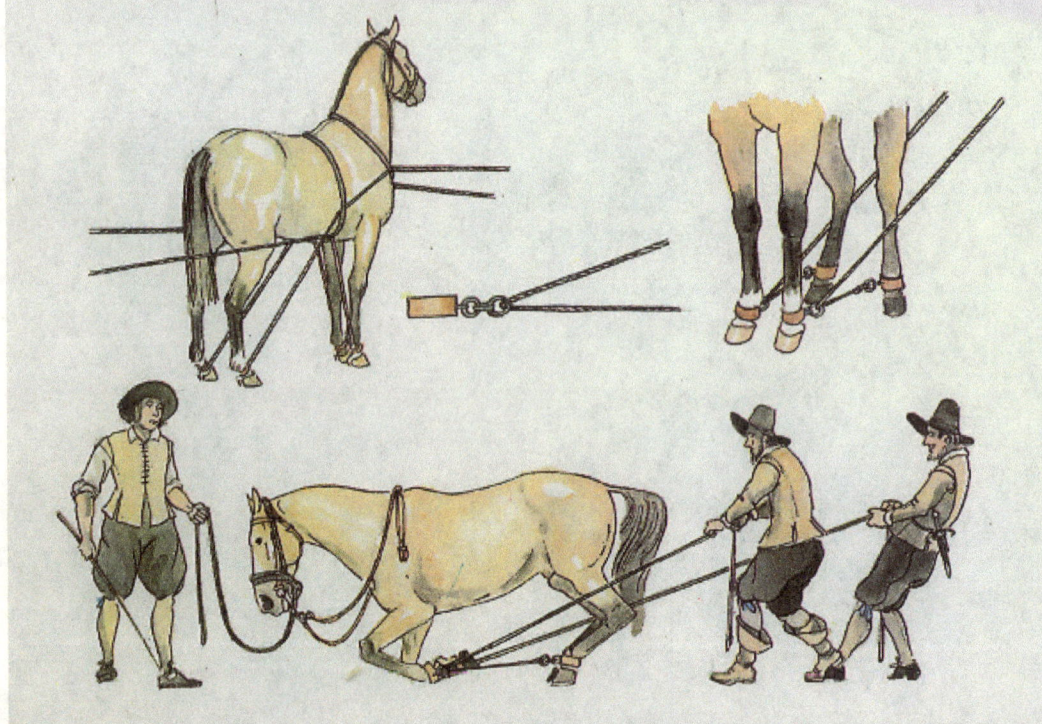

Tumbling a horse with fetters
Sometimes a horse had to be brought down for surgical treatment. The horse's legs were tied with fetters and
ropes were run through the neck and girth straps. The operation required about ten grooms and the horse to be
tumbled at a single stroke, if possible. The other, much simpler method used rope running through the leg fetters.

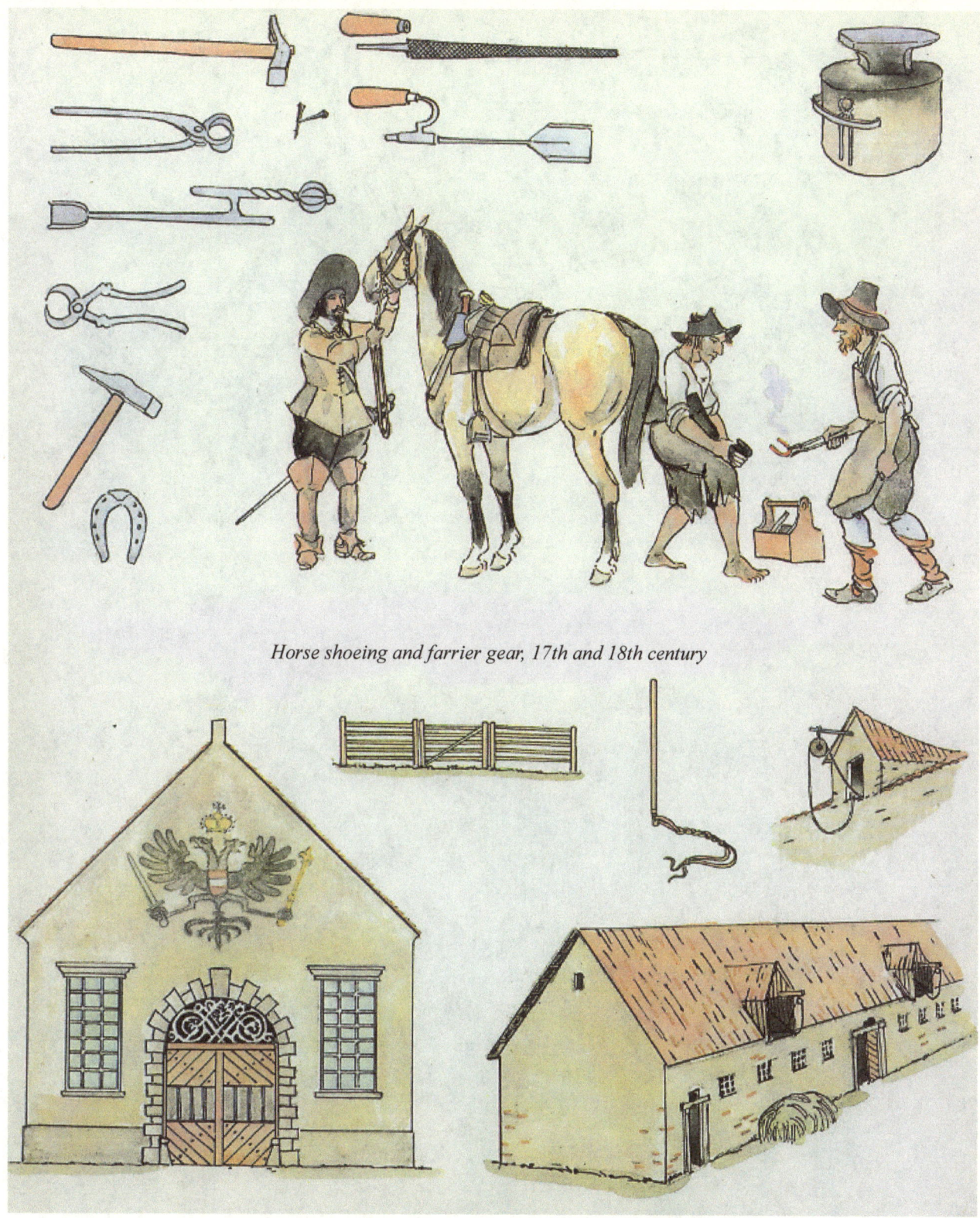

Horse shoeing and farrier gear, 17th and 18th century

Riding academy and stables, Kladruby, Bohemia 1688
Details of fence, hayloft and riding whip

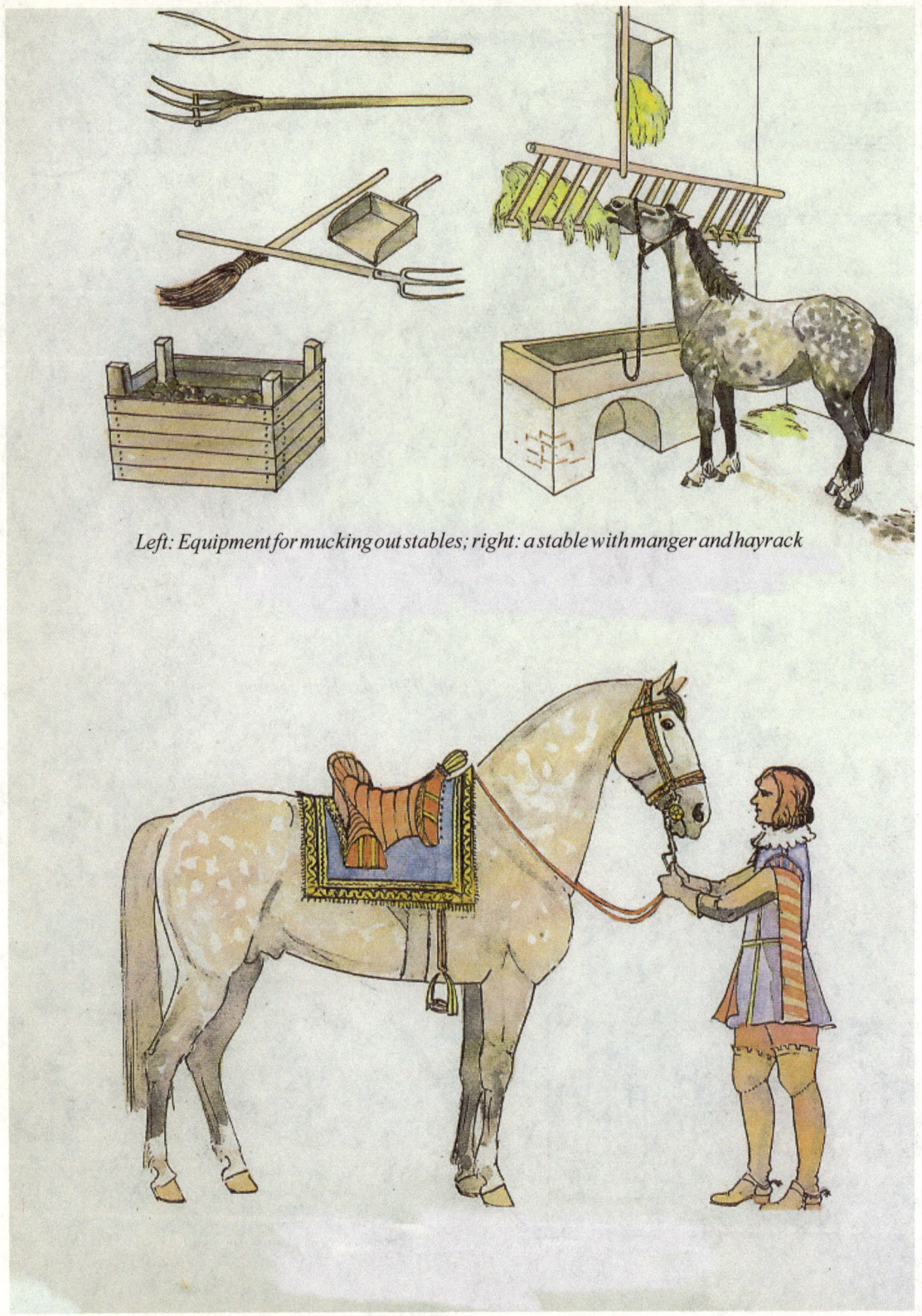

Left: Equipment for mucking out stables; right: a stable with manger and hayrack

A saddled horse ready for mounting

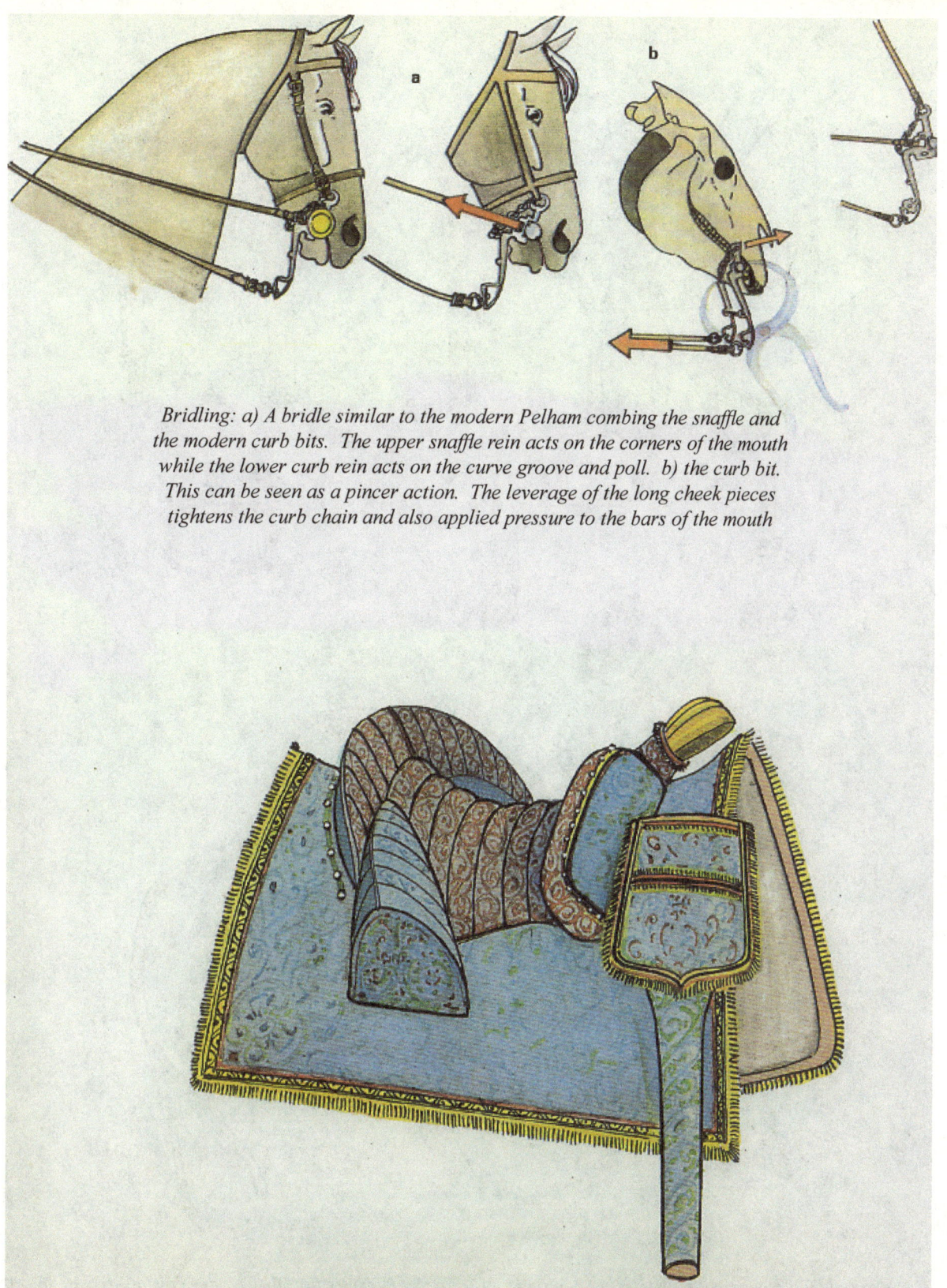

Bridling: a) A bridle similar to the modern Pelham combing the snaffle and the modern curb bits. The upper snaffle rein acts on the corners of the mouth while the lower curb rein acts on the curve groove and poll. b) the curb bit. This can be seen as a pincer action. The leverage of the long cheek pieces tightens the curb chain and also applied pressure to the bars of the mouth

The typical saddle of an officer in the early 17th century

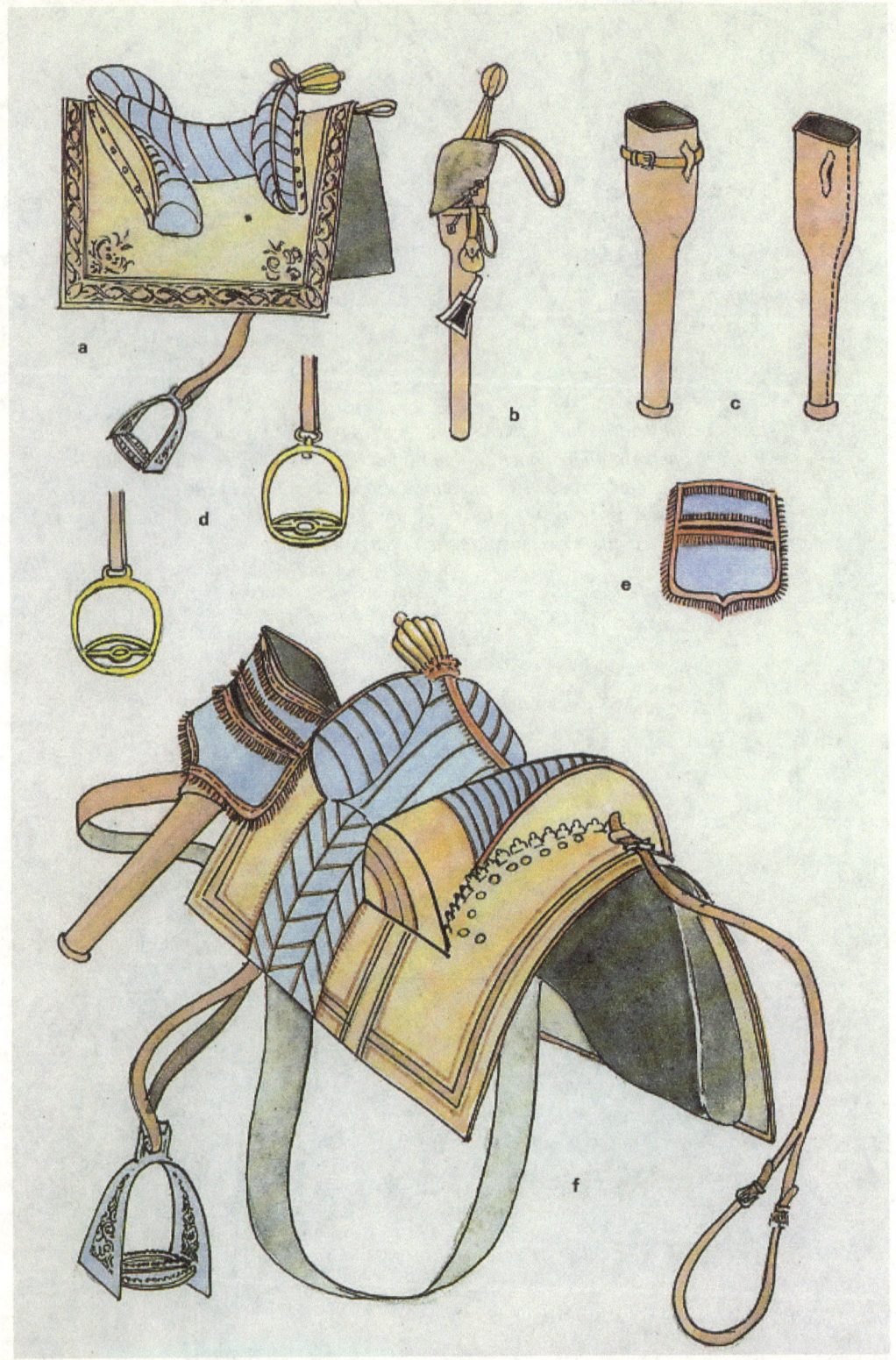

a) Cavalry saddle b)Holster with pistol, shot bag and powerhorn c) Holsters for other types of pistols d) Stirrups e) Pistol holster covers f) Complete saddler; in addition to the girth, this saddle has a breast-strap at the front to prevent it from sliding backwards and a crupper at the back to prevent it from sliding forwards on to the horse's neck

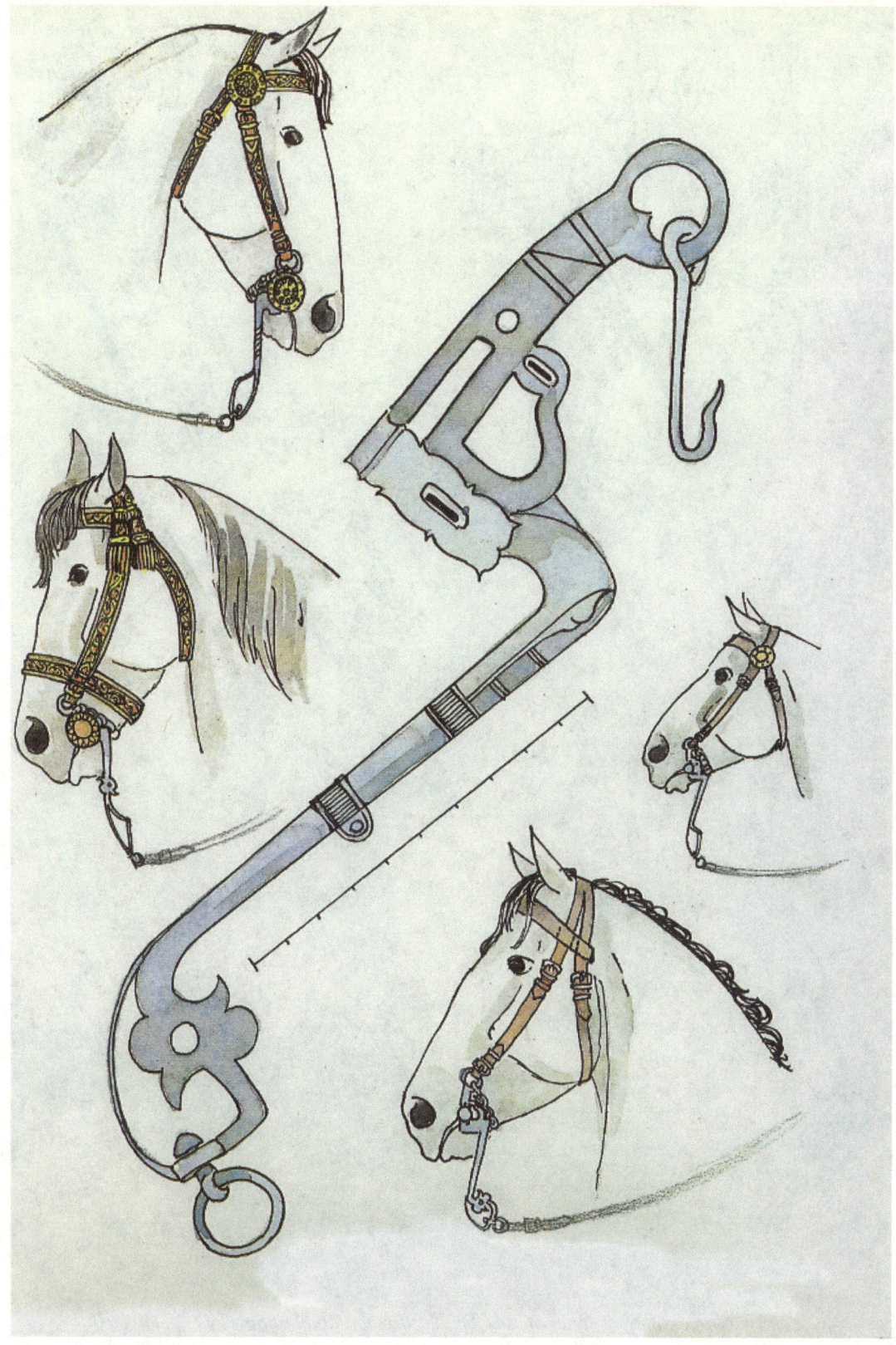

Headstalls and a curb bit cheek piece

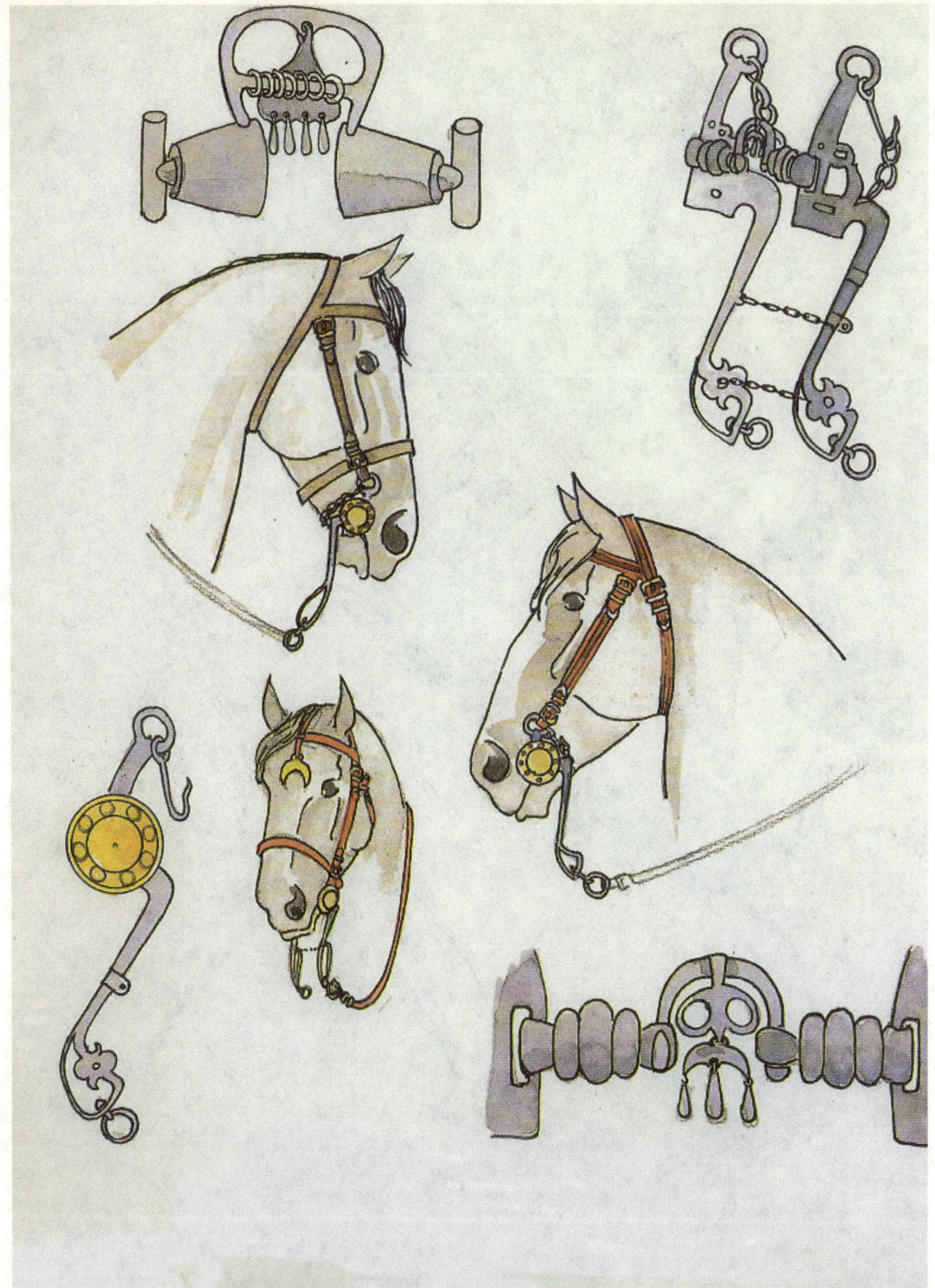

Center: Three different styles of curb bridle. Top left and bottom right: details of two curb mouthpieces showing keys to encourage the horse to mouth the bit. Top right: a curb bit showing the mouthpiece and curb chain. Bottom left: a curb checkpiece with brass trim

Correct seat according to the Pulvinel School (L'Art de Monter à chevel, Paris, 1624) – The riders face must be on the centreline between the horse's ears. CD – Both shoulders protrude evenly, forming a slight depression between the shoulder blades. EF- The left hand holding the reins must be three fingers above the pommel. G- The right hand holds a crop slightly tilted above the horses left ear. H – Both elbows held slightly away from the body. I – The legs are flexed, the knees are rigid. J – The rider's toe is near the horse's shoulder, the heel is lower than the toe and turned outward.

The rider's posture in relation to an imagined perpendicular, both at a standstill and in motion

Training a young horse a) "Breaking-in" a young horse on the lunge or long rein b) Mounting a young horse without stirrups c) and d) Simple breaking halter

Horse Combat School
Combat horses were taught to rear and attack the enemy's mount when prodded to do so, or to strike the enemy with the hind legs. For this, it was sufficient to teach the horse how to kick

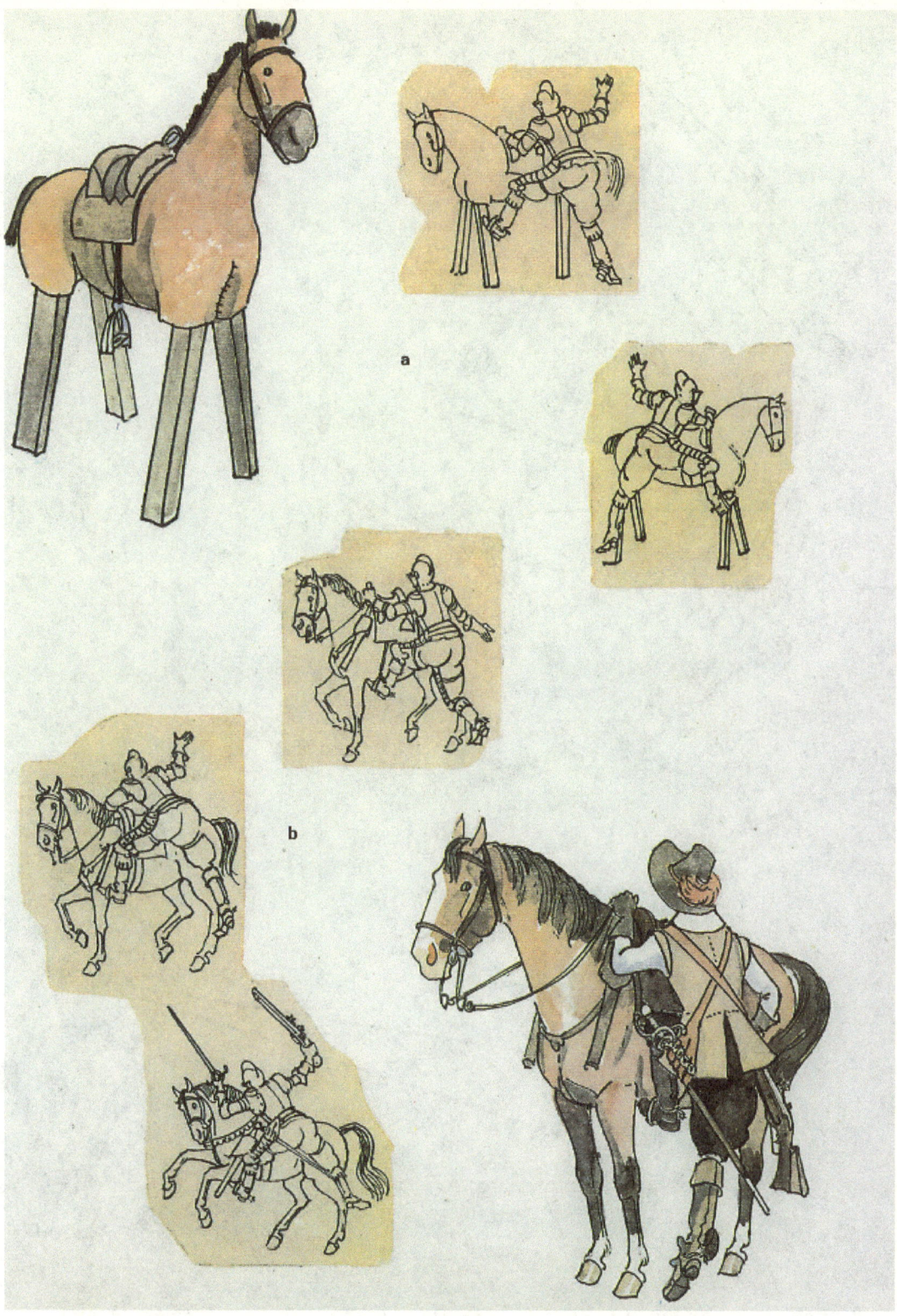

Training in Mounting
a) Training on a stuffed dummy horse b) Training on a real horse

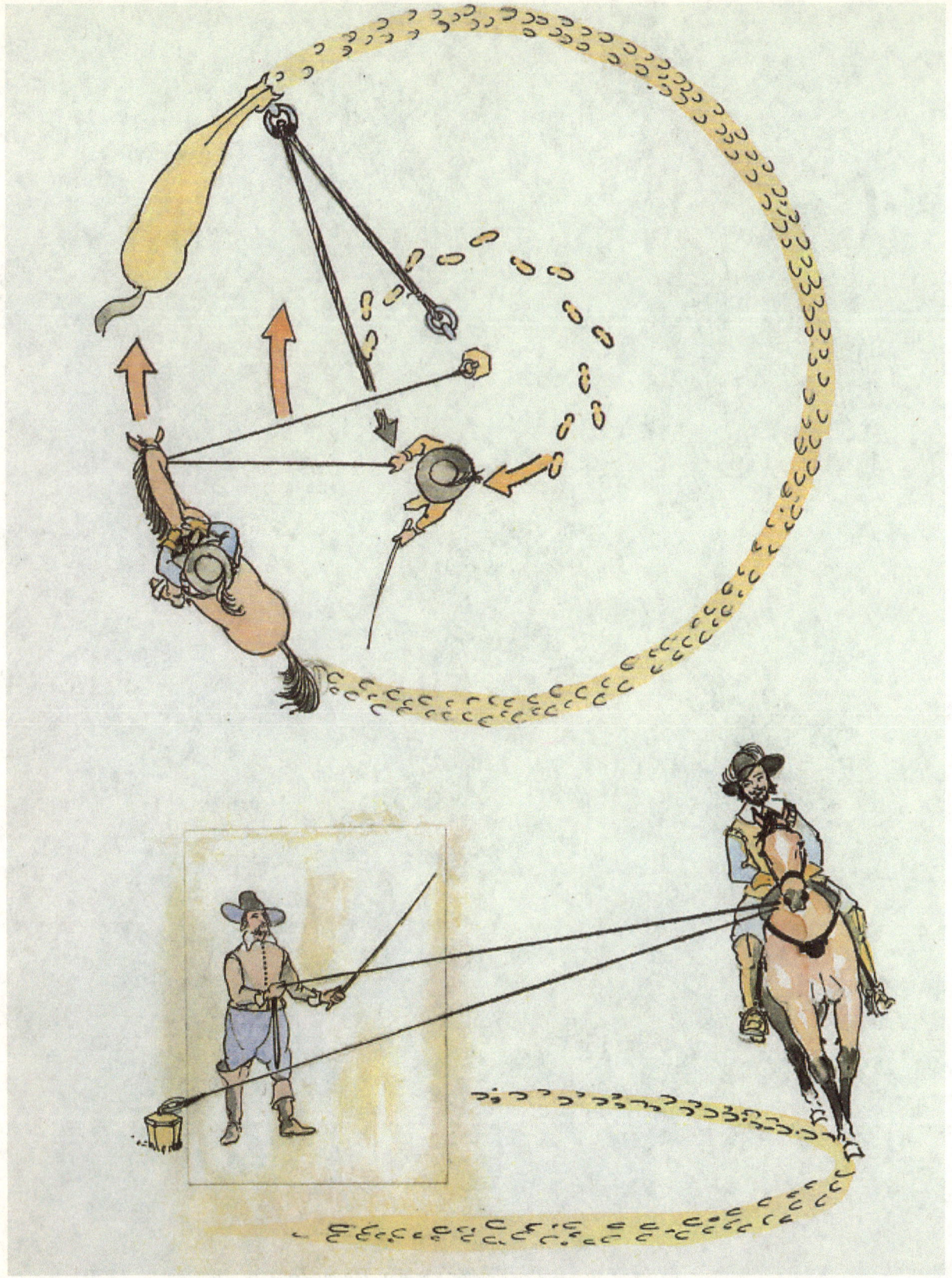

Schooling horse and rider on the lunge rein

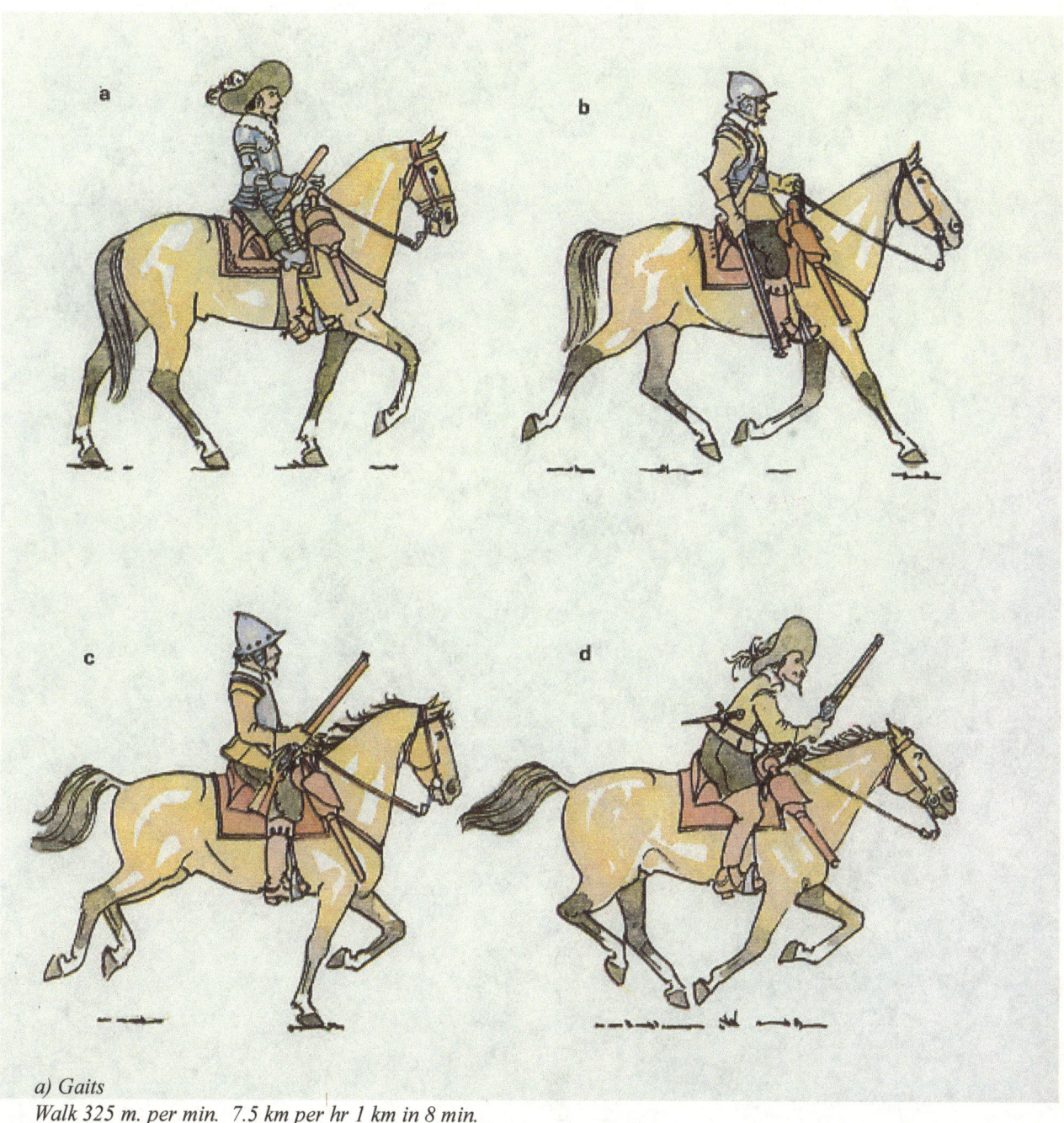

a) Gaits
Walk 325 m. per min. 7.5 km per hr 1 km in 8 min.
b) Trot
Short trot 167 – 225 m per hr. 10-13 km per hr. 1 km in 5.5 – 4.5 min. Full trot 250 -370 m. per min. 15 – 22 km per hr. 1 km in 4 – 2.7 min
c) Canter
Short canter 250 – 370 m per min, 15-22 km per hr. 1km in 4-2.7 hr. Full canter 717m per min. 43 km per hr (theoretically) 1 km in 1.14min
d) Gallop
867 m. per min. 46 km per hr (theoretically) 1 km in 1.3 min

Pistol and backsword drawing

a) Drawing pistol from holster b) Pistols were kept in holsters with grips pointing forward to ease grasping and drawing c) Drawing backsword from scabbard; the weapon was drawn over the left hand to prevent the rider from cutting himself

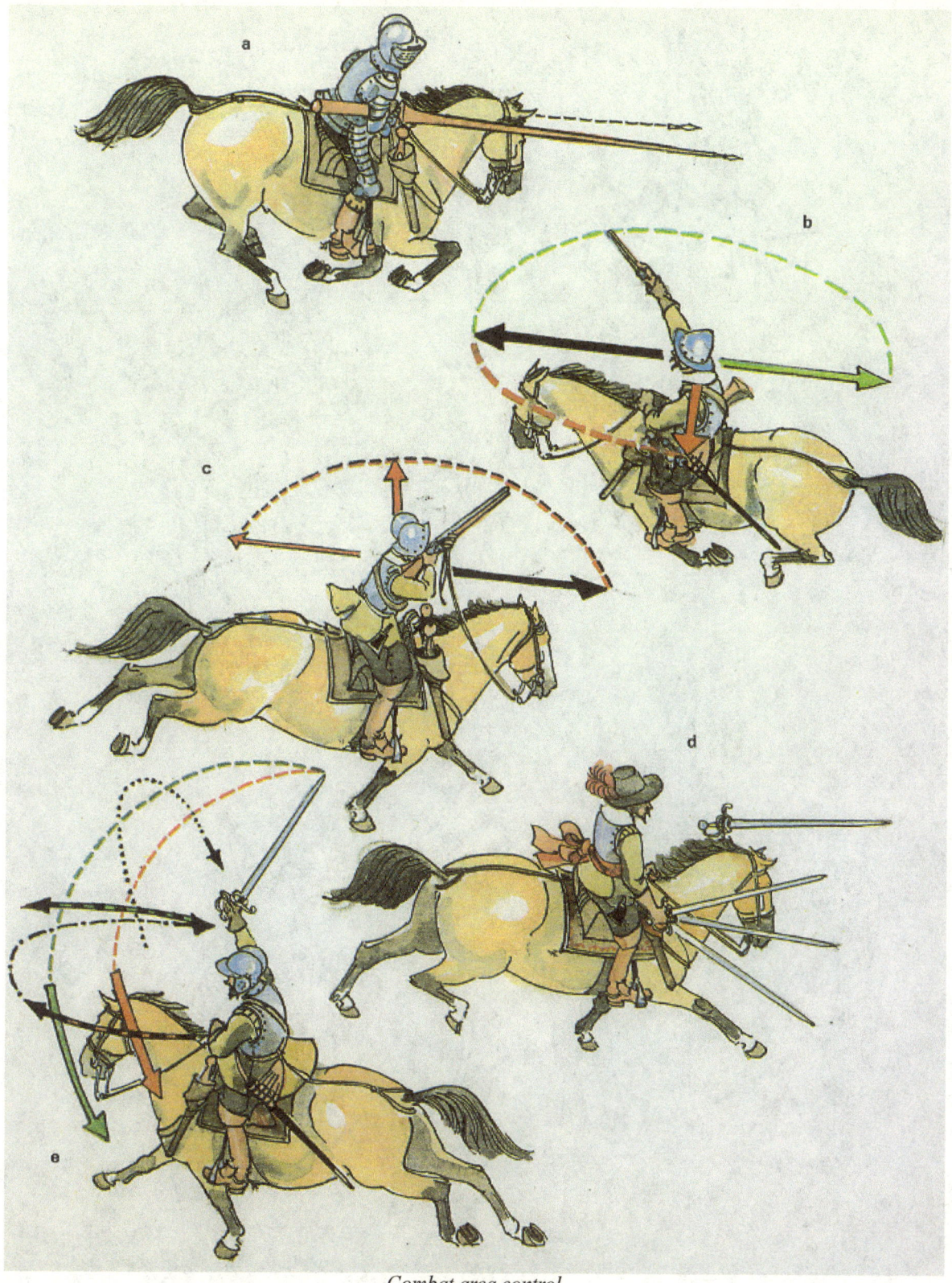

Combat area control

a) With lance along the left and right side of the horse's neck b) By rider armed with a pistol c) By rider armed with a carbine d) Using of sword for piercing e) Area controlled with cutting sword

Pistol-loading on horseback

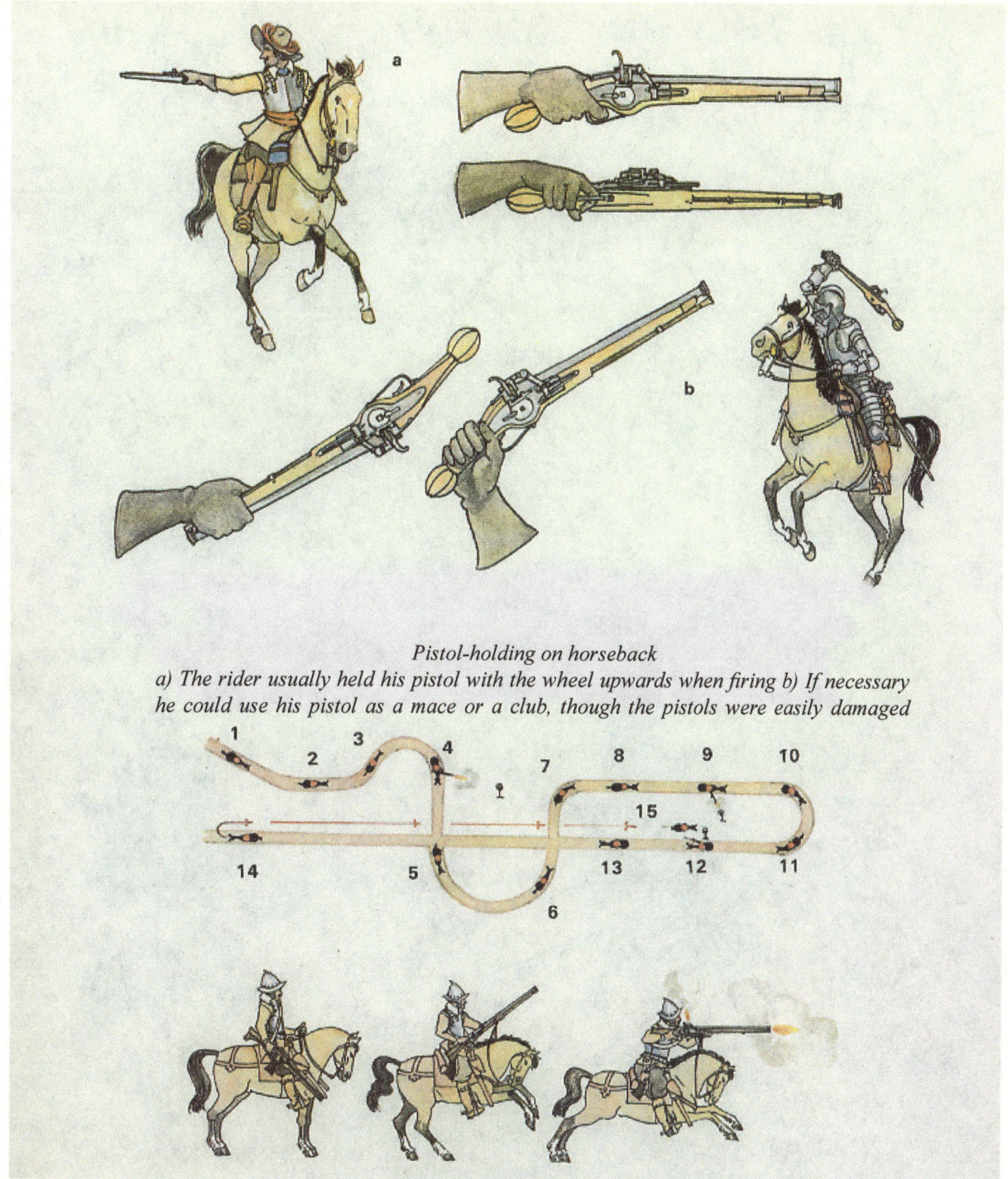

Pistol-holding on horseback
a) The rider usually held his pistol with the wheel upwards when firing b) If necessary
he could use his pistol as a mace or a club, though the pistols were easily damaged

Horsemanship training in the field riding ground

1) The rider unhurriedly drew his carbine and pistol, 2) started to trot and raised the carbine grasping it by the front grip with his left hand also holding the reins 3) switched to canter and turned to the left 4) Still canter-ing, he turned to the right and unhurriedly fired his carbine while firmly holding the reins so that if the horse was startled by fire he would not run away with him 5) He rode on, reloading the carbine 6) Then he drew the pistol, 7) raising it, with the finger ready on the trigger. 8) When he sighted the target he fired the pistol. 9) Then he began to turn his horse again, 10) making the full turn and drawing his side weapon 11) with which he was to cut into a target, 12-14) galloping to the turning point 15) and returning back to the end of the track.

Pistol-handling on horseback

a) To wind the wheellock, the rider held the pistol in his left hand together with the reins while used the spanner to turn the wheel. b) Wheellock winding key type c) Holding the pistol immediately prior to combat d) Relaxed manner of holding the pistol on horseback.

Training a horse to jump
a) Gate b) Wooden fence c) Barrel d) Fire e) Brook f) Tree g)Hedge h) Carrion heap.
The horse had to be accustomed to the smell of carrion heaps, which simulated battlefield conditions

Schooling in footbridge crossings

Tournament and riding games
a) Picking a ring hanging freely on a rope slung between two posts b) Picking a spring-loaded ring inverted in a tube hung from a horizontal bar c) Narrow-pointed lance used fo picking rings at a gallop d) Holding the lance when aiming at the ring e) Tournament game called Dzhigitovka f) Quintana riding game g) Coronet-tipped tournament lances.

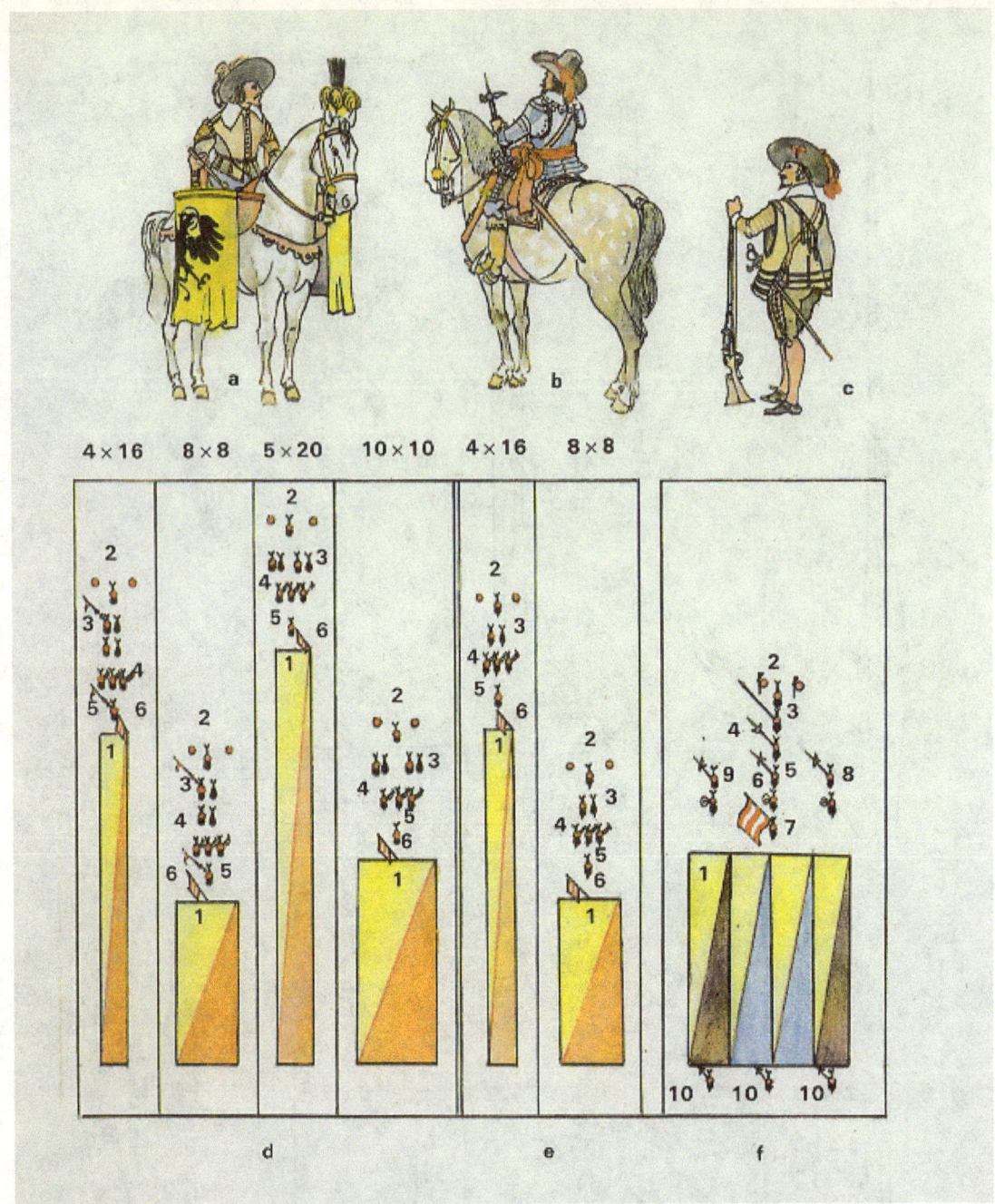

Cavalry marching column

a) Drummer b) Cuirassier colonel c) Musketeer – the colonel's personal bodyguard d) Cuirassier troops in various formations:1) Cuirassier detachment, pistol armed, 20 ranks of five riders each 2) Captain or Rittmeister, fully armed, wearing a sash and holding a staff. He was guarded by two foot carabiniers 3) Rittmaster's personal mounts led by a fully armed cuirassier and followed by a simply dressed groom. 4) Three buglers in light dress, with hats 5) Lieutenant 6) Cornet e) Arquebusiers or carabiniers in various formations: 1)Company strength: 16 ranks of 4 men each, or 8 ranks of 8 men each 2) Rittmeister with musketeer guard 3) Personal guardsman leading the horse 4) Three buglers 5) Lieutenant 6) Coronet f) Dragoons: 1) Dragoon company strength: 600 men, 100 musketeers, 20 men per rank, 10 men per file; 100 pikemen, 10 men per rank, flanked on each wing by five musketeers in line 2) Captain with bodyguard of two musketeers 3) Orderly carrying the captain's sword 4) Orderly carrying his partisan 5) Sergeant 6) Chief drummer 7) Ensign 8) Lieutenant with drummer leading the 1st detachment of musketeers 9) Sergeant with drummer leading the 2nd musketeer detachment 10) Sergeants bringing up the column rear

Cavalry first line formation

a) Grouping of 100 riders b) Position of cavalry units of total force of 500 riders. Squadron commanders, left to right: 1) Rittmister 2) Captain 3) Rittmeister 3) Captain 4) Rittmeister
The formation was followed by Quartermaster and Lieutenant

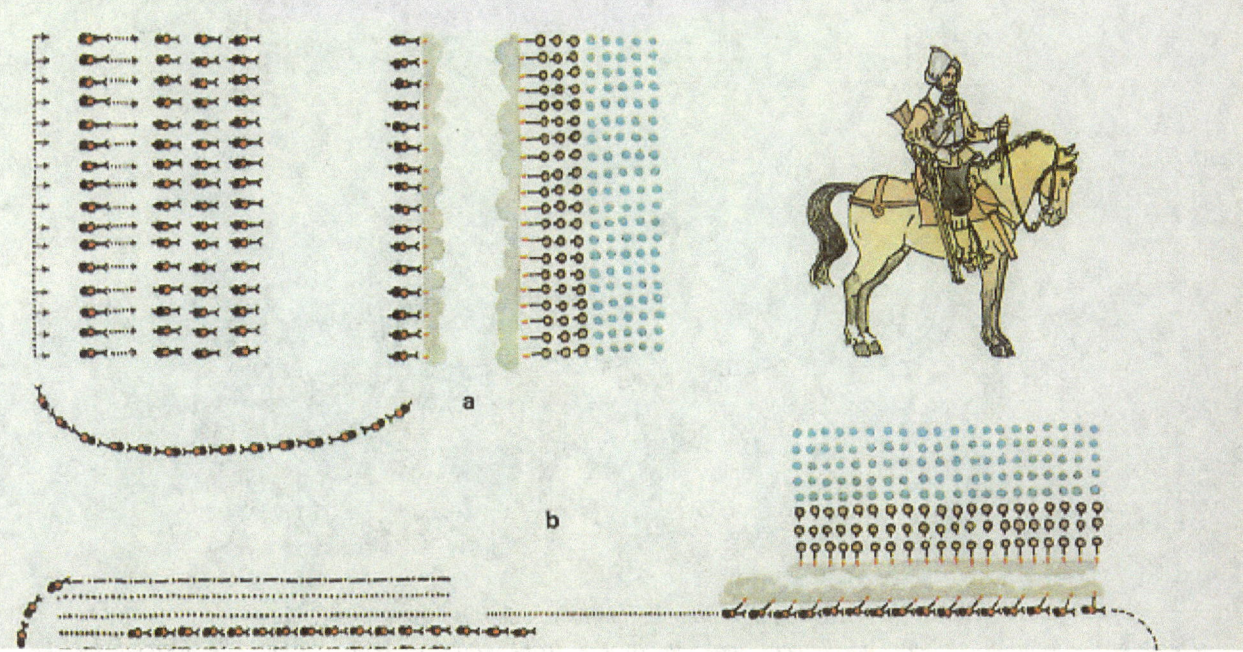

Combat tactics of firearm-equipped cavalry
a) Frontal charge: Rank after rank charged the enemy, stopping at a distance of about 30 paces and firing their weapons. Then the rank turned their horses back as quickly as possible and galloped in single file to the rear of their unit, retaking their position, having already re-loaded on the way back. As soon as the first rank cleared the field, the next rank would charge b) Flank charge: the entire file charged, riding along the enemy front and firing into his ranks. Then the file returned to its original position in the formation. Cutting weapons were used only after the enemy had been shattered by fire.

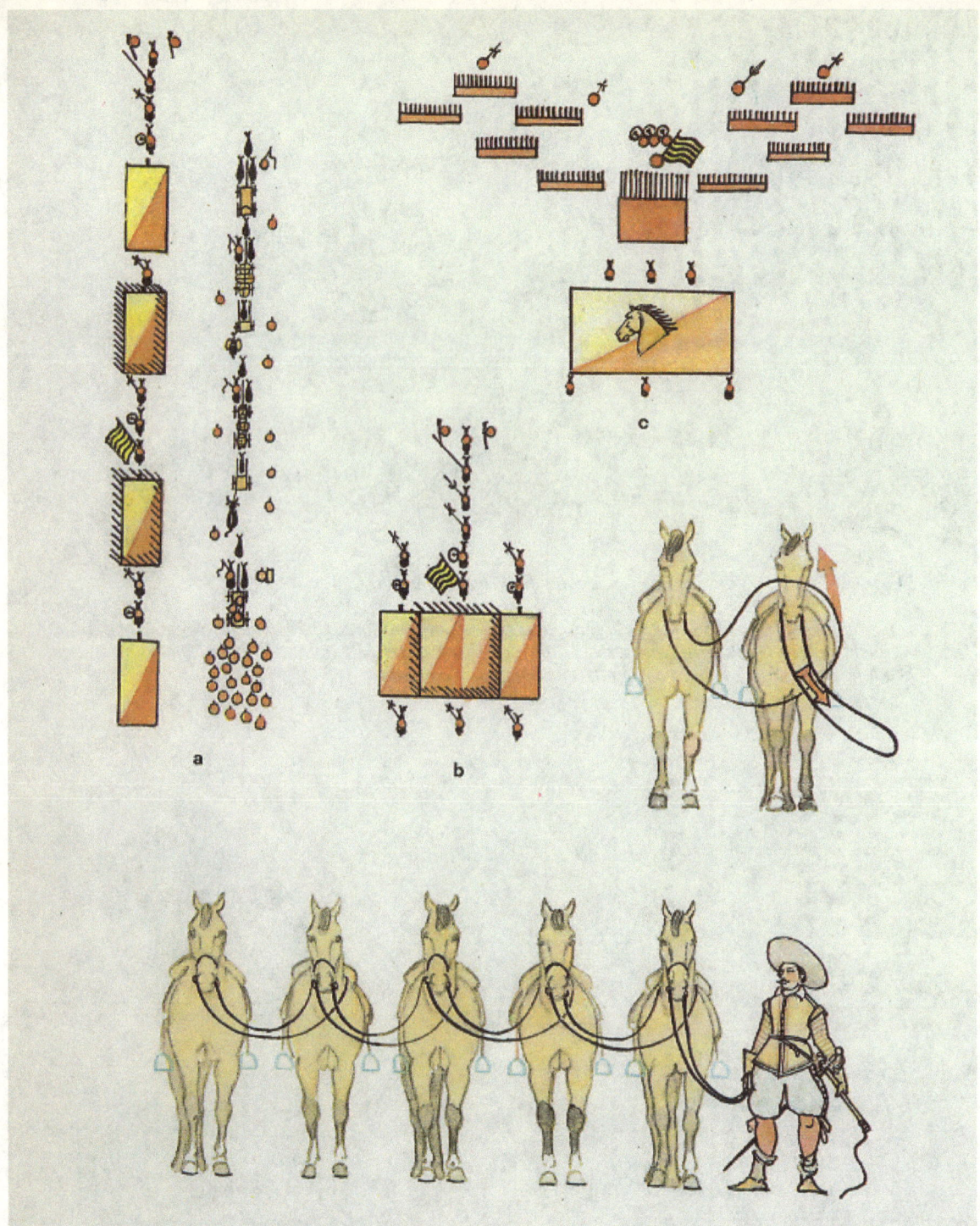

Dragoon marching column and combat formations

a) Dragoon marching column: musketeers making up the front and the rear, the middle formed by the pikemen. The supply train, pictured here on the flank, always drove behind b) In-line arrangement: pikemen again in forming the center, musketeers making up the wings c) Unit dismounted for combat: musketeers on both wings arranged in a forward-stepping echelon, pikemen forming a square center. Behind them is a square of horses tied together so that the reins of one horse are thrown over the next horse's head and so on, the last being held by a veteran horse guard. If the battle was lost, the defeated troops could not make a get-away easily because horses tied in this quite peculiar manner could not easily be disentangled. As a result, horses quite often fell into enemy hands as booty.

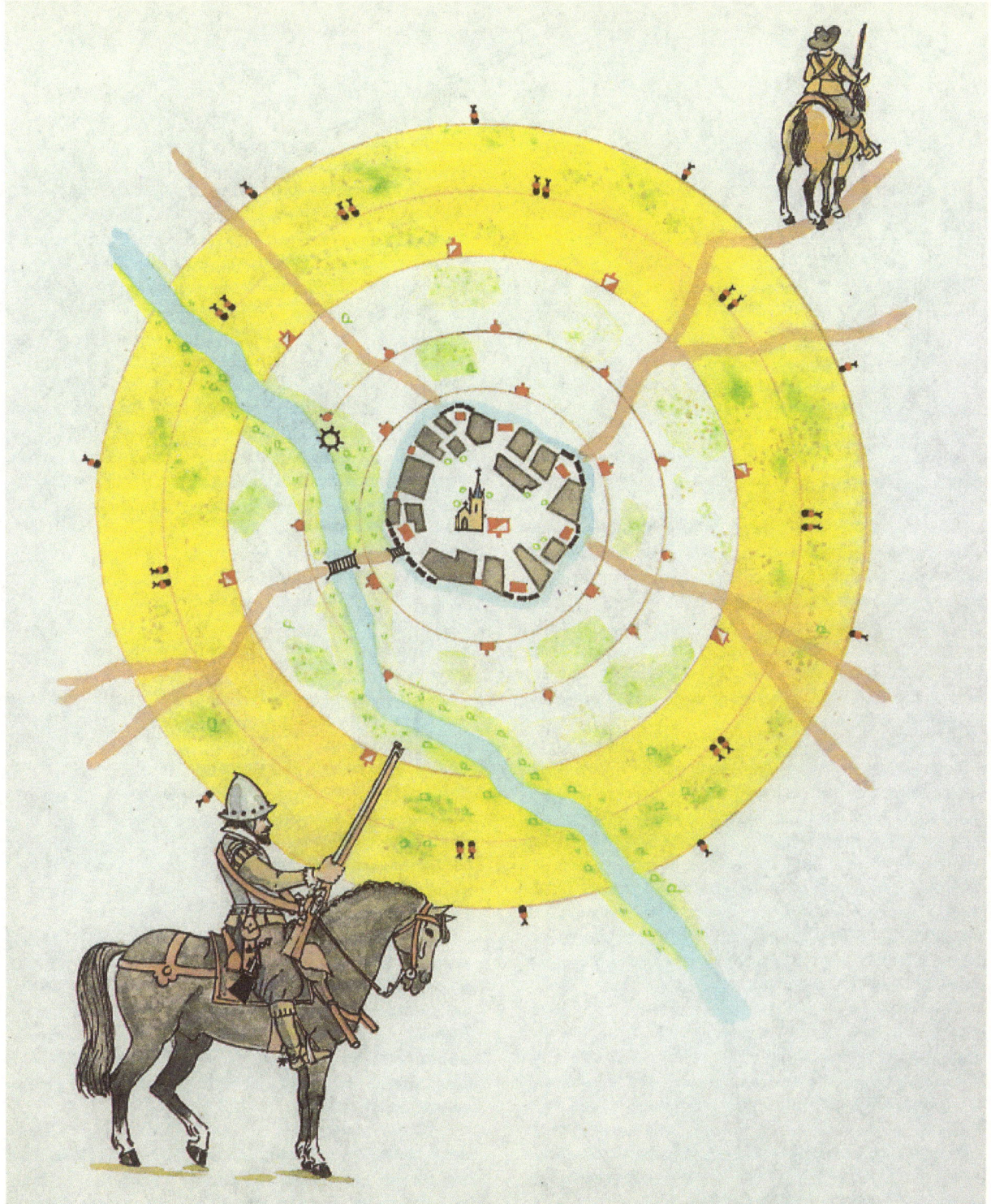

Cavalry occupation of a village – horseback and foot sentry positions

Cavalry quartering in a village had their main sentry post by the church on the village green. Mounted riders stood guard. Foot sentinels were posted at erected roadblocks at the approaches to the village. They were advanced with another circle of foot sentries, forwarded in turn by a circle of two-man foot patrols. Dragoons were best suited for this type of duty. The last circle of foot patrols were advanced with another formed by foot patrols, who in turn sent out two-man advanced patrols out front. The outer perimeter of the sentry system was manned by constantly moving single outriders.

Early 17th-century musketeers, fully armed, with kit

INFANTRY

The infantry, or foot soldiers, of the 16th and early 17th century consisted of two kinds of troops with different ordnance---namely the musketeers and the pikemen.

The musketeers were equipped with a matchlock hand-gun –the musket. This was usually 125 to 144 cm long and weighed four to seven kg, the caliber being 19 to 20 mm. The spherical lead shot weighed about 42.5 gm and the charge for one round was about 23 gm of powder. The range of the musket was 200 to 300 meters. During this period heavy muskets weighing about seven kg were supported by a forked spike called fourquette, while being fired. Later, when lighter muskets weighing four to five kg were produced, the fork became obsolete.

The musketeer carried his powder in a receptacle called a powderhorn. A measure located in the powderhorn neck gave the appropriate charge for one round. Coarse-grained powder, the so-called barrel powder, was stored in a larger horn. A smaller receptacle held the fine-grained priming-powder that was poured onto the flashpan of the musket. Both horns, slung on cords from the right shoulder, were carried on the left hip and were fastened by iron hooks to the holes in a leather tongue or flap attached to the belt to prevent the horns swinging to and fro when the musketeer was marching.

Single-round charges could be also carried in long, usually wooden, container with a lid, the containers being slung on cords from a leather strap or bandolier. The bandolier was carried on the left shoulder, and rested on the right hip, where a leather bag for lead shot was attached to it, or another bag containing such items as a small brass oil can. By the second quarter of the 17th century musketeers had already the individual charges wrapped in paper and stored in a hip satchel. These paper cartridges greatly expedited both reloading and firing.

The musketeer wore a coiled match or fuse about four to six meters long, either around his neck and shoulder or attached to his bandolier or his belt. When the troop was marching, every tenth man had to have his match lit so that the others could light theirs in case of need. When there was danger of an enemy attack, every musketeer had to have his match lit the glowing end protected against bad weather with a perforated metal cap.

Musketeers were usually armed with a side weapon: mostly rapiers and quite often daggers as well.

The pikemen, as their name suggests, were armed with the long lances called pikes, which were up to six meters in length. A pike tip had a relatively small point; the blunted butt was metal shod to allow the pike to be driven into the ground. Musketeers only wore light clothing, but pikemen were also protected by partial plate-armor consisting of a breastplate, a dossière and two plate 'tails' or tasses for thigh protection. The pikeman's head was covered with a morion or birnhelm helmet. Like the musketeer, the pikeman was also armed with a rapier, which came in handy when the pike was broken or if the pikeman had to take part in personal close-quarter combat.

The musketeer-to-pikeman ratio of an infantry unit was never stable. In the early 17th century a unit of 300 men had 160 musketeers and 120 pikemen, but the number of the latter was gradually diminishing, the pikemen being substituted by the musketeers. The long pikes of these troops had already started to be replaced with lighter, more easily handled halberds as early as the beginning of the 17th century. (Halberds were originally the ceremonial arms of officer corps or their suites.)

A typical Imperial army infantry regiment of the early 17th century consisted of five to ten battalions, each having 300 men. A unit of 1,500 to 2,000 men was already considered a strong regiment although it was not rare to have a regiment of only 800 men, or even fewer.

The battalions were further divided into small platoon-size units called korporalschafs (corporal bands) of about 24 men.

The organizational structure in those times was never fixed. Usually it was up to the unit proprietor to make it up, providing it at least conformed roughly to the custom of the period. Only the Swedish army had a regulation infantry structure, with battle orders prescribing the exact strength and organization of the battalions, regiments and brigades.

Apart from the regular infantry formed by units of at least roughly similar structure, there were also the so-called irregulars. These were the regiments raised and manned by nationalities of various Hungarian regions, such as the Hajduk and Croatian regiments, whose strength carried between 500 and 1,000 men. Also classed as irregulars were Polish infantry regiments called the 'foot Polish'.

Infantry troops were commanded by officers of various ranks. The officers differed from the rank-and-file troops mainly in the better quality of clothing and weapons, and in various kinds of ornamental trim. They wore officers' insignia in the form of colored sashes or scarves. The scarves were worn wrapped round the waist or across the shoulder and their colors varied from army to army.

A regiment of the Imperial army was led by a colonel with a lieutenant-colonel as deputy. Other regimental officers were the following: sergeant-major, chaplain, regimental quartermaster, regimental judge advocate, provost, and executioner.

The unit that came next, the battalion, was commanded by a captain, his deputy being a lieutenant. Other officers and non-commissioned staff of infantry battalions listed on the muster rolls as the prima-plana were the ensign, sergeant, leader, mustermaster, surgeon, lance corporal, corporal 1st and 2nd class, drummer and fifer.

The military service orders of the period stipulate clearly and precisely the rights and duties of each officer rank of infantry regiments. The lieutenant deputized for the battalion commander and was in charge of troop training, the ensign was elected by the enlisted men to carry the colors of the unit and in case of need he took over as deputy of the captain or the lieutenant. The sergeant supervised the guards and sentries, checking regularly that the men carried out their duties properly. Anybody who fell asleep while on sentry duty was severely punished. The mustermaster kept the unit roster and took care of the account books as well as records of provisions, ordnance and ammunition in store. The provost, who was a member of the regimental staff, was in charge of carrying out military justice. He took care that order was preserved among the troops and he checked on the quality of goods supplied to them. If the sutlers (camp followers) did not keep to the agreed prices or if they sold goods of poor quality, he was entitled to confiscate their stocks.

A newly-mustered troop underwent a thorough training. Turns of individuals and entire ranks were drilled as well as changes of front by wheeling around a flank. Drills of rank distance changes were also trained as well as turnabouts of entire files.

After mastering the close-ordering drill the soldiers learned how to drill with their weapons. The musket drill sequence was long and complicated: the musket loading and firing drill of the Imperial army during the Thirty Years' War was broken down into 99 positions accompanied by 163 orders. By the later 17th century the number of positions had been whit-

tled down to 43 although even these were too many to memorize easily. One can see that the difficulties a soldier met with during his training were enormous.

The entire complex of orders taught the musketeer to go automatically through the prescribed sequence of motions when taking the musket off his shoulder where it was carried on march or when loading his weapon, fixing the match into the matchlock doghead and, at last, firing. In the course of training the trooper had to master all the motions performed with his gun, especially the sequence of hand motions when lighting the match. Handling the burning match in close proximity to the flashpan with the fine priming-powder already poured on to it was very dangerous. The slightest carelessness or imprecision could cause a shot go off unintentionally and a comrade might be hurt or killed. All the motions the musketeers had to go through were designed to take as little time as possible. The musketeer had to learn how to wield his weapon not only in combat but on sentry duty as well.

Since musket loading took up so much time, the musketeer troops used the same combat order as the cavalry, in which the first rank of the formation was successively replaced by other ranks. The first rank fired its volley, and then split into two parts, each returning along the side of the closed formation to rejoin and reload at the rear. This maneuver was repeated by the second rank, then the third, fourth and so on. In this way continuous fire of the formation was maintained.

Upon an enemy cavalry charge or if the enemy infantry advanced too close to an infantry formation, the musketeers would retreat behind the pikemen, who were better equipped for close-order combat.

The pikemen underwent training that was similar to that of the musketeers. The complex motions needed to give the pikeman total mastery of his weapon was only slightly less extensive than that of the musketeer. In the course of his training the pikeman learned the proper battle position for his pike, how to hold the ground with his pike against a cavalry or infantry charge, how to stand on sentry duty, how to hold his pike when at ease, how to carry it while marching, how to lower it from his shoulder when the unit was passing through a gate in closed ranks, and so on.

The shapes of battle formations of the period were quite varied. One of the many formations was the so-called 'Spanish tercia', a chessboard arrangement of detachments in three successions. First came the vanguard formed usually in two detachments, then came the main forces in several parts and the rear was brought up by another two smaller units. A tercia was between 2,000 and 3,000 men strong and was divided into 70 to 100 files of up to 30 men each. Each tercia was surrounded by musketeer ranks and cavalry troops were placed on the flanks and sometimes between the individual tercias as well.

Due to the further development and improvement of hand-guns and artillery and their increasing role in warfare some of the early 17th – century European armies began to employ linear combat formations, and therefore reverted to so-called linear tactics.

These new battle formations originated in the Netherlands in the early 17th century. As was the custom of the period, the Dutch army was composed of three parts – vanguard, main forces and rearguard, the three charging either simultaneously or one after another as they approached the enemy. But, in contrast to the battle orders of other armies, the Dutch would break their formation into three lines, deploying their troops so that the width of the front would be much greater than its depth. This enabled the Dutch to use their musketry much more effectively – which they had more of than any other army of the period. Their linear formation gave the Dutch a flexibility of maneuver during battle, which helped them to defeat the Spanish, whose customary formation in a huge tercia was relatively immobile and prevented the Spanish from making full use of their musketry.

There was further development of the linear formation and tactics by the Swedish army during the Thirty Years' War, helped by the great number of muskets available to the Swedish infantry. The battle formation of every Swedish regiment usually consisted of two lines, or waves. The first line was formed by one battalion and the second, 150 to 200 meters behind from the first, was manned by the remaining two units. In battalions formations the musketeers no longer surrounded the pikemen but flanked them, usually three ranks deep. Squadrons of cavalry were positioned on the wings of both regimental lines, with artillery in front of the first line and in the gaps between the battalions.

When a continuous line of musketeers was required, both musketeer wings of the first battalion line advanced to the front and took up their position in front of the pikemen; the musketeers of both lines withdrew behind the pikemen and the second line pikemen advanced into the gaps between the first line troops.

This battle formation allowed for the greatest use of men and firepower and at the same time minimized casualties from enemy artillery. With their excellent training, more efficient and lighter weapons, and their three-rank deep formation, all musketeer ranks could fire simultaneously, the first rank kneeling, the second squatting and the third standing upright. In this way the musketeers were gradually becoming the decisive factor of any battle.

Other musketeer types and a huntsman with a hunting gun

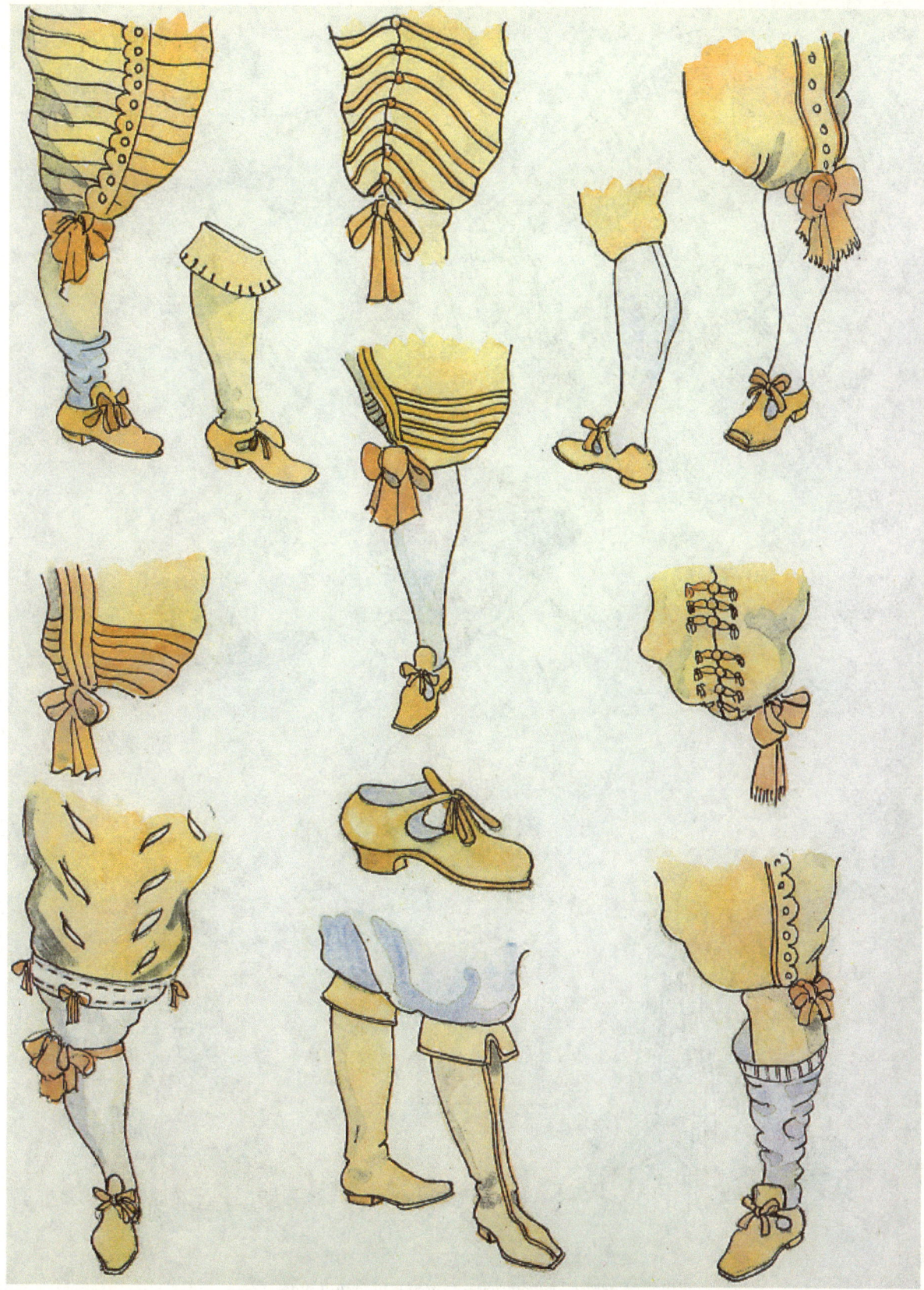

Musketeer's and pikemen's breeches, shoes and hosiery

Early 17th-century infantry tunics and hats

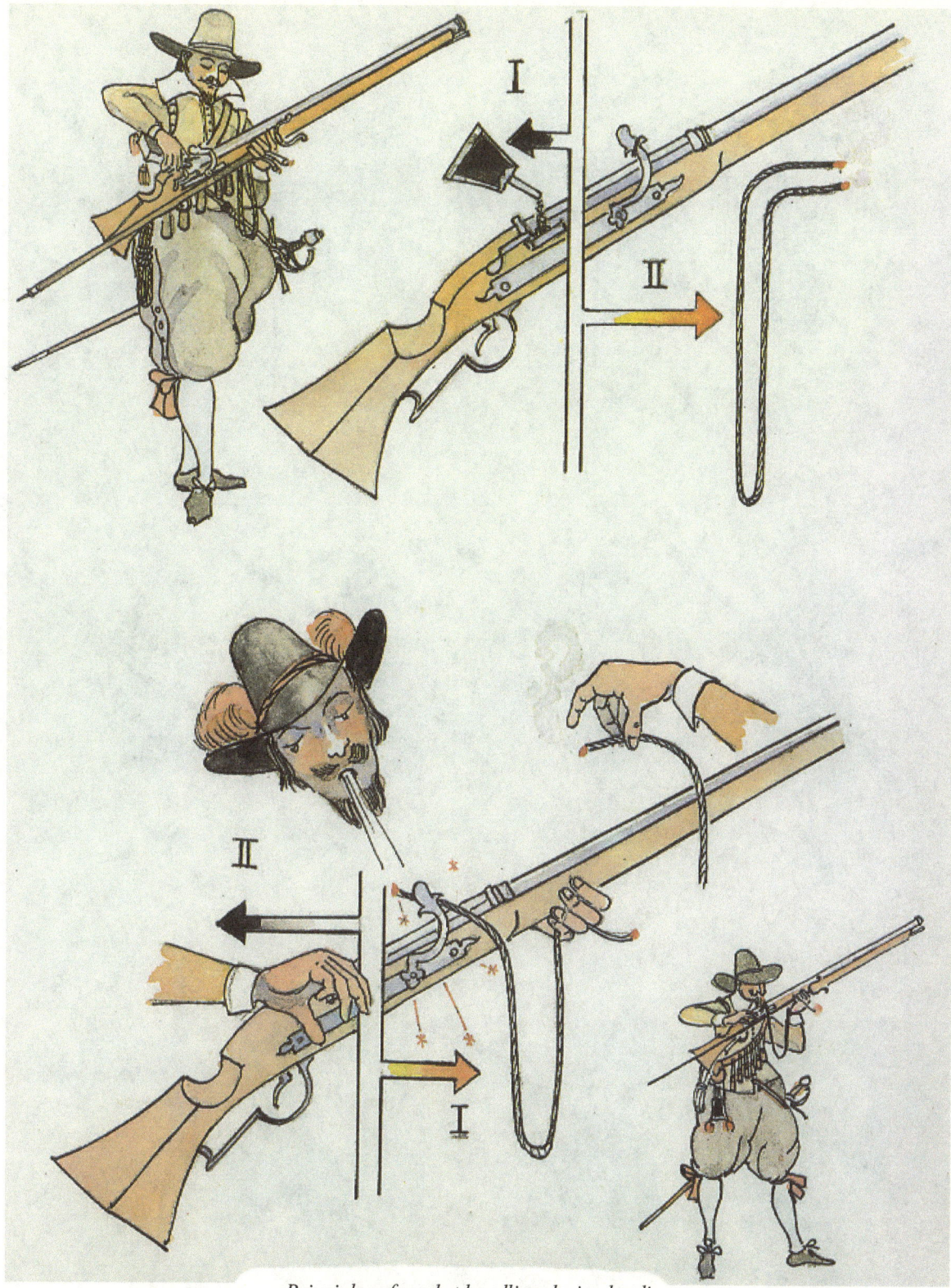

Principles of musket handling during loading.
When the musket was being loaded it was extremely important to have the match
far enough from the pan while pouring the gunpowder into the latter. Before firing
the gun it was necessary to cover the pan and to blow on the match to make it glow

Musket loading sequence drill I

Musket loading sequence drill II

Musket loading sequence drill III

Musket loading sequence drill IV

French musketeers

Detail of French musketeer dress

Foot pikeman, with ordinance and kit

Pike handling drill I

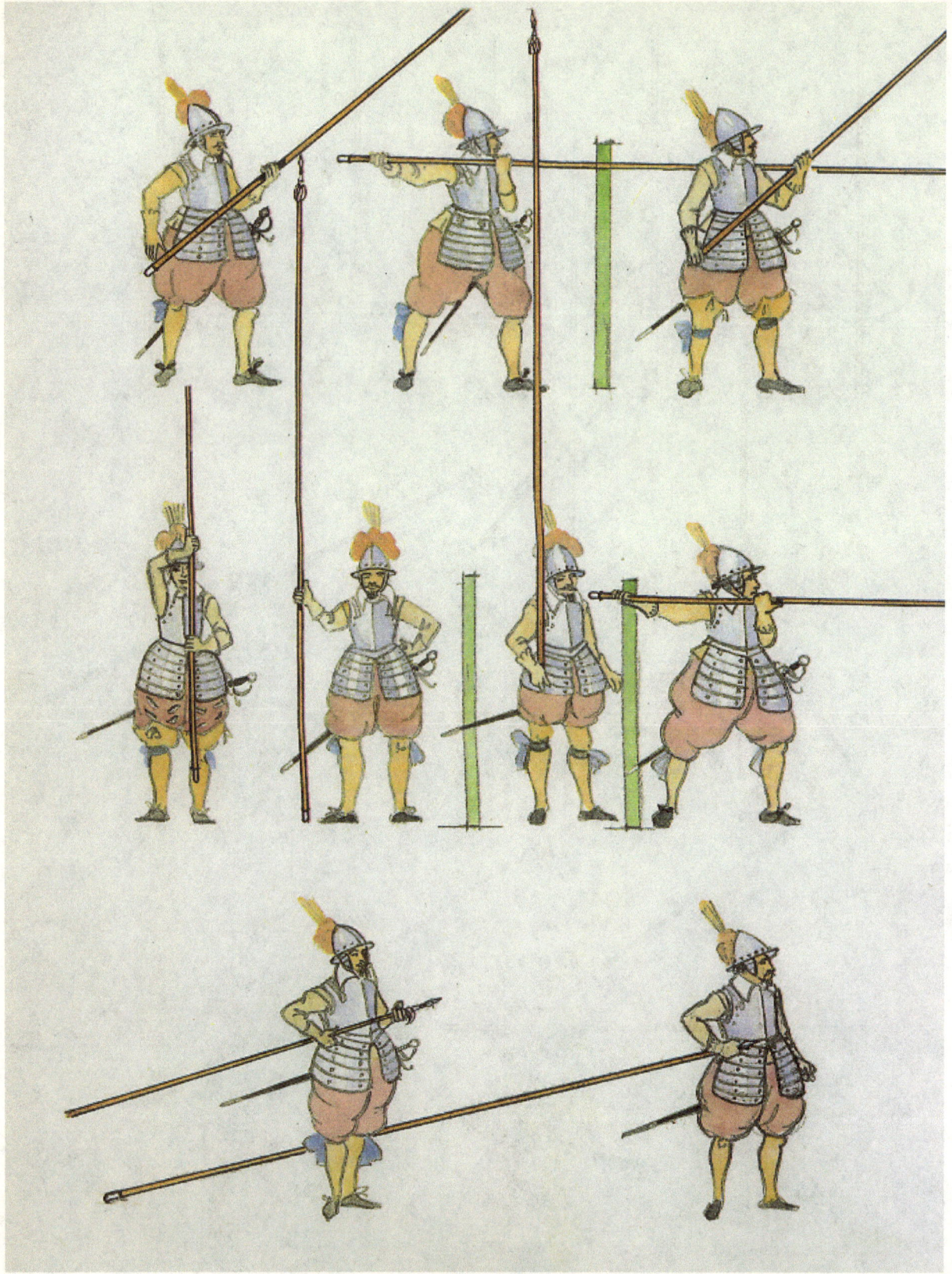

Pike handling drill II

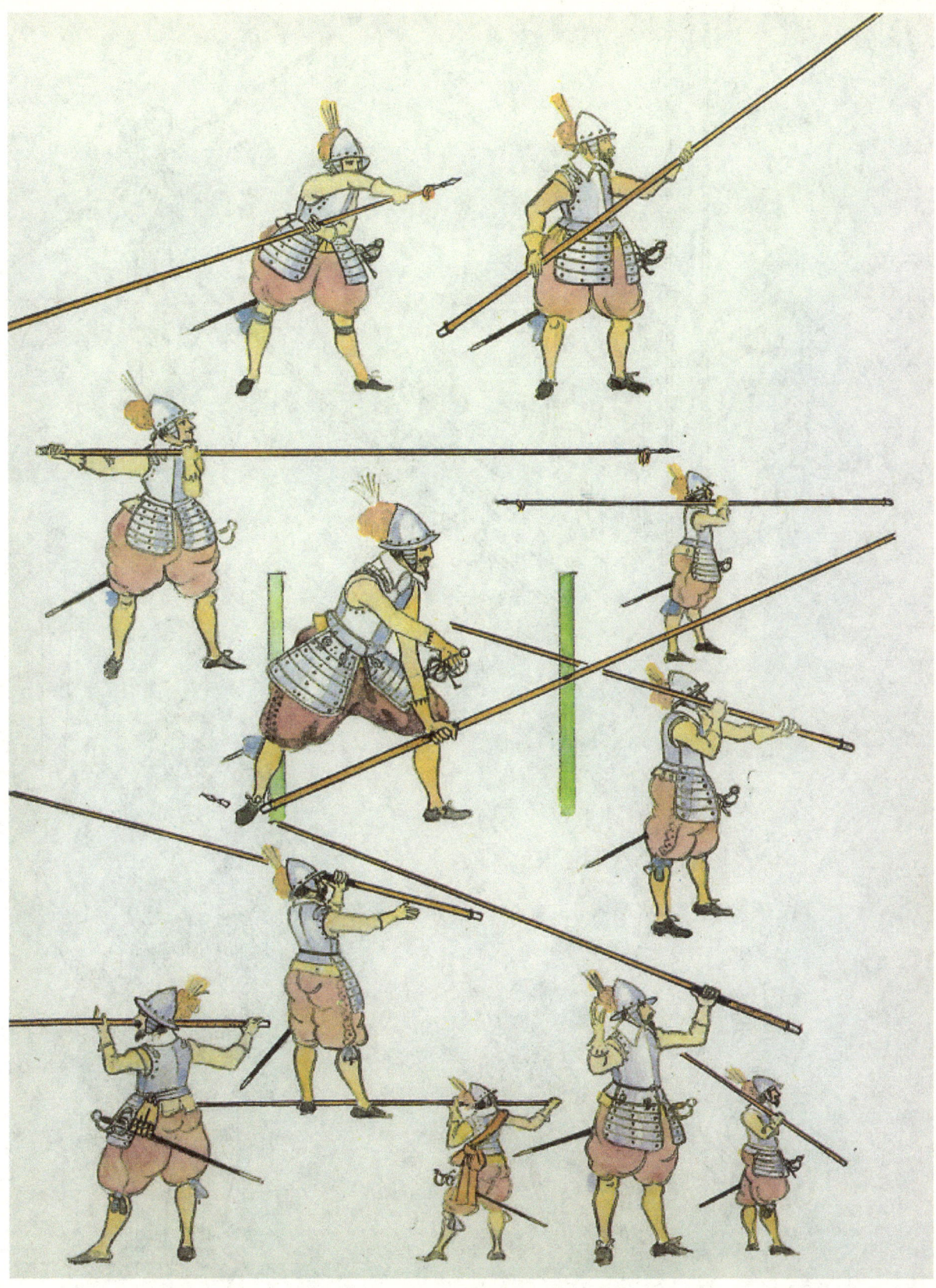

Pike handling drill III

Member of the Prince of Orange Guards, armed with a pike, sword and buckler, 1608

Officer's clothing of the Pappenheim, Jr. Regiment

Various kinds of early 17th-century military dress

Bearing Colors

a) Colors carried resting on the right arm b) Captured colors carried back to own unit. It was the privilege of the captor to bring the captured colors with the truck pointing to the ground and to display it this way at parades. c) The ensign dancing during the display of the colors, usual in the period. d) Display of the colors e) Colors carried on the shoulder

Bearing infantry colors

Drummer and fifer
a) Drummer with side drum carried on the let hip next to the sword b) Fifer c) Drum
with rope-tensioned tuning heads d) Military fife, early 17th century e) Carrying the
drum on the back while marching.

Various styles of municipal guards' costumes, early 17th century

Other types of municipal guards' dress, early 17th-century Netherlands

This is the way soldiers looked after a battle during The Thirty Years' War

Early 17th-century soldier types
a)Cuirassier in half-armor b) Pikeman c) Cuirassier in half-armor
d) Pikeman in light dress e) Officer, in half-armor

Spanish soldiers, early 17th-century, and a typical monk's habit from the same period

Scottish rifleman, early 17th-century, and a Scottish claidheamhmor sword

Infantry formations
a) Infantry troop of 144 men; 96 musketeers, 44 pikeman b) Pikeman
with his pike c) Various Imperial pikeman, early 17th-century

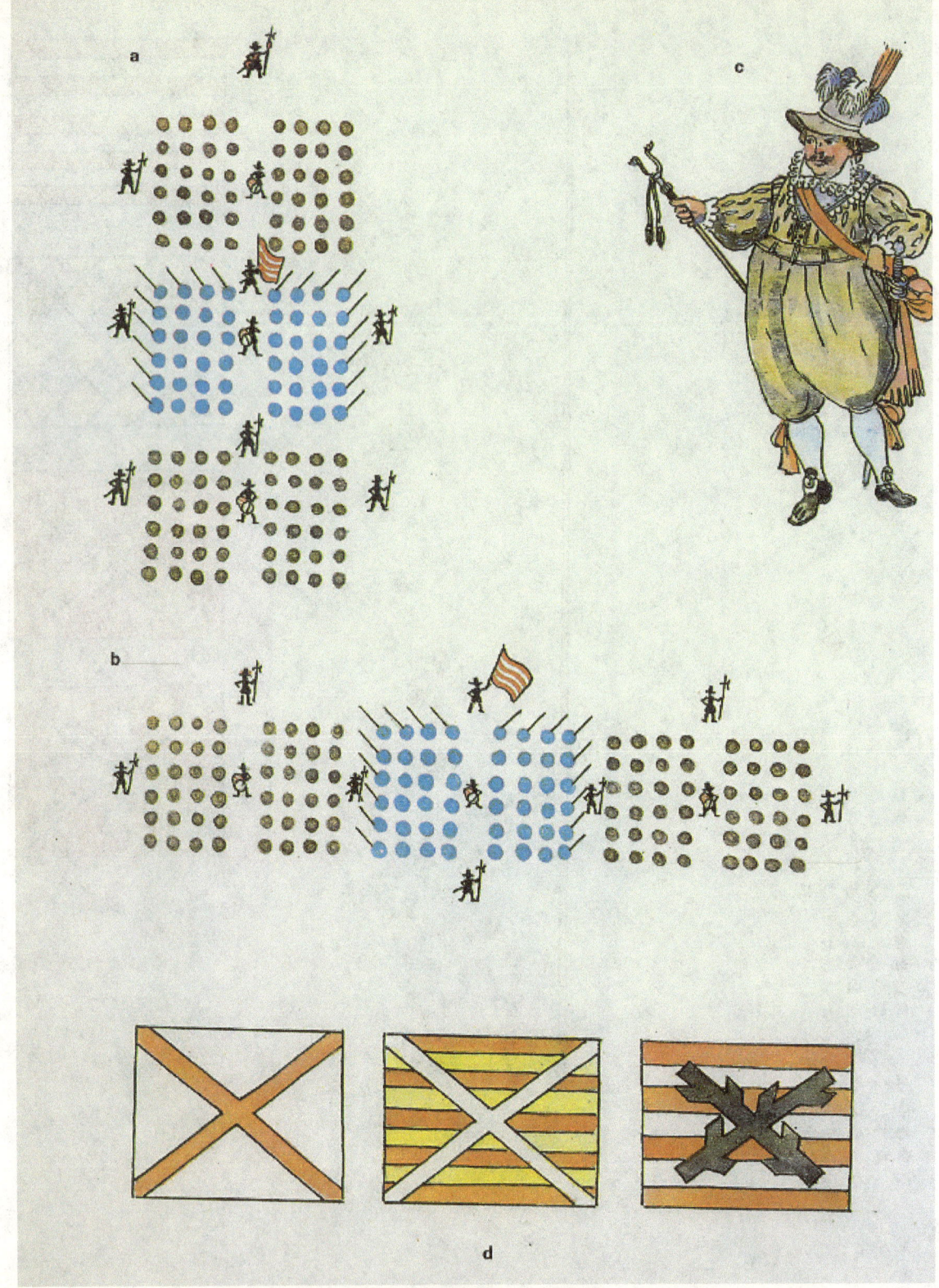

Infantry company formation

*a)Infantry company in double marching order b) Infantry company in line c) Infantry
troop commander d) Colors of various Imperial army regiments*

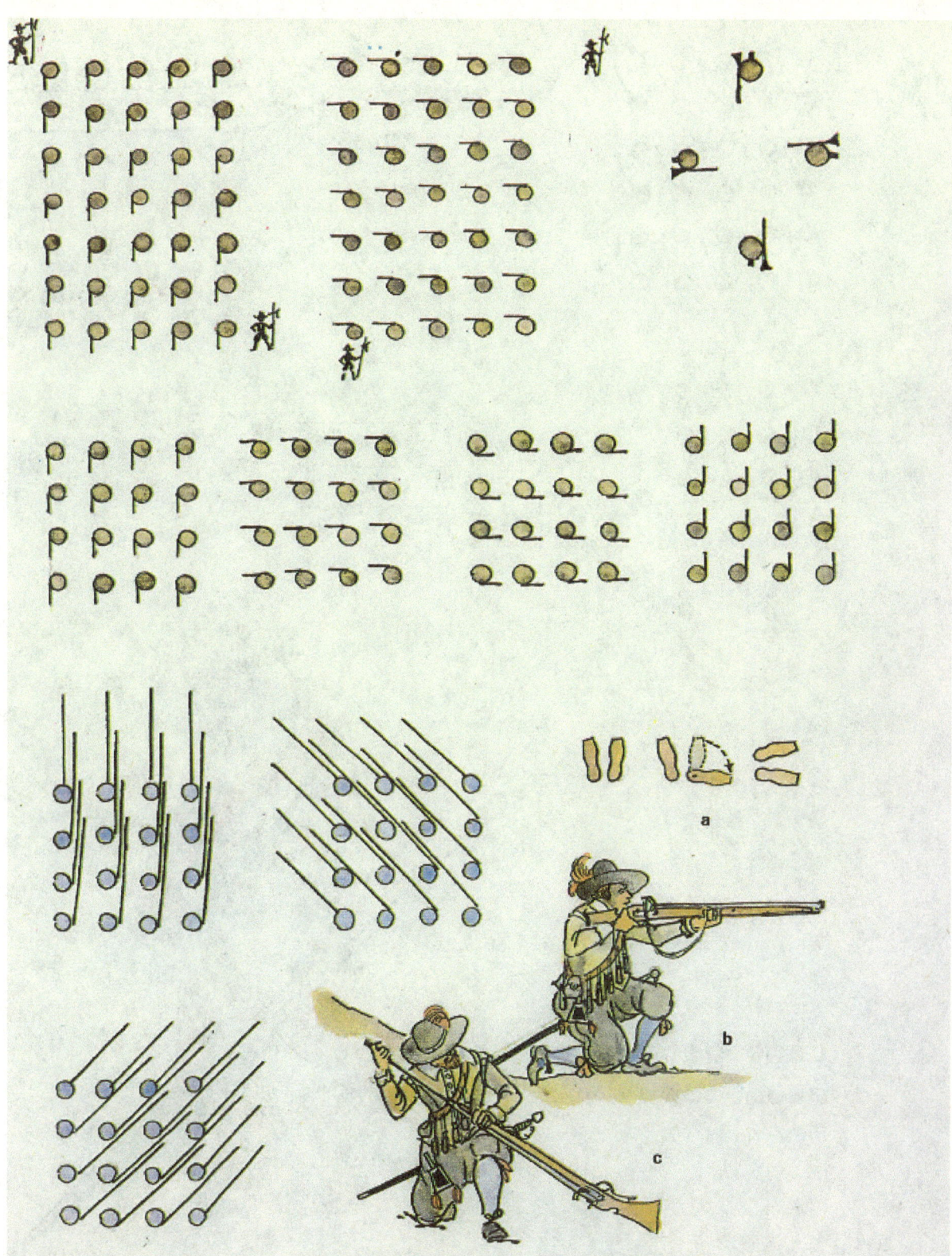

Infantry turn drills, ranks and files

a) Fleet movement, about -right b) Rifleman kneeling c) Rifleman loading in kneeling position

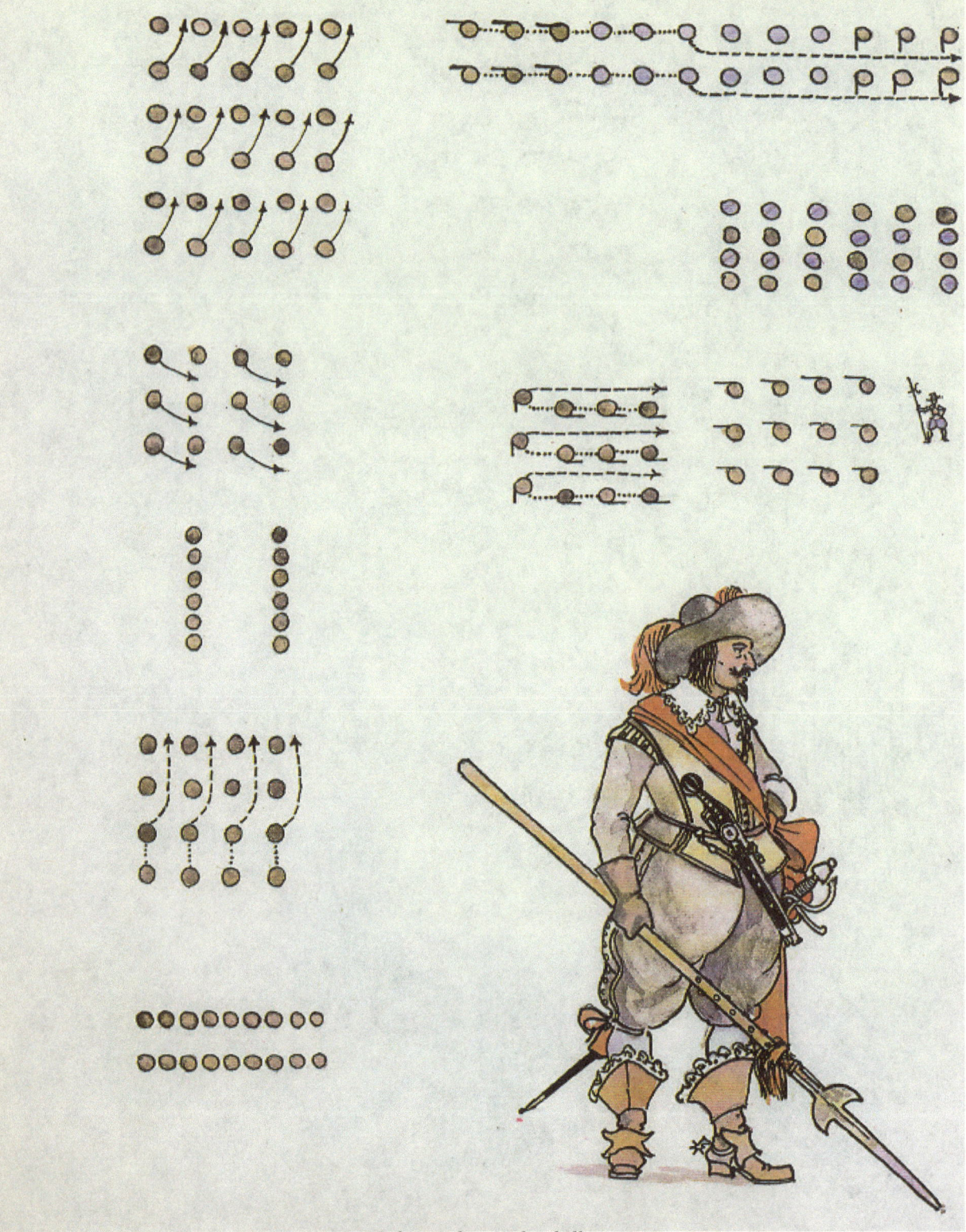

Infantry close-order drill
a) Rank and file drills b) Officer with pistol suspended from the belt with
a hoof fixed on the butt inner side

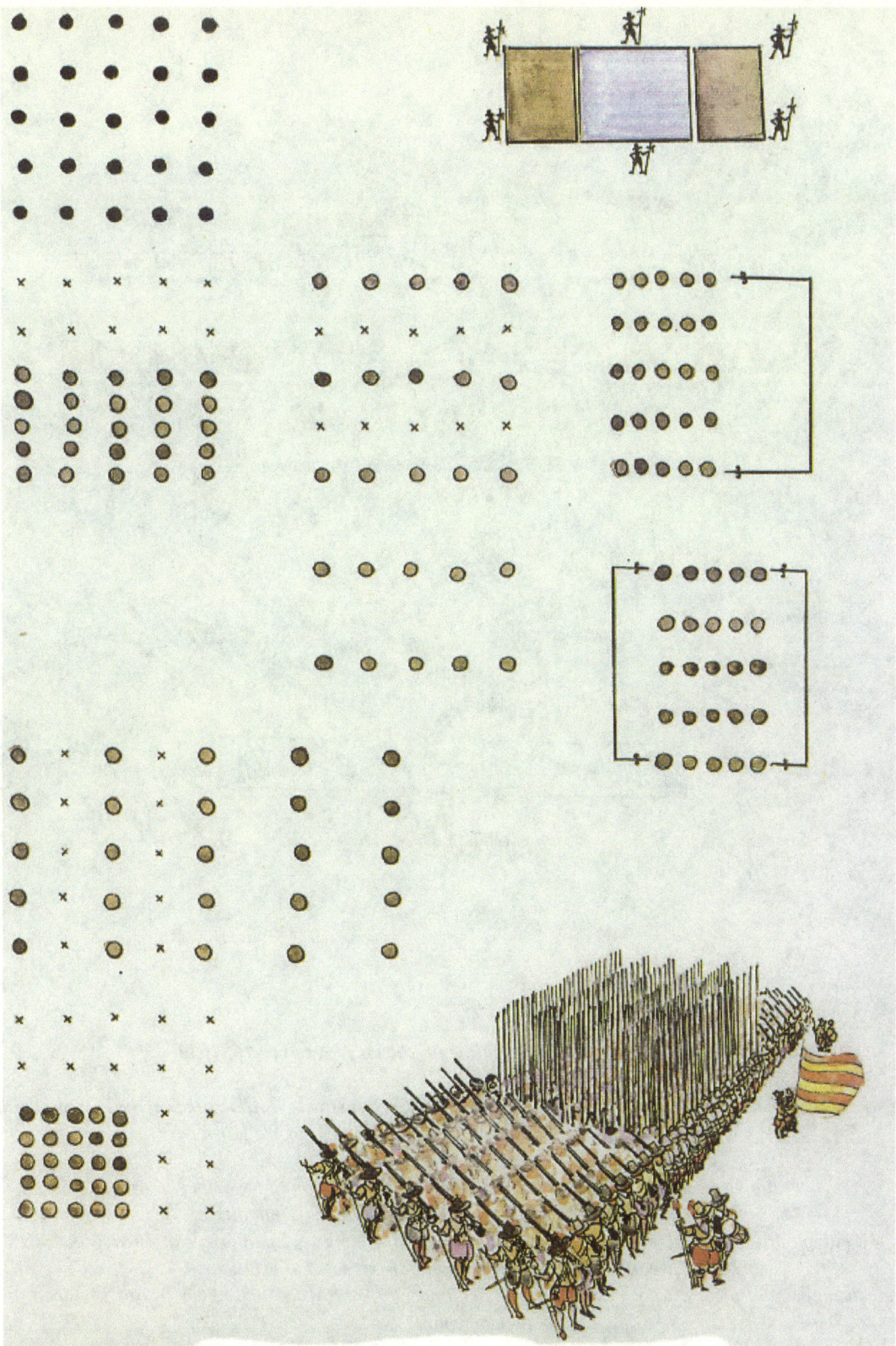

Infantry close-order infantry drill: closing and opening ranks

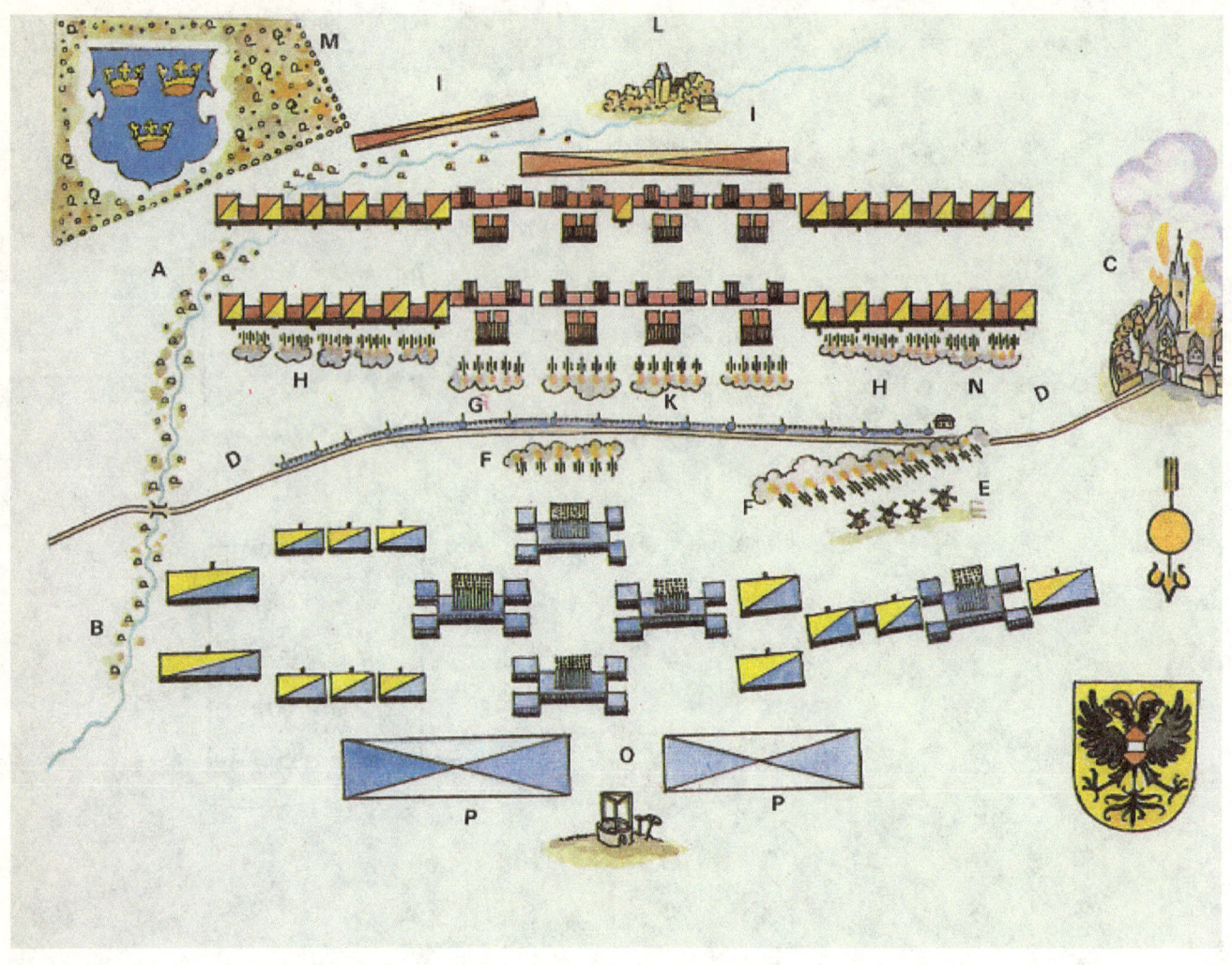

Troop positions prior to the Battle of Lützen, November 16, 1632

On the southern side are the Swedish troops commanded by King Gustavus II Adolphus, on the northern side is the Imperial army under the command of Albrecht of Wallenstein.

*A- Battle formation of the Swedish troops B-Battle formation of the Imperial troops
C-The town of Lützen D-The Leipzig road E-Windmills
F-14 cannon of the Imperial artillery, positioned among the windmills, 7 cannon positioned at the dikes
G- Swedish artillery, five cannon in front of each brigade
H -Swedish regimental pieces, total of 40 cannon positioned in front of the musketeer troops assigned to the cavalry units
I-Wagon train of the King's troops K-Moat L-The village of Chursitz
M- The village of SchölsingerHölslein N-Millers' houses O-Gallows P-Imperial army caissons*

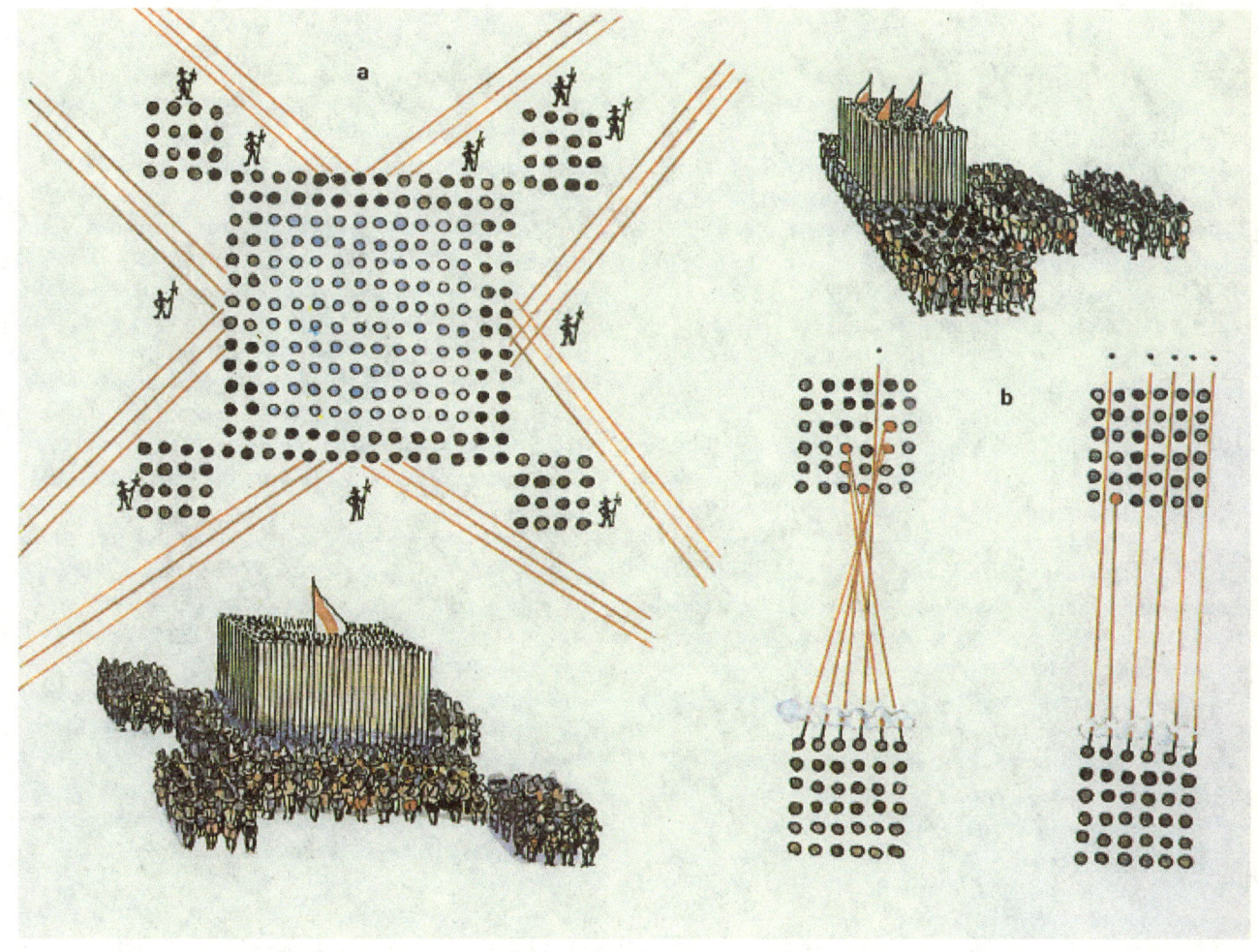

Infantry if combat formation

a)The infantry square could easily change the direction of fire for own protection as well as protection of the neighboring units

b) Concentrated fire would hit more targets than direct fire at which the individual shots might go between the rank gaps.

a)Musketeer firing his weapon supported by a fourquette b) Close order combat

CLOSE ORDER COMBAT

The military literature of the Thirty Years' War period offers illustrations of every imaginable kind of man-to-man combat. Close order combat was usual in the last part of a battle or in skirmishes between small detachments, or when an encampment was raided, a marching unit ambushed or a town or village was pillaged.

We are shown how to use a sword to parry an attack from a musket stock, and we see soldiers using helmets, musket forks or even their bandoliers as weapons. We can see combatants indulged in a fierce struggle, sometimes the quicker party ending a combat by bashing in his adversary's head with a stone. These pictorial instructions usually end by advising the victor to strip the loser's clothes off as booty.

The usual weapons in single combat were for piercing and cutting—the so-called 'cold' weapons. The growing skill in weapon design had given these weapons many new shapes; a range of specialized forms was perfected to give the user the upper hand in personal combat.

A cross guard and knuckle bow protected the swordsman's hand by catching the opponent's blade and defecting it along and off the defender's blade. Better protection was offered by the cup of the rapier, sword or saber. To stop the hilt slopping from or turning in his sweat-drenched fist the swordsman laid his forefinger on the cross guard and his thumb on the flat of the blade. On some weapons this grip led to the development of the anneau ring next to the quillon.

Some quillons were S-shaped in order to catch the adversary's blade and wring the weapon out of his fist altogether, or at least to gain a momentary advantage for counterattack, especially with a dagger held in the left hand.

The rim of the cup hilt usual on Spanish-made rapiers (but not so common elsewhere) was also valuable in fencing since it could either check the adversary's blade tip or – in case of a severe thrust – even break the blade.

Two types of cutting or slashing weapons can be distinguished depending on the blade design. Those with heavier blades of 85 to 90 centimeters in length were used mainly by the military; weapons with longer blades exceeding sometimes 100 centimeters in length featured in the personal duels and brawls which were common.

Another suitable weapon for personal combat was the dagger. Sometimes it was used in the left hand together with the rapier in the right. It served to repel the enemy's rapier while attacking with the rapier in the right hand. The dagger had to be held very firmly to withstand the heavy slashes from the adversary's weapon weighing at least a kilogram. If the two rapiers happened to lock, the quicker combatant could counterattack with the dagger.

The rapier was worn on the left hip, from a hanger attacked to the belt or to the bandolier. The hanger was fixed in so that it could easily be loosened and thrown away together with the fastening strap so that they would not get in the way of the fight. The fencer grasped the scabbard with his left hand, drew the weapon with his right, then immediately loosened both hooks and, while jerking strongly or slashing with his rapier, threw away the scabbard and the hanger.

The dagger was worn either on the left or right, always pushed slightly back. For a fencer who anticipated using his dagger in combat together with the rapier it was better to have the dagger on the left, since it could be ready in his hand even before he managed to draw the longer weapon and throw away the scabbard and the hanger. To reach with his left hand to his right hip would take too long and if he tried to draw his weapons simultaneously, his hands would cross and he would have lost the precious seconds needed to be at the ready.

The 16th and early 17th century was a boom period for many fencing schools with various masters, each employing its own system of guards and attacks. Generally the sword-fighters of the times stood facing each other and with their bodies bent slightly forward, the right hand holding the weapon close to the hip and almost fully stretched and the left hand guarding the face. The rapier point was raised to the level of the enemy's eyes. When the attacker lunged he helped his forward thrust with a strong backward jerk of his left hand. The free hand could be used to either to repel the enemy's blade or to grasp the hand which held the weapon which enabled the defender to counterattack with the right. A common feint was to entice the adversary to thrust at the defender's leg, then withdraw it rapidly and score a hit with a lunge.

This was the basic pattern, but it was left to the experience and ingenuity of the master or the school proprietor to teach his pupils those guards and figures that he considered to be of vital importance.

A clock was also valuable in combat, provided the fencer knew how to use this handy piece of clothing to his advantage. It was really impossible to slash through a heavy cloak hung loosely from the left forearm. When the enemy attacked, a quick experienced fencer could deflect the thrusting point with the cloak and counterattack. Victory was also sure if the fencer succeeded in throwing his cloak onto the adversary's blade. The cloak-and-rapier technique ranked among the most complicated fencing styles.

Halberd combat was however totally difference. To prevent the halberd from turning in the fist, the stave had a rectangular cross section. Halberds could be used for thrusting, piercing, cutting and slashing, or even for catching the enemy by the neck. A slash at the head or neck could be averted, or a thrusting attack checked, with the stave. A common feint in halberd combat was to kick the enemy in the knee, trip him and thrust or push his chest in with the stave butt.

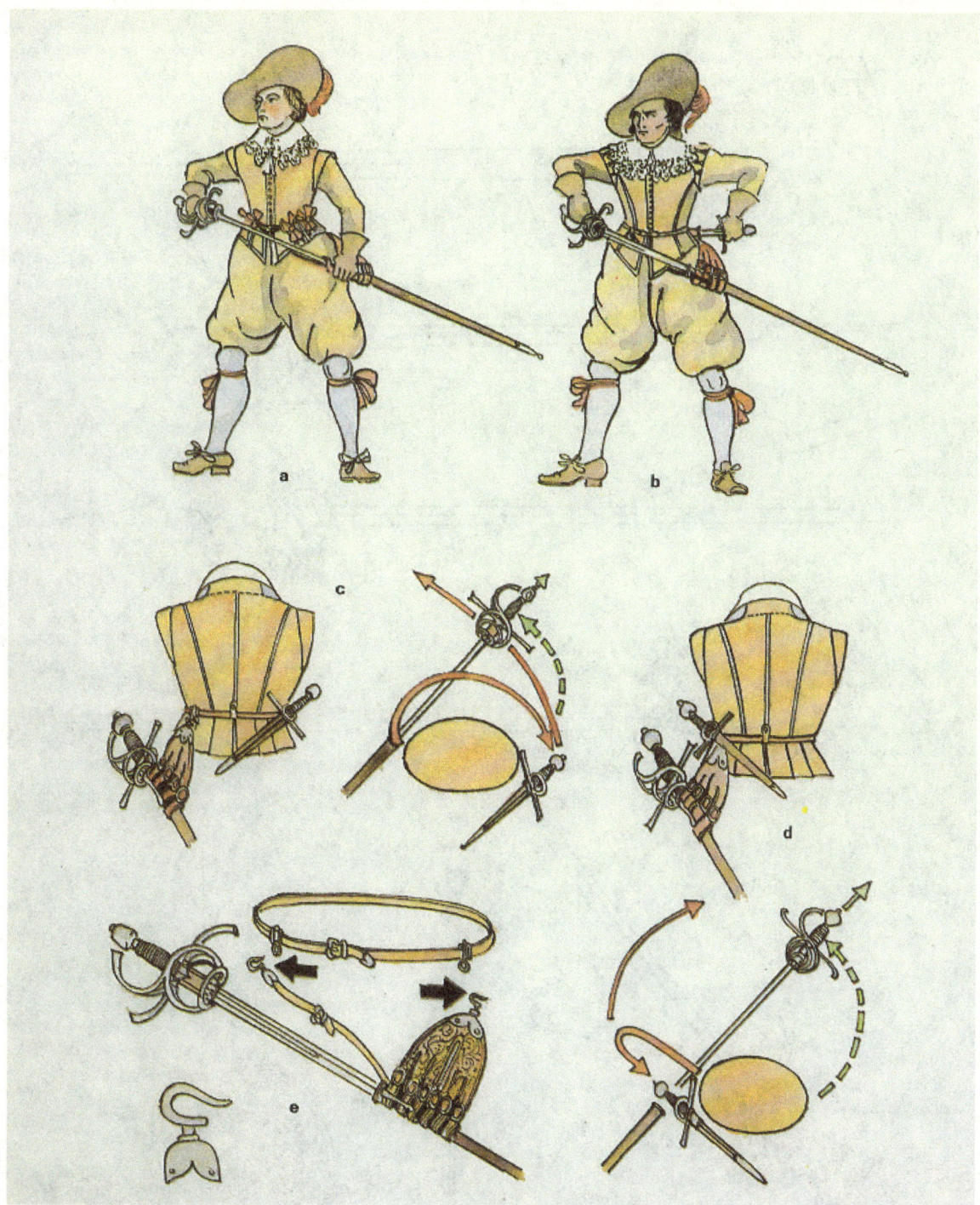

Side weapons drawing

a) Rapier drawing b) simultaneous drawing of rapier and dagger; both weapons worn on the left hip c) Drawing a dagger hung on the right, simultaneously with a rapier. This method is more complicated since the two weapons cross in the swordsman's hand. A dagger, worn on the right, could be advantageously used singly in the right hand d) Dagger worn on the left next to the rapier made simultaneous drawing easier e) Before engaging in combat, the swordsman loosened and discarded the hanger with the scabbard so as not to hinder his leg and foot work. The hanger and the strap were hung from the belt on hooks engaged in eyelets on the belt and the hanger held by mere weight. As soon as the swordsman's right hand reached the hilt, the left could easily unhook the scabbard with the hanger and discard them

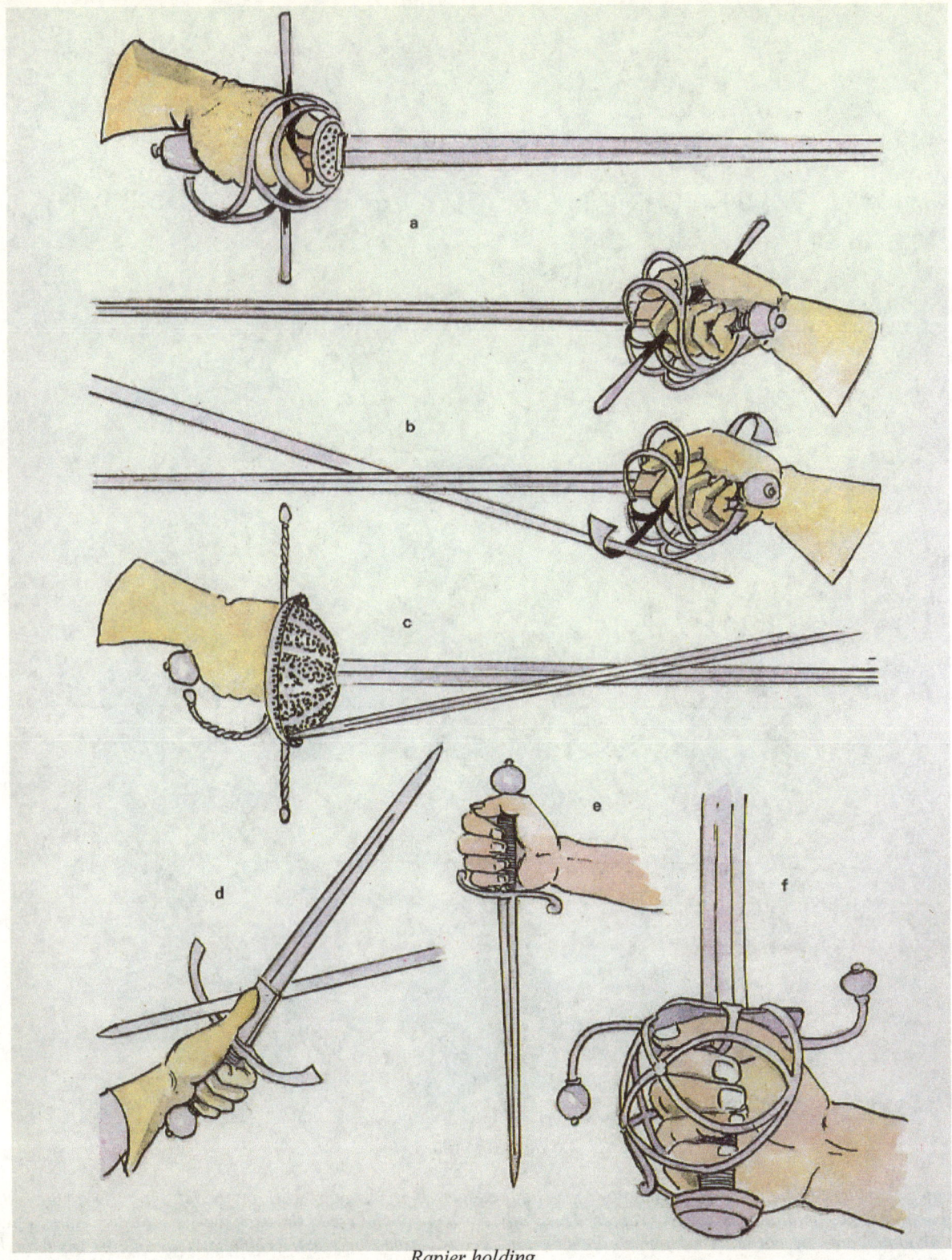

Rapier holding

a) The index finger resting beyond the quillon b) Checking the enemy's blade with S-shaped quillon c) Immobiliz-
ing the enemy's blade point in the rim of the cup guard d) Simple parry with a dagger e) Possible way of holding
a dagger if used singly in the right hand f) A grip on a sabre equipped with a massive knuckle bow and an anneau

The actual guards and parries to be employed in combat were prescribed by masters of individual fencing schools. Among the most important masters were Agrippa, Meyer, Capo, Ferro and Giganti Alfieri

a) Engarde according to Alfieri, showing the extreme caution of the fencers b) Lunge with right foot forward, body bent slightly forward, Capo Fero school c) Riposte with the left foot forward, body bent forward, the left arm guarding the trunk and face, Capo Fero school, possibly also Alfieri's d) Parry with the left leg that was being attacked into the basic position, and a high third according to Alfieri e) Rapier raised to cut f,g,) Using the left hand in fencing; the swordsman grasped the attacker's rapier-holding right hand, pushing it aside thus uncovering the attacker.

a) *Checking the attacker's arm with the left hand* b) *Engarde with rapier and dagger* c) *Engarde with sword and dagger* d) *Engarde according to Agrippa's school* e) *Fencer parries a dagger attack on his outside and riposts with the rapier* f) *Defender parries a dagger attack on his outside and riposts* g) *Standing according to Agrippa* h) *The defender parrying with the right foot back so that the attack misses the target and the assailant runs on the defender point* i) *Corps à corps; the quicker fencer using a stop thrust*

a) Swordsman with his rapier in the right hand, the left forearm wrapped around with a cloak used for parrying the assailant's thrusts b) Composite thrust; the assailant first throwing his cloak onto the defender's blade making the weapon unwieldy, and an immediate attack following c) Parry in the high third; the defender pointing his weapon down to prevent the assailant from throwing his cloak on the defender's blade d) Cutlass combat, Meyer's school; the combatant had to have great strength and a great arm span to be able to cut as well as ward off the enemy's cuts. A possible way of checking a heavy gash with cutlass was to grasp the blade near the point with the left while keeping the head covered.

123

a) Three stands used to check high thirds; the swordsman in the middle supporting his blade on his left arm b) Dagger holding if the weapon is used singly; in this case the weapon is held with nails down c) Stalemate, with both parties holding each other's armed right with their free left d) Tearing the dagger from the adversary's hand e) Raising the dagger to attack from above f) Strangling he defender with the left while the right is attacking with a dagger. The defender joined his hands and tried to knock the assailant's grip off in order to counterattack g) Disarming the assailant h) Fighting without weapons

Halberd combat according to Meyer's school
a)Raising the halberd for a great blow b)Barring the assailant's weapon with own halberd c) Tripping the enemy's leg with halberd d) Catching the assailant's nape with the axe while barring his halberd with the stave on the outside e) Halberd thrust under the attacker's chin, simultaneously kicking his left kneecap

a) Halberd stop thrust checking a riposte b) Checking a direct blow with the stave c) Tripping the enemy with stave butt thrust under the chin d) Great swing with a halberd used both for attack as well as defence

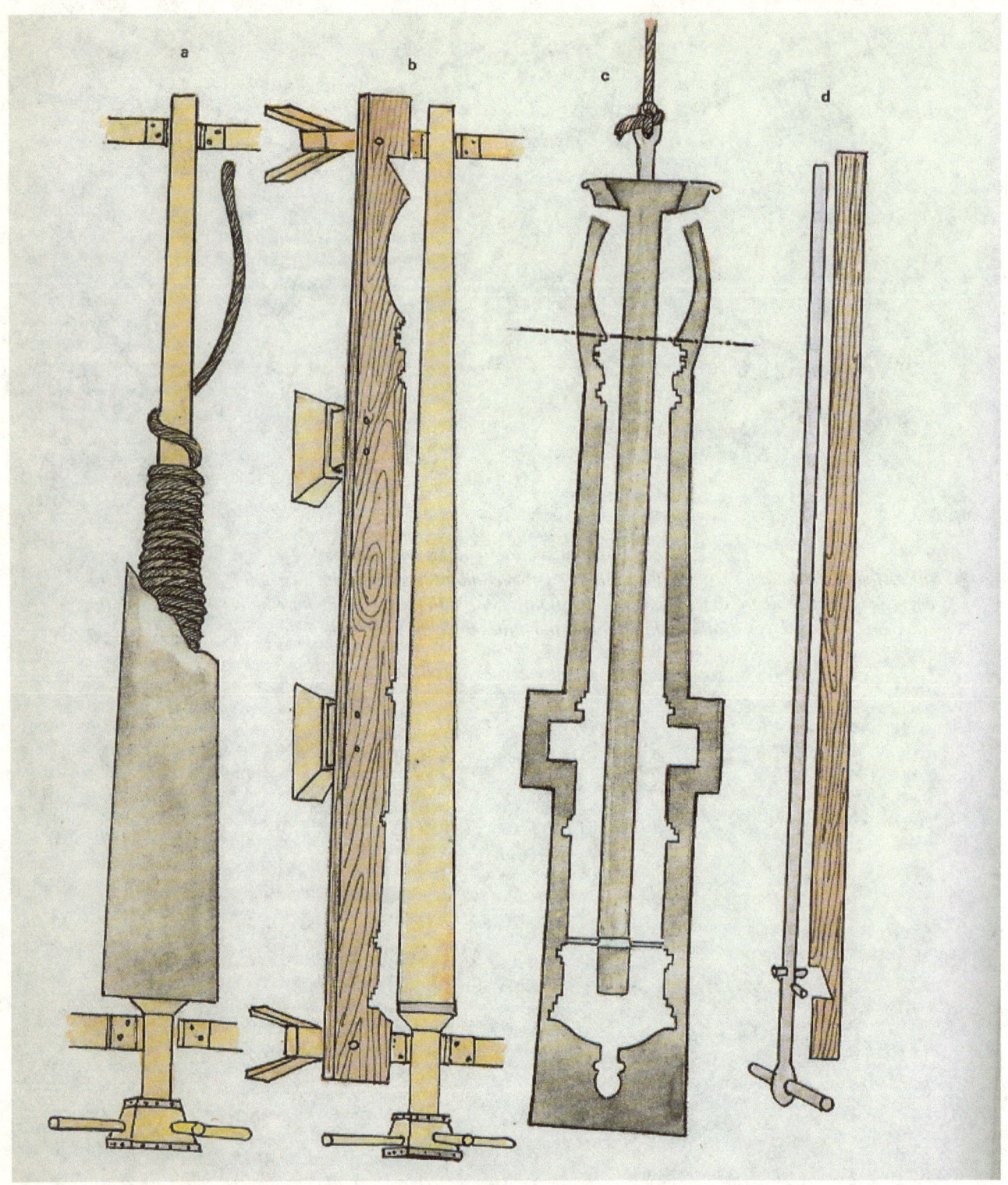

Mould for making cannon casting
a) Plastering the rope-wound shaft with soft clay b) Fixing the master template to trestles supporting the
shaft c) Barrel casting mould with inserted core d) Iron rod and master template for making the core

ARTILLERY

In the Thirty Years' War, the backbone of the artillery was the cannon.

For making the cannon barrels the so-called material known as gun metal was most commonly used. It casted well, was weather-proof and it had great strength and sufficient elasticity. Bronze guns were made by casting copper, tin and lead. Fragments of older barrels and captured church belts were often added to the mix.

To cast a battle cannon required 5,434 lbs of high grade copper, 540 lbs soft tin and 435 lbs brass to yield a batch sufficient to cast a barrel of 6,400 lbs. (Mid-18th-century manuals call for 100 parts of copper, 20 of tin, 10 of lead and five of brass. Although the exact composition of a particular gun metal always remained the trade secret of its maker, the proportions of the alloy metals would always be approximately the same.

To cast a cannon required a mold. First, a precise 1:1 copy of the barrel was made, called the pattern. The core was a long wooden shaft wound round with thick bast (barkfibre) or straw ropes. At the muzzle a funnel or barrel shaped riser fed the extra molten metal needed to compensate for solidification shrinkage and ensure that the muzzle was compact. (When the barrel had been cast, the riser would be cut off.) The ropes around the pattern were then spread with a layer of soft clay, to make a shaft, which was then turned against a master template to give the pattern the basic shape of the future barrel. Cutouts in the template molded rings on the barrel to give the piece additional reinforcement. Then the master template was removed, the pattern well spread with tallow and patterns of the trunnions, handles (sometimes called dolphins because of their shape) and relief ornaments made of a wax and tallow mixture were nailed to the barrel pattern, and the complete pattern was once again spread with a thick layer of soft clay to form the shell of the mold proper. The mold was dried above a fire, being constantly turned. The wax and tallow parts melted and the liquid substances were drained through provided ports. This technique has been known for centuries as the lost wax method. When the mold was dry enough, the pattern was removed, the mold split, re-dried and baked. Then it was reinforced with a cross pattern of iron bands and dried once again above red glowing charcoal.

Before the casting proper, a core had to be fixed into the mold. This was made of an iron rod of a smaller diameter than the required caliber, which was plastered with a mixture of clay, horse hide hair and manure and turned against a template to obtain a perfectly smooth surface. After having been dried, the core was lowered into the mould and aligned dead-centre. To position the lower end of the core firmly, a centering ring was used. The internal diameter of the ring was identical with the caliber and the ring was equipped with three mandrils forming a three point star that fixed the core. After inserting the ring into the mold and aligning it, the core's lower end was fixed into the ring, the mold parts assembled together and possible gaps filled with clay.

The finished mold of the barrel was then lowered into a pit, and the space around it filled with sand and packed firmly to five the mould greater strength. Finally the cannon could be cast. The casting pits—usually there were several —were placed as close to the furnace as possible to ensure a smooth flow of molten metal into the mould.

When the metal had solidified and cooled down, the mold was hammered off and the riser cut off. Imperfections were worked out, the surface smoothed and the reliefs inscriptions perfected with chasing. The core was removed from the barrel casting but the internal diameter of the barrel still had to be worked to the exact caliber. This was achieved by three successive boring operations using three huge drills, each of which had to be at least as long as the barrel. The barrel bore could be worked in several ways. Either the barrel was hoisted with the muzzle down and lowered against the drill, set upright into the shaft of a horse gear. Or the barrel was sunk into the ground with the muzzle up and the drill suspended from a horse-driven rig and fed into the work by block-and-tackle system. The third method used a drill set into a waterwheel journal. The barrel casting, supported on a heavy carriage, was fed against the rotating tool with a windlass or capstan. Later, in the second half of the 17th century, the practice of using a core in barrel casting was discontinued and barrels began to be bored out of a solid casting.

When the machining operations were complete and the bore cleaned, the barrel was proof-fired, using several proving rounds. The charged were greater than those used in action. For the first round the barrel was loaded with a powder charge of the same weight as the iron ball; the second charge was half and the third only a quarter of the weight of the ball. If the casting was strong enough to stand these proving rounds it was judged to be of good quality and handed over to other craftsmen who built a carriage for the barrel.

However the barrel sometimes burst during tests, usually because the gun metal was of poor quality. If the molten metal had been too hot, the constituents of the alloy which were intended to give elasticity were burned up, and a brittle barrel was the result. If the molten metal had not been hot enough, blow holes formed as the metal solidified, making weak spot where the barrel would split under the pressure of firing. A sound barrel which had been successfully tested could also burst if too much powder was used. If the charge was too strong it would eject the ball at such a velocity that the inrush of air to fill the vacuum behind the ball would split the muzzle. A cannon might also burst during test firing if the core had been incorrectly aligned in the mold prior to casting, which made the barrel walls of irregular thickness. The thinner parts of the wall would then easily give way under the pressures of firing.

Once tested, the cannon barrel was equipped with a wooden carriage. In the 16th and 17th centuries there were four basic carriage types. The most common was the cheek type, constructed of two thick board cheeks joined with wooden cross pieces. The places subjected to greatest stresses were reinforced with iron bands and pieces. The carriage was supported on wheel. So-called trucks were built for naval and casemate guns. They were very heavy and had small full disk wheels. Smaller guns used mainly to defend fortifications and ramparts were placed on mounts—wooden tripods with an iron shackle into which the barrel could be fixed. Mortars had different mounts, without wheels. The gunner's mates moved this type of ordinance with carrying poles slipped into brass bushings on the mount.

The size of the carriage was determined by the barrel size. Carriages of larger pieces were about one-third longer than the barrel; with smaller pieces the carriage was one-fifth longer.

Every piece had many accessories for loading, firing, maintenance and repairs. These included a long-handled powder-shovel made of copper sheet, and a swabrod made of sheep fleece nailed onto a wooden cylinder with a long handle. Another important part of the artillerist's kit was the ramrod. Its head was made of good strong wood and wound with thick copper wire so that the rod would not break when the charge was firmly rammed. Then there were ropes, hoists, two or three hooks, elevation wedges and crowbars, as well as a wooden board with a cut-out matching the shape of the barrel muzzle which protected the cannoneer from enemy fire while he was training his gun. Powder was stored and transported in wooden casks with a greased calf-hide top. Coarse powder for larger pieces was carried in casks holding about 100 kg; fine powder in 50 kg barrels and priming powder in 25 kg kegs. Among the accessories was also a cask of water and vinegar for cooling down the barrel when it was hot from firing. The barrel was cooled with a swabrod with a slit head holding a wet rag. The match for firing the gun was held in a forked rod or spike or in the holder of the gunner's spontoon. The breech end of the barrel was protected from rain and snow with fleece. The fine priming powder was kept in a powderhorn. The gunner also had a caliber gauge, which was a wooden, brass or ion rod with caliber marks, a set of vent-cleaning needles, three types of ball extractors, a level gauge, a quadrant and a cartabon with a series of sightholes for training the gun according to the distance of the target. Apart from all these things there were also standard accessories and tools such as various ball diameter gauges and a casket with tongs, hammers and jacks. Big artillery pieces that were extremely difficult to move were equipped with various barrel hoists.

The period was notable for its enormous variety of artillery ordinance. In the late 16th century the range of artillery pieces included 97-pounder scharfmetze, 66-pounder basilisk, 50-pounder singerin, 46-pounder nightingale, 32-pounder kartaune, 32-pounder nothschlange, 12-pounder serpent, 9-pounder falcon, 1-pounder serpentinelle and a large selection of 15 to 47 pounder mortars. The cannon were divided into siegecraft ordnance, which included the scharfmetze, basilisk, singerin and kartaune; and field ordnance which included all the other types.

However the number of gun types was decreasing throughout the period. By the early 17th century the artillery of European armies consisted of various 12-80 pound kartaunes, 10-60 pound serpents, so-called regimental pieces firing 2-8 pound shots, howitzers of various calibers shooting 6-30 pound balls and mortars discharging 40-260 pound balls. By the beginning of the 18th century, when the artillery had undergone a thorough reorganization and became a permanent service of the standing armies of Europe, even fewer cannon types remained in use, the ordnance being formed by 24, 16, 12, 8, and 4 pounder cannon and 10,9, 8, 7, 6, and 1 pounder mortars.

A gun sometimes needed several horse teams for

transport, the number depending on its weight, the terrain and road conditions. The heaviest pieces were taken apart and carried on several separate wagons. Ammunition and powder were hauled separately on caissons.

Cannon had to be hauled across rough and rocky country with windlasses and capstans. These were also used for hoisting the barrels and carriages on to ramparts and bastions. Working the capstans and hoists was not easy since the crews had to be in absolute concert. The parts of the mechanisms that were subjected to greatest friction and stress had to be moistened to increase the elasticity of the ropes and lessen the strain on the wooden parts.

The chief gunner was responsible for the organizational and tactical command of the artillery; technical matters were the responsibility of a gunsmith and later of an ordnance officer. Hauling, hoisting, mounting the gun and building the position was the job of the navies and their mates.

Before a battle started or during a siege cannon were grouped into batteries and placed in specially-built positions and emplacements, usually protected with a mound made with the earth from digging the entrenchments. The mound protected the gun and its crew not only in the front where embrasures had been made, but also on the flanks. For greater protection the mounds were topped with earth-filled wicker baskets called gabions or with sand or wool-filled bags. The floor of the emplacement was hewn from thick boards and beams, usually of oak.

Before loading a piece it had to be certain that the inside of the barrel was clean. The gun-powder charge was usually a quarter of the weight of the projectile. The gun was loaded with two bucketfuls of powder from a bucket shovel. The shovel had to be inserted in the barrel without turning in order not to spill the powder on the way along the barrel. For better orientation a groove ran along the entire length of the handle. When the shovel reached the breech, the gunner turned it and poured the powder out. After the two loadings, the charge was lightly packed with a tampion. The powder was not too compacted since a loosely-packed charge ignited better and developed greater force. The packed charge was sealed with a wad of stray or hay. The ball was wiped to remove any solid particles and dust so that it would not seize in the barrel. The loading was completed by pouring the priming powder onto the pan.

Then the gun was trained by laying it barrel

axis perpendicularly to the target. Wooden wedges were driven under the breech end to obtain the right elevation.

Cannon were rarely used throughout an entire battle. Their use was mostly limited to the initial stages when artillery was employed against the approaching enemy. During the battle cannon were used to check the enemy advance with dense canister cannonades. But, artillery was quite ineffective against cavalry troops, who moved so quickly that cannon, with their slow rate of fire, were no match for them. Before the pieces could fire a couple of rounds, the cavalry had already reached the edge of their emplacement.

Cannon were of much greater value in siegecraft. Fire against a besieged fort was directed according to the layout of the fort and the weakest parts of the defense. To breach the walls and wreck keeps or towers of a besieged stronghold, the target received cross dire from two batteries and frontal fire from a third one. Whenever a bastion was to be shot apart, fire was laid from two directions. Earthworks were reached by flat trajectories designed to hit the wall crown so that the missiles swept the packed earth off the top until a large enough breach was made to allow a waver assault of troops to cross.

If a breach showed that there were casemates behind, the artillery pieces fired into it from an oblique direction do that when the ball entered the breach it would ricochet off the inside walls, inflicting heavy casualties and damages within. In bombarding ramparts that were defended by artillery, part of the attacking forces' artillery was used for making a breach and the rest tried to silence the enemy batteries within.

Whenever a big fortress was to be taken, a general battery was set up. This effective array of cannon of varying caliber consisted of eight kartaunes (42 pounders), six half-kartaunes (24-pounders) and four quarter-kartaunes (12-pounders). The battery was usually placed about 300 paces from the fort walls. The kartaunes made the breach and any remaining masonry that might obstruct the smooth progress of the infantry attack were taken care of by the half-kartaunes. The task of the remaining pieces, the quarter-kartaunes, was to prevent the defenders from stopping the breach, digging a defensive entrenchment or erecting a gabionage (earth filled cylinder of wicker or metal bands).

The time it took to make a breach varied greatly. When Tilly laid siege to Minden in 1626, his artillery breached the town walls in a day. Firing opened at 5 a.m. and ended at 9 p.m. In this time more than 1000 rounds hit the wall. On the other hand, when Magdeburg was besieged in 1630, three batteries fired constantly for six days before even a tiny breach could be made.

Even though a piece might have been constantly trained on the same target and always returned to the original firing position after discharge, the next round might be still off target. The cause could be an incorrect charge or strong side wind, or a faulty carriage. If one of the pair of carriage wheels was seizing, instead of moving backwards on the recoil, the gun could swivel slightly as well, changing its aim.

Great problems were caused if the ball seized in the barrel and could not be rammed home onto the charge. The barrel would have to be hoisted with the muzzle up and oil poured into the bore. After the oil had had time to act, the barrel was turned with the muzzle down and knocked on the sides with a wooden pole until the ball fell out.

If a piece had not been fired for a long period or if it was to be transported across water, the charge and the projectile was also extracted. To prevent the enemy from using captured artillery, gunners would drive a nail or spike into the vent before retreating.

It took a long time to make a spiked gun usable again. The ball had to be removed from the barrel and the charge sealed with a wooden packing seal. Sometimes it was enough to fire the charge to drive the spike out of the vent, but usually the vent had to be re-drilled.

The main kind of artillery missile of the period was the cast-iron cannon ball, which kept its priority until the early 19th century. It was strong, heavy and fairly cheap, and its damaging effect was quite considerable.

Canister or case shot was used as anti-personnel ammunition. It consisted of canvas or leather bags or wooden or sheet cylinders, filled with rocks, iron or lead pellets, nails or iron scrap. Canisters were always stored close to the piece to be used whenever the enemy waged an unexpected attack against the emplacement.

Grenades were another common kind of artillery ammunition. They were hollow spheres filled with explosive which was detonated with a fuse ignited by the explosion of the charge before the grenade left the gun barrel. The fuse was housed in a wooden bushing in a hole in the ball. Some grenades had a special detonator consisting of a rough striking steel and flints. On the impact of the ball the steel

a) Measuring the barrel calibre b) Measuring the barrel outer diameter surface c) Bore regularity gauge in the form of a rod with slip-on disks or isosceles crosses d) Barrel bore inspection with a sun-reflecting mirror e) Rod for measuring the barrel calibre f) Instrument with barrel calibre measures

struck a spark from the flints, detonating the charge.

So-called chain shot was used against infantry as well as cavalry. Its two chain-linked hemispheres detached after discharge and, with their fast spinning, inflicted great damage and casualties. Chain shot continued to be used until the early 19th century by navies to destroy and riggings of enemy men-of-war.

The artillery had also incendiary ammunition. Usually this was nothing but an iron ball which was heated for about thirty minutes until it glowed cherry red, and placed into the thoroughly-cleaned barrel. The powder charge was protected against self-ignition with a seal of a wooden disk and soft-clay. Stone incendiary missiles were also used. The stone core was plastered up to the bore diameter with incendiary material which was ignited by the powder discharge.

By the early 17th century illumination or star balls filled with pitch and turpentine, were in use. Poison ammunition and various asphyxiating, blinding, stinking and smoke bombs were used in the war of the Netherlands against Spain. These kinds of ammunition were later forgotten, but they were reintroduced in the 20th century during the First World War.

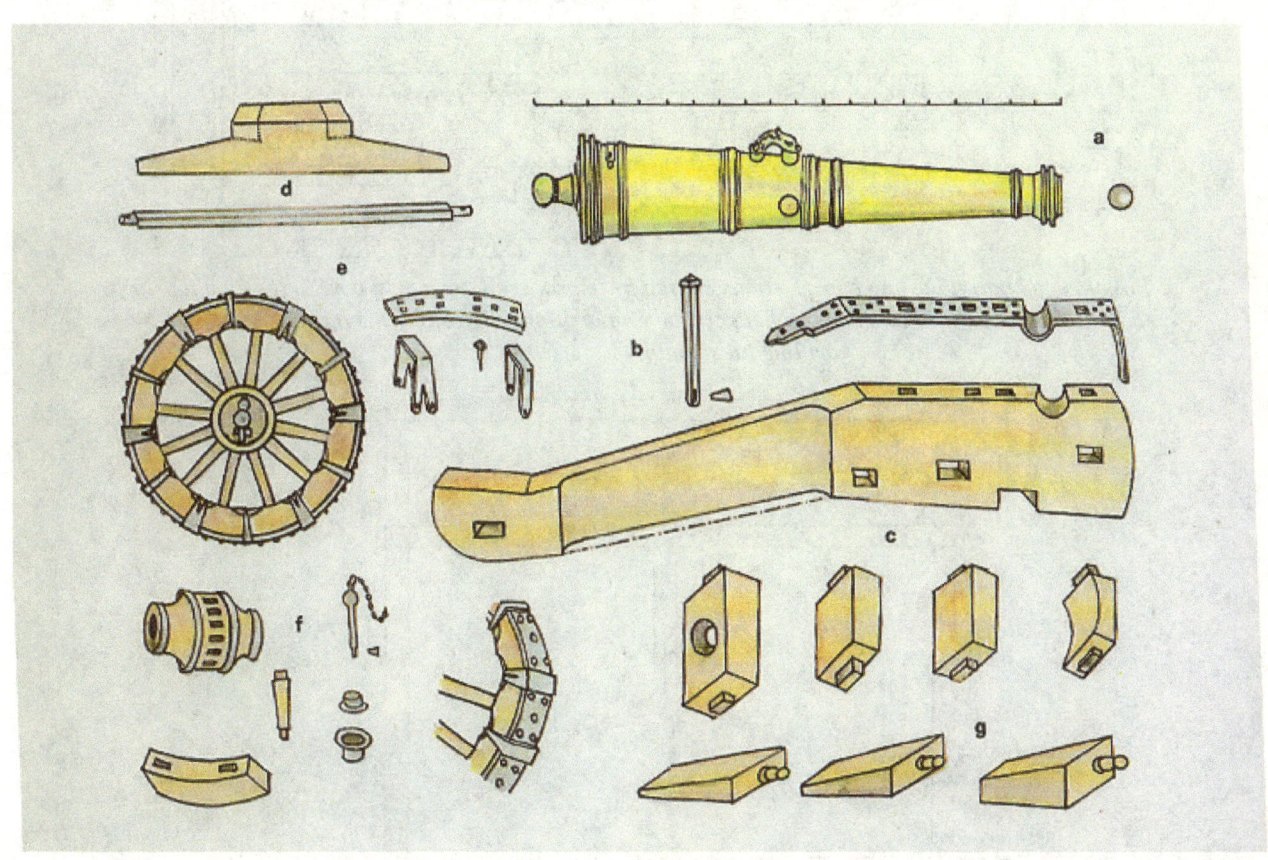

Cannon assembly
Barrel length determined by calibre a) Cannon barrel with a calibration scale showing the barrel type also according to the calibres b) Left cheek of the gun carriage, with an iron band reinforcement and recesses holding the barrel trunnions. Another shorter iron band cap held the trunnions from the top. The band shown here is forged onto the cheek and secured with four clamps c) Wooden cross-pieces joining the cheeks d) Gun carriage axel joined by an iron rod e) Gun carriage wheel section: the rim consisting of iron hoop sections nailed onto the felly and reinforced with clamps f) Wheel hub with lynch pin and detail showing the fastening of the rim section onto the felly g) Wooden elevation wedges

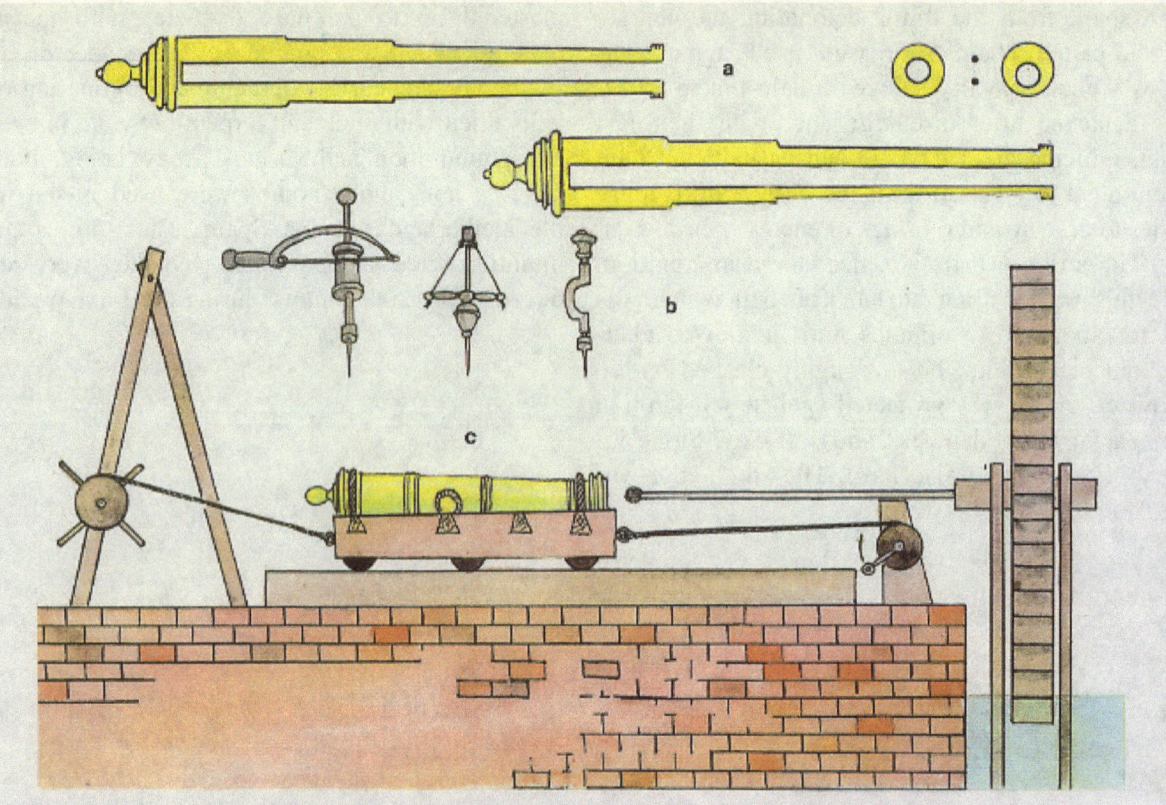

a) Possible gun barrel casting imperfections caused by improper alignment of core in the mould prior to and during casting b) Various types of augers for vent drilling c) Working the barrel bore with a huge drilling bit set into a waterwheel shaft

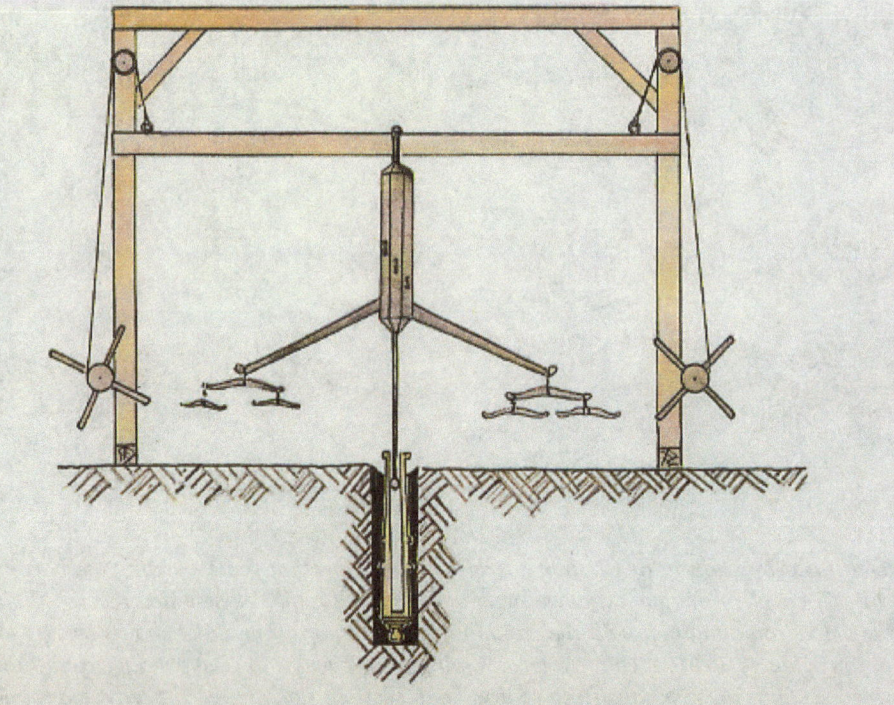

Working the barrel bore with a huge vertical drilling rig driven by horse gear

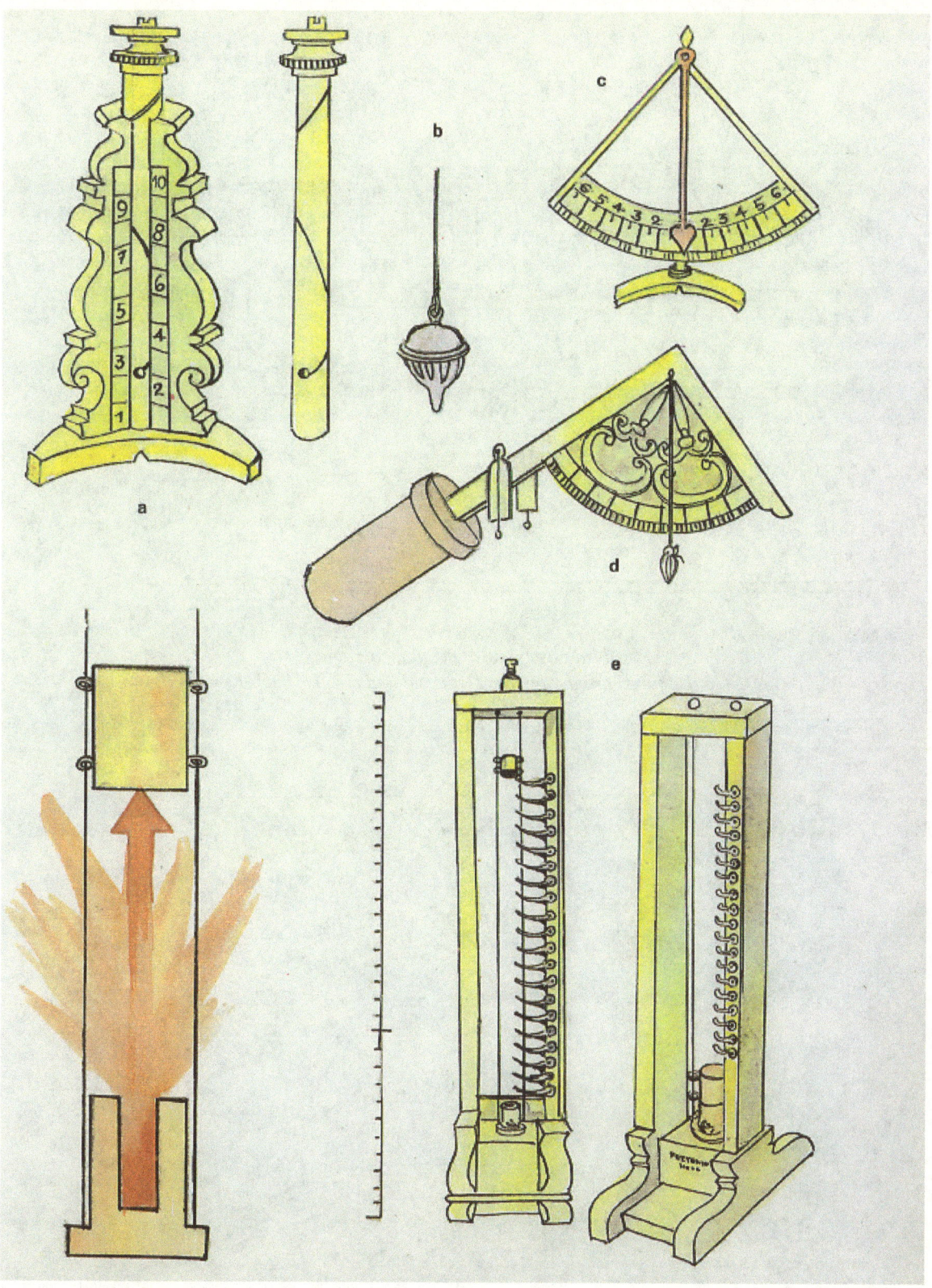

Gunnery Instruments
a) Cartabon with a small vertical adjustable sighthole b) Plum line and bob c) Inclino*meter d) Plummet with quadrant e) Instruments for measuring powder blast effects*

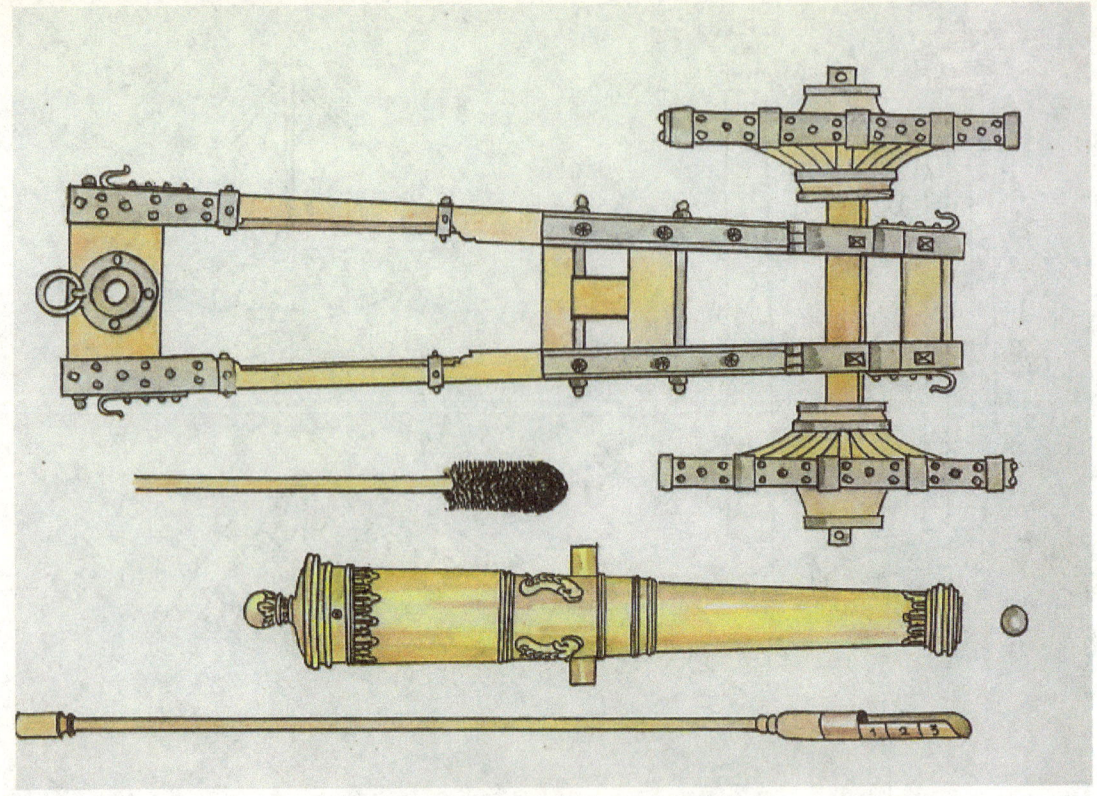

A bird's eye view of the gun carriage
Next to the barrel are the swabrod, ramrod and powder bucket shovel

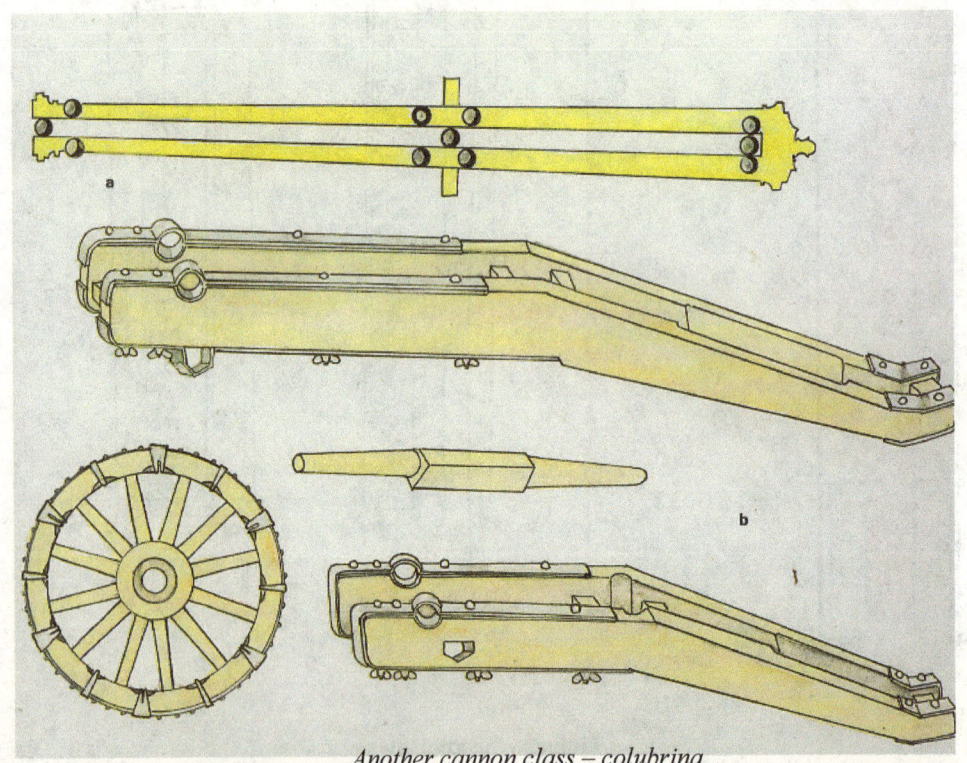

Another cannon class – colubrina
a)Determination of barrel wall thickness according to ball calibre b) Larger and small
gun carriages with axels and wheels

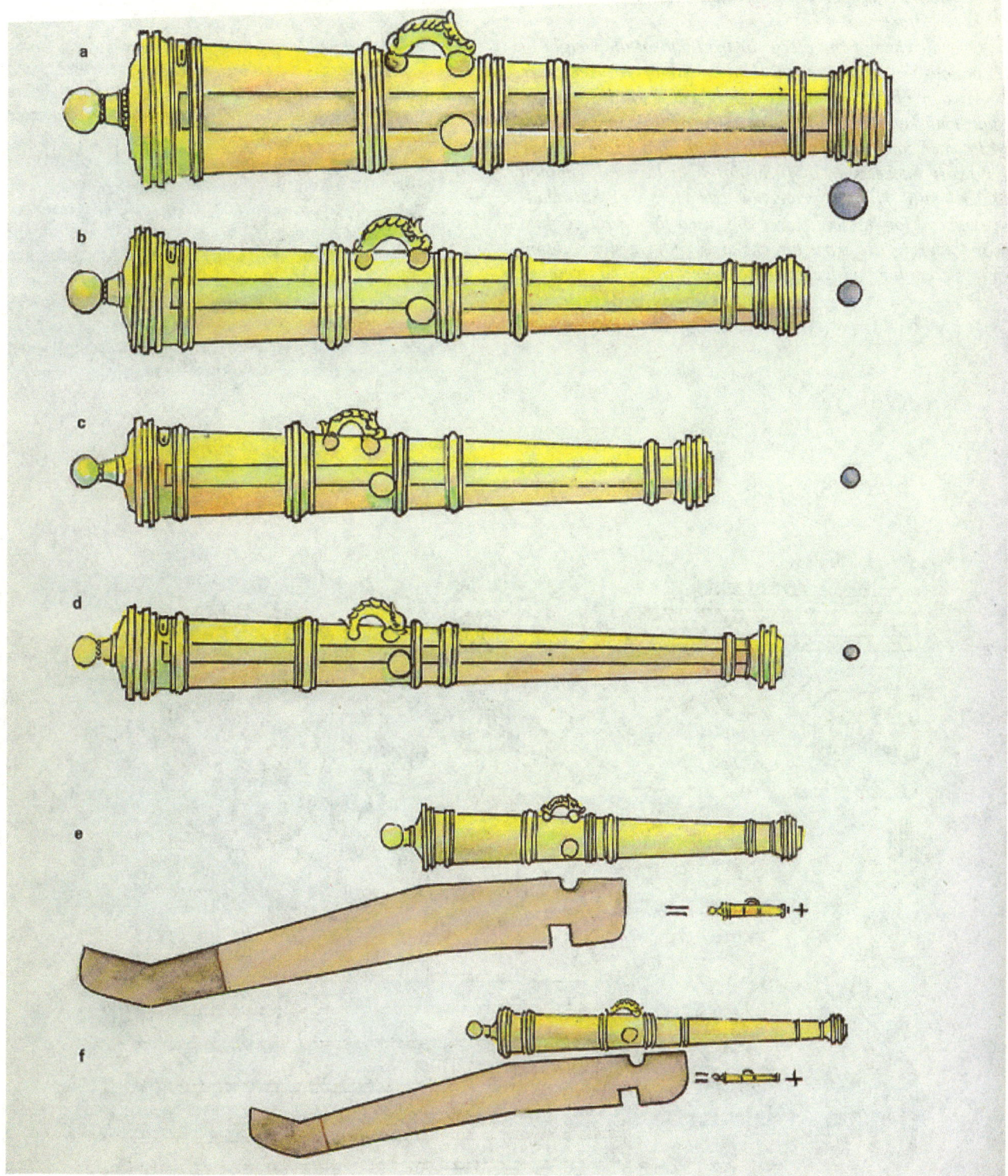

Typical Central European gun classification based on gun calibre, circa 1600

a) Kartaune – 42-pounder (cannon)   b) Halb-kartaune – 24-pounder(demi-cannon)
c)Viertel-kartaune – 12-pounder (culverin) d) Acktel-kartaune – 6-pounder (saker)
e) Barrel-to-carriage length ratio, heavy ordinance f) Barrel-to-carriage length ratio, light ordinance

European Weapons and Warfare, 1618 - 1648

Heavy class cannon – kartaune – 42-pounder

a) *Overall view of the piece* b) *Iron ball of the weight of 42 pounds* c) *Iron crowbar and ancillary wooden bars* d) *Wooden block serving as a protection for the gunner against musketry fire* e) *Quadrant* f) *Cartabon sighting device* g) *Powder keg* h) *Powderhorn with fine grain primer* i) *Powder bucket shovel* j) *Swabrod* k) *Ramrod* l) *match holder* m-n) *Helical projectile extractors* o) *Slit-headed swabrod for holding a wet rag, used for barrel cooling* p) *Spoon projectile extractor* r) *Barrel with vinegar solution for barrel cooling* s) *Fleece used to protect vent in bad weather*

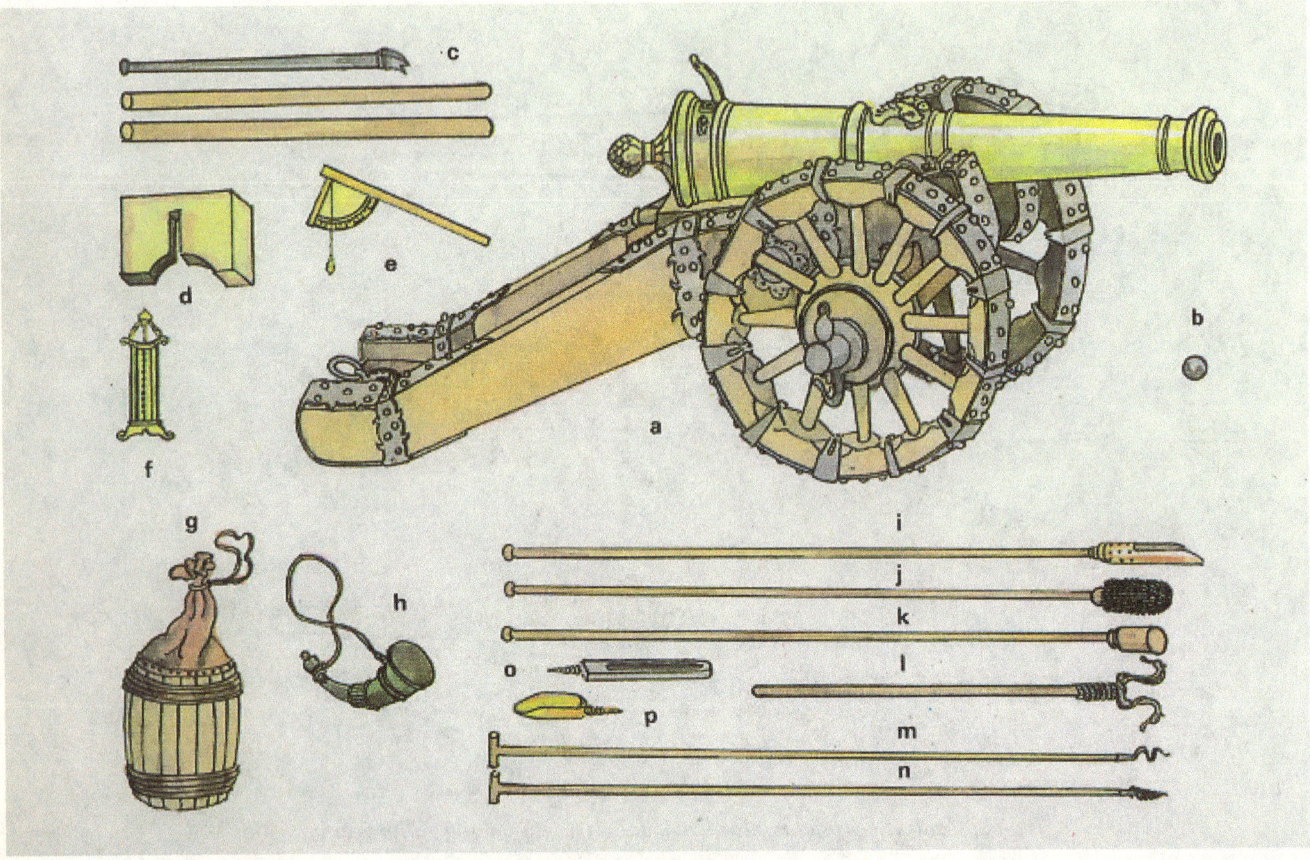

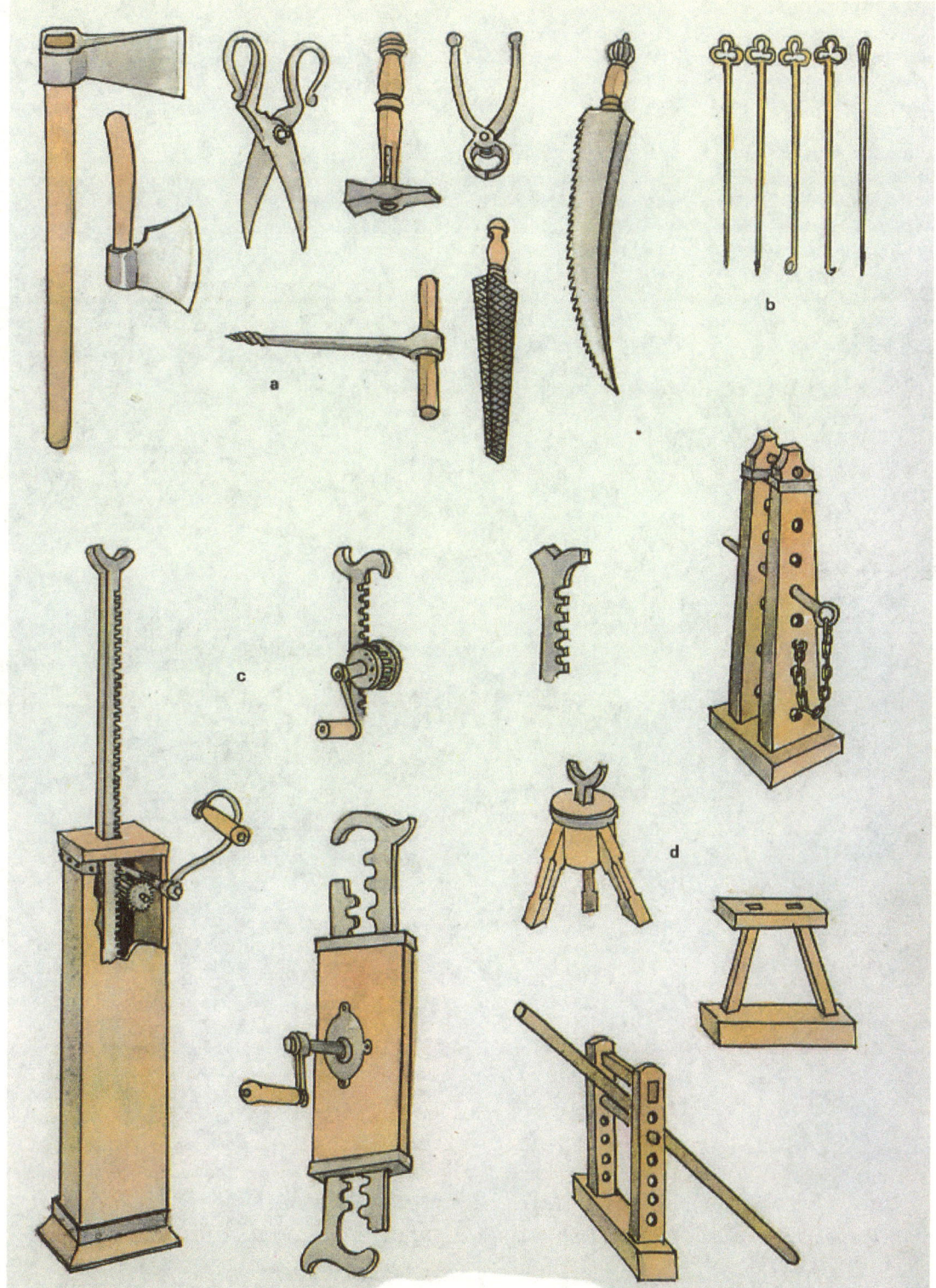

Typical gunnery kit

*a) Accessories and tools b) Vent-cleaning needles and a needle for leather gear repairs
c) Various jacks d) Various level fulcrums*

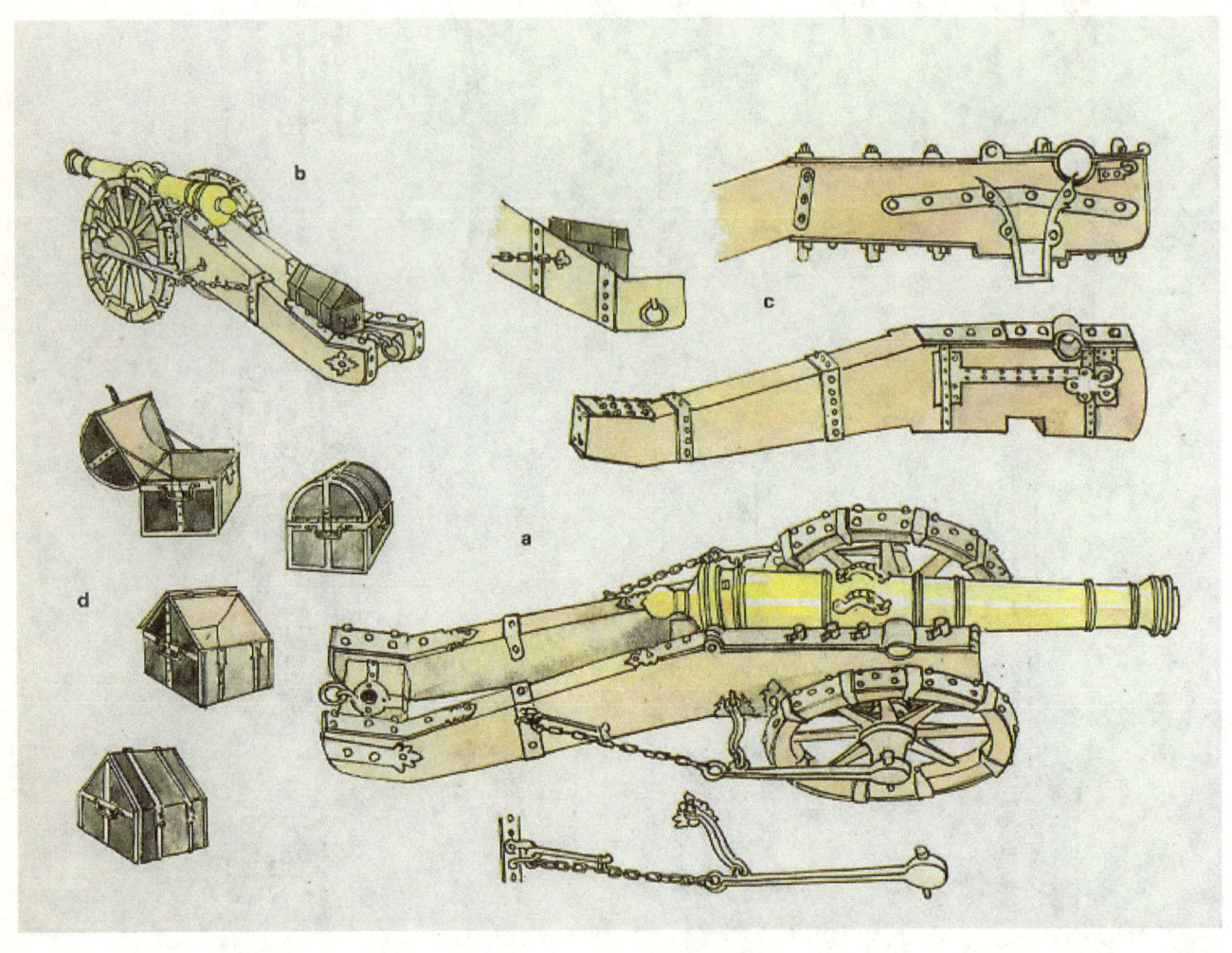

Gun carriage models

a) With chain reinforced axel b) With built-in tool box c) Various gun carriages d) Gunnery kit chests

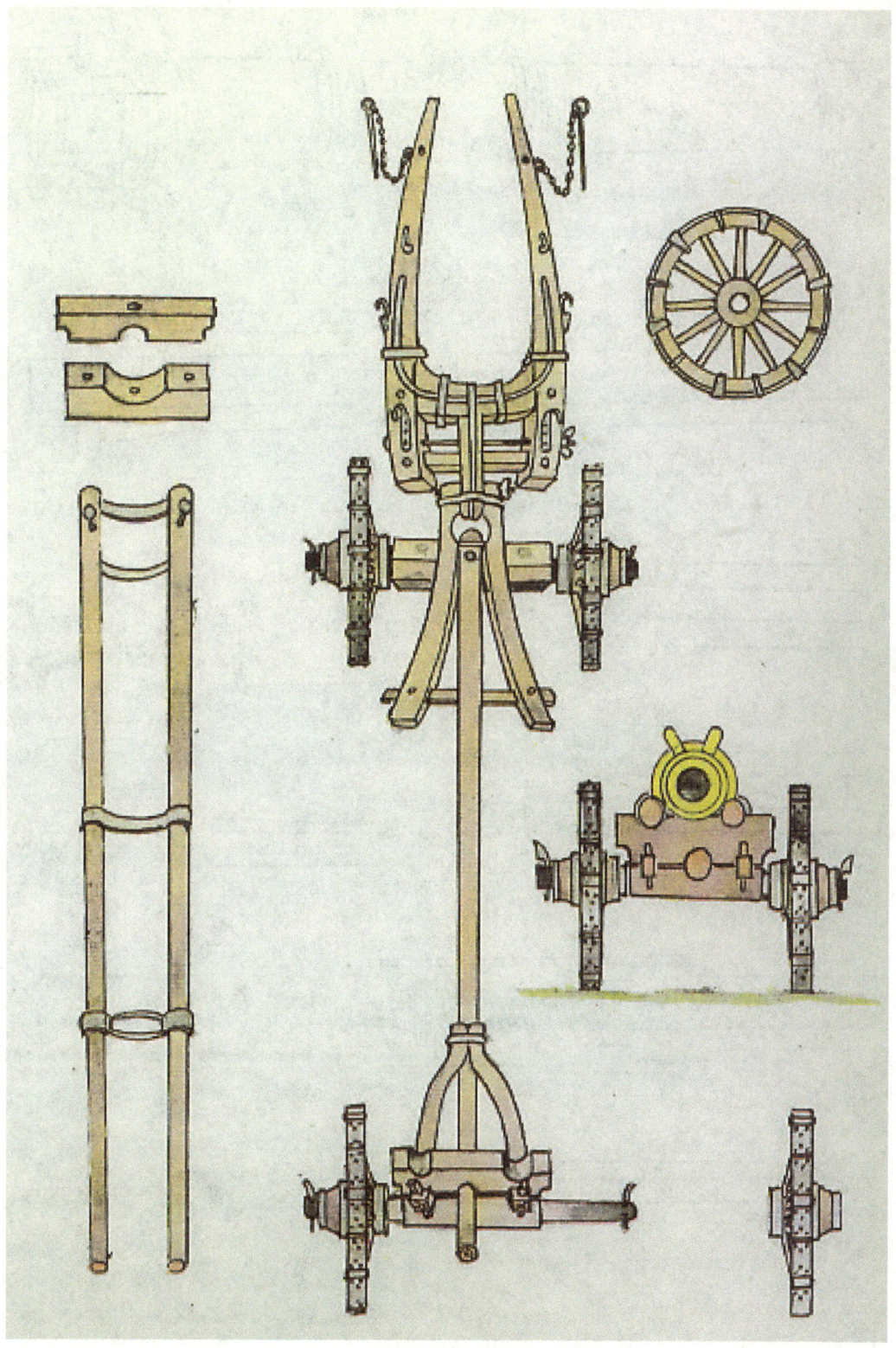

Wagon for gun carriage transport

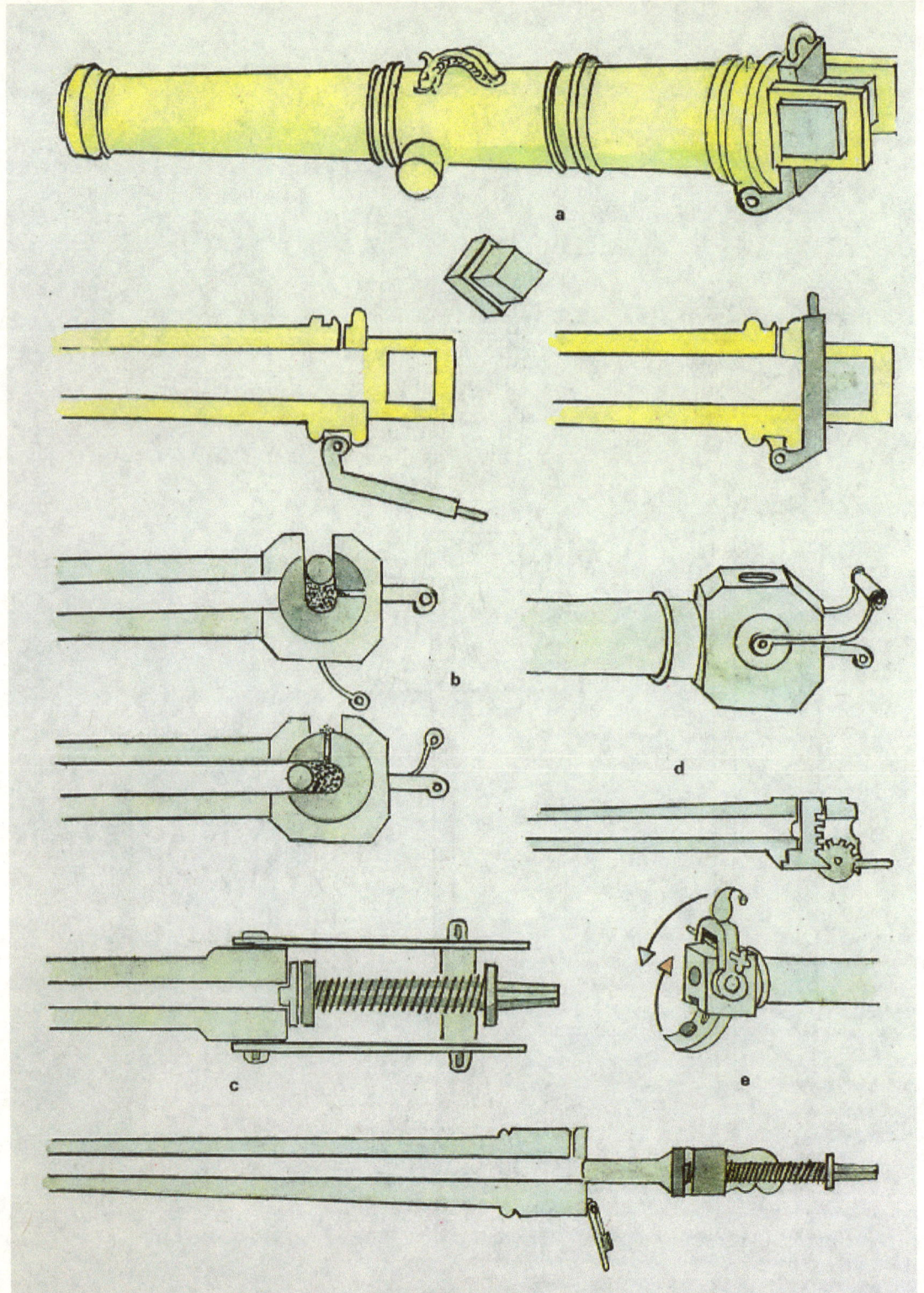

Breechloaders

a) Bronze barrel with iron breech plate and block b) Iron barrel with turning breech block c) Screw type breech block d) Opening the breech with a gear meshing with geared breech block e) Two part tilt breech block

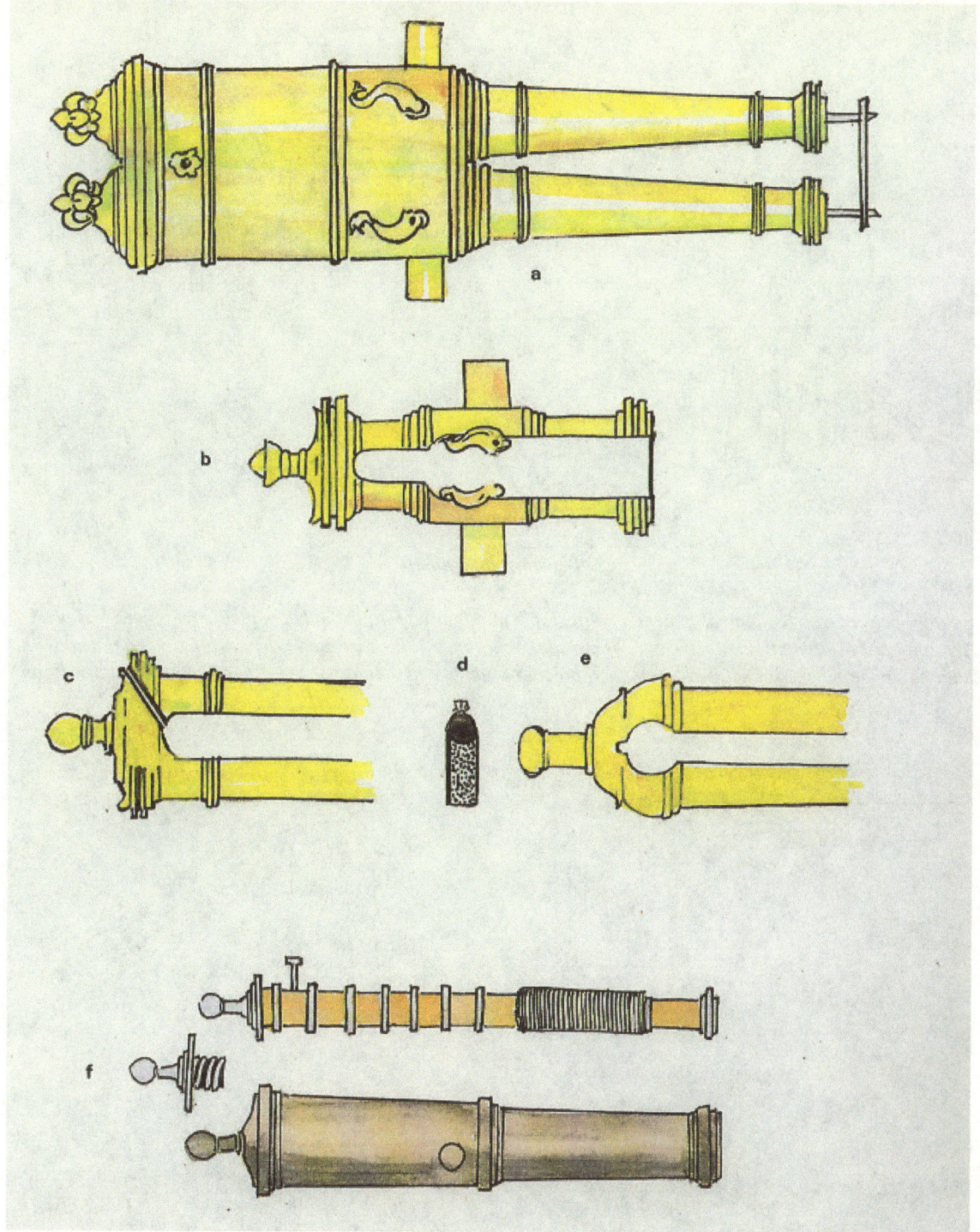

Unusual gun barrel types

a) Double barrel with central vent, used for firing four pound iron balls b) Howitzer barrel with narrowed powder chamber for 12-pound iron balls c) Vent drilled obliquely into the barrel powder chamber d) Ready-made shot of iron ball and powder charge e) Spherical powder chamber barrel f) Leather cannon, the iron tube is reinforced with iron rings and wrapped with ropes and leather

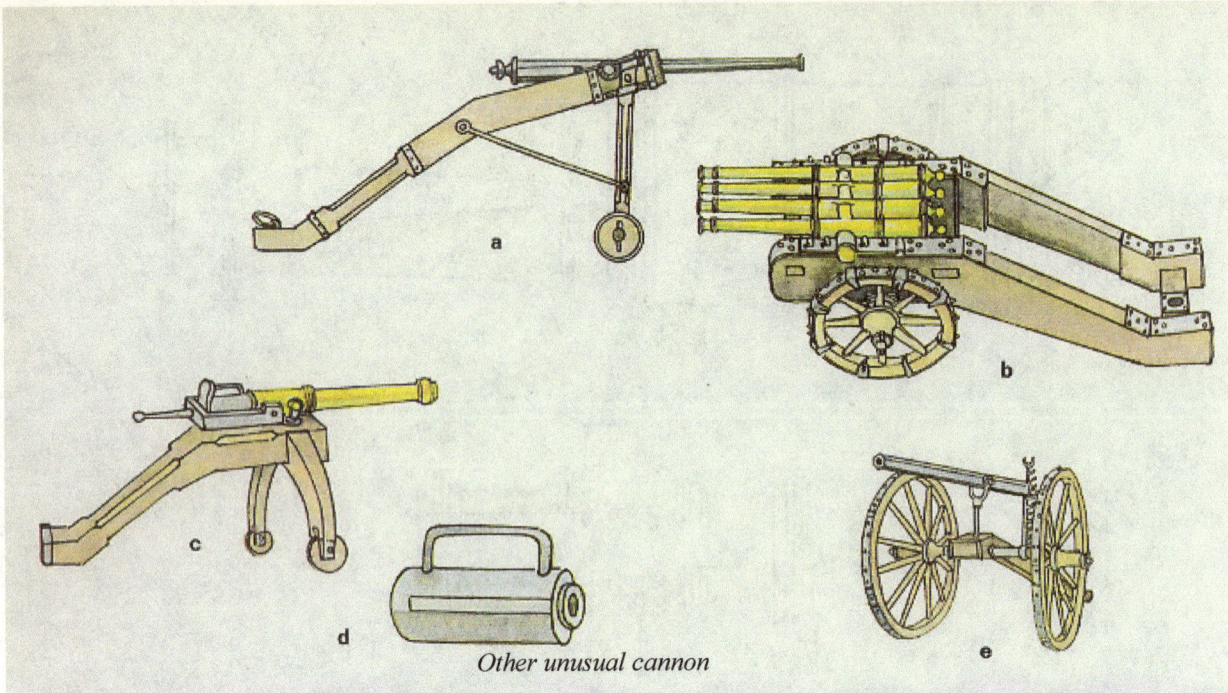

Other unusual cannon

a) Small calibre iron battlement gun on an adjustable mount used for castle defence. Barrel length was about 180 cm, calibre approximately 20 mm b) Carriage-mounted four barrelled cannon c) Breechloader with detachable chamber d) Detailed - detached powder chamber assembly e) Small calibre bronze barrel gun on adjustable mount used in castle defense as late as early 17th century

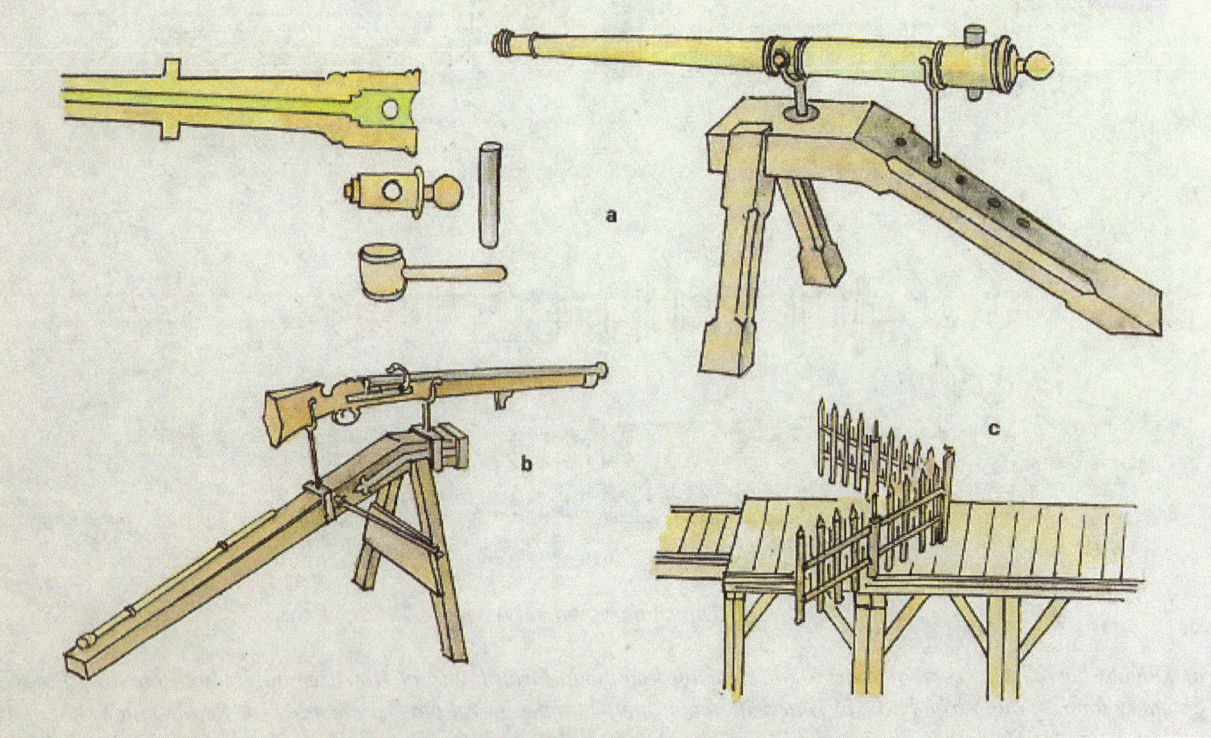

a) Small calibre bronze barrel gun mounted on a tripod. The breech is closed with a bronze plug secured with a large iron cotter pin b) Battlement gun with match-lock, tripod mounted c) Bridge block at the spot covered by battlement gun fire

Fire at casemates
a)The most effective system of fire b) Less effective system of fire c) Cross-section of walls with casemates

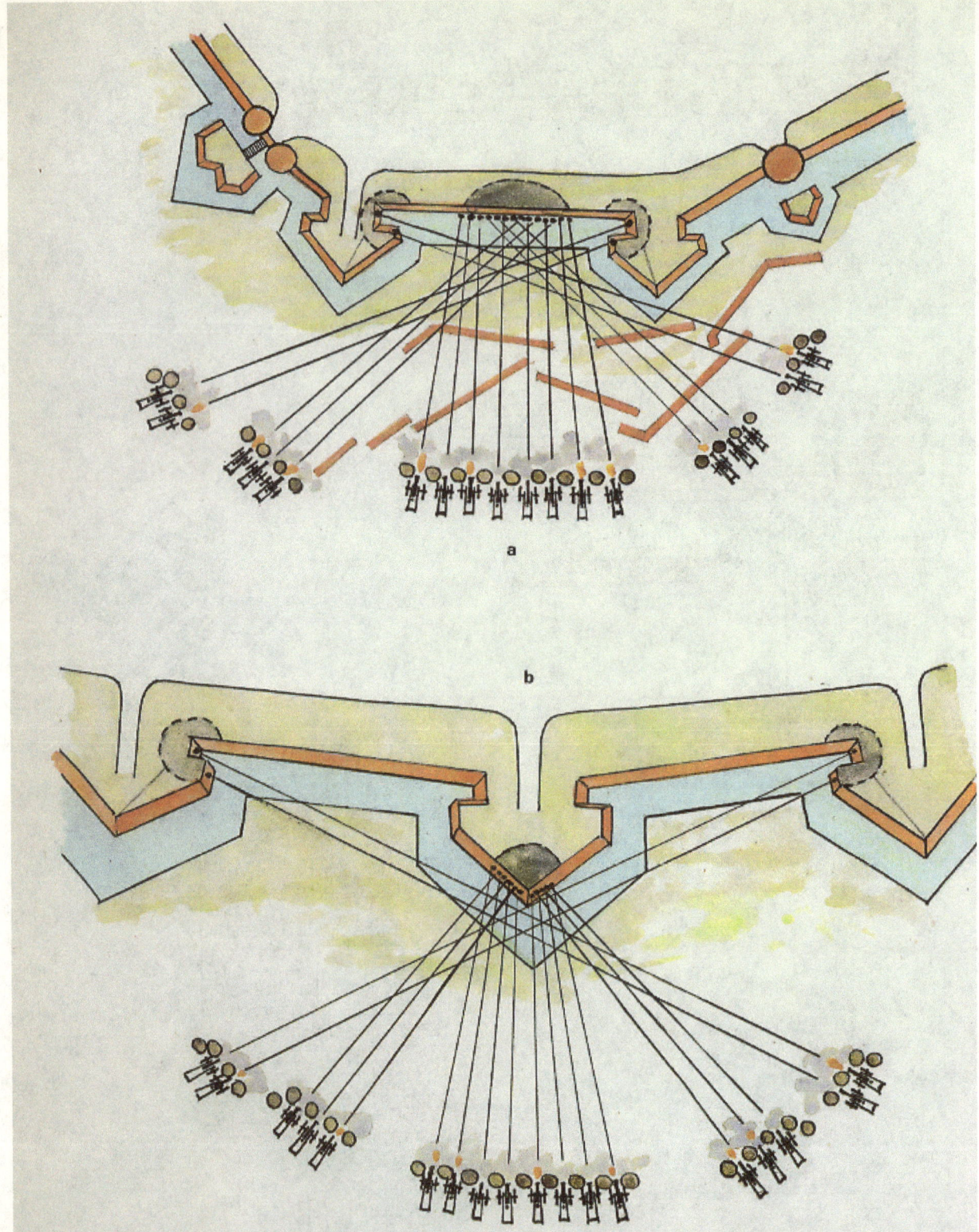

a

b

Battery position breaching a fort's walls and silencing enemy artillery emplacements

a) Battery position and system of fire to breach a curtain b) Battery position and system of fire at bastion salient

Gun carriage hitch according to weight

Gun carriage hitch according to weight with accessories of the piece

a) Auxiliary horse team hitched in front of a single beast harnessed in between the thills (shafts)
b) Thill-equipped gun barrel wagonc) Tripod mounted jack loading barrel onto the gun carriage
d) Thill-equipped limber

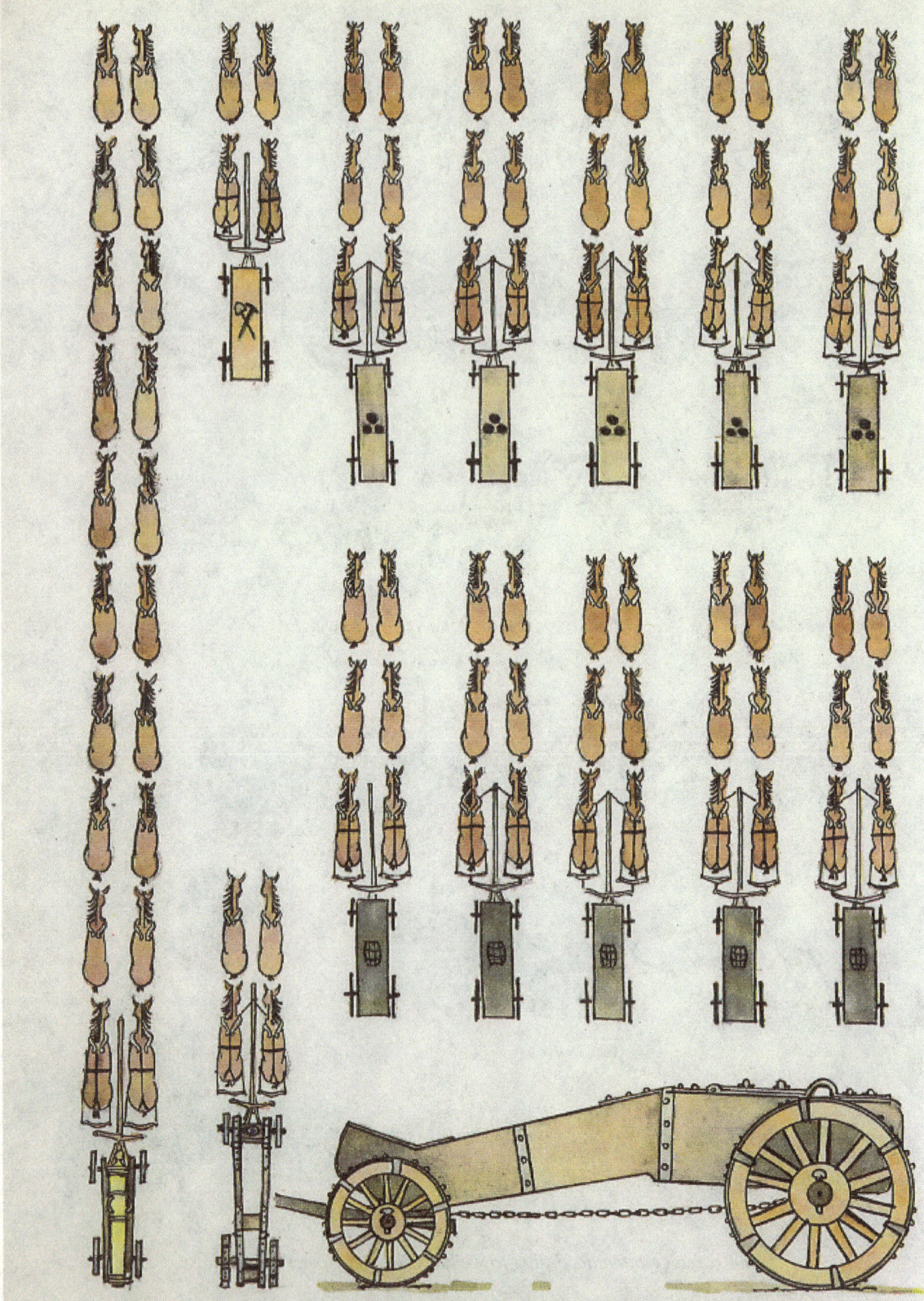

Number of hitches for transport of a 50-pounder nightingale. The number of hitches required for the transport of the carriage, barrel, ammunition, gun powder and kit

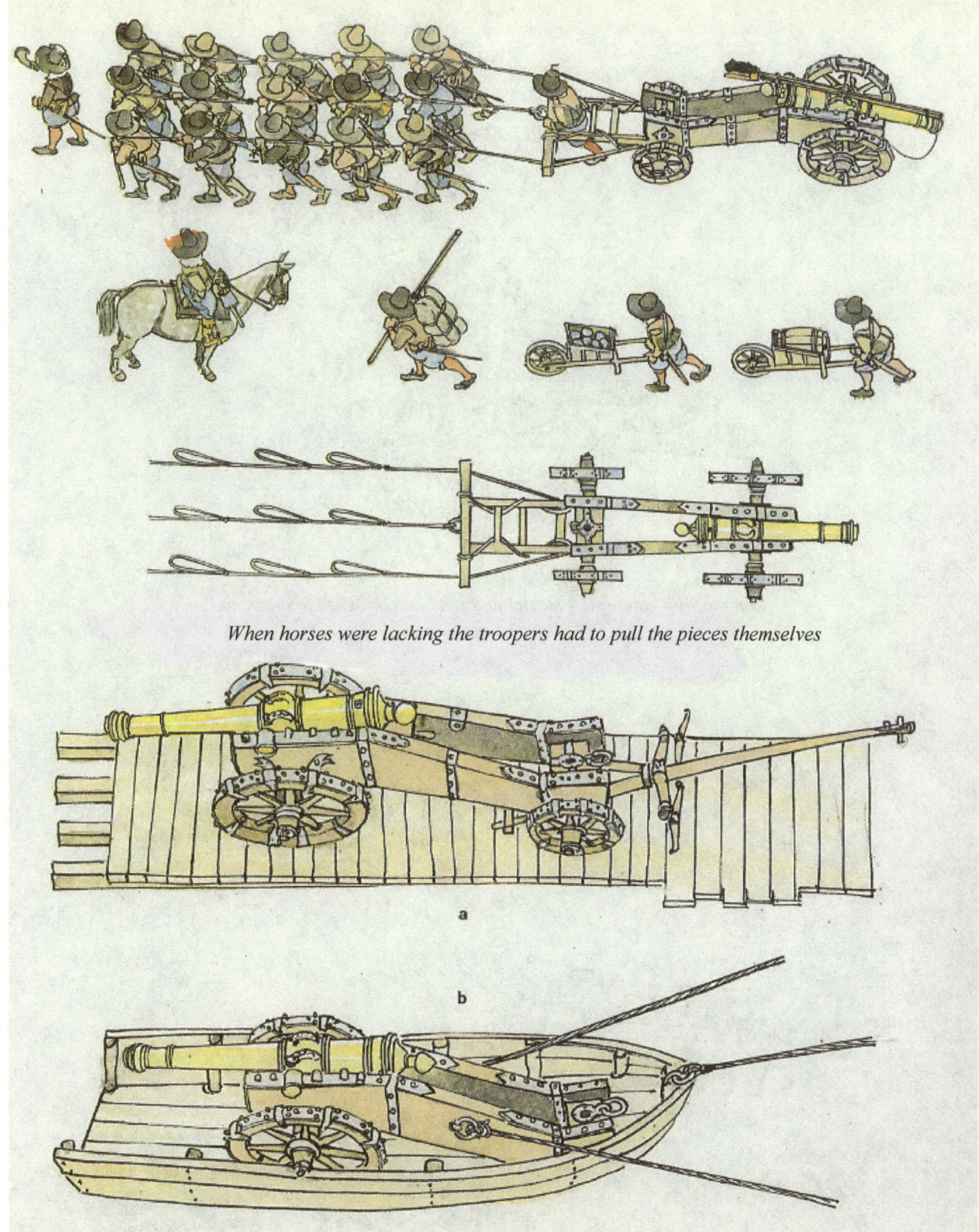

When horses were lacking the troopers had to pull the pieces themselves

a

b

Gun transport in soft terrain
a) Gun transport on soggy ground b) Gun hauling on muddy trench floor or on extremely soggy ground

Cannon with gunpowder shovel and swaband attached to the barrel

Gun hauled with capstan
a) Capstan b) Gun sledge c) Another type of gun sledge with loaded barrel d) Gear needed for capstan loading

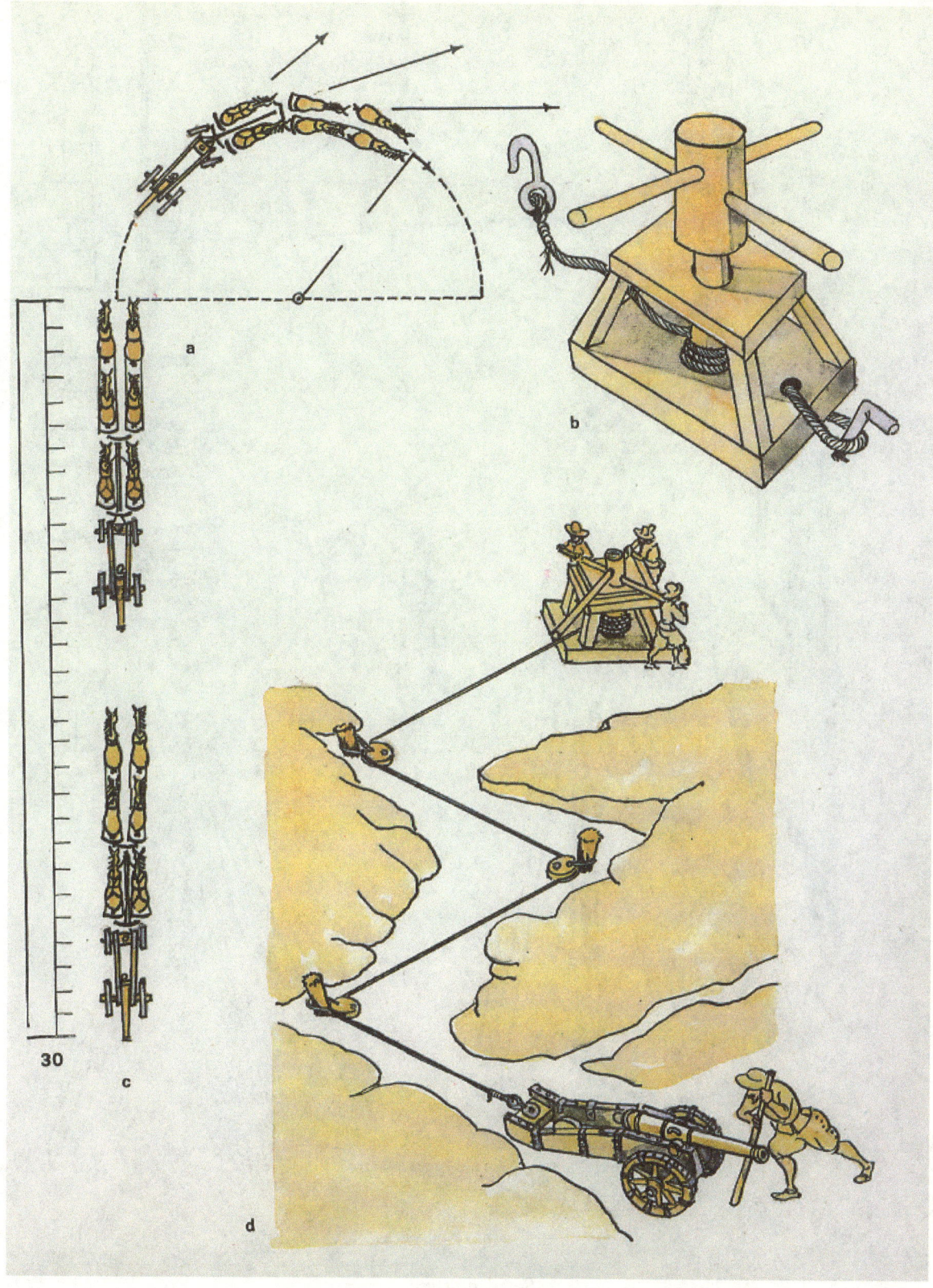

a) Turning radius of a six-horse team (on level ground it was 7.5 m) b) Capstan c) Length of six-horse gun hauling teams d) Gun hauled with capstan on even uphill road

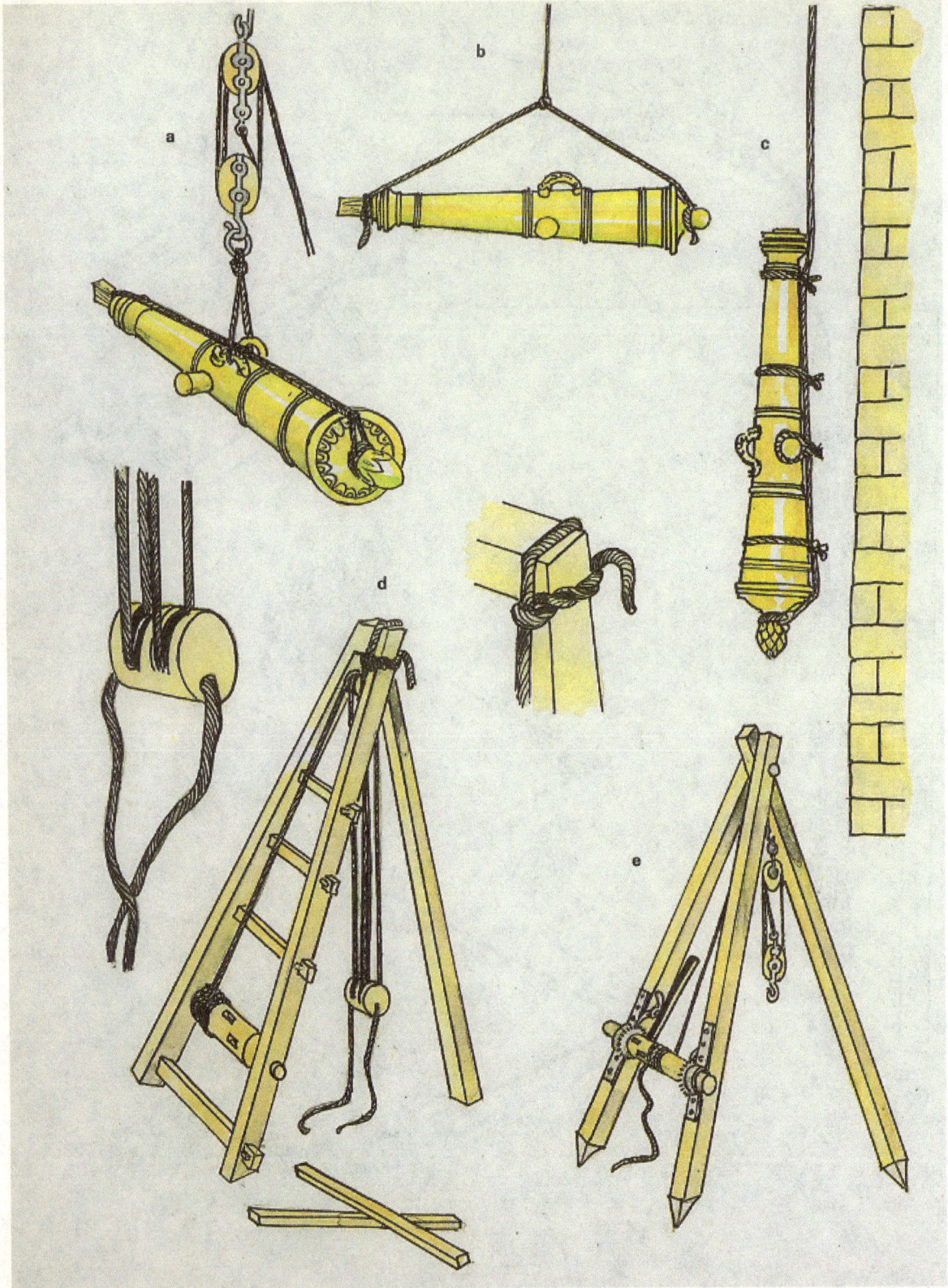

Barrel hoisting
a) Block and tackle b) Barrel fastening for lifting c) Method of hoisting the barrel and system to secure the barrel d) Gun barrel hoist, with details of rope hitching to hoist and the block e) Another type of hoist

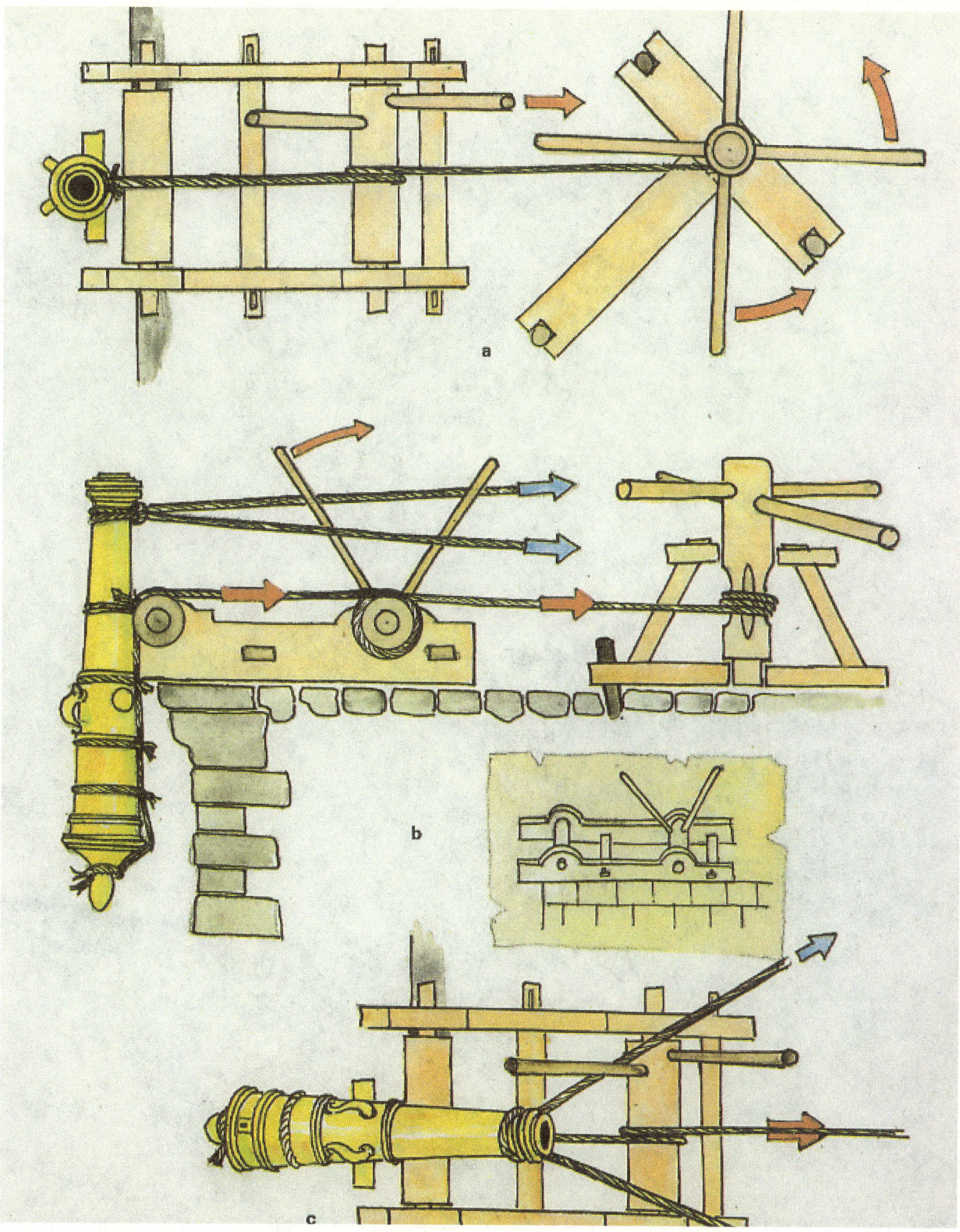

Hoisting a gun to the top of a keep
a) Windlass and capstan during the hoisting operation b) Side view of the two mechanisms when the
lifted barrel has been just secured with a rope c) Lowering the secured barrel onto a windlass

Field gun positions and location of kit

Position of the Swedish field gun crews at fire, usual in the Thirty Years' War b) Gun positioned on emplacement floor and protected with gabions. In the rear is a low fence to check excessive recoil. To the right of the carriage is a barrel and bucket for vinegar-and-water coolant, further right is a powder keg and a powder bucket shovel. Ammunition is placed near the left

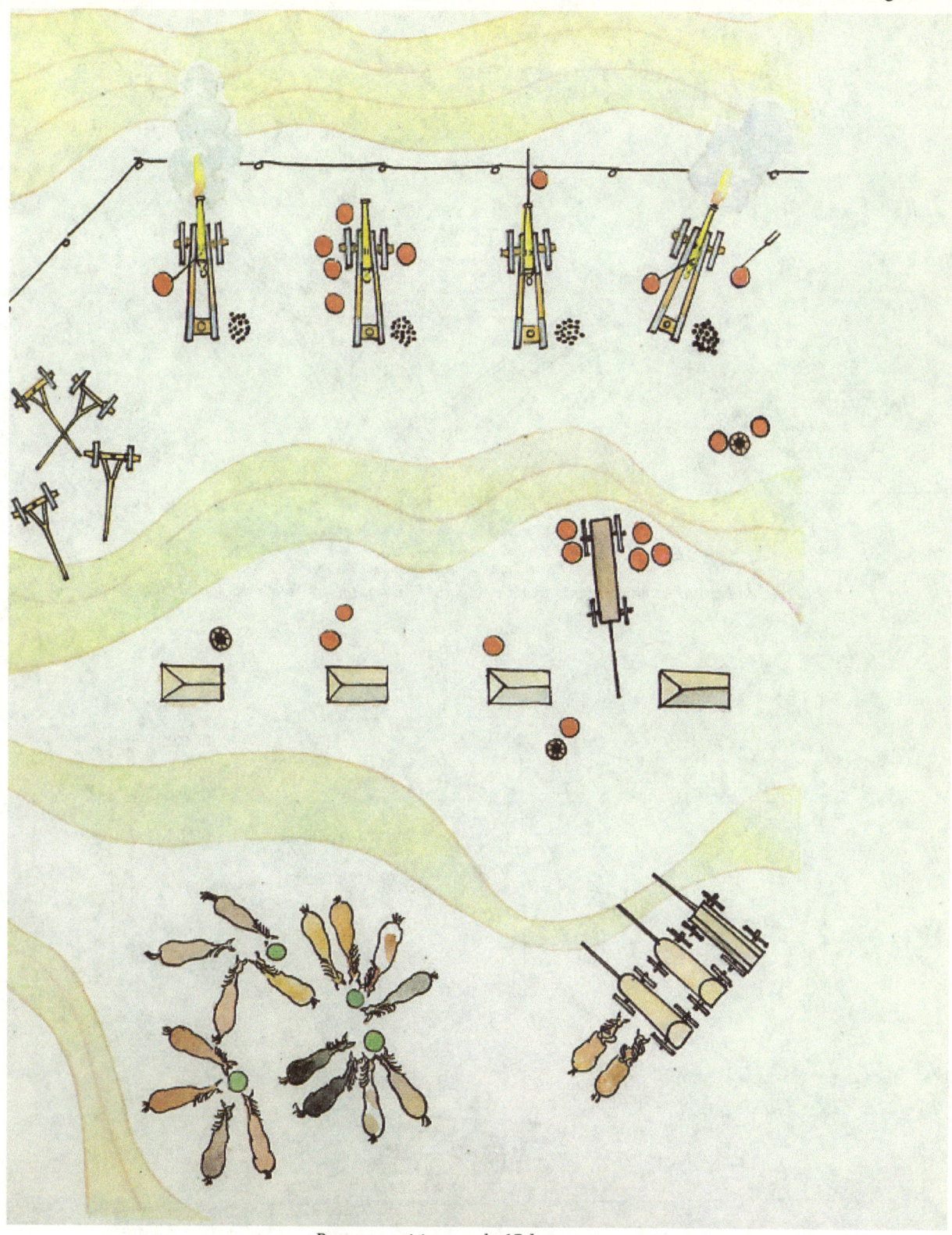

Battery position, early 17th-century
The guns follow an in-line arrangement. The fire sector of the gun on the right wing differs
from that of the rest of the battery. In the rear of the battery there are tents, powder kegs and
a caisson. Further back are the horse teams and wagons guarded by the drivers.

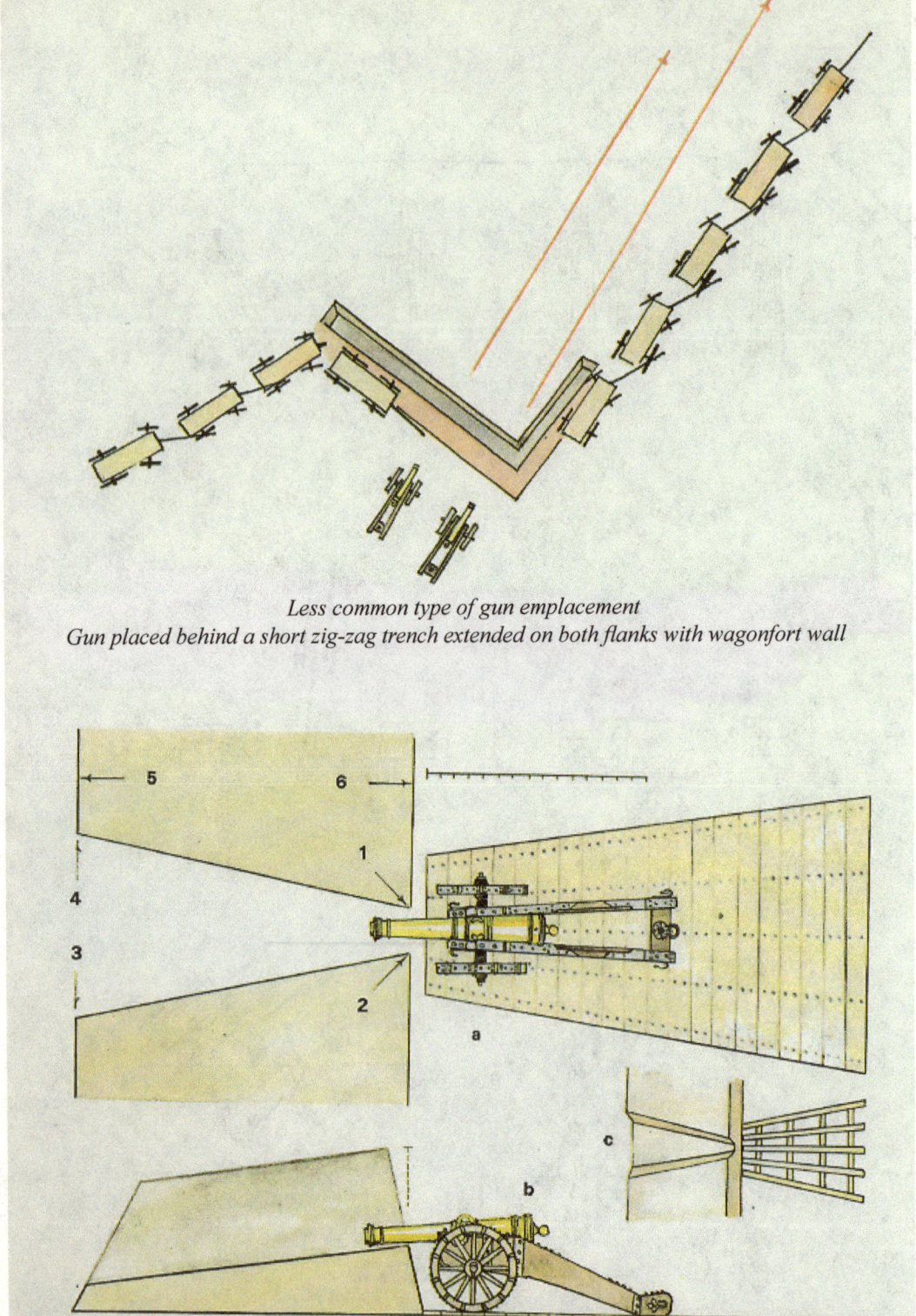

Less common type of gun emplacement
Gun placed behind a short zig-zag trench extended on both flanks with wagonfort wall

Emplacement embrasure and floor
a) Parapet embrasure dimensions and emplacement floor 1-2) =3 feet, 3-4) = 12 feet, 5-6) =23 feet
b) \Cross-section of embrasure and floor (height 11 feet) c) Floor timber frame

Fort gun position

The gun is positioned on inclined floor. Recoil from firing forces the gun up the slope. When the slope checks the recoil, the gun easily returns down the ramp to the original firing position b) Same floor design with inclined ramp at the end of the floor c) Gun positioned on a wheeled barbette equipped with small access ramps d) Laying the gun with a sighting disk

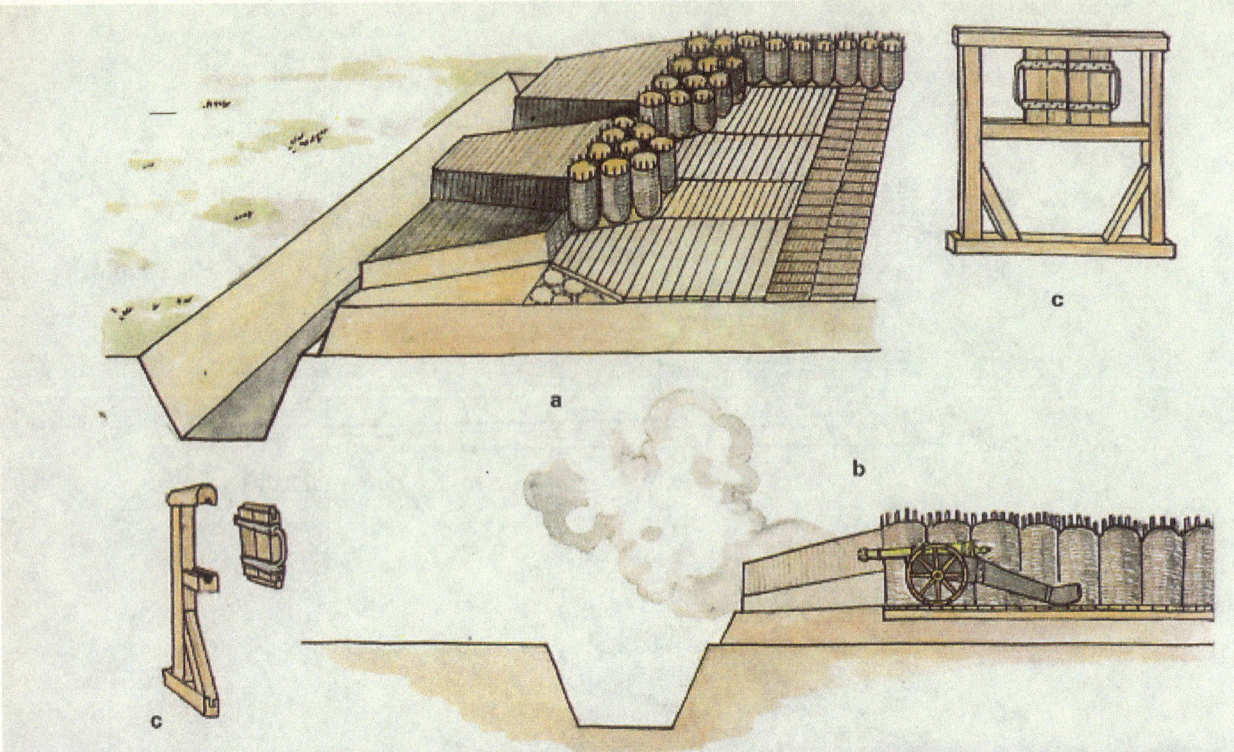

Built-up gun emplacement with gabions and floor

a) The guns are protected with earth-filled wicker gabions. The earth forming the parapet is rein-forced with wickerwork woven into a frame of wooden poles b) Cross-section of an emplacement be-hind a ditch and lay-out of gabions c) Sliding window embrasure used in this type of emplacement

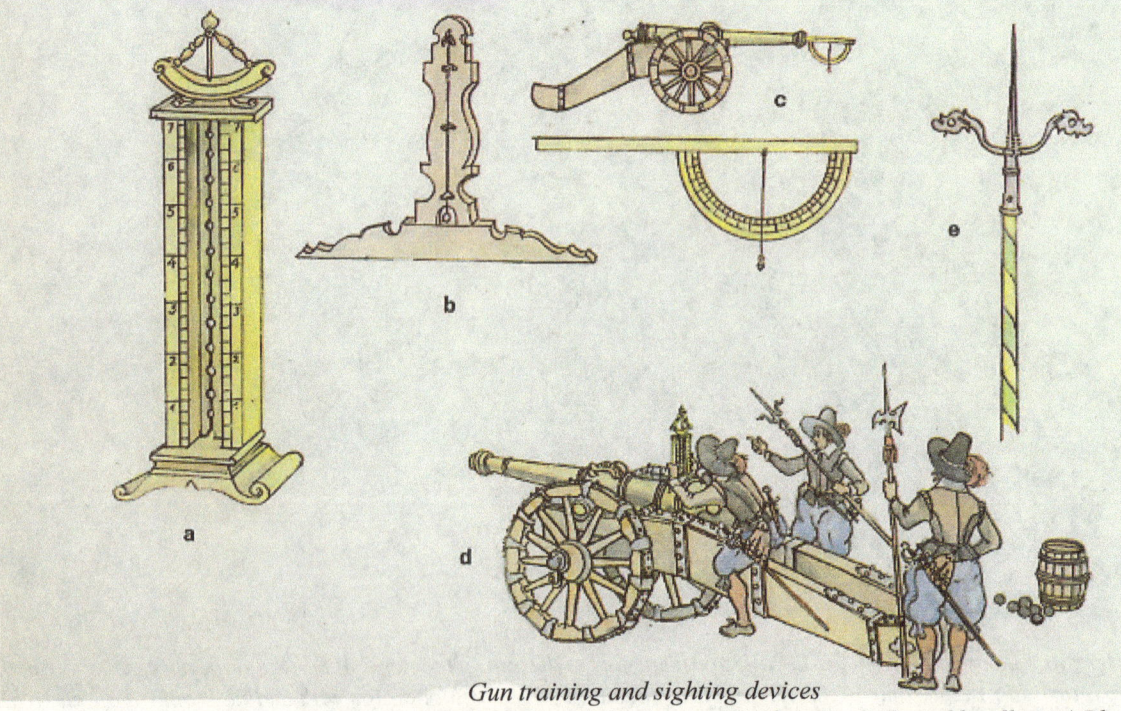

Gun training and sighting devices

a) Cartabon device with small sight-holes and a simple plummet b) Plummet for barrel levelling c) Plummet with quadrant fro barrel elevation check d) Gun training with a cartabon device e) Gunner's spontoon with match holder

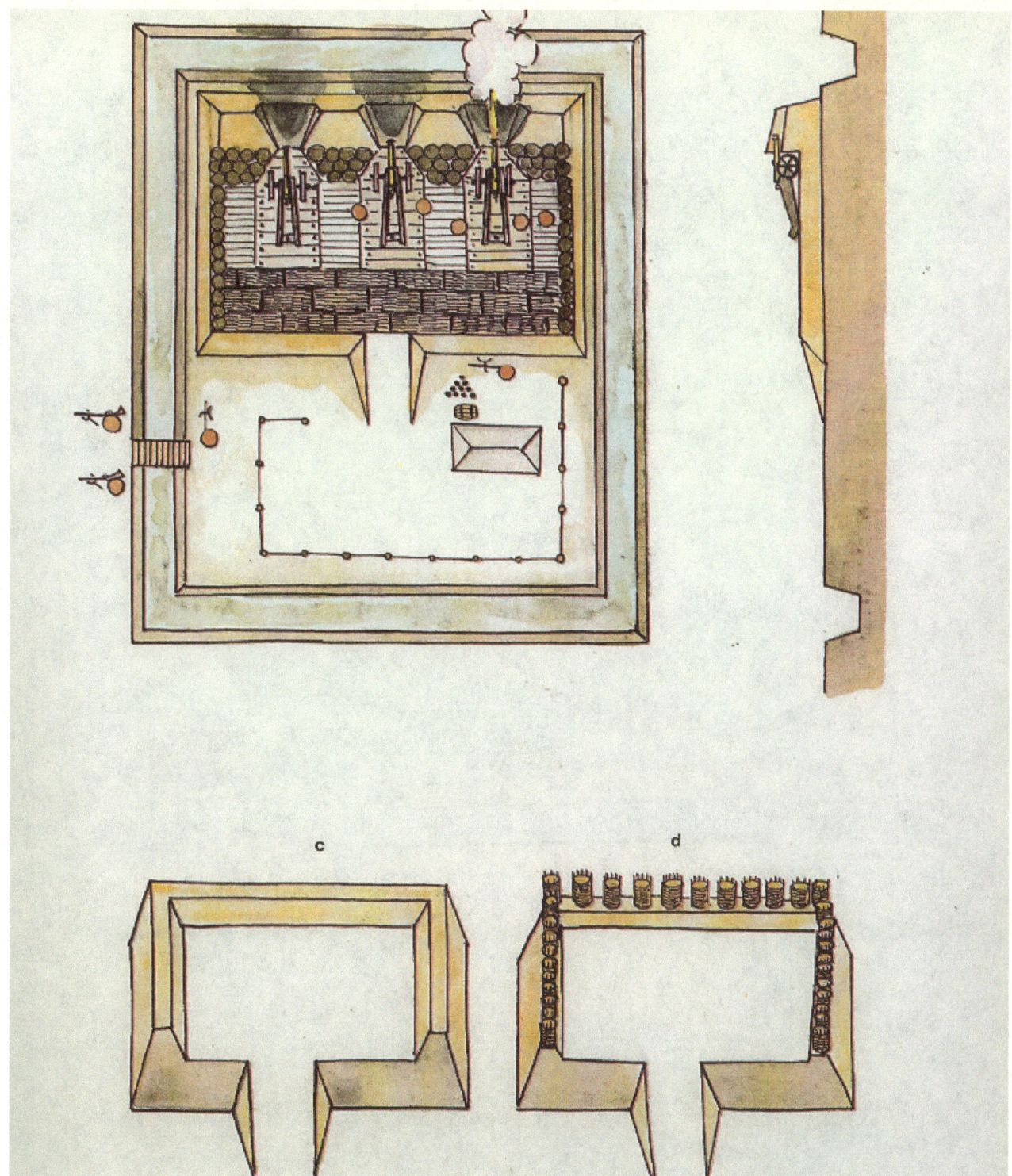

Other types of gun emplacements

a) Gun emplacement on a parapet with a breastwork reinforced with gabions also protecting the battery flanks. In the rear is a ramp for hauling the guns onto the parapet. Behind, under the emplacement is an ammunition tent. The area around the tent is further protected with a low fence. The flank ditch is spanned with a guarded footbridge b) Cross-section view of the emplacement described above c) Gun emplacement protected merely with an earth parapet d) Gun emplacement with low breastwork topped with gabions.

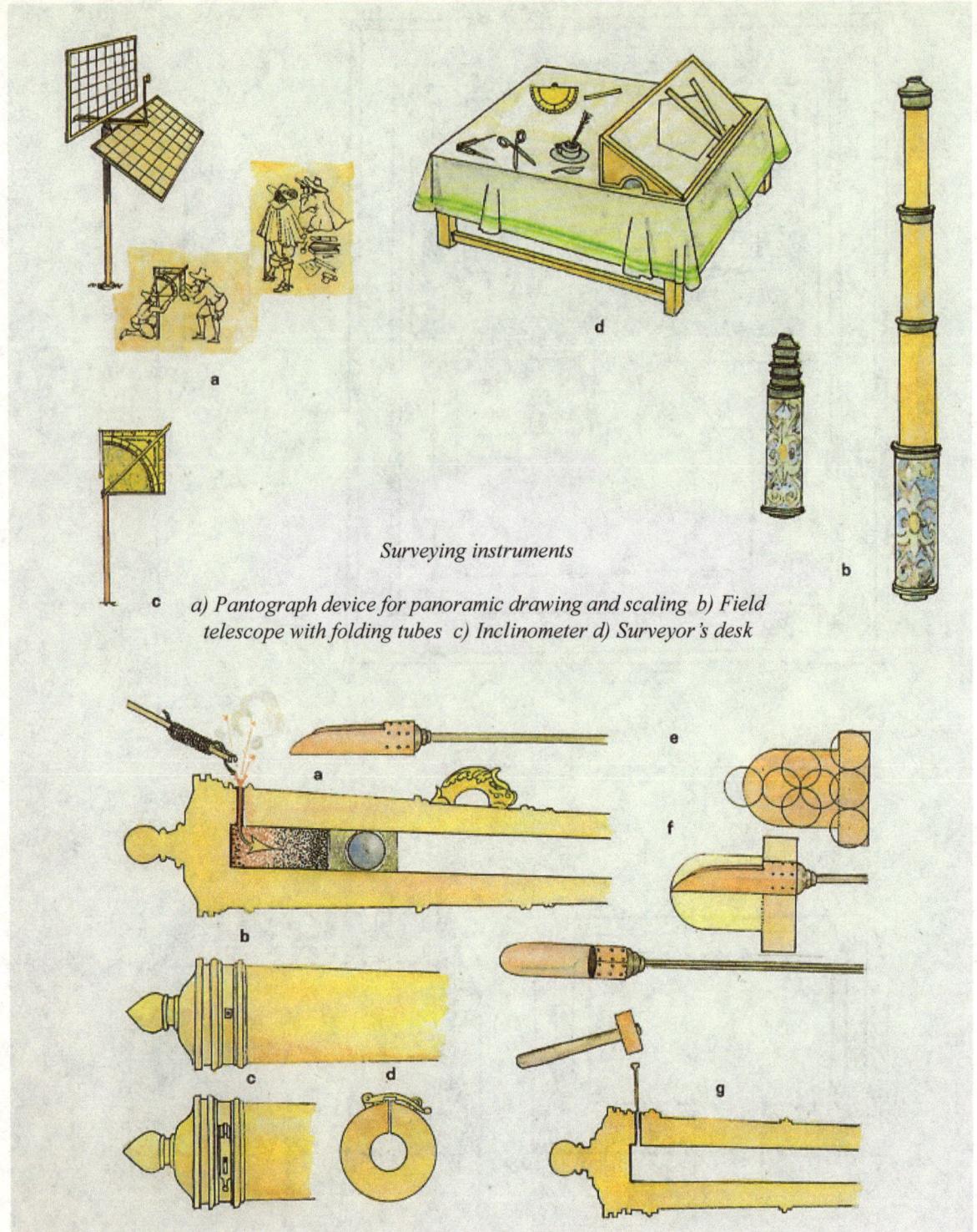

Surveying instruments

a) Pantograph device for panoramic drawing and scaling b) Field telescope with folding tubes c) Inclinometer d) Surveyor's desk

Barrel vents and gun firing

a) Cross-sectional view of the breech end of a loaded cannon and firing with a match b) Bird's eye view of gun barrel vent c) Vent cover d) Cross-sectional view of barrel, with marked vent and vent cover e) Unfolded skirt of powder bucket shovel, designed individually for each calibre class f) Powder loading bucket shovel with a groove along the handle to facilitate loading at night. The groove provided orientation as to whether the shovel is being held in the proper position g) Spiked vent; vents were spiked when the piece was in danger of being captured by enemy troops.

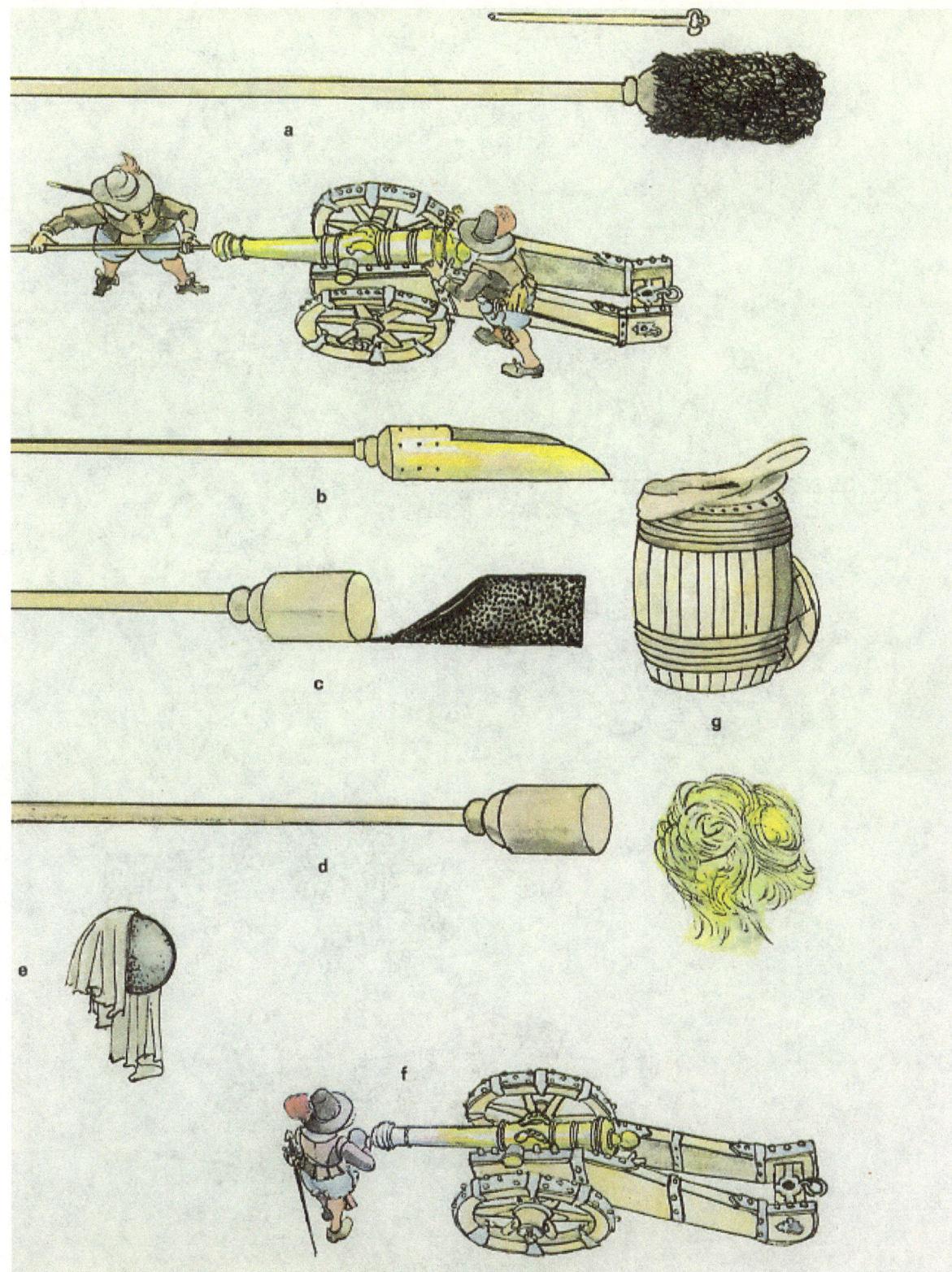

Gun loading
a) Barrel and vent cleaning b) Powder pouring c) Powder tamping d) Charge packing with
a swab of hay or straw e) The projectile was wiped with a rag to remove sand and other solid
particles to prevent seizing f) Ball placed in the barrel g) Barrel with powder

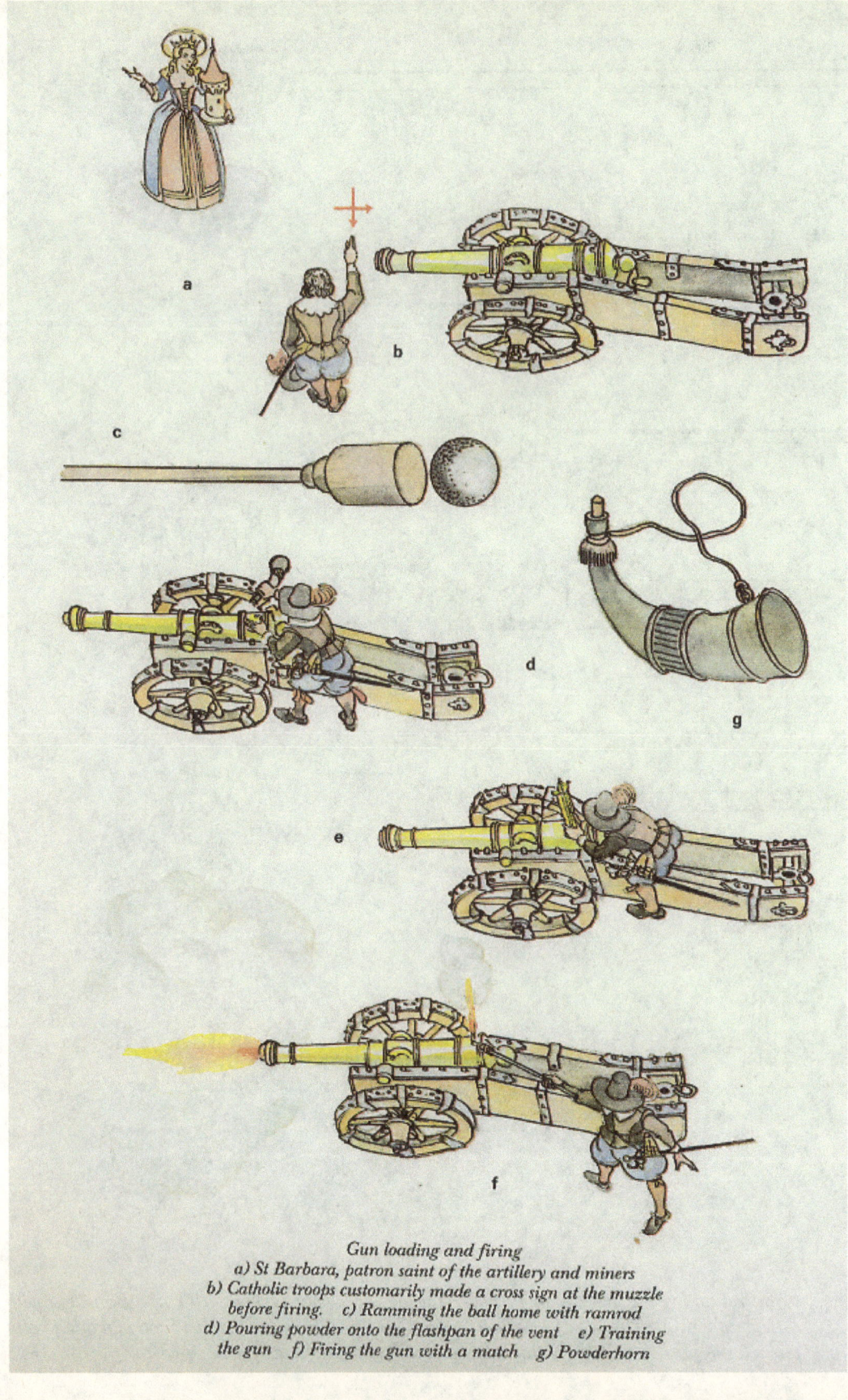

Gun loading and firing
a) St Barbara, patron saint of the artillery and miners
b) Catholic troops customarily made a cross sign at the muzzle
before firing.   c) Ramming the ball home with ramrod
d) Pouring powder onto the flashpan of the vent   e) Training
the gun   f) Firing the gun with a match   g) Powderhorn

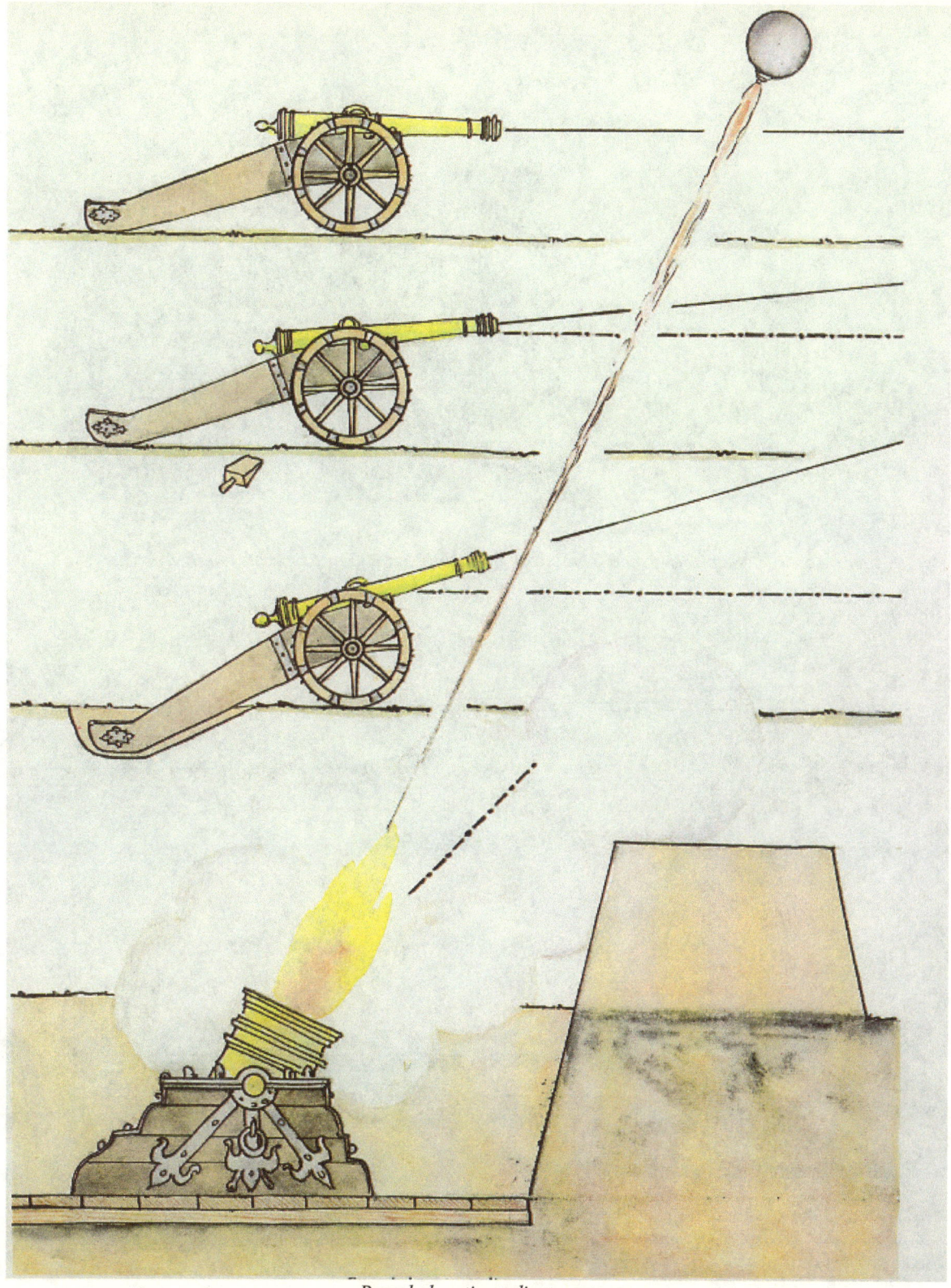

Barrel elevation adjustment
If a piece was to fire at steeper trajectories, the elevation required was obtained either by raising the wheels with a support or by lowering the carriage trail into an excavated pit. A siege mortar (below) was designed for high-trajectory firing.

After discharge, the pieces would be ready to fire another round in 12 minutes at the earliest

a

b

Systems of fire at fortification works
a) Firing at a parapet to 'wipe off' the packed earth from the top b) Firing at a wall to topple the crown into the ditch

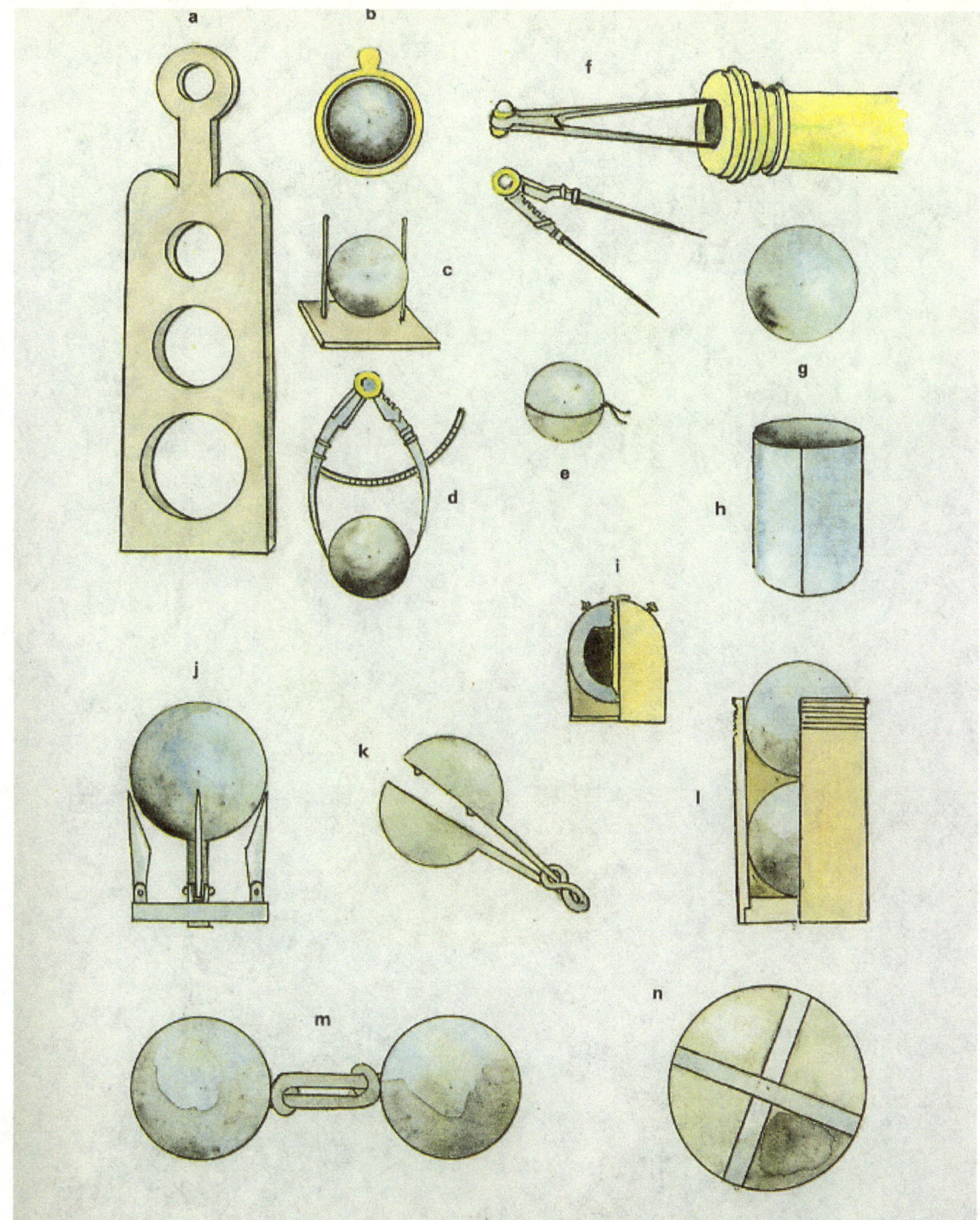

Artillery ammunition and ammunition gauges

a) Four calibre gauge plate b) Single calibre ring gauge c) Single calibre calliper type gauge d) Checking the ball calibre with compasses e) Checking the ball calibre with a knotted rope f) Checking the bore calibre with compasses g) Usual solid iron ball h) Metal sheet container for iron pellets or scrap – a canister shot i) Grenade (inside the missile is a powder charge detonated with a burning fuse) j) Knife shot with four knifes inside that opened after ejection. Used mainly for the destruction of men-of-war rigging k)Shot consisting of two folding hemispheres opening after discharge l) Chain shot in a wooden container protecting the chain against damage during discharge. After the shot left the barrel, the two chain-linked balls flew apart gained rotation and thus inflicted considerable casualties in the closed enemy ranks m) A pair of balls linked with interlocking sliding rods and eyelets. A variation of chain shot n) Stone (marble) ball reinforced with iron hoops

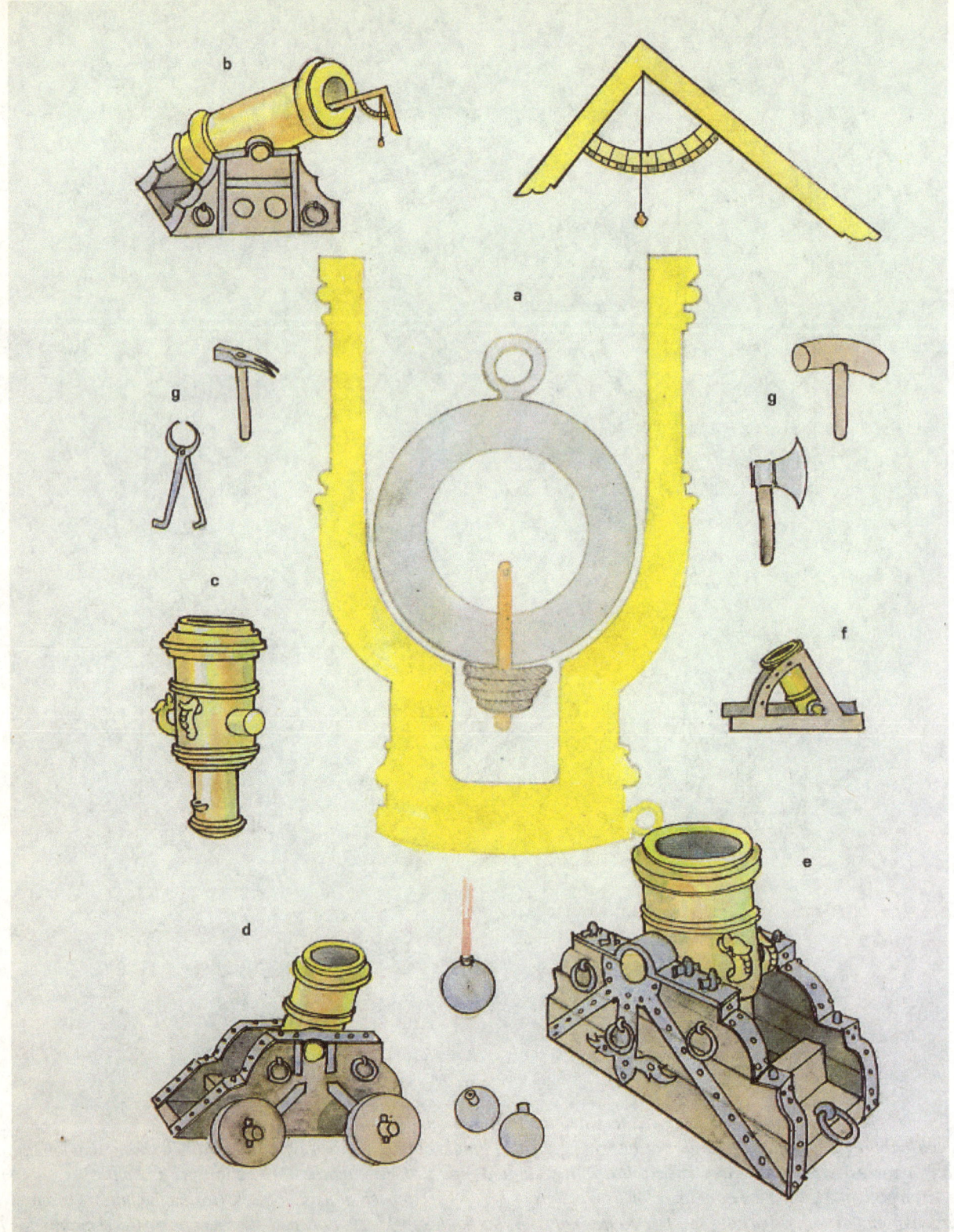

Siege mortars used for high-trajectory firing inside besieged cities and forts
a) Cross-section of mortar barrel, with grenade inverted b) Mortar with elevation quadrant inserted in the barrel and detail of the device c) Mortar barrel d) Wheeled mortar cradle mount e) Typical mortar type f) A less typical mortar, circa 1600 g) Accessories

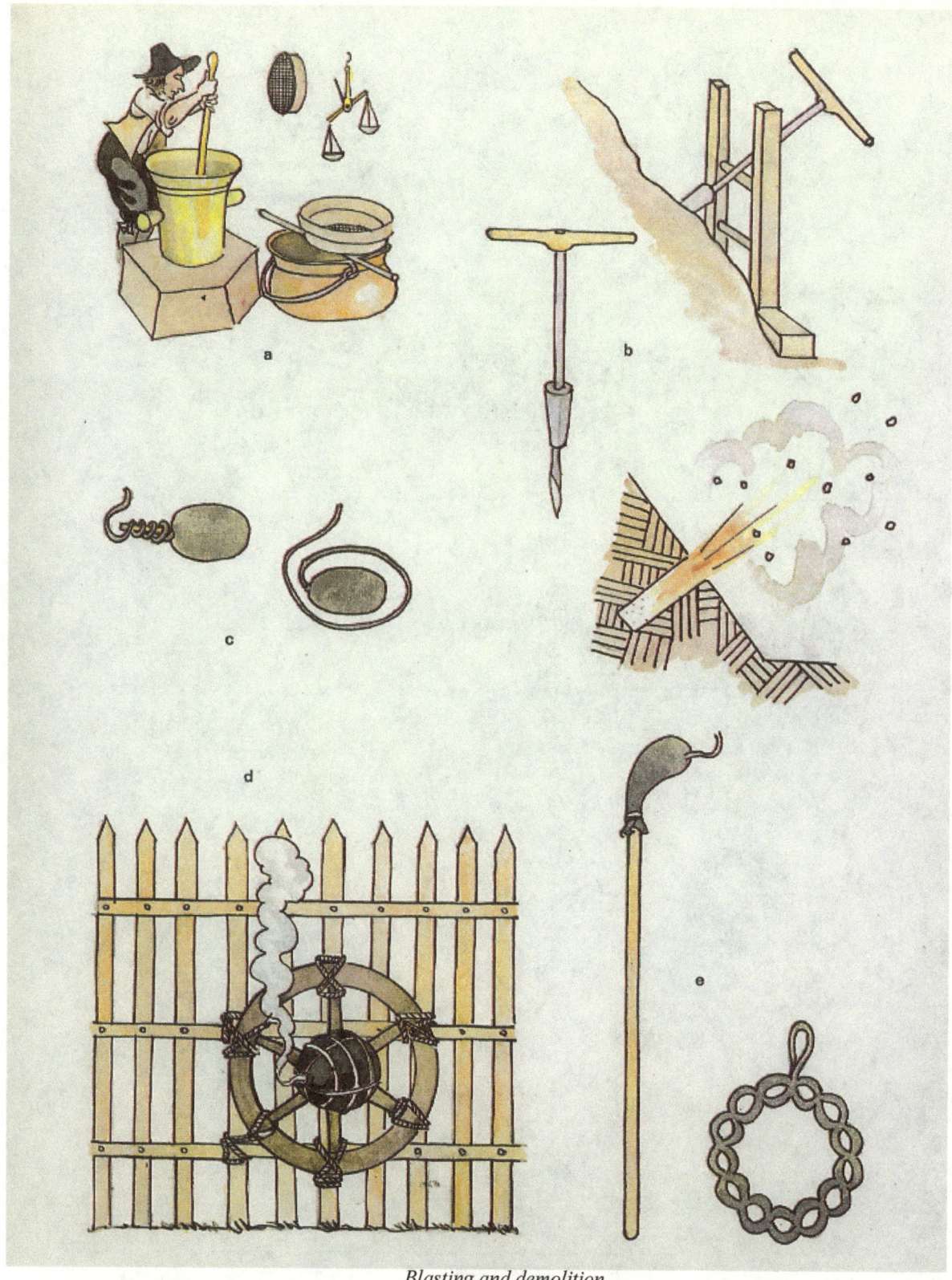

Blasting and demolition
a) Simple gunpowder manufacture b) Auger fro drilling blastholes in the ground, and blasting a charge
c) Charge with fuse d) Explosive wheel; the force of the exploding powder charges mounted on the wheel
rammed the wheel into the fence, breaching it e) Explosive tipped rod and so-called incendiary wreath

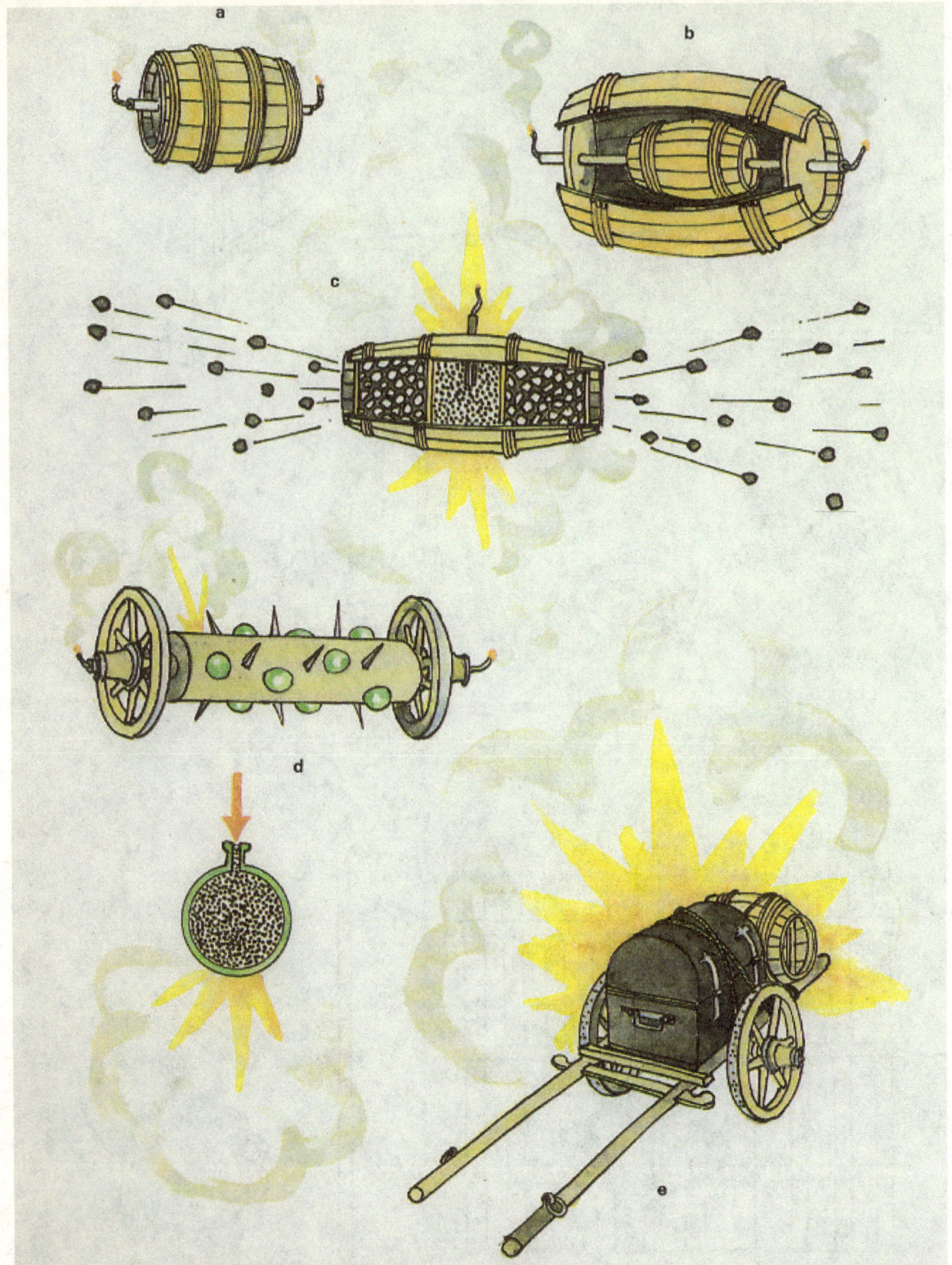

Blasting and demolition
a) Keg with an explosive charge inside b) Combined incendiary keg c) Explosive keg with a charge in the middle and packed with rocks. When the charge exploded the rocks were hurled around, inflicting casualties and damage d) Cheval de frise, with spikes and explosive glass ball. The powder charge is inside the cylinder e) Coffre d'artifice, or infernal machine

Using the petard

Petards were used for blasting gates, and portcullises a) Petard mounted on a base plate designed to be hung on the gate of the besieged structure b) Cross-section of a petard c) Bronze petard body d) Circular petard packing disk e) Ironshod wooden petard mounting base; the cut-out on the underside houses the petard body f) Hook nails for fixing the petard onto the face g) An example of placing a petard onto a face to be blasted. The face lies beyond an obstacle which in this particular case is negotiated with a ladder mounted on two wheels.

THE SUPPLY TRAIN

Provisions, ammunition and other military supplies were indispensable to any army, though in the early 17th century the supply train still had not been made an integral part of the army structure. Instead, wagon drivers were hired with their wagons and teams for a specified period of time or for a campaign.

The entire wagon train (though mostly hired) was subject to strict organization, especially during troop movements. Setting the march route, and grouping and forming the train, was in the charge of the wagonmaster, who decided who should drive which wagon and in what order. Many drivers did not even know what they were carrying.

In a train of more than 200 wagons, the wagon-master's orders were relayed from wagon to wagon by a trainmaster. One wagonmaster was in charge of about 200 wagons; his duties were to hire the wagoners, if possible those who were familiar with the roads and terrain of the planned route. His place was usually at the head of the wagon train, riding together with the commander of the sappers as a part of the cavalry vanguard.

The route was chosen according to the composition of the train and the type of artillery carried. In places where wagons were liable to get stuck or where there were steep slopes to be negotiated the trainmaster had to get auxiliary teams from other wagons as quickly as possible.

In difficult country bulky and heavy cargoes were unloaded and distributed among lighter wagons. This was done by journeymen, smiths, carpenters and wheelwrights. For these operations, various types of jacks hoists and tackles were used.

Great care was taken over the caissons laden with gunpowder. At stops, they were stationed at places chosen well beforehand by a detail officer, either a quartermaster or an armorer. The caissons were protected by a ring of wagons, and sentries were immediately posted.

When the wagoners' hire contract was up, they were free either to leave the troops and return home, or to sign up for another period. The chance to be rehired was especially welcome if the army had won a town or fort, and gained booty that had to be transported away.

Supply wagons were of numerous designs and types. Experience had shown that the most suitable wagons were the types used locally in the area the army was passing through, since these were built to suit the particular terrain.

Heavy carrier wagons were the basis of military supply trains of the period, but carts, packed asses and mules were also employed. Coaches and sedan chairs were used for personal transport.

According to their weight and type, the wagons were drawn by a team, or three or four horses. Extra teams were added for rough country and heavy loads. The driver either rode one of the team, the so-called near horse, or sat on the box. The team was easier to control from horseback since the driver could follow the preceding wagons and the road better and did not tire so easily from the monotony of the drive.

Draught horses pulling heavy freight carriers were harnessed in collar harnesses since the beast could lean into the collar and pull better. Carriage horses were hitched by so-called breast harnesses.

The pulling harness of the wheeler pair was designed to enable the horses to use their weight for braking the wagon when going down a short slope. One longer slopes, brakes were used.

The simplest method of braking was to stop the wheel turning by tying it to the perch with a rope. But iron rim of the wheel could be damaged by friction on rocky roads. Another method was to tie a strong drag pole with one end to the wagon body, running it under the rear axle next to the wheel so that the trailing end would act as a brake. The most reliable brake was the so-called wheel or skid pan which was fastened onto the rim like a shoe, so that the wheel would skid on it rather than the rough road; the other rear wheel could turn freely. A wagon braked in this way could easily and safely descend even a steep slope.

Provisions and supply wagons were usually fitted with rack superstructures. The racks were covered with planks, wicker-work or basketry. The cargo was usually protected by a canvas, either thrown over it and fastened or supported by several wooden arches.

Part of the matériel, especially lighter cargoes, was transported on carts suitable for the plains. These usually had large wheels and were drawn by a single animal hitched between a pair of thills.

Carriage bodies were suspended on strong leather straps from rigid corner posts topping the axles. To prevent a considerable side swing, the body was loosely tied on the bottom to the perch. Various types of sedan chairs, mainly used by higher officers, were carried either by horses, mules or human bearers.

In places inaccessible for wheeled vehicles cargo was carried on pack animals, usually jackasses or mules, saddled with simple pack saddles.

Wagons were also used to carry sapping equipment and specially built chassis were used to haul disassembled bridging devices, such as pontoons, balk and chess.

The wagon train of every army was followed by a band of women, wither riding or simply on foot. These were the wives and mistresses of mercenaries, who took care of their washing and cooking and other domestic work at the rest stops or in between battles.

The women carried their bundles, kegs and panniers on their backs, shoulders and heads, in every conceivable way. Wives and mistresses of high-ranking soldiers differed from the others not only in their dress but also in having more ornate saddles. Often they were accompanied by maids also following on horseback. The whole band of wives and mistresses trailing the train was in the charge of a veteran officer called the wenchmaster.

Field medical service

a) Surgeon examining the depth of a wound b) Sponge, bowl, wine and oil flasks and a bandage wetted with the healing mixture of the two liquids c) Surgeon's jug d) Surgeon's satchel and surgery instrumental case e) Medicament receptacles f) Amputation hacksaw, scissors, scalpel, bandage roll, sponge, surgical suture and needles, odds-and-ends box

a) Broken leg fixed with splints b) Arm and head bandages c) Enema syringe d) Tooth extraction forceps e) Amputation hacksaw f) Leg bandage g) Thumb being nipped off with bone nippers h) Bandaging the stump of an amputated arm

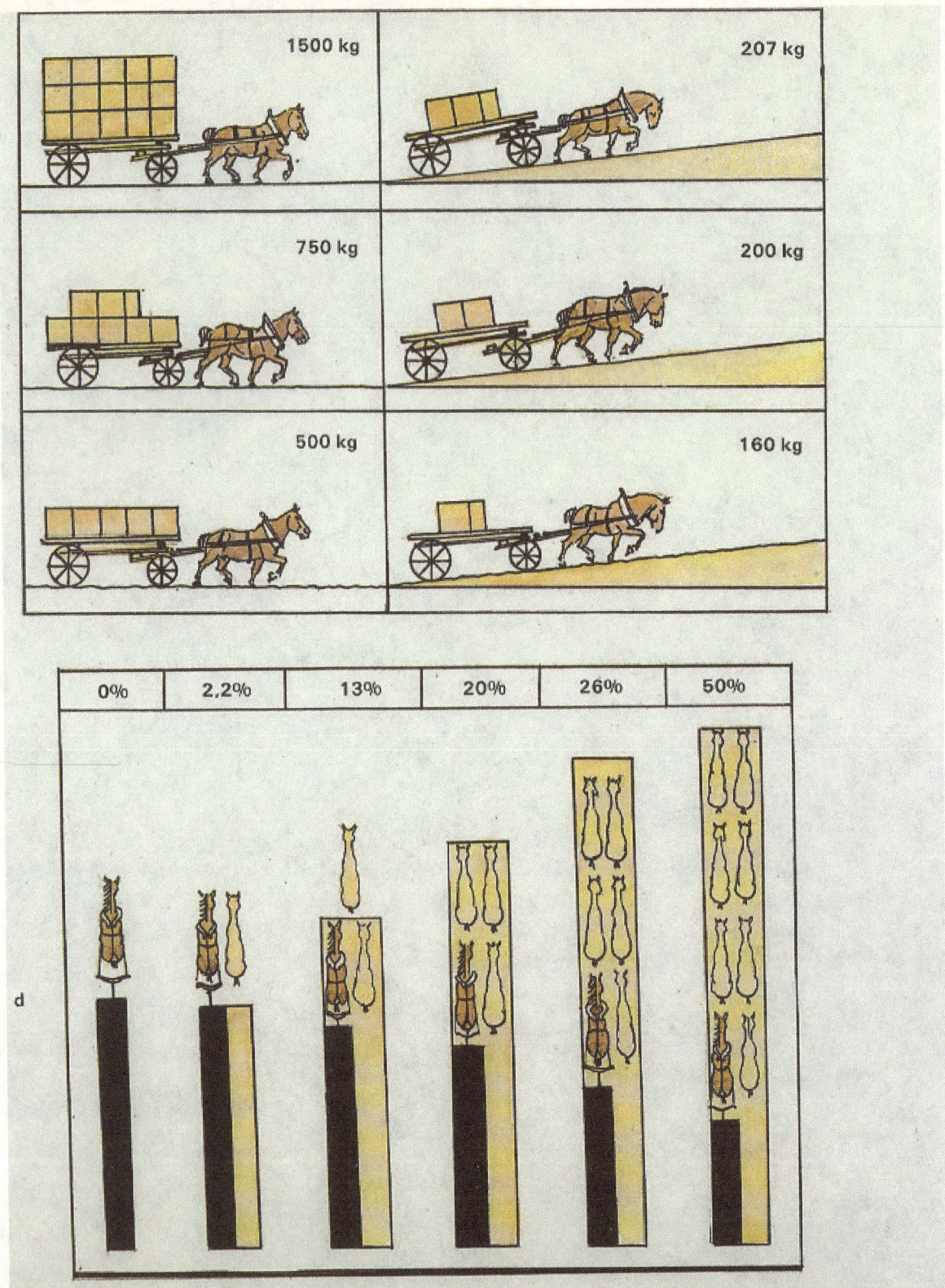

Horse pulling force for various road surfaces and slopes
*a) Good surface road and slope b) Bad surface road and slope c) Rutted gravel surface road
and slope d) Drop of pulling force requirement with additional auxiliary teams being hitched*

Wheel size

a) *A large wheel requires a smaller pulling force, it sinks into the ground less and negotiates obstacles better* b) *a wagon with smaller wheels has greater stability than one with larger wheels* c) *A small wheel has greater rigidity and strength than a large one* d) *The turning radius of a small wheel, smaller than that of a larger wheel*

Braking
a) On descending a short slope, the wagons were braked by the wheeler pair, acting on the shaft with their harness straps
b) Braking by means of a pole drag c) Tie rope d) Skid pan and its fastening to the chain e) Skid pan fixed onto the wheel

Freight and military supply wagons

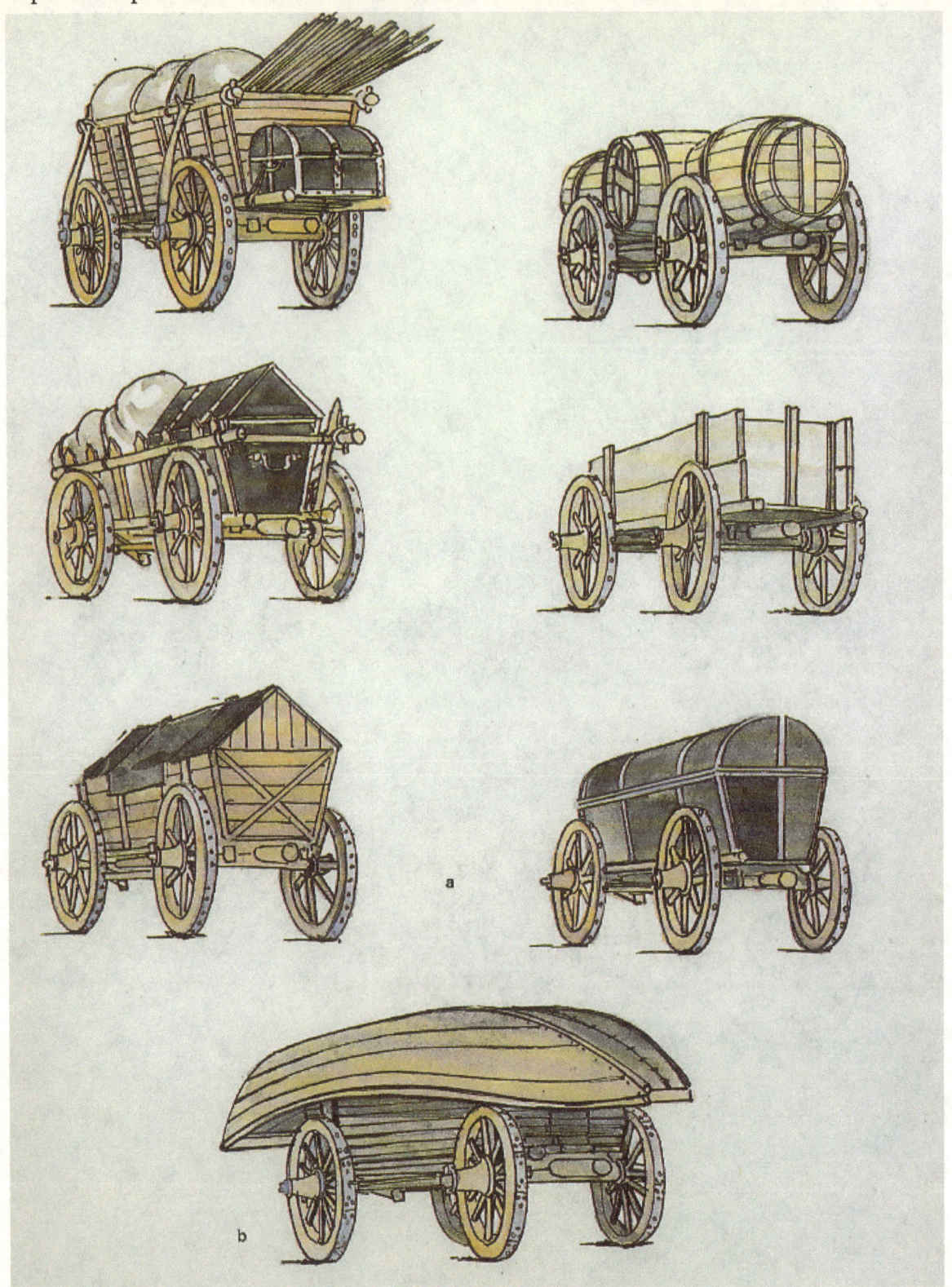

Military wagons
a) *Various types of wagons carrying arms, powder and other military equipment* b) *Engineers' wagon, with boat and bridging material*

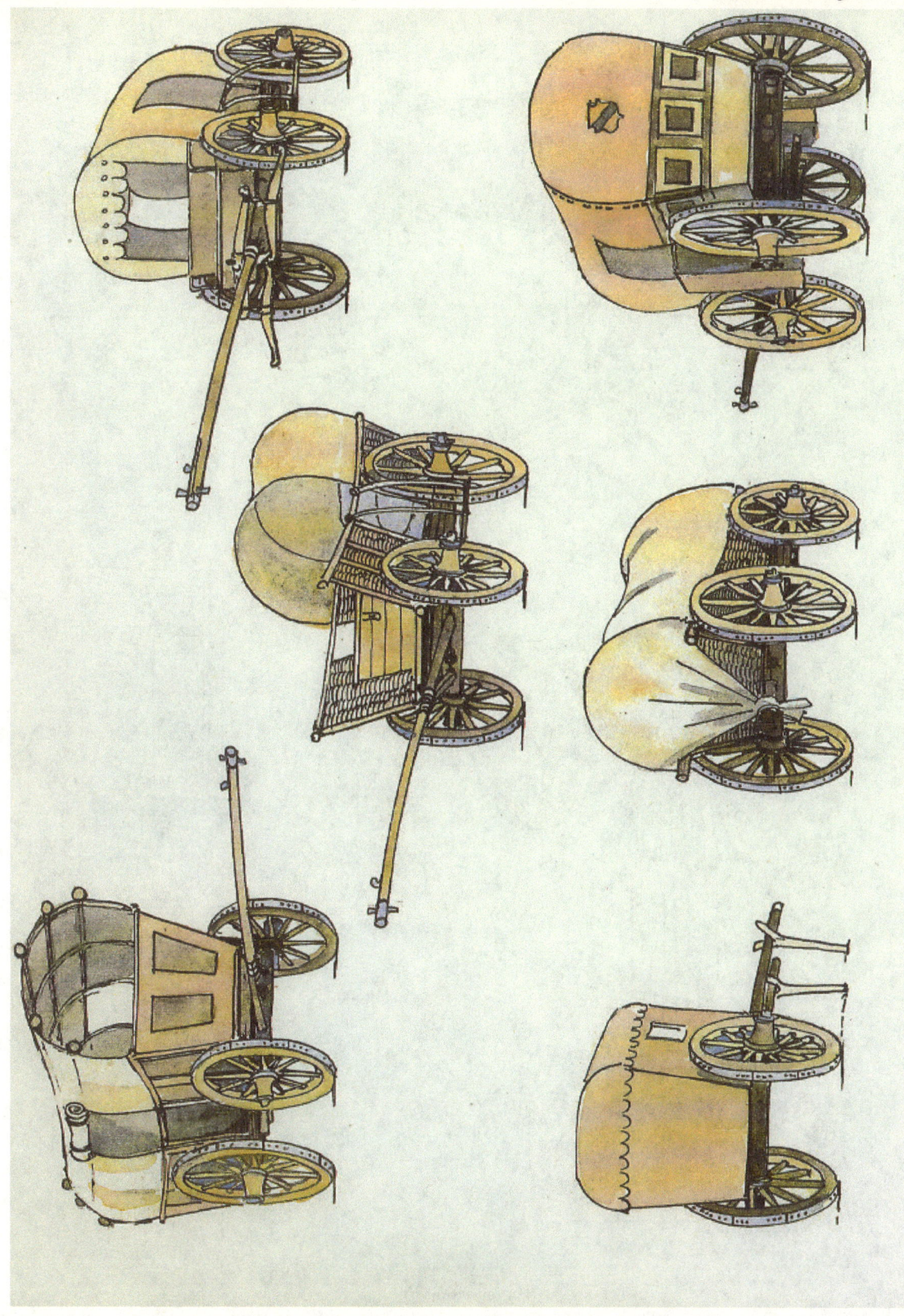

Four wheeled passenger vehicles and a two wheeled cart

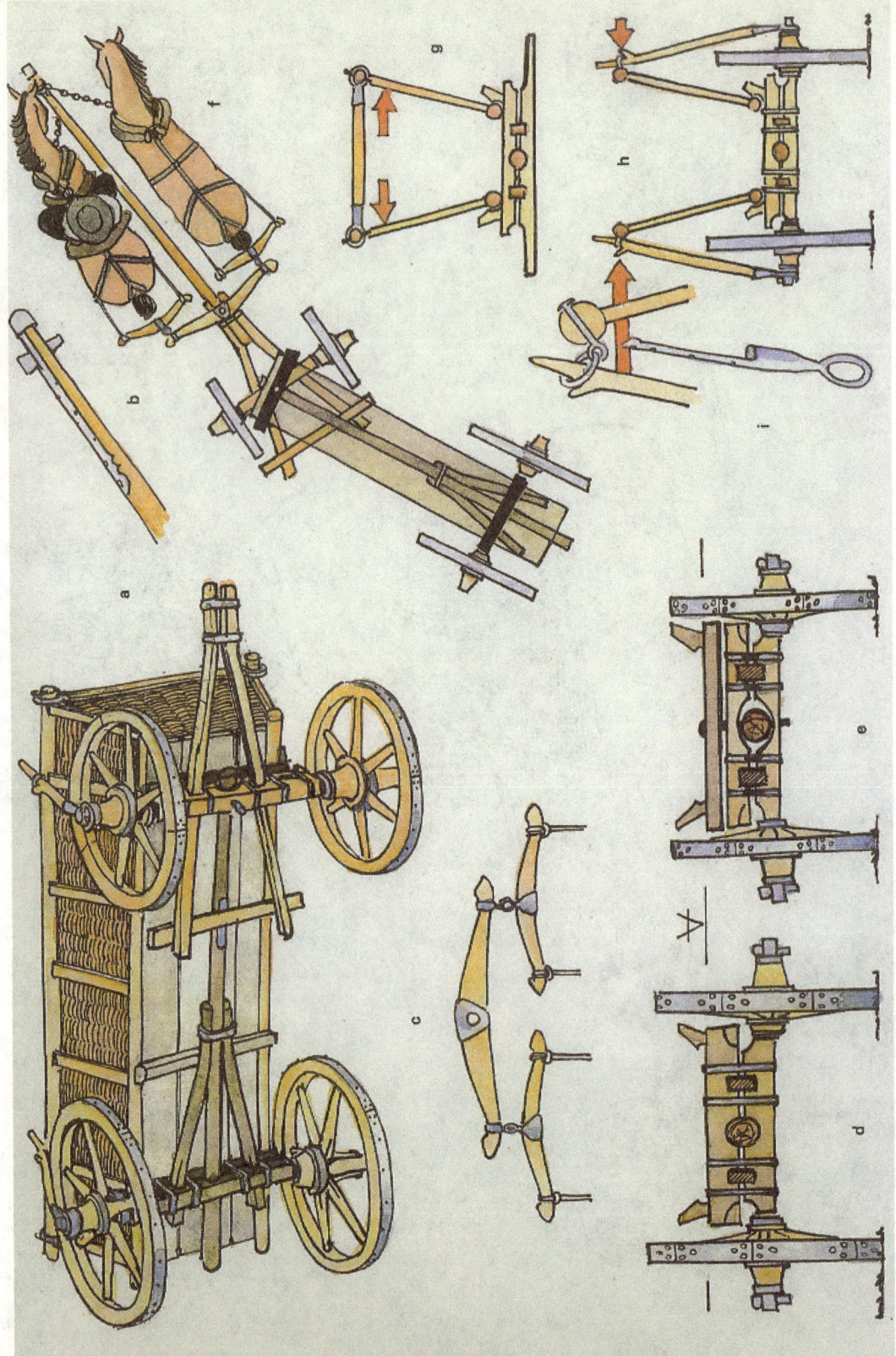

Wagon assembly
a) Chassis b) Shaft shod with iron c) Whippletree d) Wagon rear assembly e) Wagon front with swivel assembly f) Wagon turning g) Cross-bar holding the sides open h) Sides reinforced with strake braces i) Details of stake braces

Harness and wagon teams
a)Unicorn team, the driver riding the near horse of the wheeler pair and controlling the leader b) Typical seat of the driver on the near horse c) Horse harnessed to a cart d) Pack mules with cargo, led by a muleteer

Farm wagon and hitching

a) Farm wagon with a three-horse hitch b) Country style collar harness c) Snaffle bridle

Draught horses in collar harness a) Off horse b) Near horse

Various collar types
a) Near horse in draught collar harness b) Collar c) Shaft or tie rope
d) Collar pad stitching block   e) Off wheeler with holdback strap

Other methods of harnessing
a) Horse harnessed in between thills b) Horse harnessed to bear a sedan chair

Carriages
*a) Gentleman's coach with leather strap suspension b) Carriage of King Louis XIV c) Hackney
for hire d) Cross-sectional view of the carriage shown under "a"*

Carriage team harness
a) Carriage breast harness for a team of six b) Detail c) Other types of breast harnesses

Various carts
a) Cart with a harnessed horse b) Carette with barrel c) Wicker body cart d) Wooden body cart

Various other types of carriages and sedan chairs

a) Nobleman's carriage drawn by a four-in-hand, the driver controlling the team from his box with long reins Reins from the leader pair run through the rings on the headbands of the wheeler pair b) Simple sedan chair
c) Mule harness for bearing ornate sedan chair d) Mules bearing ornate sedan chair

*a) and b) Details of two types of harness fro draught horses c) Troughs for food and water
d) Food bag e) Mangers*

*Other cart types
a) Covered cart b) Open cart c) Tilting cart d) Rock cart*

Ladies' saddles

a) View of ladies riding sidesaddle, early 17th century b) Horse with sidesaddle c) Lady's palfrey with two riders, the woman sitting sideways d) Peasant woman on a horse bearing a simple sidesaddle

Mule saddles
a) Loaded pack mules with nose bag b) Sutler with laden pack horse c) Mule with pack saddle d) Country rider
e) Pack saddle types

PERMANENT FORTIFICATIONS

With the development of artillery permanent fortifications began to change significantly. Old medieval town walls which had withstood even the fiercest pounding of the old siege engines, now proved to be ineffective against artillery fire. The only feasible and practical solution was greatly to lower the town walls and to reinforce them with earth banks and mounds. While the fortifications of the medieval towns were being modernized the original ramparts were also lowered and filled with earth so that gun emplacements could be built there. Nevertheless, all these measures were nothing but an emergency solution.

Modernizing old town walls presented a whole range of new problems. It was very expensive and yet ineffective since even reinforced walls up to 10 meters thick still could not hold against a prolonged and systematic cannonade of siege batteries. Apart from that, the new huge earthworks exerted too much pressure on the foundations of the old walls.

In the 16th century, new strongholds or fortresses were built as an integral part of the defenses of many countries. This was a new development in the field of military engineering. The new fortresses had ample space for the living quarters, storerooms and other military buildings. Their designers envisaged new towns being built in the space enclosed by the ramparts.

This kind of permanent fortification originated in Italy in the late 15th century. The original walls were replaced with great earth mounds, with a new name, curtains. Instead of the old ramparts new huge bastions were built, and the barbicans that had protected the medieval walls were replaced with ravelins. From all these new fortification engineering features – the curtains, bastions and ravelins – a new defensive system was created, a modern polygonal-plan fortress surrounded with wide ditches.

The basic feature of the new fortification design was the large bastion. This system was to prevail from the 16th to mid-18th century.

In the 16th and 17th centuries the new bastion system spread throughout the entire European continent so that today it is impossible to say who invented the bastion. It may have been the famous Italian sculptor, painter and architect Michele Sanmicheli who built bastions in Verona in 1527, or it was possibly somebody long since forgotten. At any rate, among the first to apply the idea of the bastion to fortification was the outstanding architect Francesco Paciotto of Urbino, who built fortresses featuring the new bastion in Turin, Cambrai and Antwerp.

On the top of the bastions or inside their valued cellars, the casemates, there was space for artillery emplacements from which the guns could both cover the perimeter with direct fire and the area along the curtains and ditches with flank fire. Inside the bastions there were shelters for the cannon crews and storage space for ammunition. The huge bastion structures were usually placed on the points of the polygonal-plan fortresses. The bastion plan was usually pentagonal, the ramparts being protected against collapse with masonry walls. The individual bastions were connected with curtains – straight sections of the earthworks which formed also the sides of the fortress.

The bastions and curtains were in turn protected with a ditch three to five meters deep and 20 to 30 meters wide. Both the inner and outer walls of the ditch were protected from collapse by a masonry lining the inner wall being called the escarp and the outer the counterscarp. Beyond the ditch there was a wide mound sloping outwards, the glacis.

The road from the fortress led across another bridge and through a cut in the glacis. Where the road left the defense system there would be another small defense mound or palisade or a combination of both.

Since the access route to the fort would be guarded by a series of sentries, there would be several sentry boxes and guard houses placed along the way. The latter were sometimes erected even on the bridges. Sentry boxes stood on bastion horns as well to allow the guard to watch the area along the fort walls. Where enemy infantry fire was expected, the ramparts were equipped with banquettes running along the parapet, from which the defenders could return fire with their hand-guns.

The simple design of the 16th-century polygonal forts was constantly changed and modernized. The general trend was to advance the individual defensive features to the front of the basic fort polygon. But there were many different schools of military engineering, based on totally different theories and principles, so that engineers of the same generation, sometimes even working for the same state, were building fortresses of entirely different designs.

Until the 1550's, bastions were built with their flanks perpendicular to the curtains, the salients forming obtuse angles. The curtain sections between the individual bastions were about 500 meters long which, because the short range of the period's artillery, made the mutual defense of the bastions with gun fire almost impossible. Therefore smaller bastions were built in the centre of the curtain section. The bastions and curtains were about nine meters high, the counterscarps about seven meters.

From the later 16th century on, fortress design followed the so-called neo-Italian school. Its major Italian representative included Nicollo Tartaglia, Errard de Barle-Duc, Antoine de Ville and Daniel Speckle. The new school built the salients of its bastions at an acute angle. The school also created the so-called horned bastion, with rounded flanks. The curtain was shortened from the original 500 to 250 meters, and the height of the curtains and bastions were both increased to 12 to 15 meters, measured from the ditch bottom, so that the bastion and curtain parapets topped the glacis by three to five meter. Other smaller works called cavaliers were built on the top of the bastions and curtains, serving to protect their gun emplacements. Engineers of the period also advanced the glacis to about eight to nine meters from the counterscarp, making a covered way so that the defensive troops could move along the ditch without being seen to the position where an attack was expected.

At the same time an advanced defensive line was created. To protect the fort gates and curtains, earth embankments called ravelins were built in the ditch. Originally they were rounded, but later they became triangular, forming a salient.

By the start of the 17th century the new type of fortress following the principles of the neo-Italian school was already being built all over Europe, modified according to local conditions of individual countries.

The period saw also the spread of fortresses influenced by the Dutch engineering school, whose chief representatives were Simon Stevin and Henne van Coehorn. These forts were characterized by much simpler design, and they cost much less to build than Italian-style forts. The works were usually made of earth only, without brickwork supporting them, and without casemates inside. The ramparts were surrounded with a ditch about 20 meters wide and three meters deep, half to three quarters full of water. To prevent the earthwork from collapsing, the ramparts were advanced with the so-called faussebraie. The bastions and curtains were about six meters high and the faussebraie about four meters, measured from the foot of the ramparts. Typical of the Dutch school were features similar to ravelins built in the front of the bastion salients. To eliminate the so-called dead space along the works, that is, the space that could not be controlled by fire from the fort, extensive structures called hornworks were built. To defend bridgeheads or the space next to the approaches to the fort, and sometimes also to protect the outskirts of fortified cities, the Dutch school built so-called crownworks, usually in the form of an independent bastion flanked by with two demi-bastions.

The bastion system reached perfection in the later 17th and the first half of the 18th centuries in the ingenious French military engineer, Sebastien Le Prestre de Vauban (1633-1707), who built more than 30 new fortresses, while some 300 were rebuilt under his guidance.

Vauban strongly opposed the geometric patterns that had prevailed until then. His designs were strictly subordinated to functional needs and to the local terrain. In Vauban's time many other European engineers built works according to his principles. The Vauban school is characterized by the following features. In contrast to previous practice, Vauban's bastions were much more extensive, so that their vauntmures and barbettes could hold more troops and guns; the greater size allowed also for the construction of cavaliers. The salient angle of the bastions was less than 90 degrees and the flanks were almost perpendicular to the curtains. Behind the bastion, in its gorge, Vauban provided another, usually circular, work where an extra gun battery was placed. Great bastions were also built in the ditch, but the length of the curtains between each bastion did not exceed 11 meters, measured from the bottom of the ditch. As before, a 24 to 32 meters-wide ditch ran along the entire works. Apart from the bastions also other structures were built in the ditches. These had been already known from the Dutch school. The access road o the fortress was protected by two longitudinal mounds called caponiere, which were erected where the road crossed the ditch. Vauban also followed the Dutch in building extensive horn and crownworks in the perimeter, and the curtains were sometimes advanced with so-called tenaille structures. These were basically inverted triangles or V's, the angle pointing inward to the wall and the flanks outward to the perimeter.

The principles of Vauban's bastion system were to survive essentially unchanged until the first half of the 19th century.

If a fortress was to hold out against a siege, it required strong defensive works and a sufficient number of defenders, guns and ammunition. Moreover the defenders had to be well-stocked with food and water. To grind enough flour to bake bread from, windmills would be erected in besieged forts.

To safeguard against a possible future siege, stocks of gunpowder and the ingredients for its manufacture were made already in peacetime, as well as sufficient amounts of other materials for various coffres d'artifice and similar devices such as fire balls.

Whenever a town or the fortress was in danger of a siege, the materials for stopping breaches in the walls and ramparts were made ready. The necessary precautions against the fire were taken, fire-guards posted and enough hides prepared. Wet hides were used to extinguish fires. Various sapping implements had to be also collected, such as shovels, spades, axes, hoes, carts and water buckets. There had to be sufficient stocks of construction timber, stakes for making palisades, boards for gun emplacements and for shoring underground galleries.

Well-equipped and fully-manned forts and towns could withstand even very long sieges. For instance, Ostend was besieged by Spain from 1601 till 1604; between July 1601 and March 1603 the Spaniards fired about a quarter of a million artillery rounds at the city.

In the event of a long siege a large number of rules or articles were published to inform the fort population what to do in various circumstances. The citizens were ordered to stock themselves well in advanced with enough firewood and charcoal to last the siege, and cover these inflammables with boards and manure to prevent fires. Hay, straw and gabionage wicker had to be also covered with earth or manure. In every house a fire-guard had to be selected from among the adult males. Citizens assigned to fire-guard duty were equipped with water buckets and wet hides. Street corners were lit by resinous kindlings so that hurrying people would net bump into each other. Every able-bodied citizen was ordered to present himself with his weapon for the defense of the walls and ramparts, whenever an alarm was sounded, usually by a drum. He was bound to come, totally sober, to a pre-selected rallying point, where he was incorporated into a fighting unit. No-one was allowed to fire a gun without the commander's permission; a breach of this order was especially heavily punished. Women, children and foreigners had to stay indoors at night to keep the streets clear for the defending troops. All public houses were closed.

If the enemy artillery succeeded in breaching the fortification, the defenders dug ditches along the breach and put up a gabionage of baskets or barrels filled with earth or sand, or wool filled bags. However, to stop a breach under constant enemy cannonade was an extremely dangerous job.

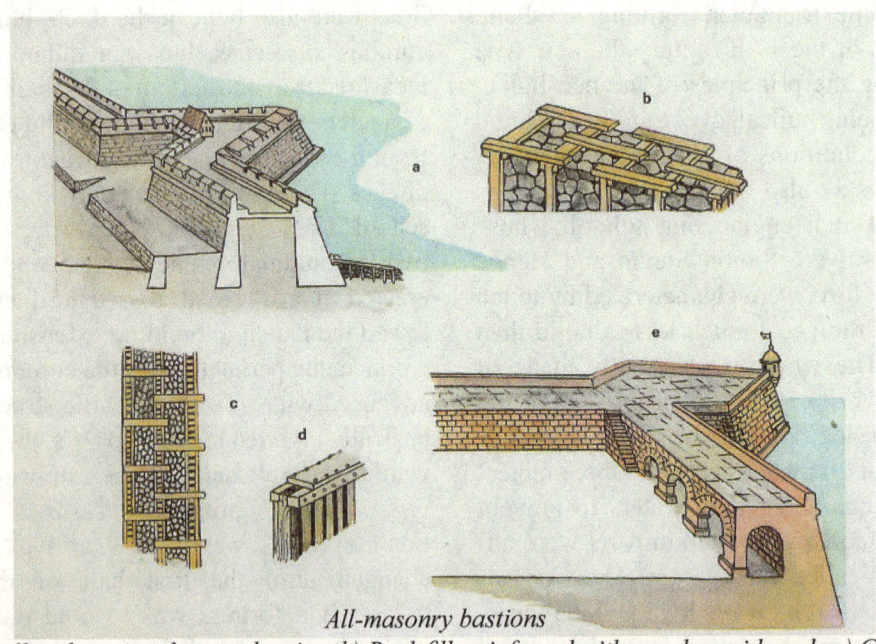

All-masonry bastions

a)Stone wall with a triangle trace bastion b) Rock fill, reinforced with wooden grid work c) Grid detail
d) Pilot embedment e) Brickwork wall with a bastion, watch tower, staircase and inner gallery

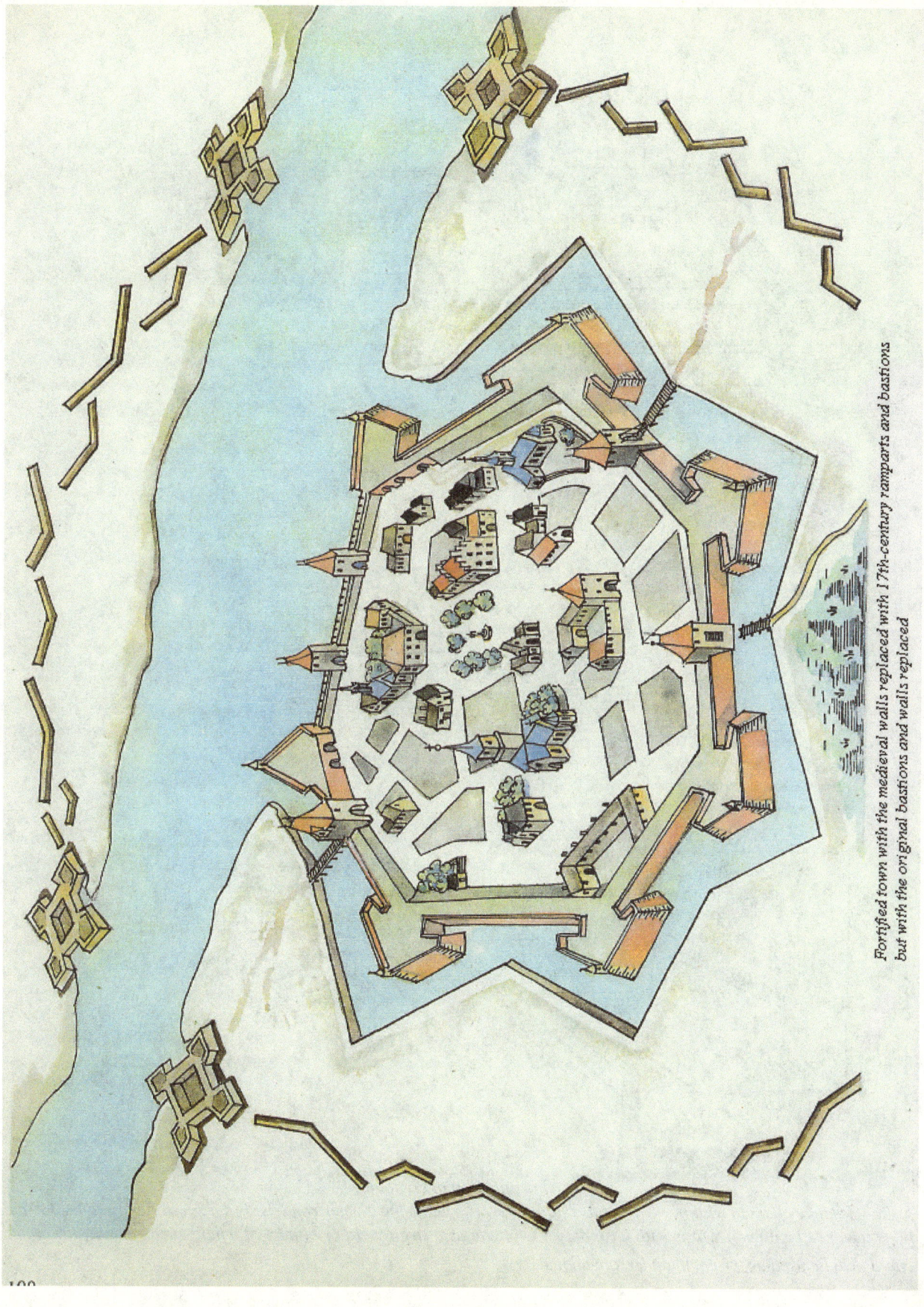

Fortified town with the medieval walls replaced with 17th-century ramparts and bastions but with the original bastions and walls replaced

Fortification of châteaux

a) *Renaissance château with newly built fortification works featuring corner rondels* b) *Original Renaissance fortifications advanced with new works with a rondel* c) *Château as a stronghold or citadel of a field encampment; the château could also be used as the commander's headquarters.*

New fortification works advancing the old walls
a) The new part of a town's fortification system b) Gate fortifications c) A new fortification system using the original town gates

a) Hornwork bastion with a cavalier according to Specklin's engineering school b) Barbette or battery position: Under the embrasures runs a corridor, the center of the courtyard is equipped with a drain. The area is accessible along a staircase built in between the walls. The material was supplied down the ramp (not seen) c) Horn bastion with guard tower in the salient

Artillery barbettes in bastion corners

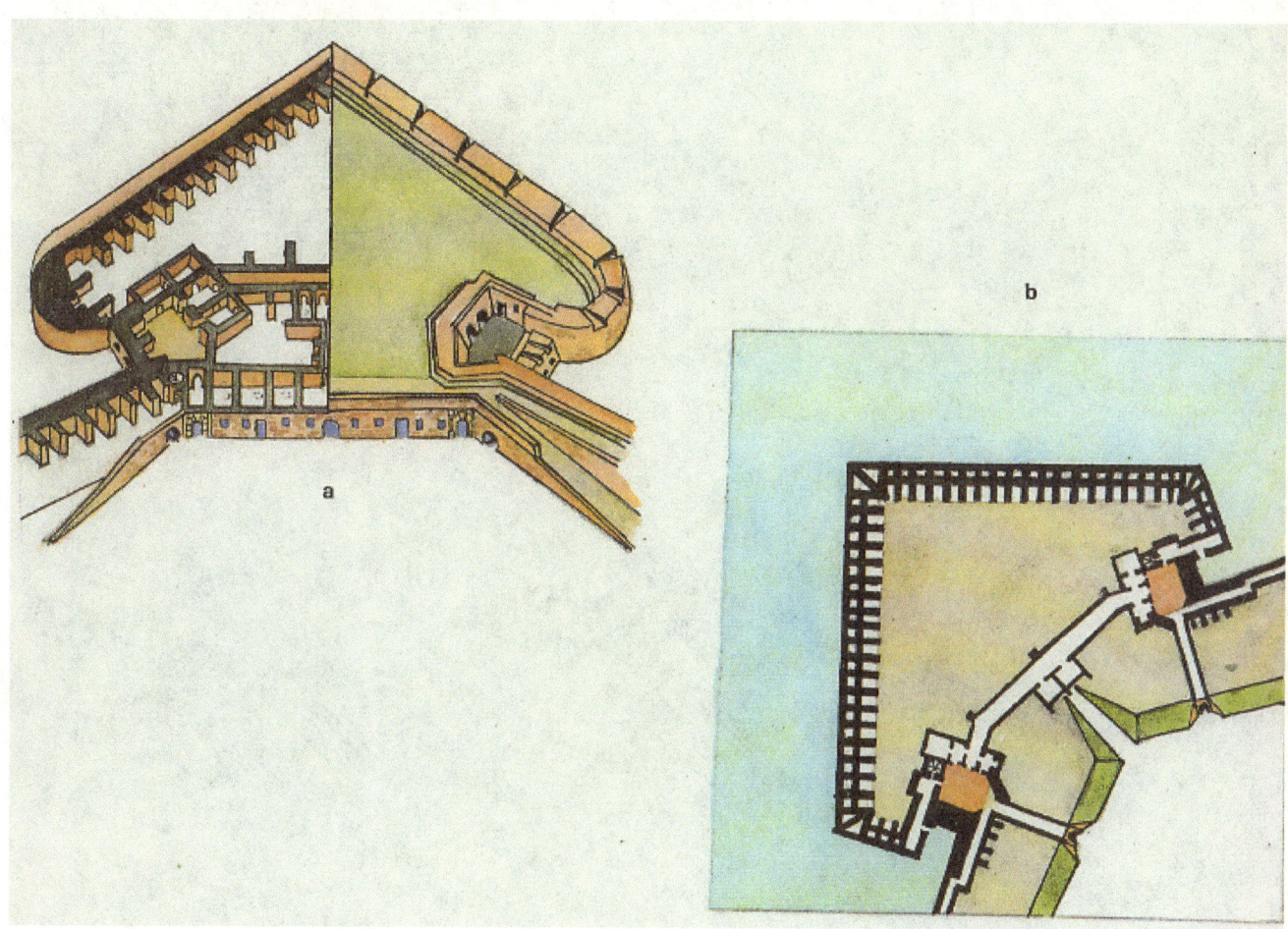

Bastions and casemates
a) Bastion with wall in the gorge. The wall has doors and windows from the rear and the space inside is divided into several rooms and cells b) Bastion rear is reinforced with an earthbank, a ramp is cutting through the bank, and two postern passages for transportation of supplies up to the barbettes located behind the bastion horns. Both barbettes are connected by a casemate

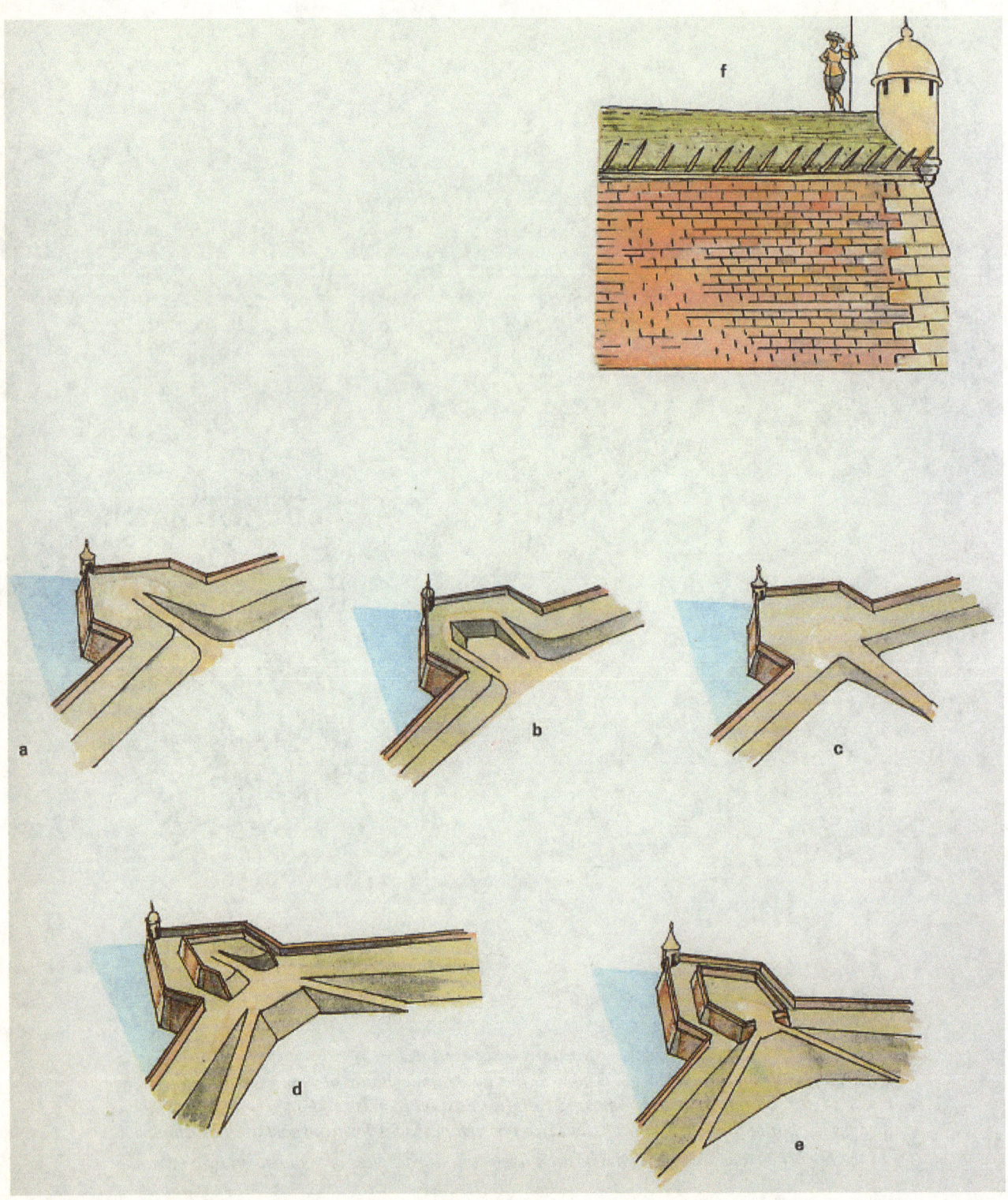

Bastion ramp types
a) Ramp cut into the bastion b) Hollow bastion with two ramps c) Postern ramp perpendicular to the gorge d) Pair of upslope postern ramps and a ramp cutting into the cavalier e) Pair of postern ramps leading directly into the cavalier f) Salient and tower

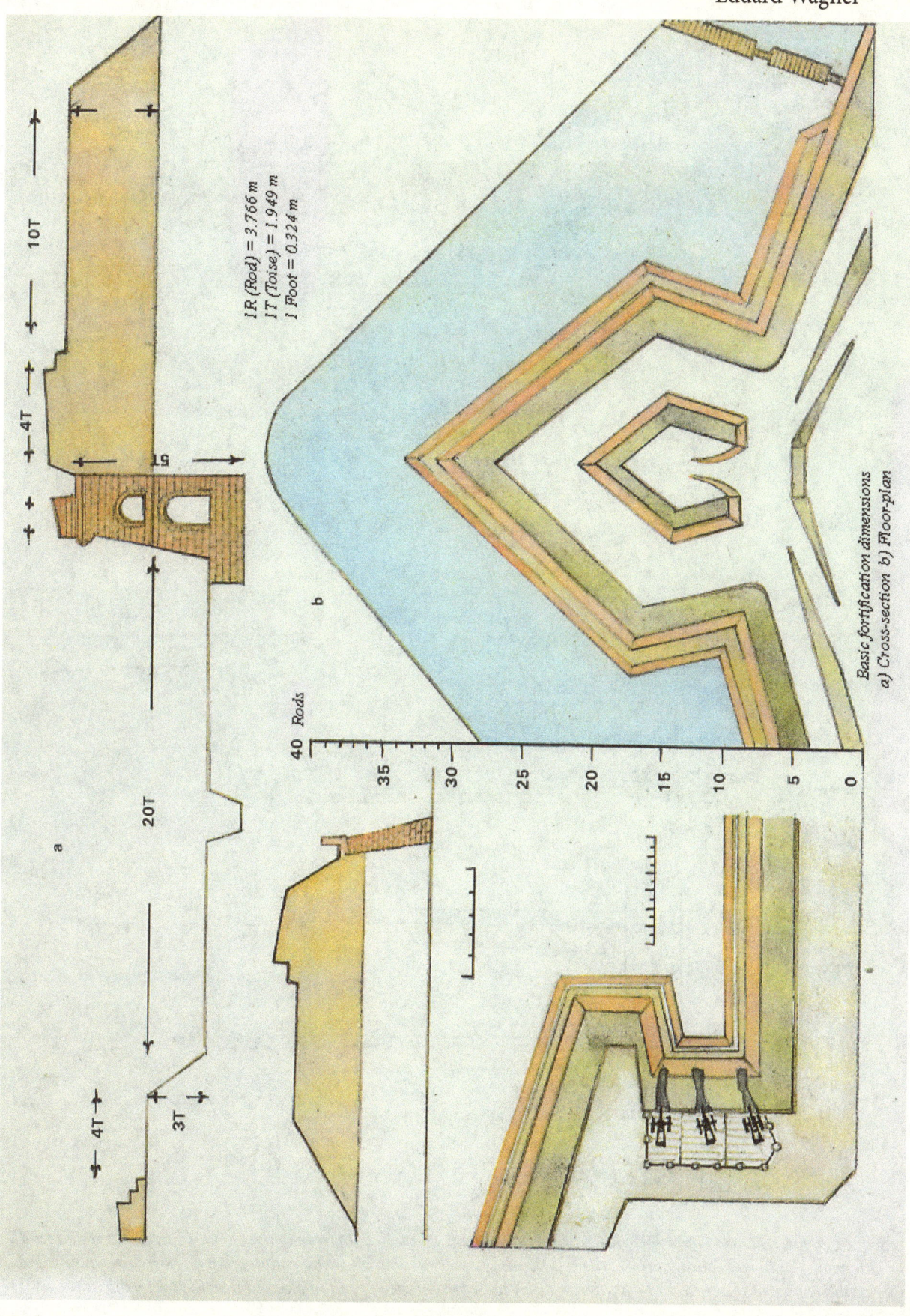

1 R (Rod) = 3.766 m
1 T (Toise) = 1.949 m
1 Foot = 0.324 m

Basic fortification dimensions
a) Cross-section b) Floor-plan

Rods

One of the many fortification systems

a) Section of fortification works with two bastions, each with a cavalier. In front of the curtain center is a ravelin with a battlement gun in each corner. From the rear leads an access ramp allowing a cannon to be positioned on the parapet at the center of the curtain b) Battlement gun used for defence of both field and permanent fortification works

Ravelin
a) Cross-section of the work   b) Detail of a low parapet at
the foot of the works   c) Ravelin, a small fortification work
built in the ditch either in front of the curtain or between two
bastions

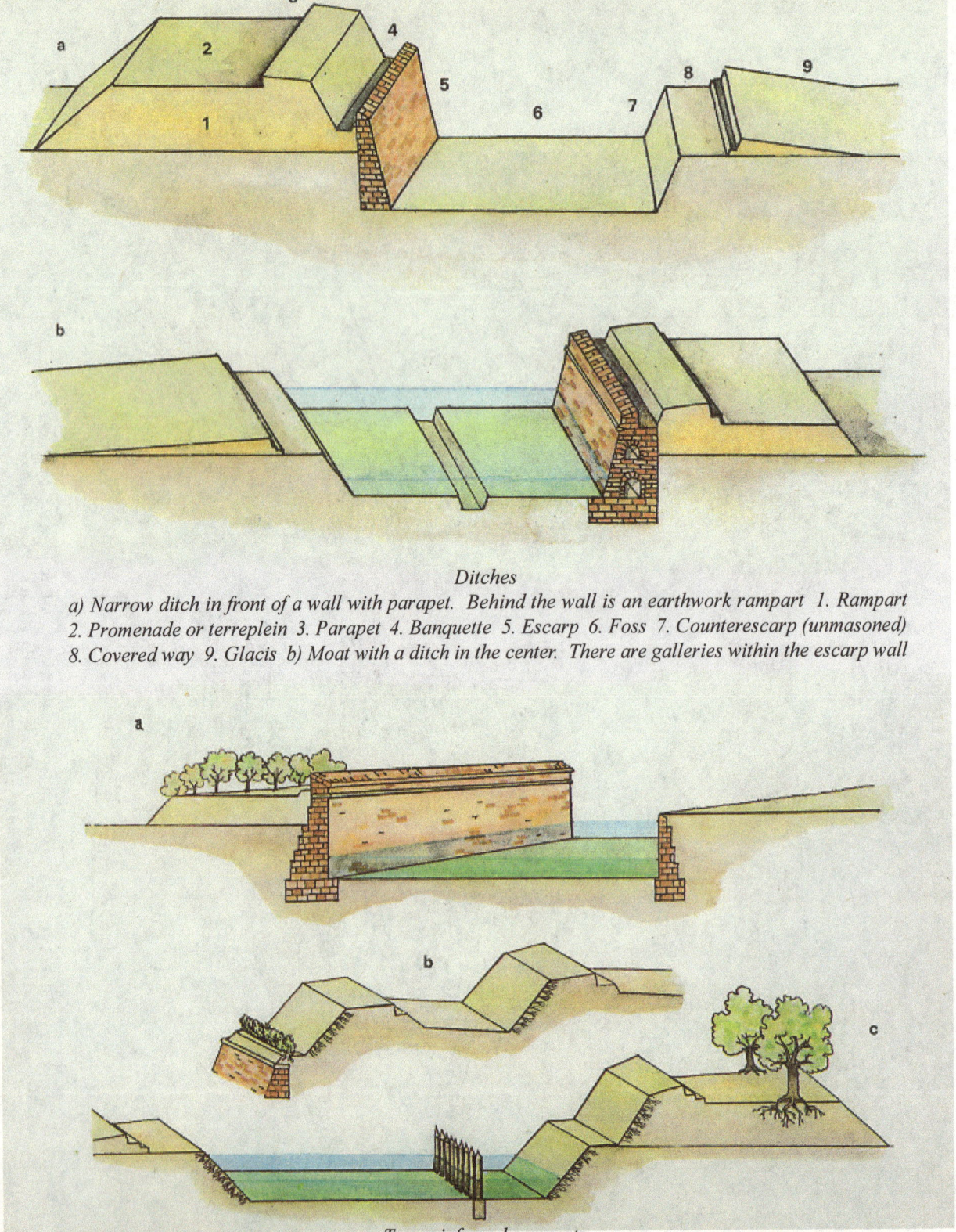

Ditches
a) *Narrow ditch in front of a wall with parapet. Behind the wall is an earthwork rampart 1. Rampart*
2. *Promenade or terreplein 3. Parapet 4. Banquette 5. Escarp 6. Foss 7. Counterescarp (unmasoned)*
8. *Covered way 9. Glacis b) Moat with a ditch in the center. There are galleries within the escarp wall*

Tree reinforced ramparts
a) *Ramparts with arboreal alley. The trees are planted some distance from the wall so that their roots*
would not damage the masonrywork b) Double ramparts, with the wall topped with a hedge c) Tree
reinforced ramparts. The earthworks are protected with a palisade embedded in the bottom of the moat

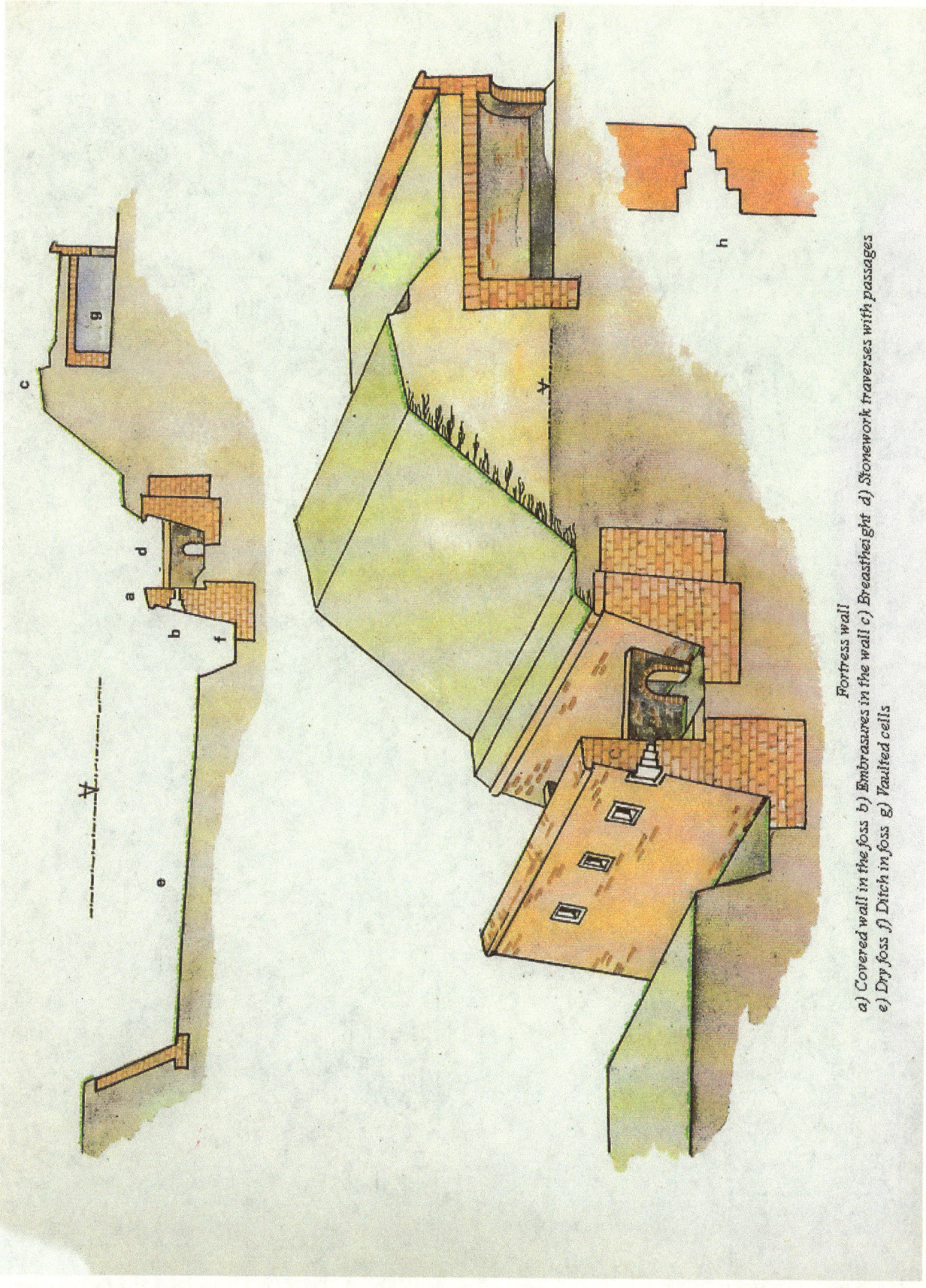

Fortress wall

a) Covered wall in the foss b) Embrasures in the wall c) Breastheight d) Stonework traverses with passages
e) Dry foss f) Ditch in foss g) Vaulted cells

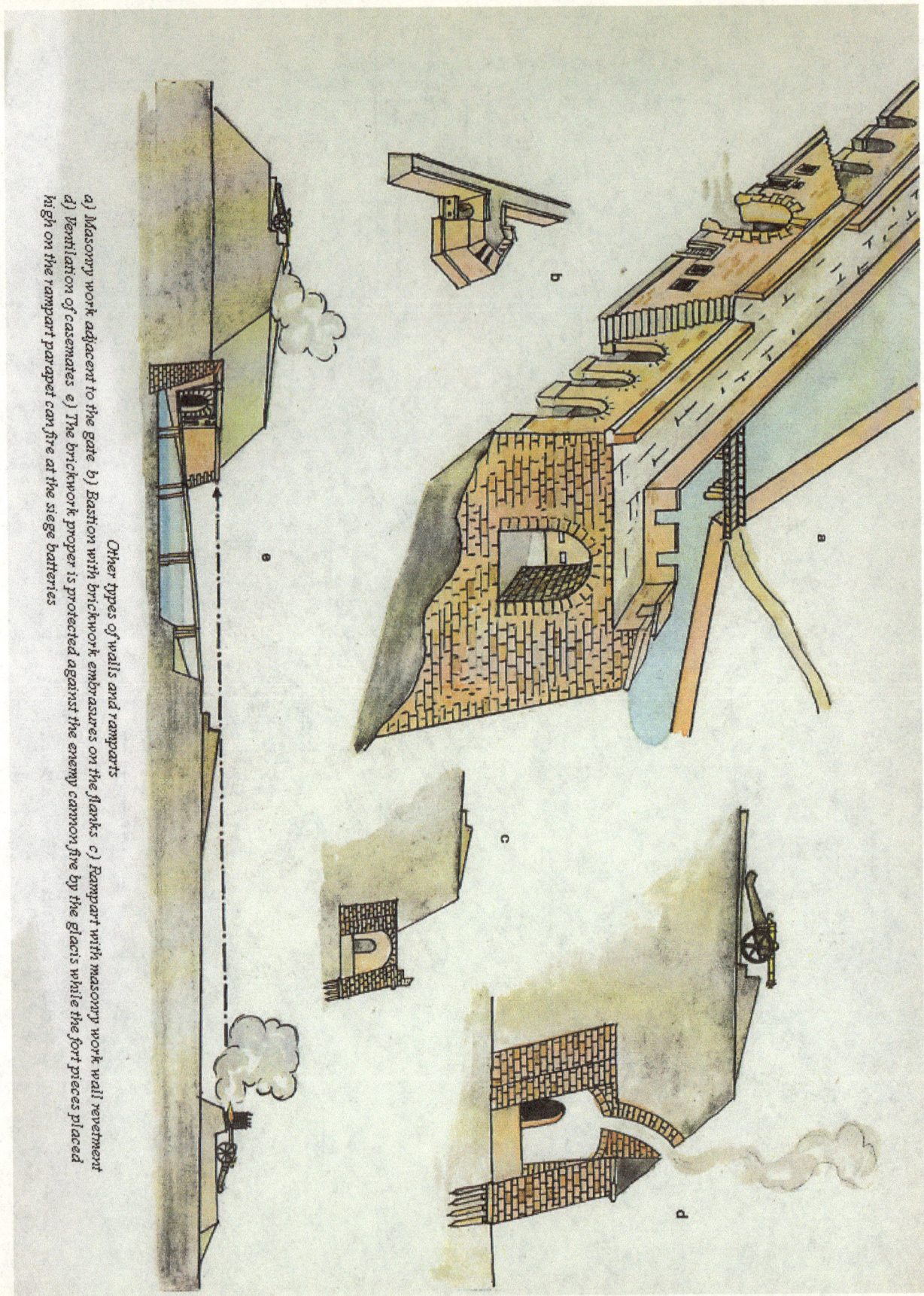

Other types of walls and ramparts

a) Masonry work adjacent to the gate b) Bastion with brickwork embrasures on the flanks c) Rampart with masonry work wall revetment d) Ventilation of casemates e) The brickwork proper is protected against the enemy cannon fire by the glacis while the fort pieces placed high on the rampart parapet can fire at the siege batteries

Masonry work revetments
a) Wall corner reinforced with hewn stone ashlars b) Wall with casemate and buttresses c) Detail of wall reinforced
with an earthfilled rampart

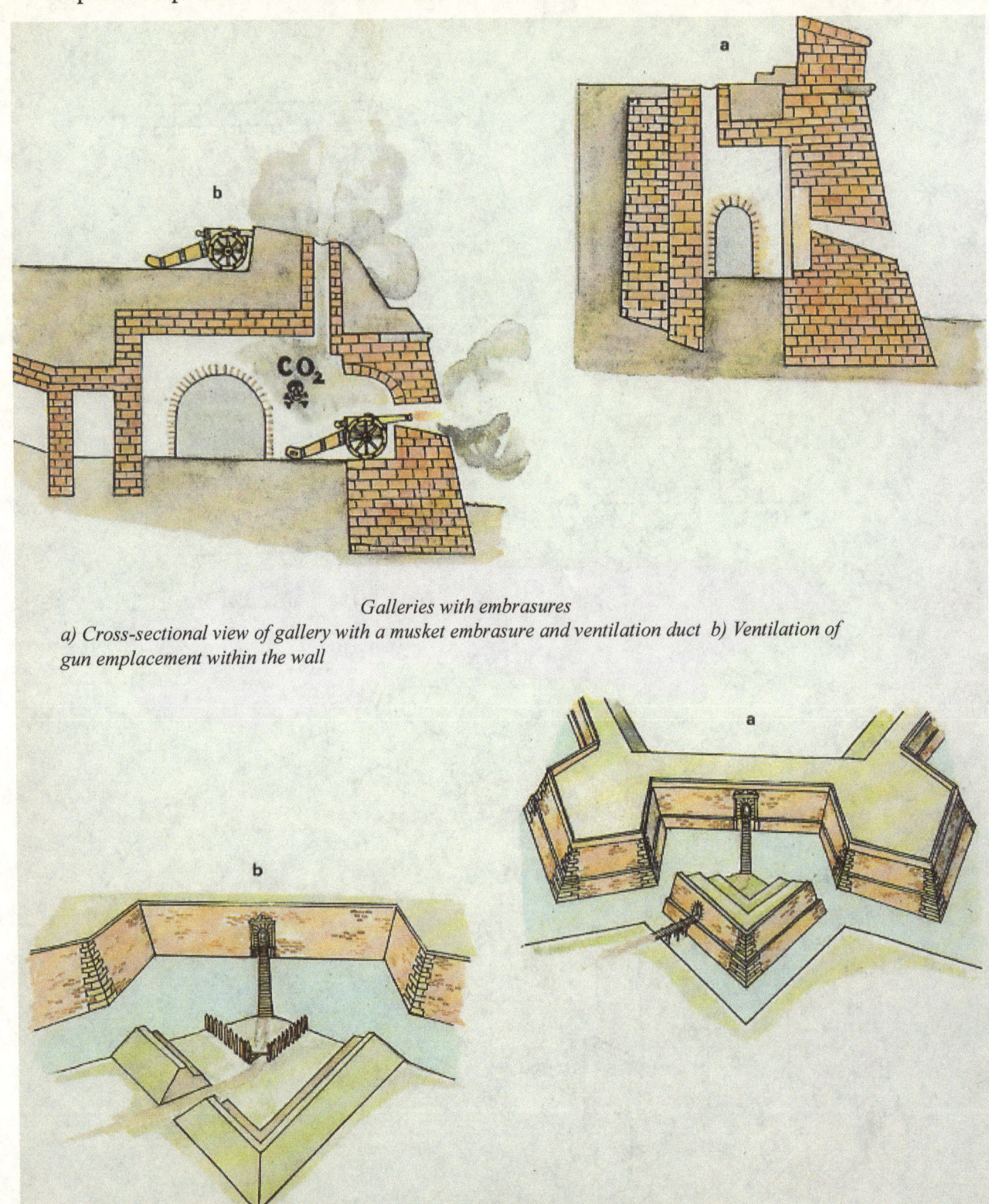

Galleries with embrasures
a) Cross-sectional view of gallery with a musket embrasure and ventilation duct b) Ventilation of gun emplacement within the wall

Connection of fortress with perimeter
a) In between two bastions; there is a bridge extending from the gate to the ravelin and another from the latter onto the glacis b) In this case the bridge leads straight from the gate across the ditch to the other bank, the bridgehead being protected with an earthfilled parapet and palisades covering the approach to the bridge.

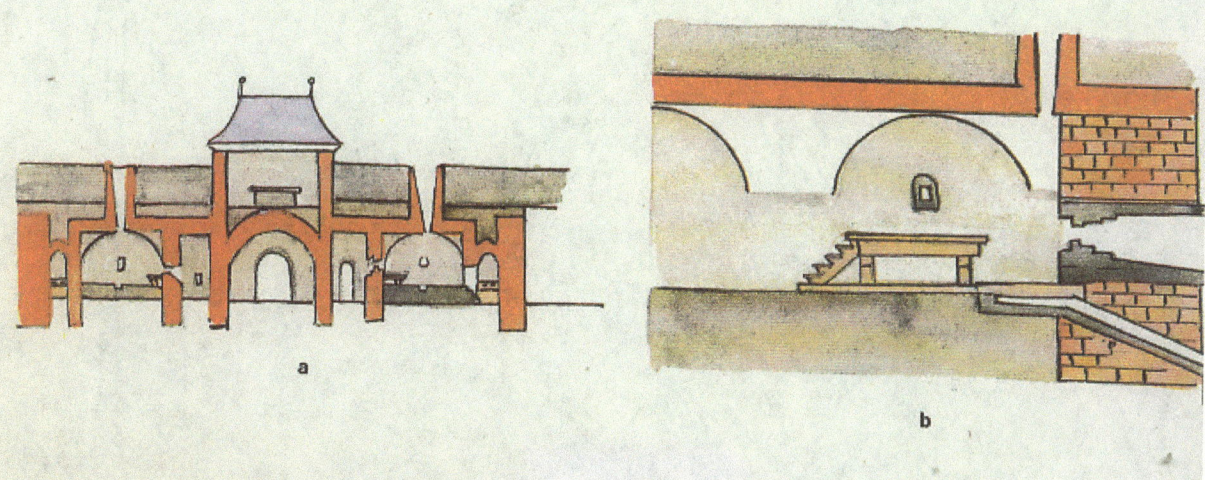

Baroque gate and its ground-plan

a) Longitudinal section of gate, inside face b) Vaulted cell within the outside part of the gate

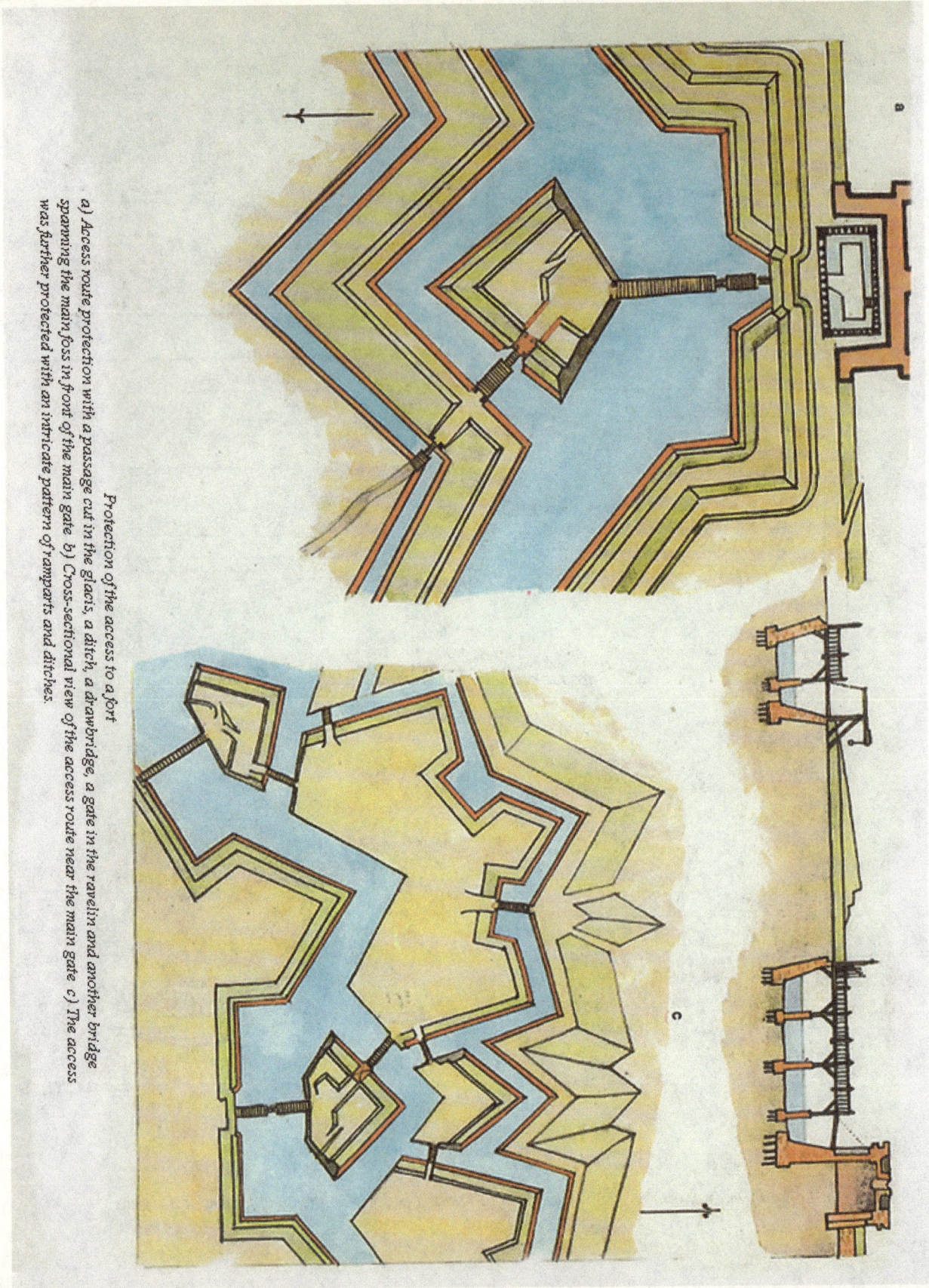

Protection of the access to a fort

a) Access route protection with a passage cut in the glacis, a ditch, a drawbridge, a gate in the ravelin and another bridge spanning the main foss in front of the main gate b) Cross-sectional view of the access route near the main gate c) The access was further protected with an intricate pattern of ramparts and ditches.

Another system of access route protection
The wooden bridge connecting the fortress with the perimeter incorporates a drawbridge, a full tilting barrier, a guardhouse located in the center of the bridge and two drawbridges.

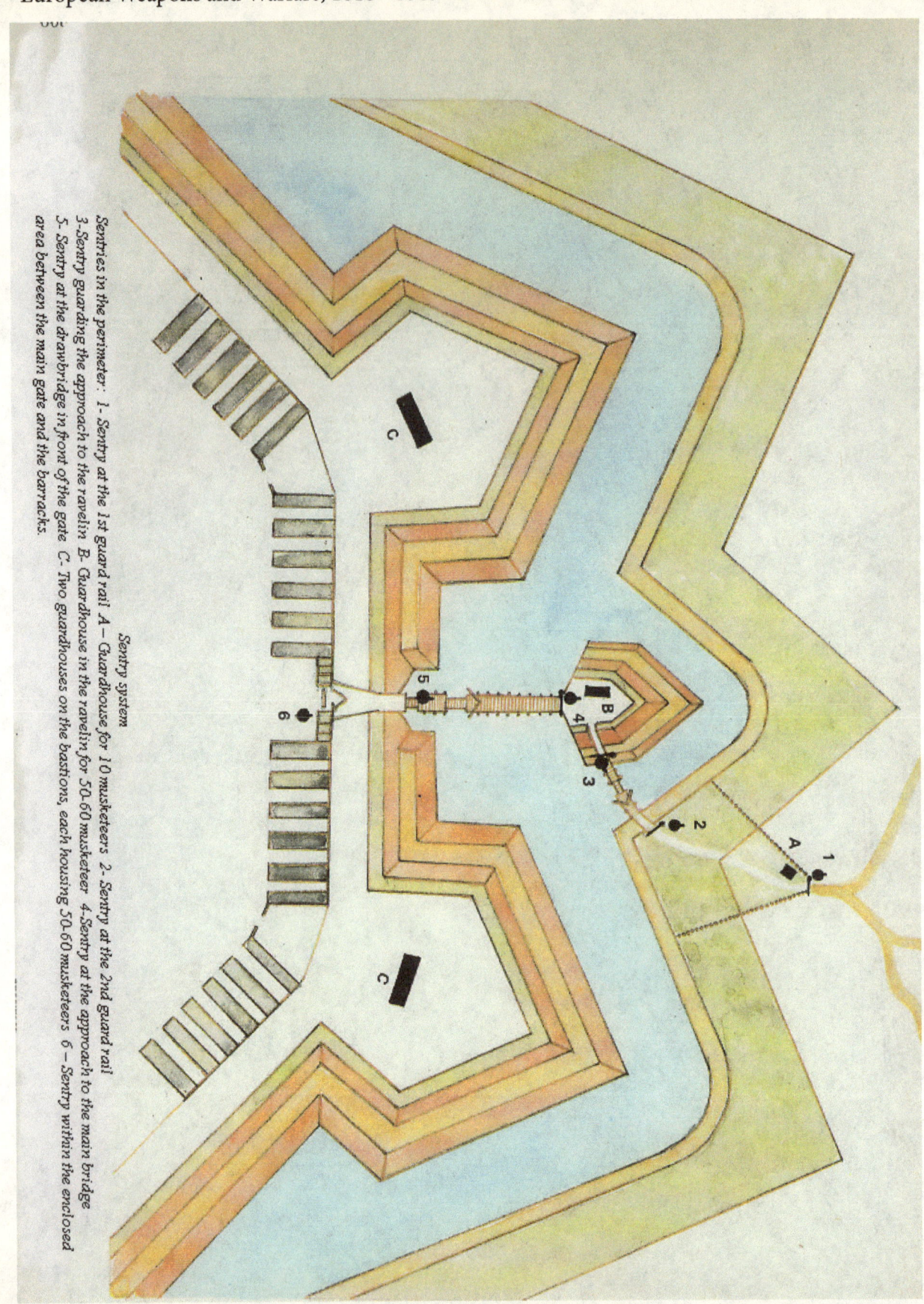

Sentry system

Sentries in the perimeter: 1 - Sentry at the 1st guard rail A – Guardhouse for 10 musketeers 2- Sentry at the 2nd guard rail 3- Sentry guarding the approach to the ravelin B. Guardhouse in the ravelin for 50-60 musketeer 4- Sentry at the approach to the main bridge 3- Sentry guarding the approach to the ravelin B. Guardhouse in the ravelin for 50-60 musketeer 4- Sentry at the approach to the main bridge 5- Sentry at the drawbridge in front of the gate C. Two guardhouses on the bastions, each housing 50-60 musketeers 6 – Sentry within the enclosed area between the main gate and the barracks.

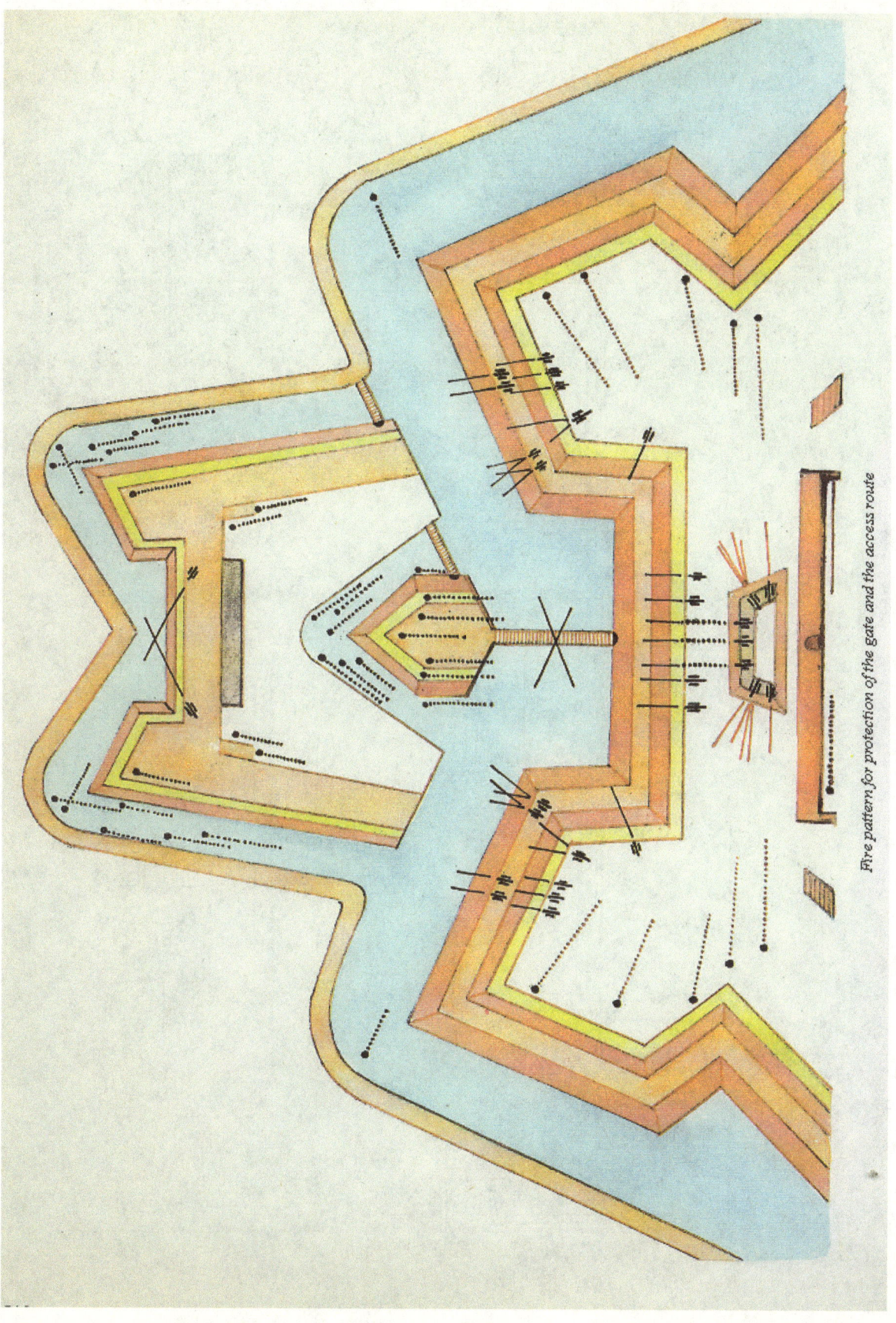

Fire pattern for protection of the gate and the access route

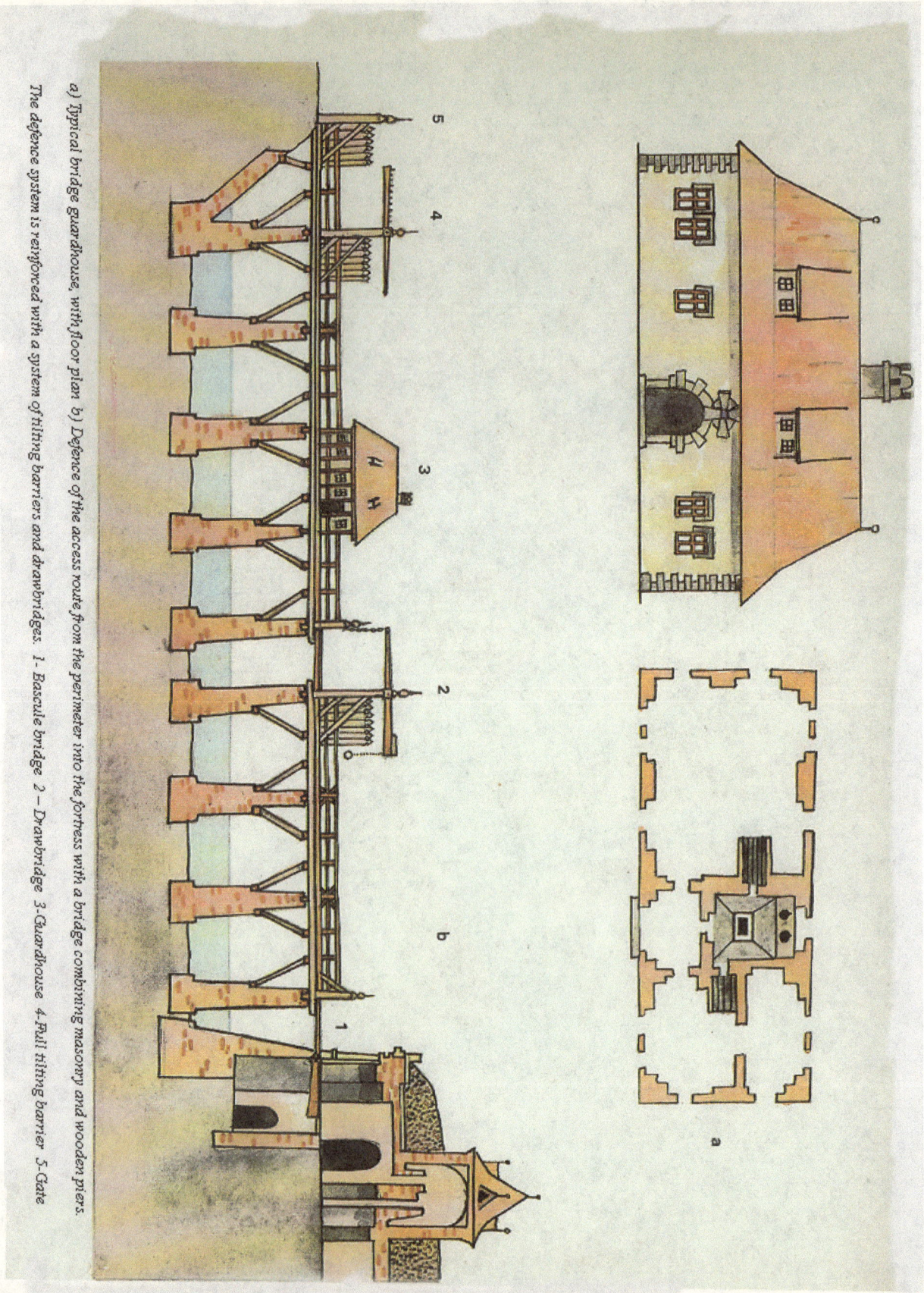

a) Typical bridge guardhouse, with floor plan b) Defence of the access route, from the perimeter into the fortress with a bridge combining masonry and wooden piers.
The defence system is reinforced with a system of tilting barriers and drawbridges. 1 - Bascule bridge 2 – Drawbridge 3-Guardhouse 4-Full tilting barrier 5-Gate

Using older keeps in the 17th century
a) Old keep connected with the ravelin by a wooden bridge b) Gothic keep with the original drawbridge
incorporated into the 17th-century defence system

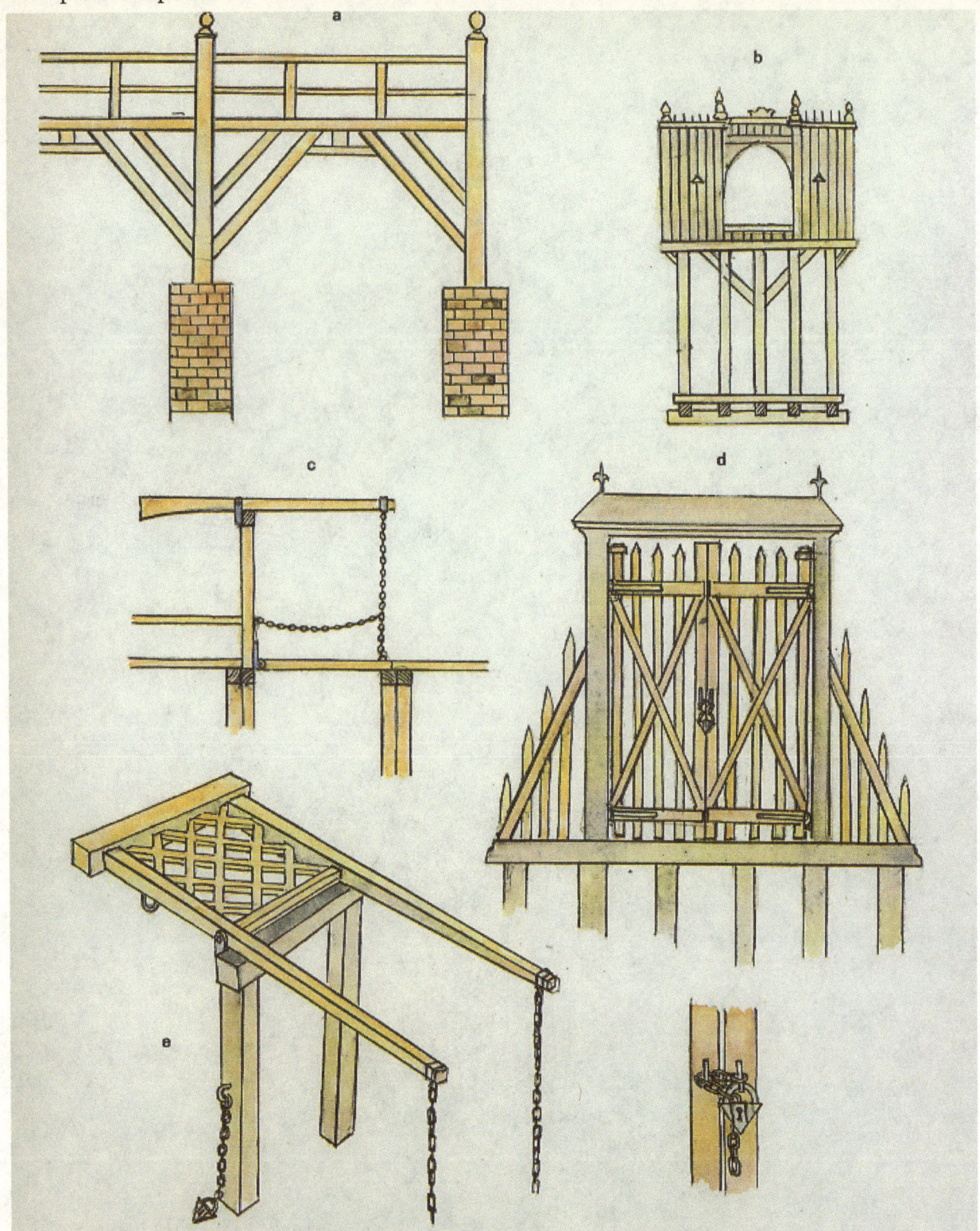

Details of bridges
a) Brickwork piers combined with wooden piles b) Bridge gate with palisade c) Wooden bridge with a draw
section d) Two-leaf lattice gate with lattice wings and detail of padlock fastening (below) e) Lattice barrier; on
the left is an iron ring which would be linked with the ring on the gate post with a chain and a padlock

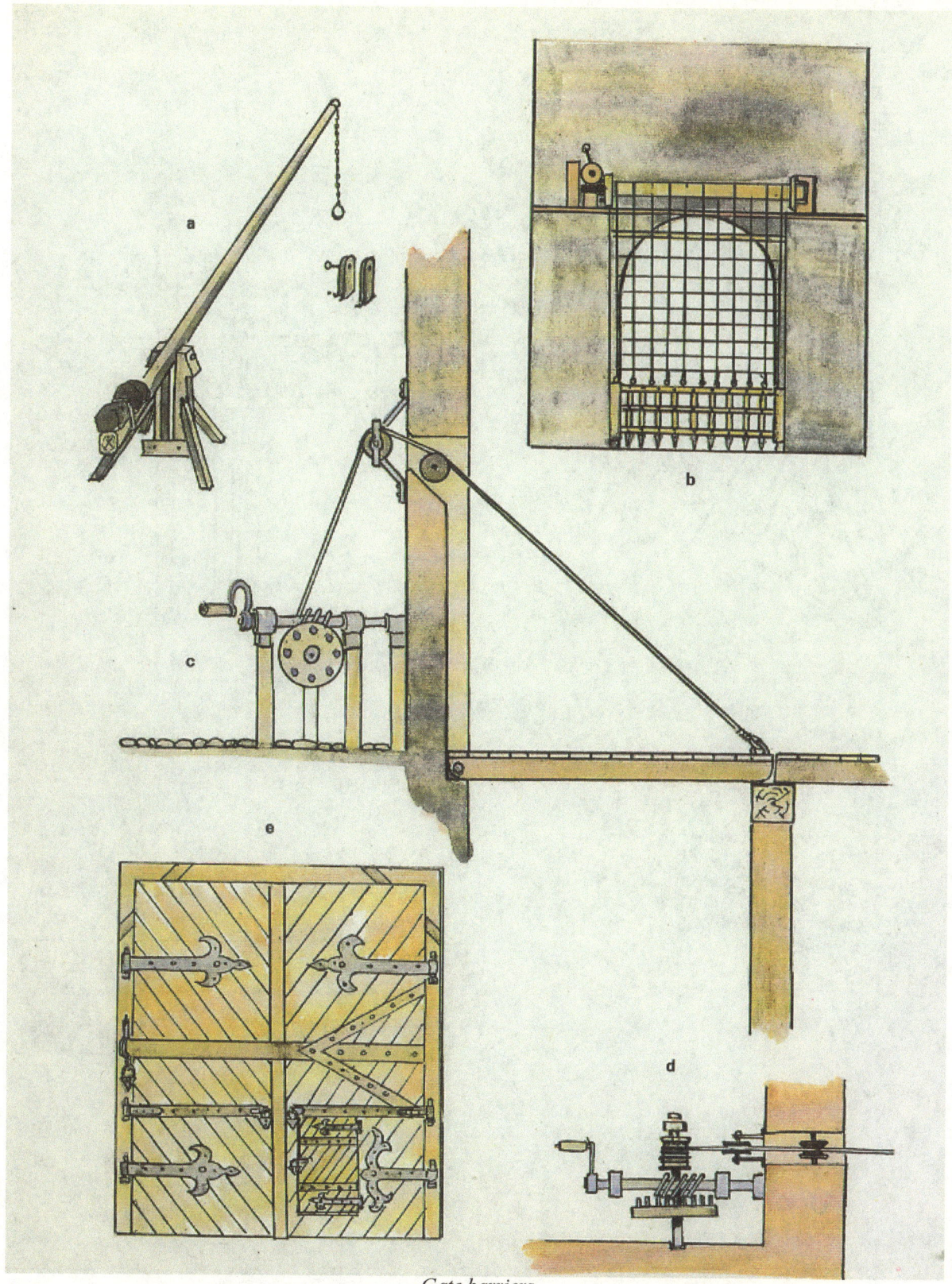

Gate barriers
a) Gate with a guard rail b) Portcullis c) Cross-section of a drawbridge raised
by a wormgear d) Bird's eye view of the hoisting gear e) Ironclad fort gate

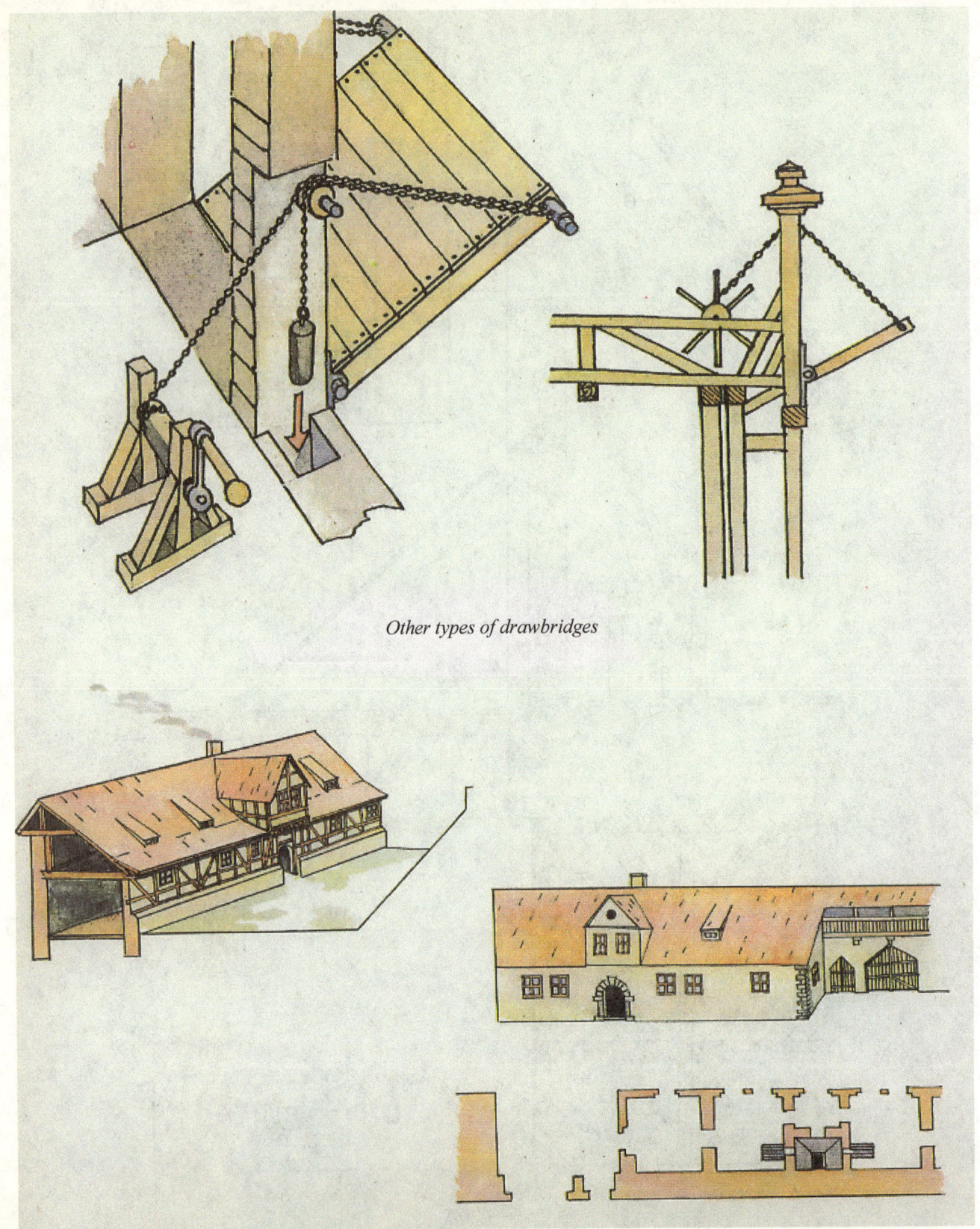

Other types of drawbridges

Fort caserne types

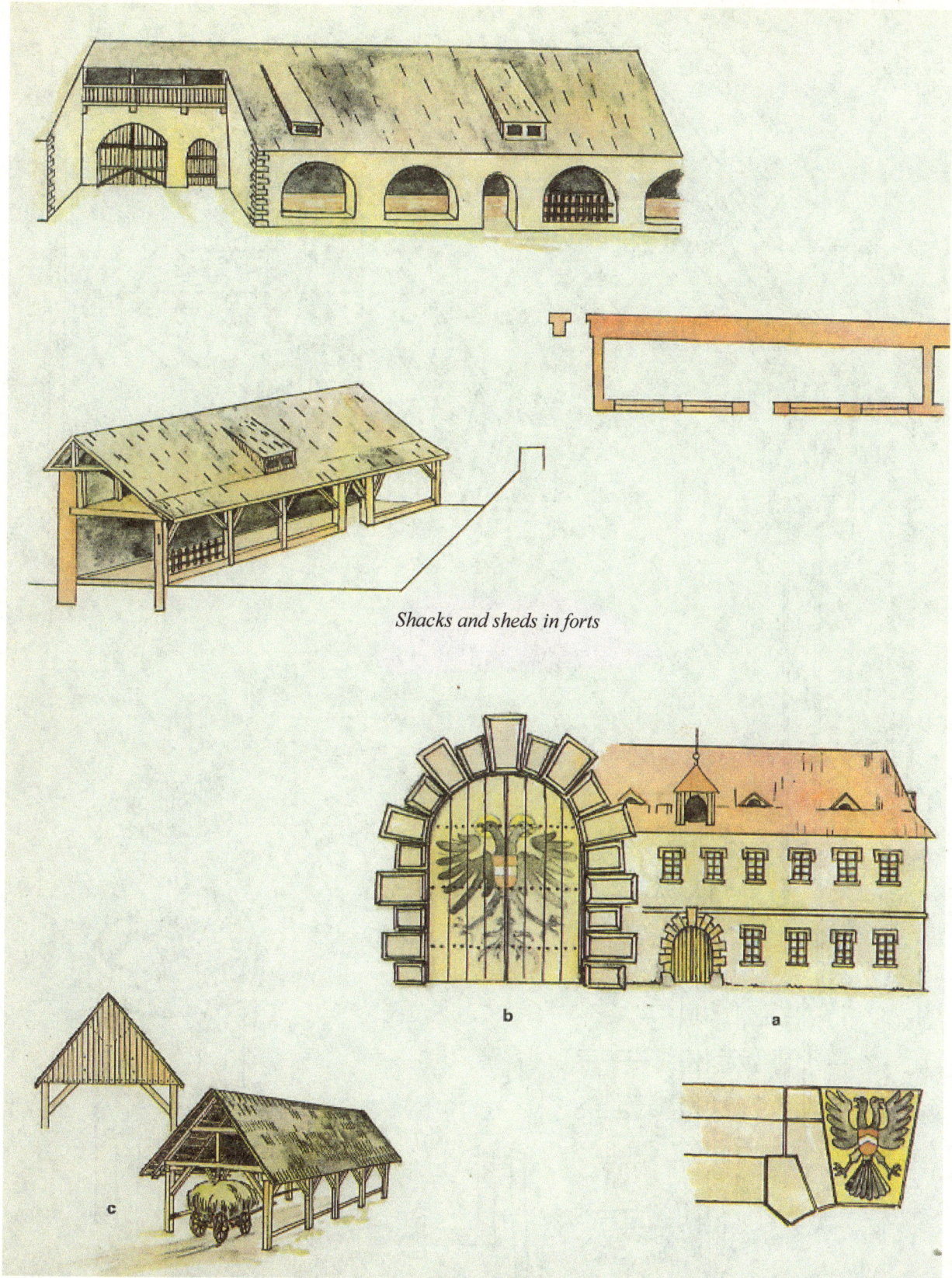

Shacks and sheds in forts

Fort caserne
a) Front view of caserne b) Caserne gate, 17th and 18th centuries c) Shed

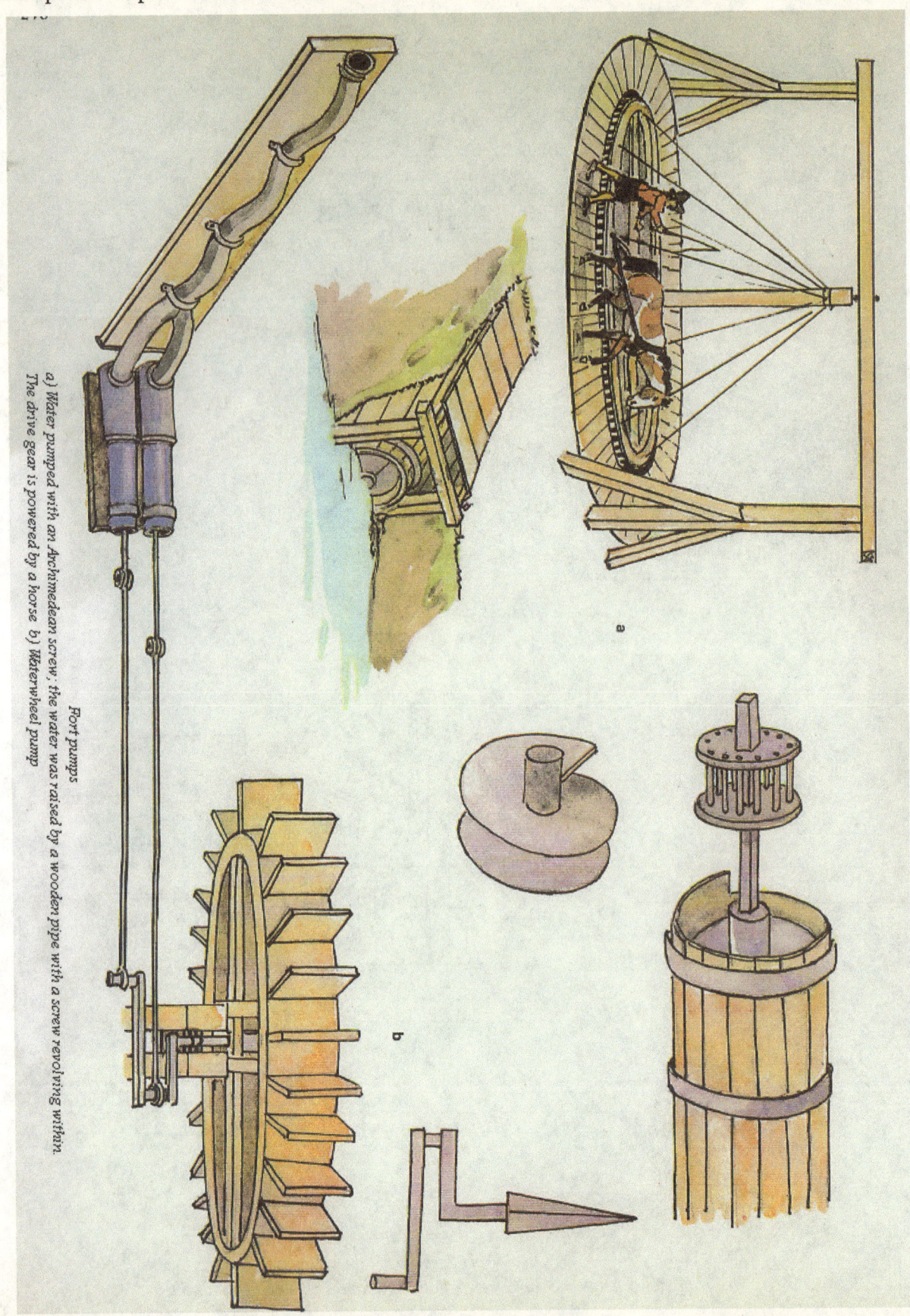

Fort pumps
a) Water pumped with an Archimedean screw; the water was raised by a wooden pipe with a screw revolving within. The drive gear is powered by a horse b) Waterwheel pump

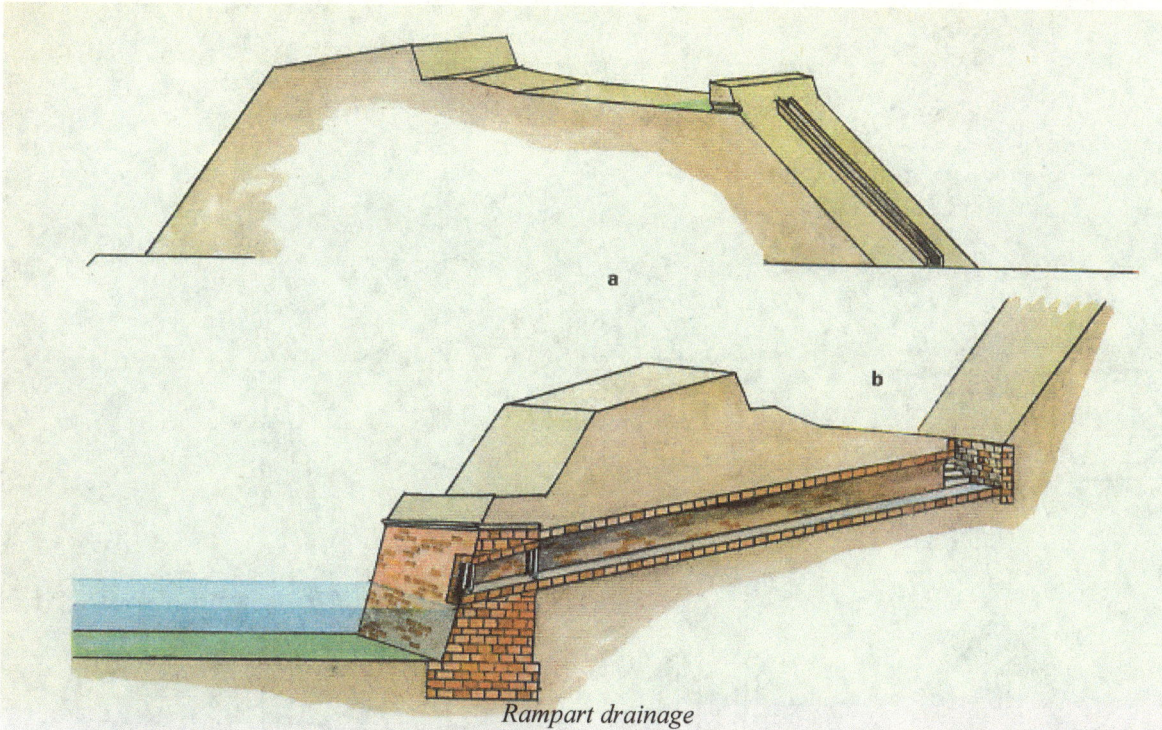

Rampart drainage
a) The rear face of the rampart is drained with a pipe and gutter b) Drainage between two ramparts.
Through the front rampart a masonry tunnel was cut through the counterscarp wall, with the outlet into the
ditch. The outlet is equipped with a grille

Mills
a) Permanent masonry water mill on a riverbank b) Floating water mill

Windmills and their mechanisms

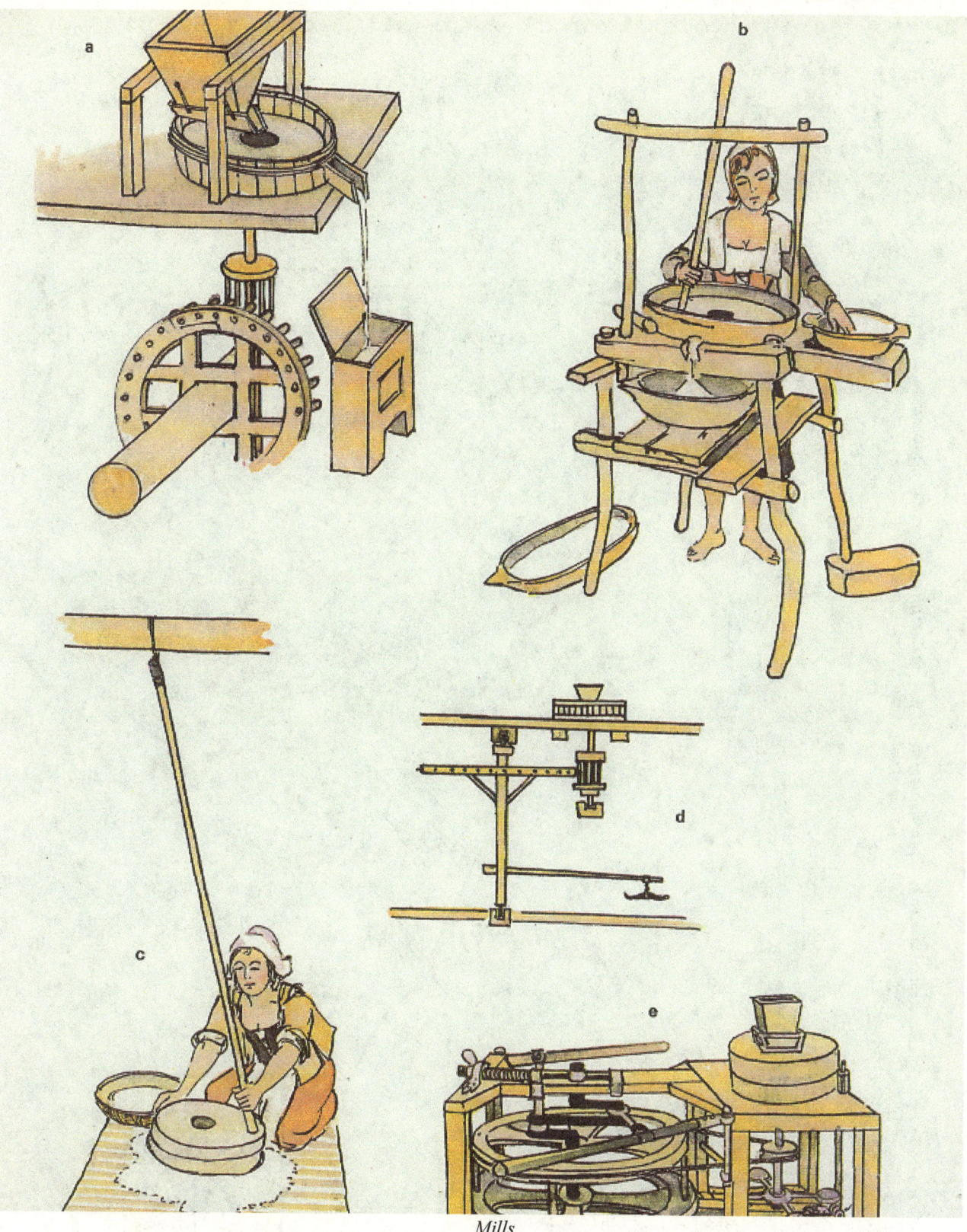

Mills
a)Milling mechanism driven by a waterwheel b) Hand mill mechanism c) Hand mill mechanism dating from as early as the 14th century d) Mill driven by a horse gear e) Hand mill (Designs have been preserved that suggested that the mill be placed on a wagon and powered from the rear axel)

Siege of Imperial troops against the Turkish Army in Nové Zámky, Slovakia, 1683. A—cannon emplacements B—mortar emplacements

Siege entrenchments

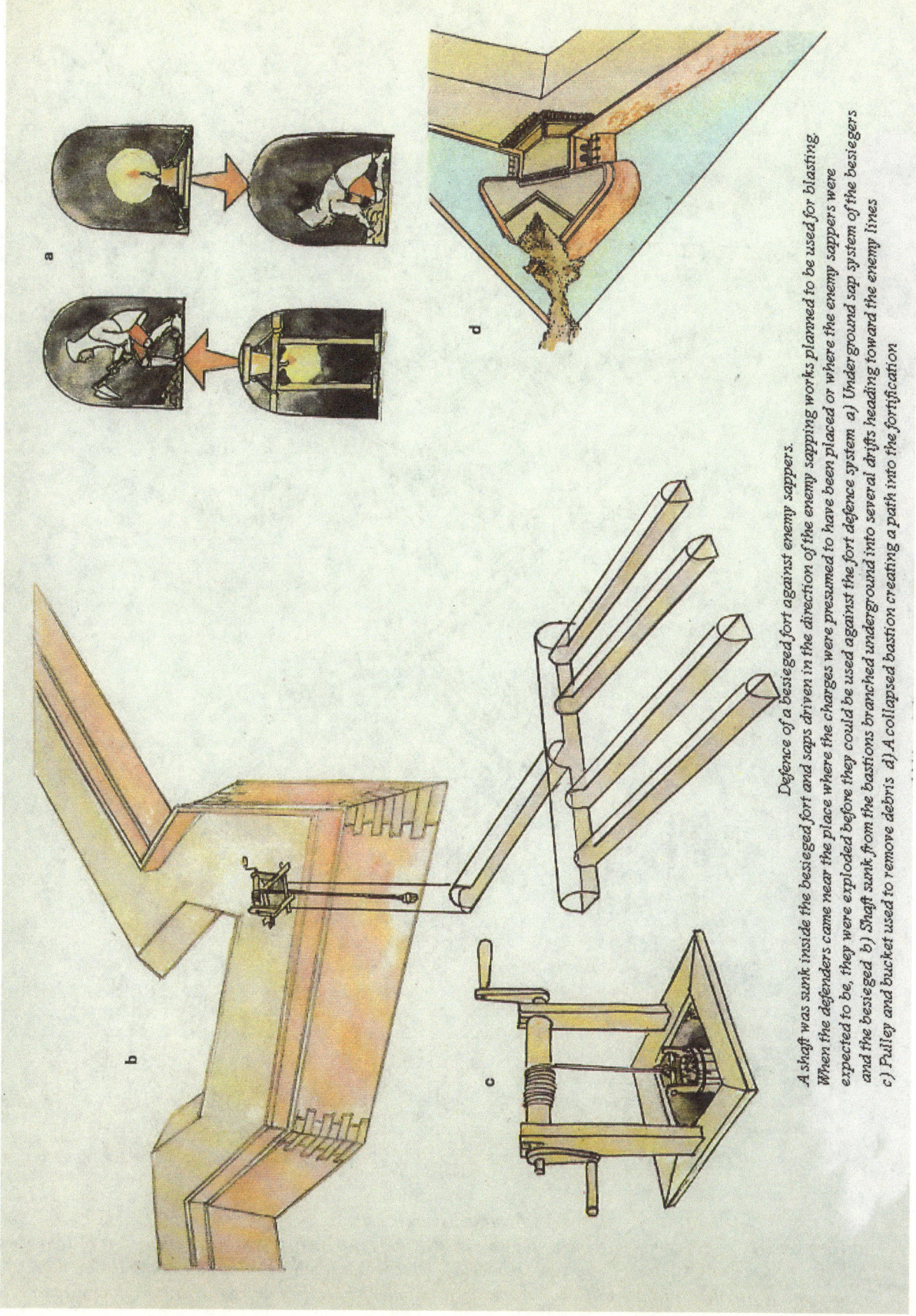

Defence of a besieged fort against enemy sappers.
A shaft was sunk inside the besieged fort and saps driven in the direction of the enemy sapping works planned to be used for blasting.
When the defenders came near the place where the charges were presumed to have been placed or where the enemy sappers were
expected to be, they were exploded before they could be used against the fort defence system a) Underground sap system of the besiegers
and the besieged b) Shaft sunk from the bastions branched underground into several drifts heading toward the enemy lines
c) Pulley and bucket used to remove debris d) A collapsed bastion creating a path into the fortification

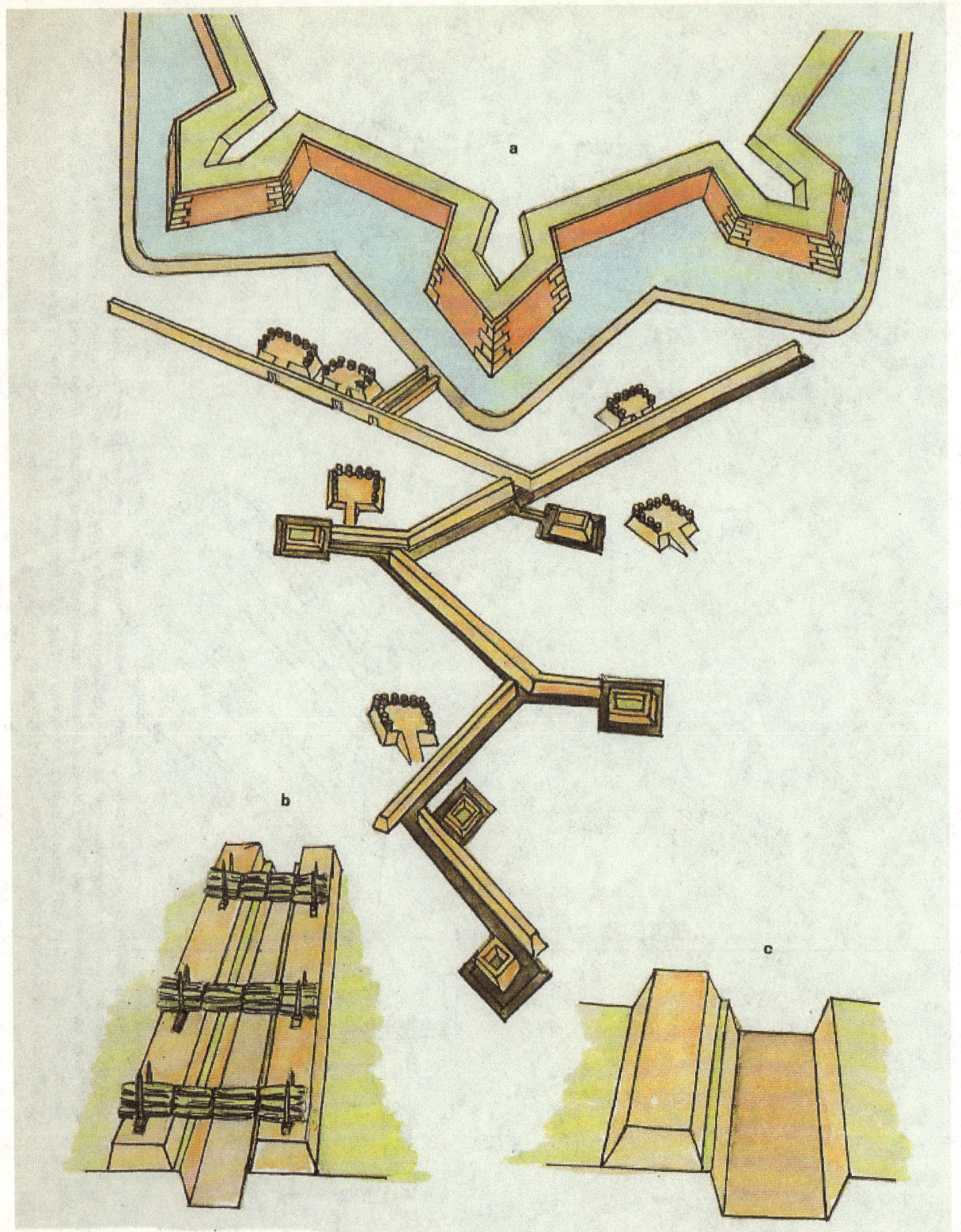

Approach entrenchments
a) The zig-zag course of approach trenches allowed assault troops to reach right up to the enemy fort b) Trench with parapets covered with fascines; the picture shows the fascines made ready for covering of the individual stretches of the approach trench c) Trench with one parapet only, the latter facing the side from where an attack was expected

FIELD FORTIFICATIONS

There were two basic kinds of field fortifications: defensive and offensive. Defensive fortifications were built by every army whenever it interrupted its march. Their quality depended on the length of stay. Offensive field fortifications were systems of trenches and shelters built during a siege of an enemy stronghold.

When the marching column stopped, a suitable place for the camp was chosen which would defend well and also provide water for the cavalry mounts and the train teams. For an overnight stay a simple wagon-fort wall and tents and shelters would be whipped up. If a longer stay was planned, work on trenches and ditches would start first thing in the morning. The excavated earth was piled to form a protective parapet. For an extended stay the parapet and the ditches were reinforced and the parapet and the ditches were reinforced and the parapet was equipped with small bastions. The ground-plan of such field earthworks often followed the lay-out of permanent forts. It was quite common to incorporate into the encampment and its fortification any structures that existed in the place before the arrival of the troops. Châteaux, castles and citadels were used in this way because they offered lodging for the troops and their commanders and because of their strength. Whenever such structures had masonry fortification walls, these were incorporated into the field fortification system.

Quite often an army could stay encamped in such fortifications for a long time, using them as an operational base for sorties into the surrounding country-side.

When a siege of an enemy-held fort or town was laid, the besieging army tried to get as close to the fort ditch as possible and build permanent artillery emplacements there to enable the guns to fire at close range at the ramparts to make a breach for the assault troops to penetrate the besieged fort.

To achieve this, a system of inter-connecting trenches, called saps, were dug in front of the besieged fort or city. These allowed movement of troops and equipment to the front lines immediately under the enemy's ramparts. To give enemy fire as few targets as possible the saps followed a zigzag course. Where the sap changed course, gabionage was erected, and the entire sap or at least some sections of it were covered with faggots or fascines.

To prevent the besieged seeing what was going on in the entrenchments, fences and screens were run along the works. Earth-filled gabions were thrown up to protect fun emplacements against enemy fire. Their manufacture, as well as building all field fortification works proper, was in the charge of the work-master or chief sapper. The gabions were five to seven feet round and six to ten feet high, with frame posts from two to four-and-a-half inches thick. The frame was interwoven with wicker, with the posts extending at least one foot at the bottom to allow the gabion to be firmly embedded in the ground. The baskets were then filled with earth and the earth packed with a hand rammer.

The besieged had usually ample means for repairing their defensive works damaged by enemy artillery fire. If the attackers saw there was no chance of getting inside through a breach in the works, they would hire miners to dig galleries to undermine the ramparts. Underground saps leading from the attackers' positions to under the besieged ramparts had a least one corner immediately before the target area to damp the blast wave from the explosion to prevent it blowing back through the galleries. At the gallery face beneath the walls of the besieged structure, a chamber was cut in which kegs were packed, as tightly as possible, to maximize the effect of the blast.

If the defenders realized that the attackers planned to mine their ramparts they would drive their own saps from inside the walls into the enemy positions and try to gas or blow up the enemy miners. (The gases used were antimony gases.)

Life in military encampments was subject to the strictest discipline. Any mutiny or riot by the troops met with severe penalty. Leaving camp without permission, stabbings or shootings in brawls etc, were often punishable by death. It was expressly forbidden to talk to enemy troops unless approved first by the supreme commander. Whenever both cavalry and infantry were established in one camp, infantry were bound to clear space for the horses. No shooting or campfire was allowed without permission. Drunkenness and all felonies committed under influence of liquor were severely punished. If a spy was suspected in the encampment, an alarm was sounded upon which everybody was supposed to hasten to his tent so that the stranger's presence could be easily determined. Special care was paid to regular observation of picket and sentry duty.

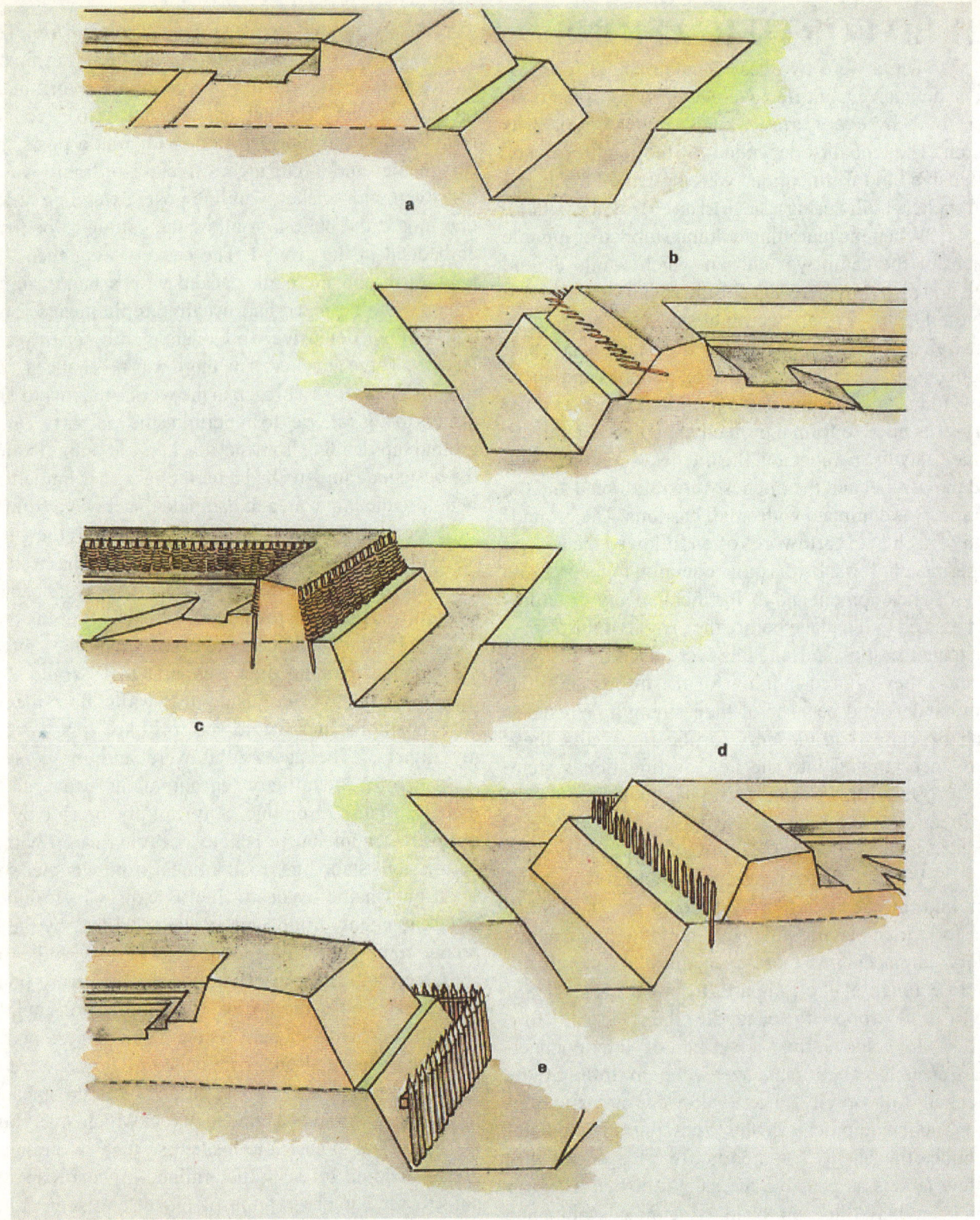

Parapets
a) Simple earthwork parapet b) parapet with fraise c) The loose packed earth of the parapet was usually reinforced with gabion revetments d) The approaches to the parapet on the side facing the enemy were also protected with a fraise and sometimes with palisade embedded in the firm ground in front of the parapet e) Another method of stake defence: the stakes are driven into the moat bed and joined with the horizontal beams

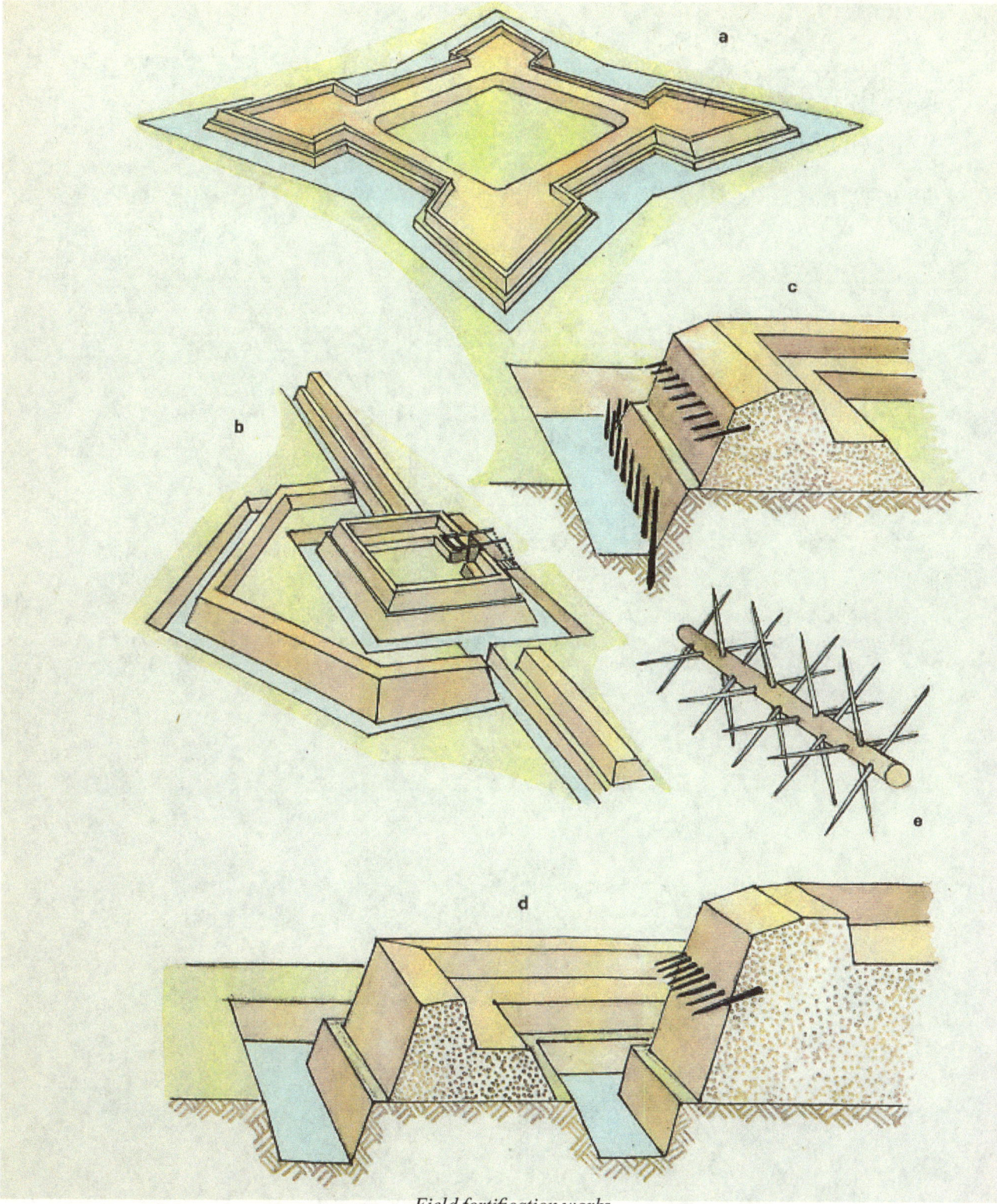

Field fortification works

a) Redoubt – an enclosed fort with four bastions b) The straight-line field fortification system also incorporated these forts with a moat and drawbridge c) Parapets piled up from the excavated earth, protected with stakes. One line of stakes, the fraise, was embedded directly in the parapet face, the other formed a palisade driven into the moat bed d) Double parapet with moats and a fraise in the main parapet e) Entanglement with spike iron bars

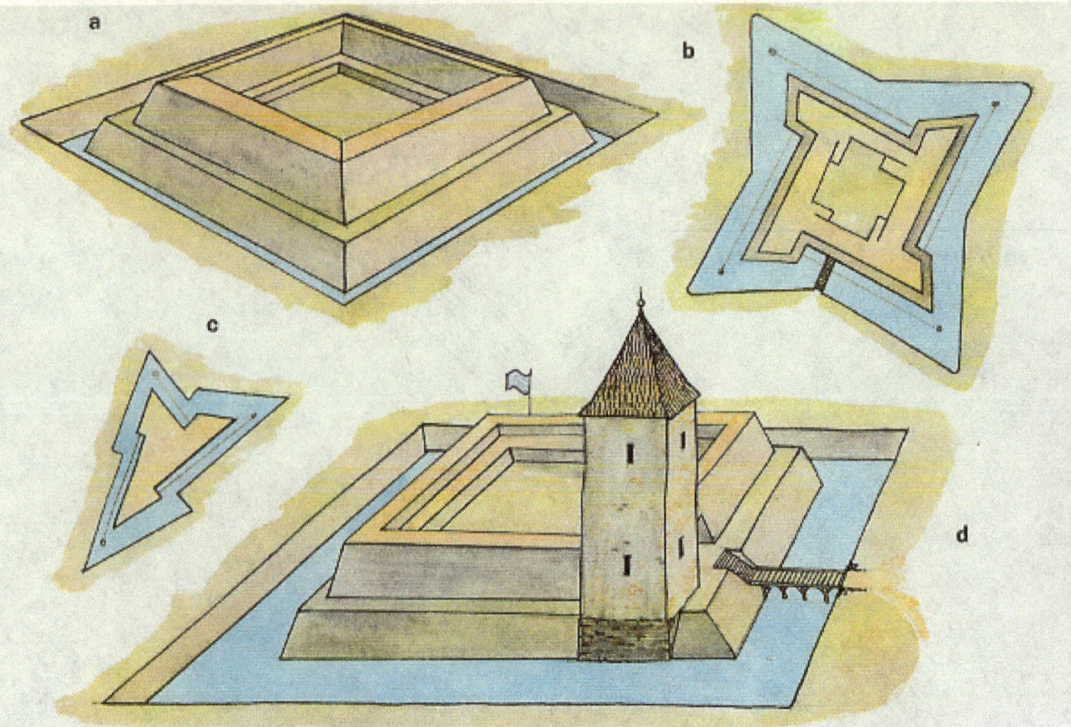

Other field fortification works
a) Square lay-out work, with a ditch b) Irregular star-trace redoubt c) Triangle-trace redoubt
d) Square-trace redoubt incorporating an existing medieval keep. The keep serves as an
observation point as well as a defence work protecting the near-by bridge spanning the moat

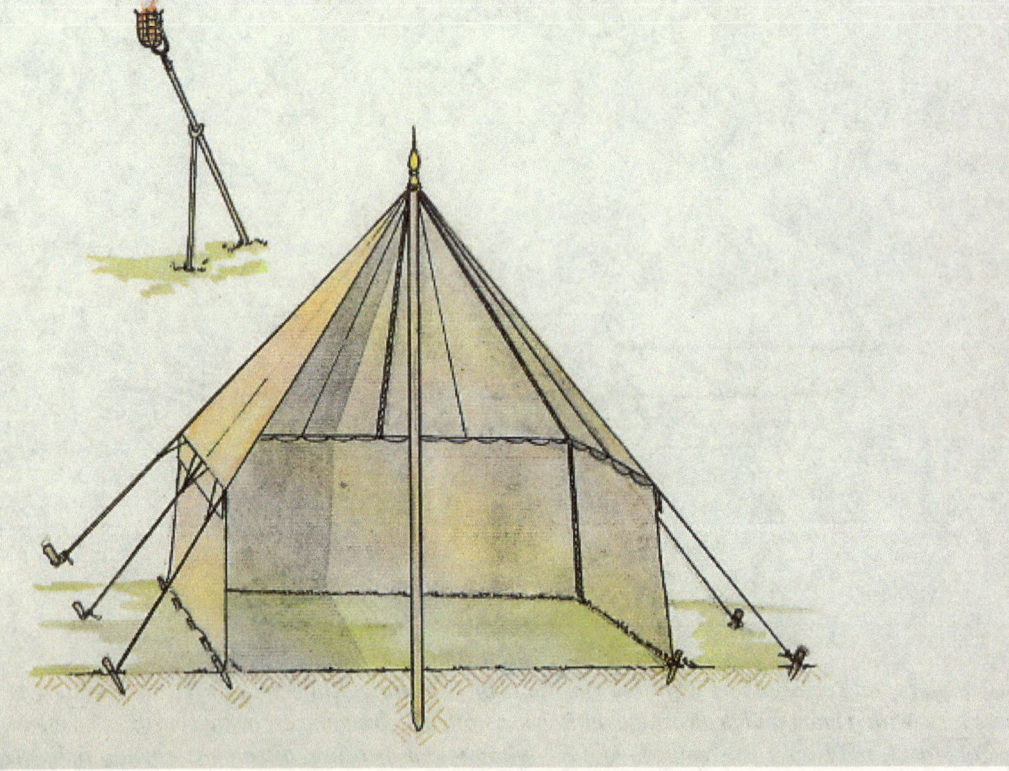

Common tent design, mid-17th century

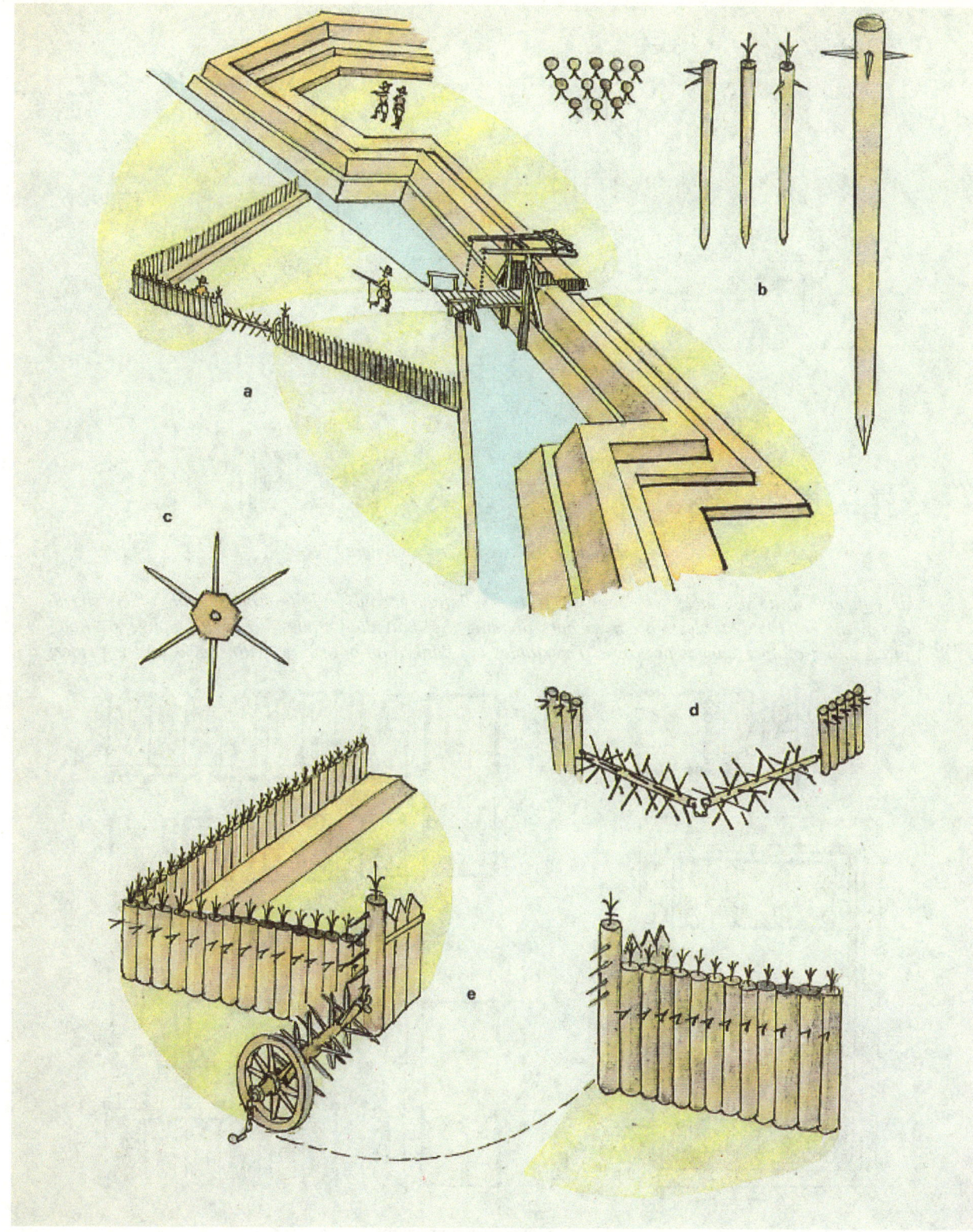

Detail of field fortification works
a) Parapet with a drawbridge across the ditch. The bridgehead is protected by a triangular palisade with
a wheeled cheval de frise b) Barbed spikes used for the construction of entanglements c) Cheval de frise
used for barring palisade entrances d) Chain linked chevaux de frise barring the entrance of a palisade
e) Wheeled cheval de frise used as a palisade entrance barrier

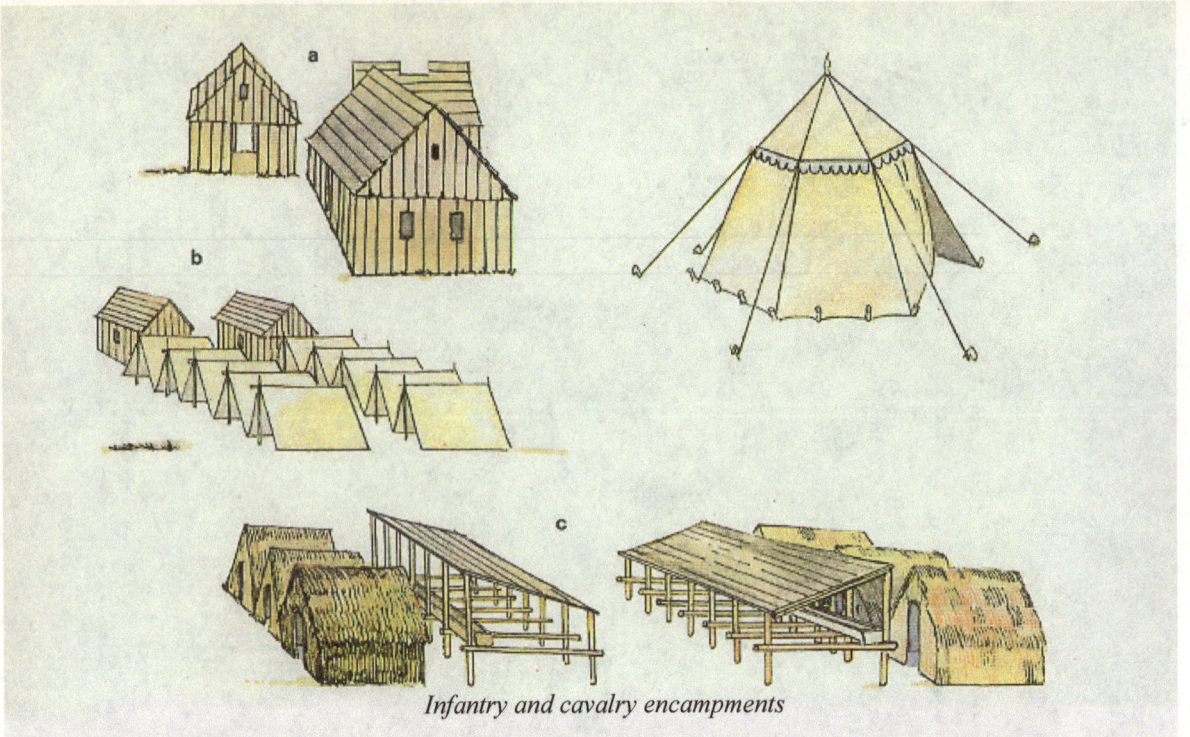

Infantry and cavalry encampments

a) Officers' wooden shacks b) Row of tents for infantry rank-and-file troops, with office shacks at the end c) Field stables with cross bars dividing the individual stalls, fitted with mangers. Roofing is either of thick canvas or straw. The stables are flanked on both sides with shacks housing riders

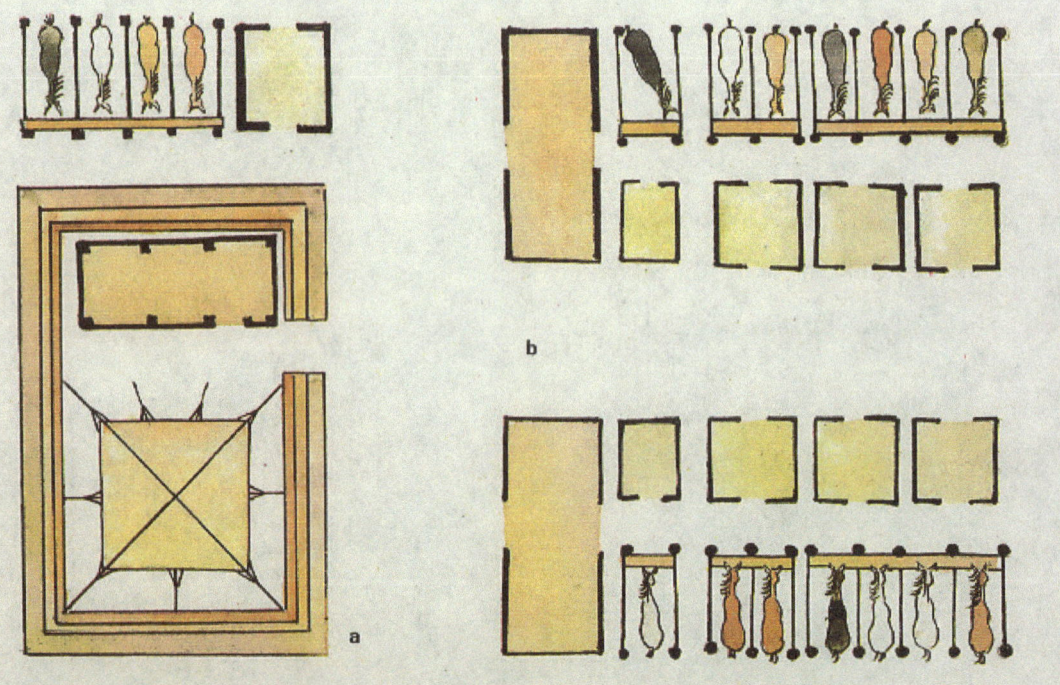

Cavalry encampment

a) Captain's tent, with a field kitchen, protected with a simple breastwork; lieutenant's and ensign's shacks have their entrances facing the captain's tent b) Horse stalls fronted with riders' shacks. At the head of each row is a wooden shack or cottage housing officers. The regulations called for an aisle allowing passage of a regiment between each 5-6 shacks; the width of the aisle was to be 8 feet.

Field encampment tents and shacks
a) Infantry tents with supporting spiked fork, which could be also used as a weapon b) Infantry shack and frame
c) Cavalry shack and section of field stable

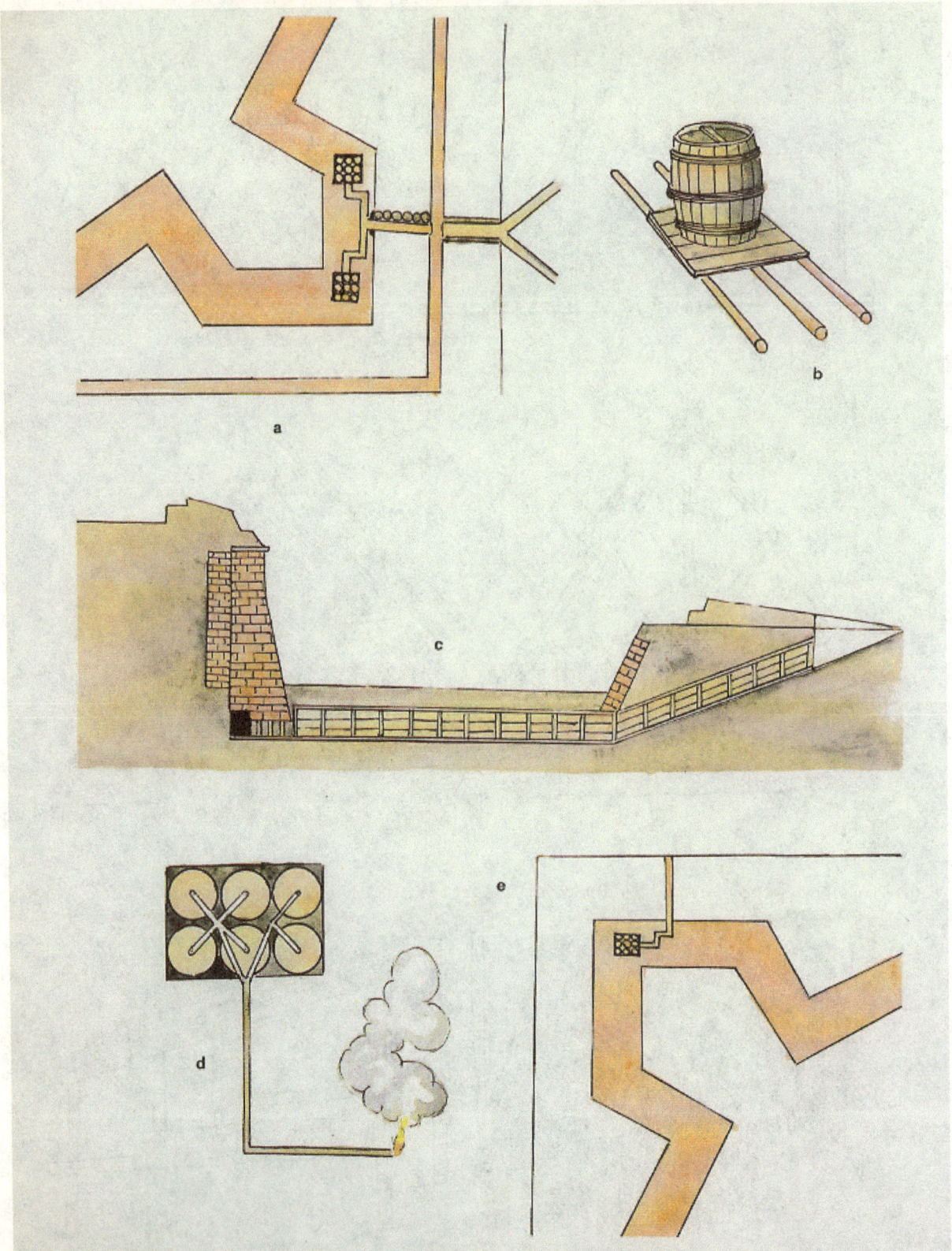

Saps driven under permanent fortifications works (The army laying in siege dug saps under the enemy works) a) Saps dug under the corners of a bastion b) Powder barrel with stretcher c) Sap course and timbering of the rampart wall in the blast chamber location d) Fuse branching to individual charges e) Sap driven under a bastion salient

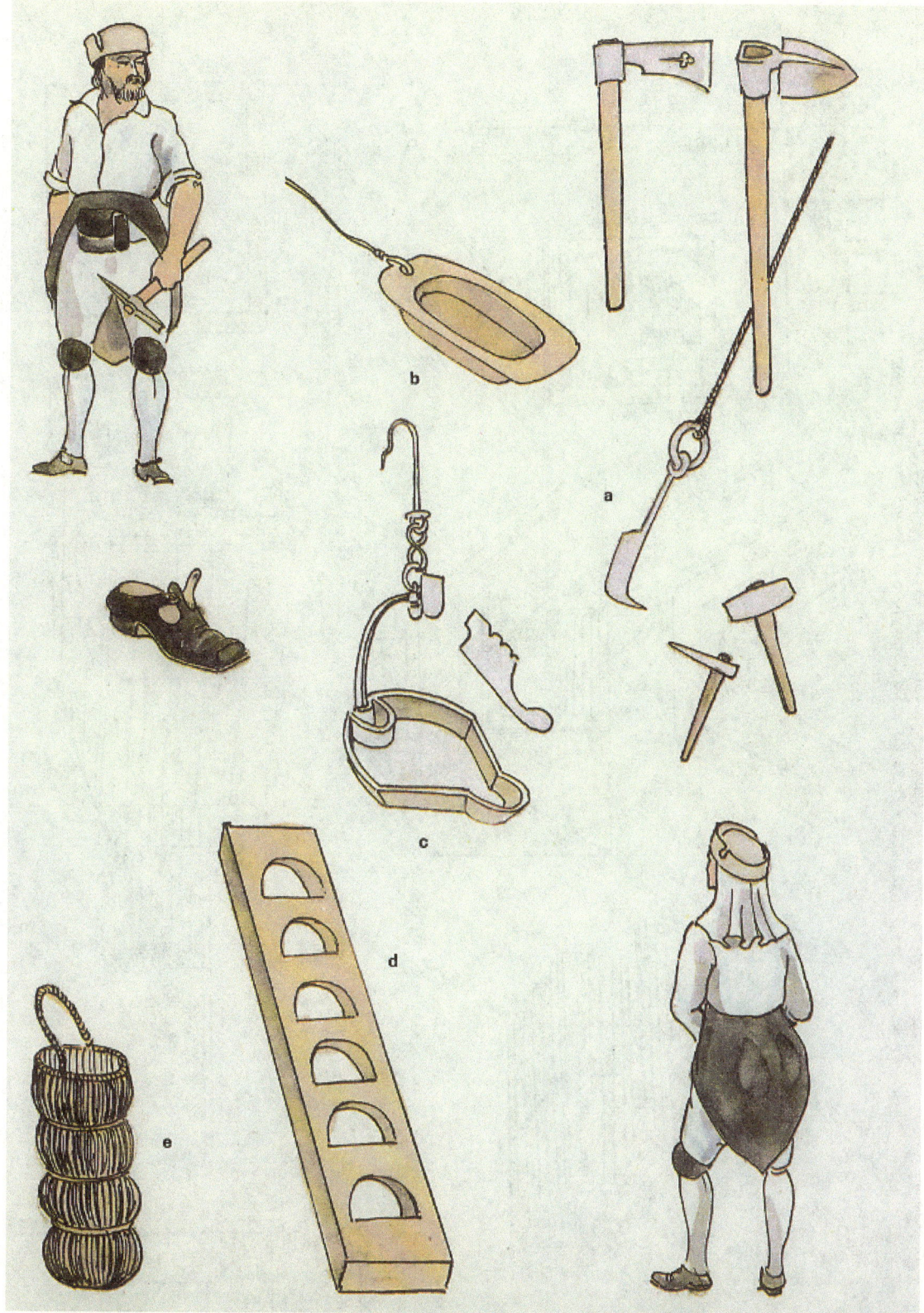

Miner hired as sappers and their gear   a) Hook for underground timber haulage and other tools   b) Wooden sled container for removing earth   c) Tallow burning lamp d) Ladder hewn from   single piece of wood   e) Wicker-work tub for removing earth

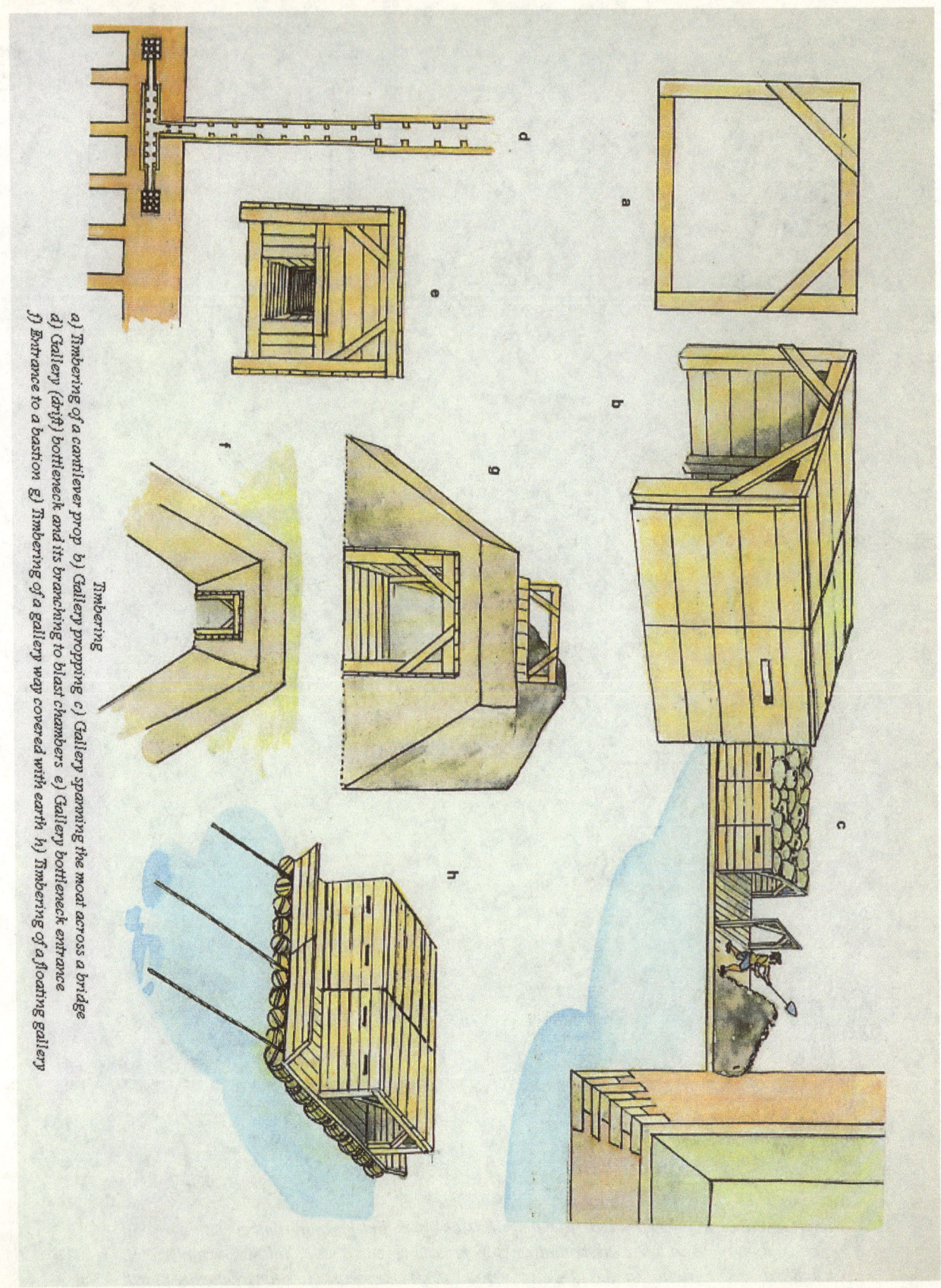

Timbering

a) Timbering of a cantilever prop b) Gallery propping c) Gallery spanning the moat across a bridge
d) Gallery (drift) bottleneck and its branching to blast chambers e) Gallery bottleneck entrance
f) Entrance to a bastion g) Timbering of a gallery way covered with earth h) Timbering of a floating gallery

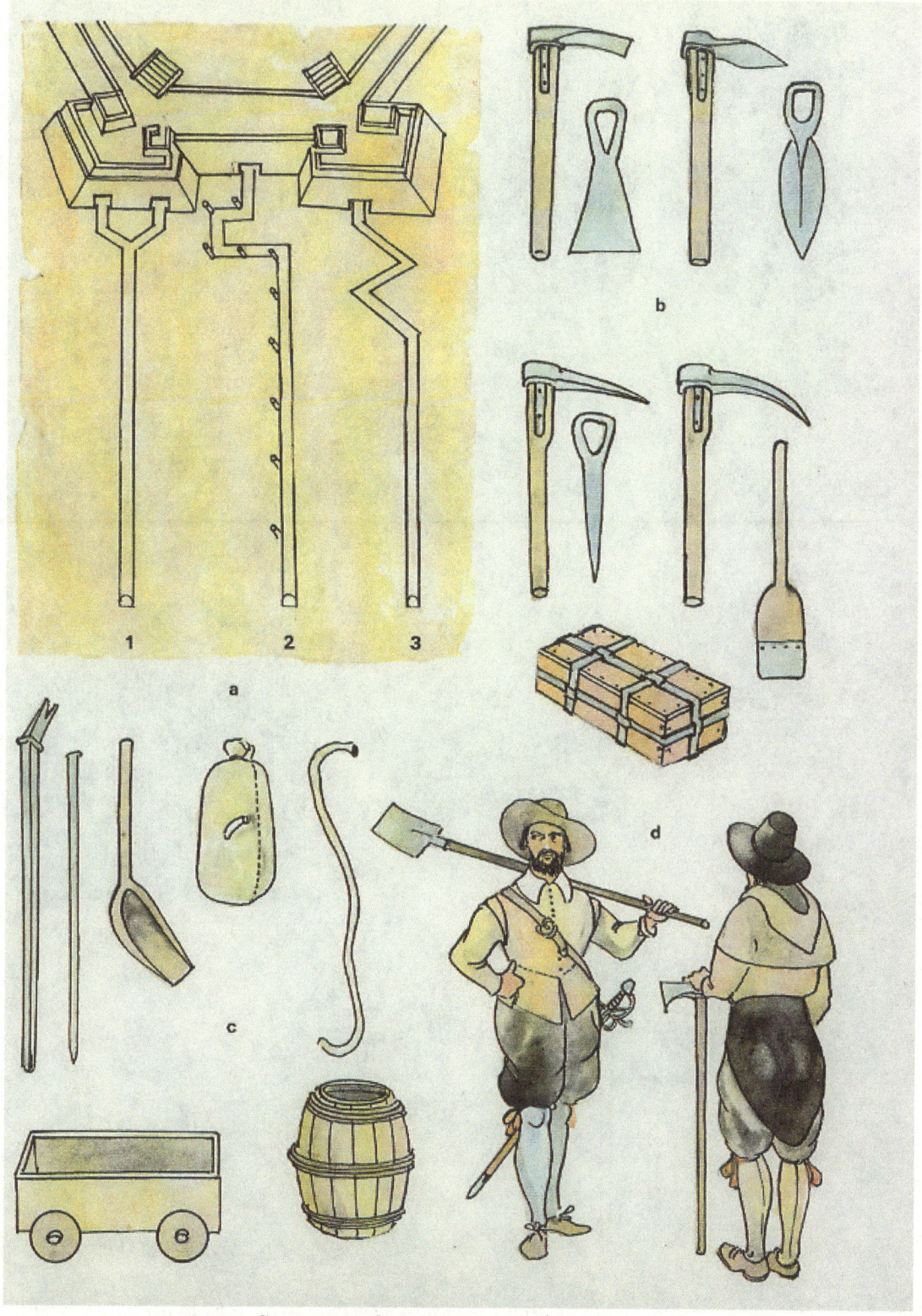

Sap types and sapping implements
a) Sap types 1 – Fourquette (forked sap) 2- Royal 3 – Serpentin b) Short handled
gear for work in narrow space and ironclad powder box c) Iron crowbars for prying
rock loose, wooden shovel, powder bag, fuse, haulage tub, powder keg d) Sappers

Gabions, fascines and other methods of wood reinforcement of siege works a) Gabions in three sizes b) Wicker baskets filled with earth, forming a loophole c) Wicker screen, of stakes driven into the parapet and interwoven with wicker d) Sandbag loophole, covered with turf e) Stone loopholes f) Fascine screen supported by portable brackets g) Screens from vertically arranged fascines fastened to a horizontal brace tied to stakes driven into the ground i) Fascines laid across a trench and supported with two low holders embedded in the breastworks j) Low fascine support

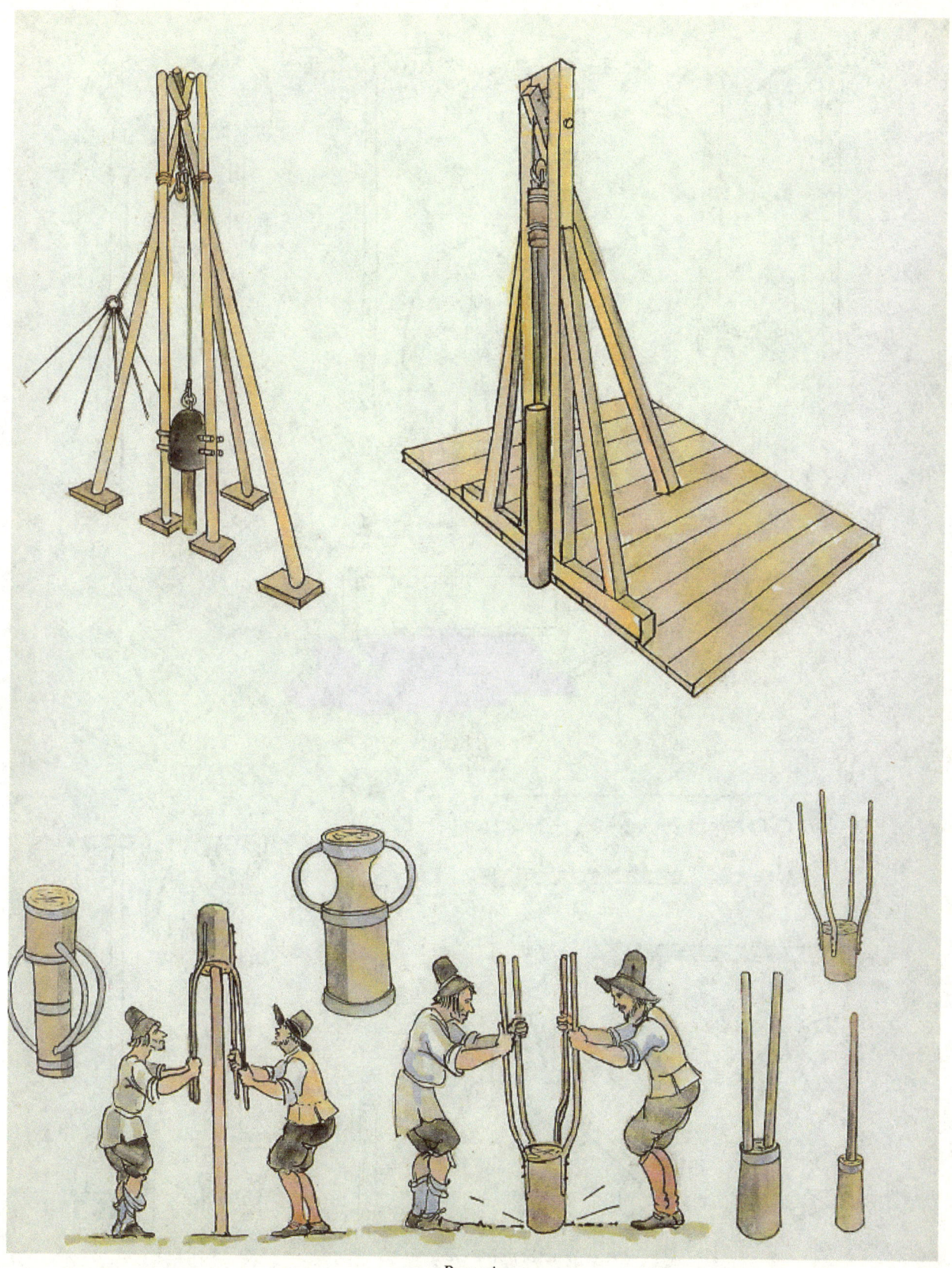

Ram rigs
Hand rammers and their use

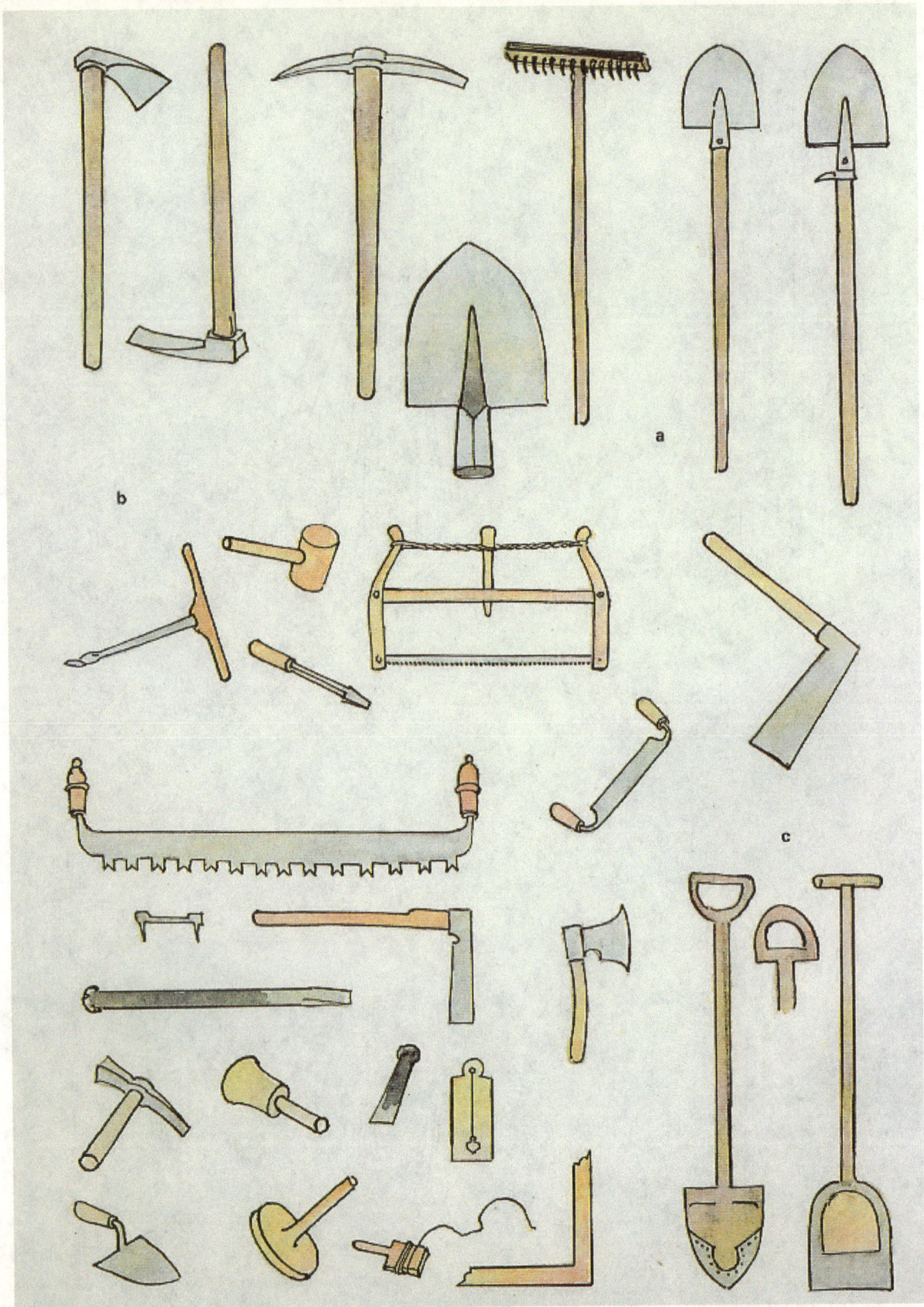

Sapping Gear

a) Hoes, pick, rake, spades, spade detail b) Auger, mallet, chisel, frame saw, axe,
drawknife c) Other tools, cross cut saw, axe, hatchet, construction and masonry tools

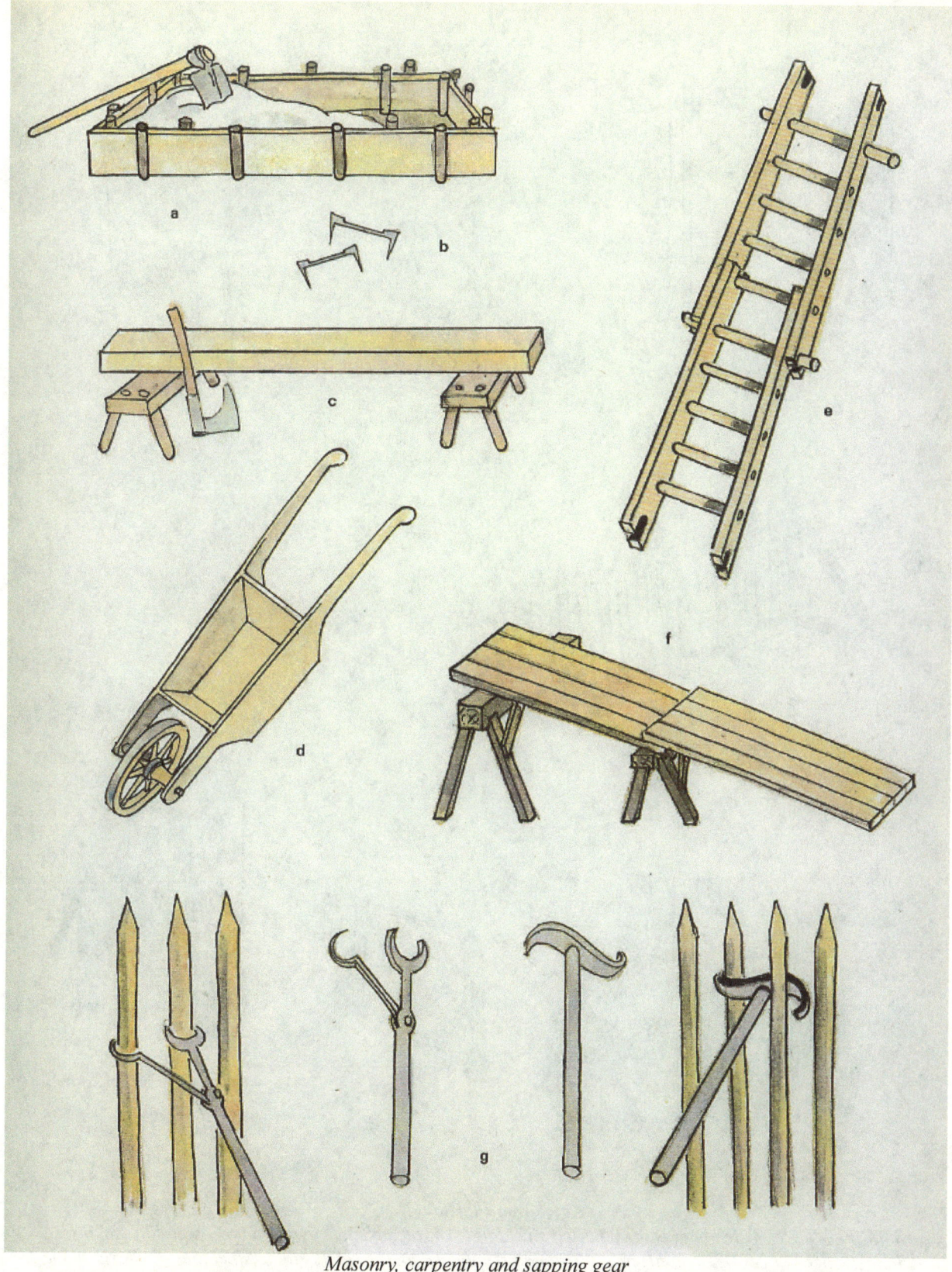

Masonry, carpentry and sapping gear
a) Lime slaking trough b) Dogs c) Beam with carpenter's axe d) Wheel barrow e) Extension ladder
f) Simple trestles g) Fence breakers

Wood shielding

a) Wood shielding of nailed boards b) Wheeled shielding c) Protective fencing with braces d) Star snares used for road blocks against cavalry but effective also against infantry troops e) Portable shielding f) Shield made from boards on a wagon chassis g) Protective screen from boards and wet cowhide used for extinguishing incendiaries h) Wheelbarrow mounted lighting device with a metal reflector

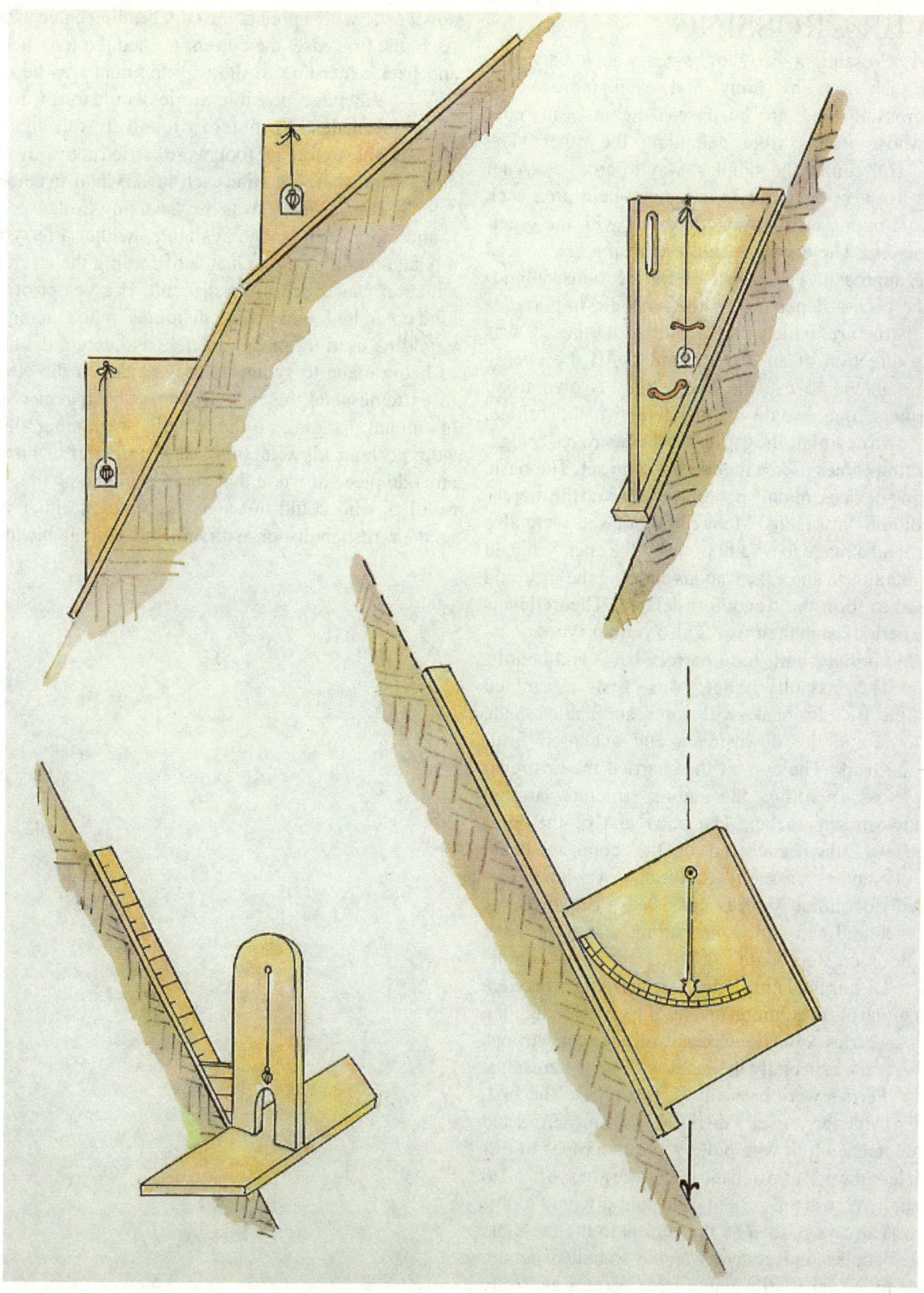

Inclinometers used for parapet construction

RIVER CROSSING

Crossing a body of water was a very difficult task for any army and even more so if the crossing had to be forced against an enemy whose troops were defending the other side.

Of course the simplest way to cross a stream was t use a bridge. But in an enemy-held area such strategic points were always defended with the greatest tenacity. The enemy would establish a bridgehead at the approach. The extent of fortifications defending the access depended on the strategic importance of the structure, which was greatest if the bridge was in the direction of an expected attack. If the enemy did not intend to use the bridge for his own troop movement, they would simply demolish the bridge.

To negotiate the gap left by the destroyed bridge, assaulting forces used a mobile bridging set. The basic bridging devices, mainly pontoons, followed the marching column on wagons. Mobile bridging sets were also of great advantage to assault troops if the enemy staged a counterattack, since the wagons carrying the rig could be used to form the wagonfort defense. Theoreticians of the period list in their works also various types of assault footbridges built form barrels, balks and boards.

The assault bridge was first assembled along the friendly bank, with ropes and cables made fast to it and the downstream end anchored firmly to the bank. The current then carried the upstream end across, pivoting the entire structure around the downstream anchor. The outer end of the footbridge was then anchored at the opposite bank.

Another assault footbridge design, earmarked for infantry use, consisted of two thick, well-anchored and taut cables strung across the river with floor or step-boards fastened across the cable.

During the Thirty Years' War period, ferries were still a much more common means of river crossing than bridges. Ferries could be also easily used to carry troops across rivers, especially in places with strong currents.

Ferries were basically of two types. The first, called a cable ferry, used a thick cable strung across and a punt attached to it with pulleys and two ropes of different lengths that allowed the punt to be always headed diagonally across the current. The punt oriented in this way was always pushed by the current to the far bank.

The second system was the so-called pendulum or flying ferry, in which a large barge was firmly anchored in midstream and a rope was paid out from it down river with a punt at the end, heading again aslant. As in the first case, the current pushed the ferry across and back according to the way the punt was headed.

Whenever possible, armies would ford. Cavalry and freight-laden wagons forded relatively well; infantry, when unable to ford on foot, were carried across by cavalry, one musketeer behind each cavalryman, in tandem.

But if there was no standing-bridge to be found, no assault bridge available, neither a ferry nor a boat, and not even a chance of fording the river, the situation was much more difficult. If a vessel of any kind could be found and requisitioned in the vicinity, it would be used to transport riders and cargo, the horses being made to swim along the sides of the vessel. In extreme need the rider had to swim together with his mount, hanging on the mane or swimming alongside, pushing his weapons and kit in front of him on any odd piece of wood that could be found on the spot. Soldiers who could not swim kept afloat either with reed or rush bolts or with inflated animal bladders.

Boat bridge construction with girders laid directly on the bulwarks; and (below) ferrying troops across a stream

241

Bridgehead establishment (bridge defence) a) Bridgehead established on the Rhine b) Bridgehead established at the confluence of the Elbe and Mulda Rivers

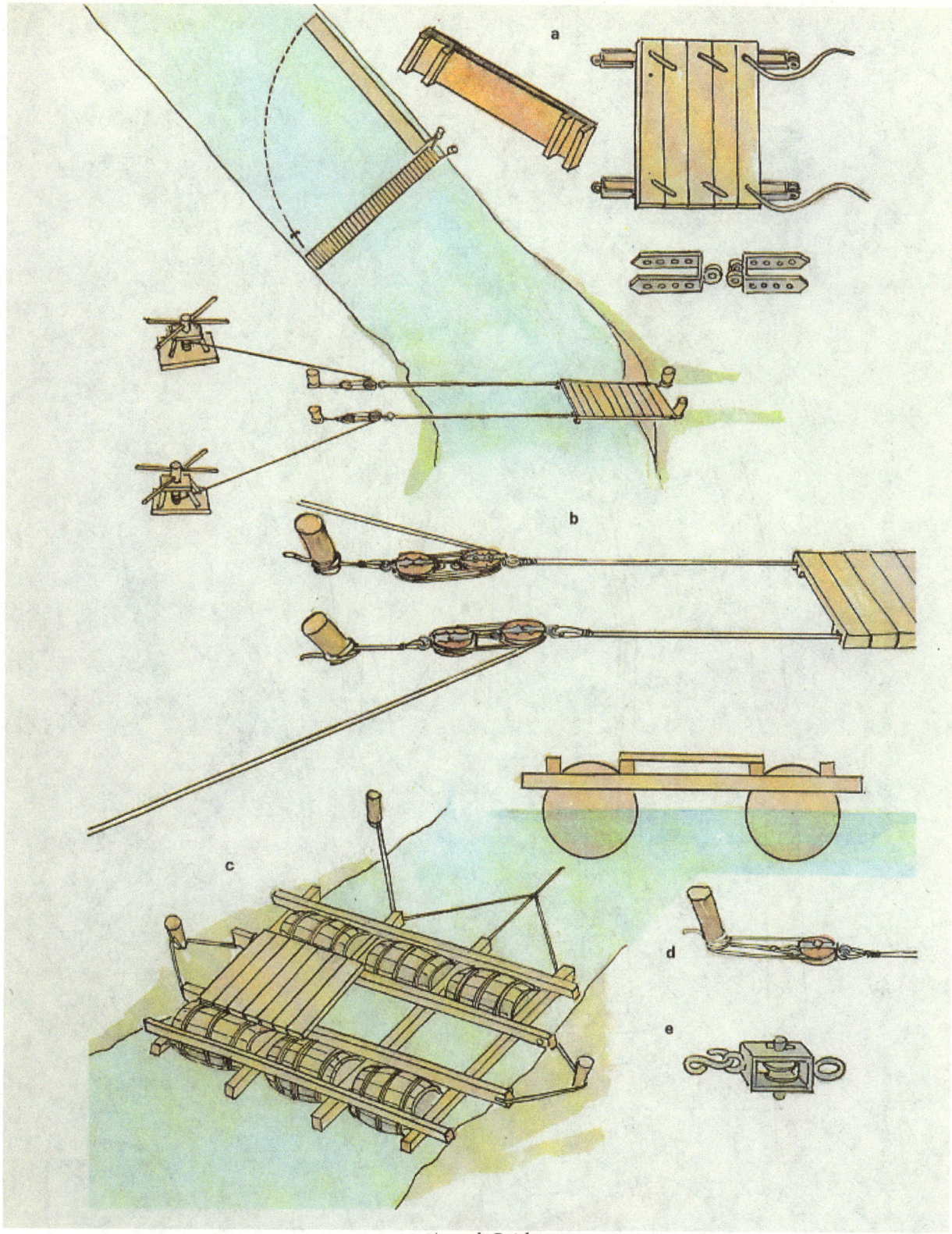

Assault Bridges
a) Assault bridge on girders joined with iron shackles. The chess sections were tied to the girders b) Assault bridge supported by cables strung across the stream with napstans c) Assault footbridge constructed from beams and barrels; the construction could also be used as a raft d) In this way a block was made fast to a bollard e) Iron block

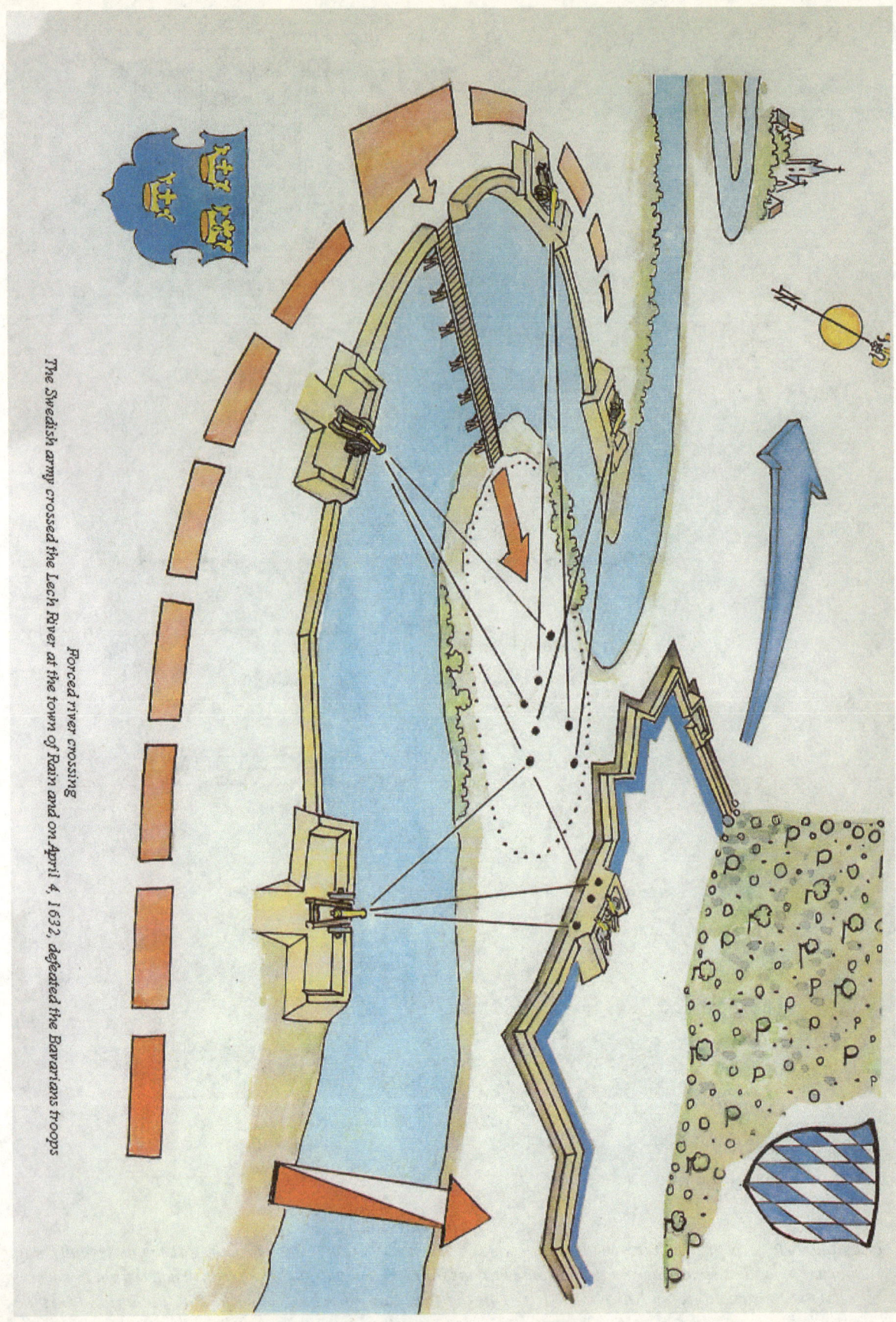

Forced river crossing

The Swedish army crossed the Lech River at the town of Rain and on April 4, 1632, defeated the Bavarians troops

River crossing

a) Crossing horses by swimming them alongside a boat b) Crossing troops by swimming c) Rider swimming with his horse d) Horse swimming and the rider holding his horse by the tail e) Fording on horseback f) Trooper swimming on inflated animal bladders g) Swimming stroke of the period – dog paddle

Fording
a) Musketeer transported across water behind a cavalryman b) A musketeer fording on foot c) First aid to a drowning man

CLOTHING, ARMOUR AND WEAPONS

If the troops were to fulfill important and often demanding combat tasks and objectives, they had to be properly armed and outfitted. The standard and quality of the troops' clothing, weaponry and armor were often the decisive factors of the fighting morale both of the land reserves and mercenary armies of the Thirty Years' War period.

Troops' clothing did not differ substantially from civilian clothing although the cut and quality of officers' dress naturally reflected the standards of the higher social classes. Generally, the clothes of the rank-and-file were identical with the dress of town and country people, although sometimes perhaps it was of slightly better quality.

Military clothing also followed the trends of civilian fashion especially before the introduction of uniforms. At the beginning of the 16th century military dress was characterized by rich, sometimes even ornamental slashing patterns, revealing a silken undergarment of rich, often contrasting colors. However, in time the Spanish fashion conquered Europe, introducing its characteristic feature, a cone-shaped padded jacket called the 'wamus'. The cone was inverted, that is the base was formed by the shoulders and the apex pointed between the breeches. Higher officers, like the upper classes, wore fashionable knitted hosiery and richly-folded breeches tied either above the ankles or below the knees. Infantry wore shoes and cavalry, if not clad in plate armor, wore high leather riding boots.

The Spanish fashion had also introduced rich adornment of dress with embroidery, ribbons and all kinds of other, often superfluous, trimmings. The popular Spanish folded ruff was worn around the neck and the head was covered by a small hat. In the late 16th century wams of the so-called goosebelly shape was typical.

The shape of plate armor also followed the line of the dress style. Today it is difficult to say whether it was the wams that copied the shape of the front of breast plate or vice versa. Officers' armor was beautifully embellished, especially in the later 16th century. Etching was the most common technique of plate armor embellishment since it did not affect the strength of the plate. Quite often etching was combined with hammering, embossing and chasing; gilding and silvering was also common. The ceremonial armors of rich noblemen and sovereigns were especially exquisitely embellished. These masterpieces of the outstanding European armorers and armor-smiths of the Thirty Years' War period are today among the most prized items of the world's great collections. Plate armor of this type is often adorned with mythological scenes, classical figurative and plant decorative patterns, fruit garlands, mascarons and fighting scenes.

The ranks were equipped with cheaper, less fancy plate armor. If there was any decoration at all, it was on the breast plates, commonly in the form of a pattern of burnished and black surface.

In the course of time plate armor was gradually made less burdensome. By the late 16th century cavalry no longer wore the three-quarter plate reaching down to the knees. The tasses which had been short until then, became longer and wider to protect the popular wide-trunk hose. The feet were still covered with high leather boots. But the infantry were gradually getting rid of plate armor altogether because it slowed their marching. The only feature of plate armor that was kept was the helmet, either in the form of the pikeman's pot or the morion adopted from the Spaniards, or the birnhelm that had developed from the Gothic iron hat or chapel-de-fer.

At the turn of the 17th century a more sober fashion was adopted, especially in Protestant countries, of simple-cut and dark materials, with linen or cambric collars and cuffs trimmed with lace. Officer dandies of both Catholic and Protestant armies, however, continued wearing dapper and richly-ornamented clothing.

At the beginning of the Thirty Years' War and especially in the 1630's both civilian and military fashion began to be influenced by the German and Swedish styles. Instead of the restricting wams freer doublets with long front tails were worn, often made of silk or atlas. A manly touch was lent by large epaulettes. Doublets were adorned with wide lace collars. The original wide trouser legs had begun to acquire a pipe-like shape by the mid-17th century, reaching generally down to the knees. High boots replaced Spanish shoes. Officers and dandies of the time wore broad-brimmed hats, richly adorned with plumes. Long, free hair was also very fashionable. In colder weather soldiers kept warm with simple capes, reaching usually down to the hips; in winter they wore short fur coats or fur lined cloaks of thicker cloth.

Armor was also undergoing further development. Cavalry switched to wearing free-face helmets, at first similar to the infantryman's iron hat, later adopting the schischacke originally of Turkish origin and popular especially with heavy cavalry. During the Thirty Years' War cavalry were also gradually getting rid of individual components of armor. Apart from the helmet, only the breast and back plates remained in use, sometimes also articulated shoulder pieces. A shallow impression can be sometimes found on the left side of the front plates. These impressions are marks of test proof bullets fired from pistols at 20 paces. (The proof fire was a sort of quality inspection of the plates.) However, light cavalry of the period finally got rid of plate armor altogether, wearing merely short buffalo hide coats called buffcoats. At the beginning of the 17th century only a few pikemen continued wearing partial plate armor among infantry troops and by the mid-17th century only the English pikemen remained faithful to body armor.

Since the late 16th century some sort of hand-gun had become the main ordnance of both mercenary and land reserve troops. At first this had been the arquebus, but later the musket was adopted by infantry and dragoons, and pistols by cavalry. The introduction of hand guns into army ordnance resulted in a huge increase of fire power.

` The musket stock could be firmly rested against the shoulder and the weapon could therefore be better aimed. Musketry shaped varied greatly according to the countries of origins and place of manufacture. There were substantial differences between muskets of German, French, or English make but throughout the period all the weapons of the type followed roughly the same design as the matchlock. In the first stage of musketry development, dating from about 1600 to 1635, the matchlock was equipped with a long action lever protruding from the stock. When the lever was pressed upwards, the motion was transferred via the bent end of the lever onto an iron ring fixed firmly onto the doghead pin; the action tipped the latter down to the flashpan. The burning match clamped into the doghead vice jaws igniting the priming powder in the pan so that the flame flashed through the vent into the barrel, setting off the main charge. A later type of matchlock, with which infantry were equipped after the 1630's, had a short-action lever protected with a trigger guard, rather than a long lever. The trigger transferred the motion onto lever which in turn

tripped the doghead via the ring on the pin in a similar way to the earlier design. The entire mechanism was mounted on an iron plate fixed to the side of the stock.

The musket was approximately 140 cm long and the weight was at first eight to ten kg, later four to five kg. The heavier models had to be supported with a fork when being fired.

The wheellock did not need a burning match to ignite the priming powder and facilitated the design of weapons that could be carried either under the coat or, more often, in saddle holsters. This meant that cavalry could now also be armed with hand-guns and by the beginning of the 17th century pistols for some time had displaced 'cold' weapons with the cavalry.

The principles and design of the wheellock were somewhat more complicated than those of the matchlock. The wheellock action is based on a serrated iron wheel mounted on a square pin. Using a winding key or spanner the wheel was wound back by one third of its circumference. This action simultaneously pressed—through a linked chain fixed to the other end of the pin—the main or strike spring. A butt on the trigger clicked home into a hole on the inner face of the wheel. When the trigger was pressed, the trigger lever support shifted aside and slipped from the hole, freeing the wheel. The spring-loaded wheel would release and start quickly turning, its serrationed circumference striking sparks form a pyrite pressed against it by doghead jaws. The sparks then ignited the primer in the flashpan.

Although the wheellock principle remained more or less constant the design varied according to the manufacturer and use, so that wheellock with uncovered, externally-mounted mechanisms were known, as well as designs with the wheel placed either outside or inside. There were many French, Spanish, Dutch and Italian wheellock designs. Wheellocks were used not only for cavalry pistols but also for some types of cavalry carbines.

A heavy musket called the battlement gun could be also classed among infantry ordnance. It was used to defend stronghold, and its length varied from 190 to 210 cm, the caliber being 24 to 25 mm and the weigh 20 to 25 kg.

Generally speaking, the common usage of body armor had also influenced the basic shape of cold weaponry. The mighty cut with the Gothic broadsword was ineffective against plate armor and therefore cold weaponry blades were becoming gradually narrower to make it easier to get the tip through the plate gaps. This in turn meant that the grip on the weapon had to be changed rather than gripping the sword firmly in the fist which had been necessary for the heavy blow; the weapon now had to be held in a subtler fashion dictated by the prevalent piercing techniques. The hilt of the weapon was laid diagonally across the palm and the index finger placed on the guard close to the blade. Iron gauntlets were no longer suitable and were replaced by leather gloves. The hand of the combatants were at first protected by simple, later by ever more intricate and effective knuckle bows, swept hilts and cup guards. At first these devices protected only the fingers, but later the entire fist was guarded in this way against the rival's slashes and thrusts. Sword and rapier guards of the period had a great number of variants. In Central Europe swept hilts prevailed but cup guards were more common in Italy and Span. Sometimes they were quite simple but quite often they were beautifully embellished by the leading masters of the craft. The best blades of the period were made in Toledo, Spain. The Toledo masters specialized in blades that allowed for easier handling.

The 16th and 17th centuries saw the manufacture and use of a great variety of cold side weapons. Apart from the common swords and rapiers weapons of totally different shape were also made, such as the Scottish claidheamhmor, the Swiss sword, the Italian storta, the German and Czech dusack and so on. In southeast Europe sabers were common. When cold weapons were reintroduced in the 1730's as the basic cavalry weaponry, when heavy plate armor had already disappeared from the battlefields, a new weapon was employed both for piercing and slashing – the backsword.

Long stave weapons had also undergone some changes. The lance that had been the mainstay of the cavalry arsenal until the early 17th century disappeared when pistols were introduced as the main cavalry weapon. Lances survived only in units of the Polish hussars and with the Cossacks and cavalry units of some other Eastern nations.

The infantry pike remained a regulation weapon of the mercenary troops until the introduction of the bayonet, but their numbers were gradually decreasing while firearms were rapidly gaining prominence. The halberd was also increasingly popular, first as the weapon of palace and household guards, later as regular infantry ordnance. Apart from halberds all kinds of other stave weapons were used in the period, for example scythes, spontoons and partisans.

Colors, or flags, form a self-contained group of military matériel. The first mercenary troops had flags with short, simple staffs with firmly-attached cloth blades of two or three bright, conspicuous colors. The size was usually two by two and a half or three meters. The flag of a regiment was quite often designed by the commander himself, following the color scheme of his family coat of arms or the colors of the country. Very popular blade designs were those with flames or stripes. Battalions of a regiment often displayed the same color-scheme on their flags, but the arrangement of the colors would differ. The colors had to be conspicuous to facilitate signaling and relaying orders. Specially-trained flag bearers with broad shoulders skillfully played the flag according to a pre-set order code. Since the mercenaries often changed sides and masters according to who was able to offer better and more regular pay, it was sometimes quite impossible to distinguish whether the colors belonged to friendly or enemy troops. In the 17th century this lead to the introduction of flags bearing the coat of arms of the unit, the proprietor or military entrepreneur.

The flags of the cavalry units, the standards or cornets, were smaller than infantry colors and banners. They were of an oblong shape with rounded corners, or the fly end had swallow tails. Most common were the square cornet, that is standards with ribbons, symbols, insignia and various mottoes. The original simplicity of design disappeared in time and many symbols and scenes began to appear. Sometimes the latter were even humorous, serving to ridicule the enemy, and the bands of women trailing the armies had their flags bedecked with symbols that were anything but pure or decent.

The Imperial army used to have an eagle on its colors and after the victory over the Czech estates in the Battle of the White Mountain (1620), which ascribed to a direct intervention of Virgin Mary, the standards also bore her image. Cavalry standards were adorned with the likeness of St. George, while the artillery and the miners displayed St. Barbara on theirs, flown permanently from their wagons. The riflemen had St. Sebastian as their patron saint and the sappers had St. Joseph.

The Mansfield army had the motto 'For Faith and Liberty' on their colors; the flags of the Catholic League proclaimed to be fighting 'For Church and Imperium'; while the Croatians proclaimed 'I Yearn for Booty'; and the banners of the Lisowski regiments that 'The Great Eagle Bird Shall Vanquish His Enemy'. The troops of Albrecht of Wallenstein bore flags with the images of Mars and Venus and under which was the motto 'With Art and War'.

The banners of the Swedish troops that entered the European theatres of the Thirty Years' War in 1630 already had long flagstaffs. Their symbol, displayed on the blade, was usually three royal crowns on a yellow background. This type of banner was to be commonly used later, and has survived essentially until our own times.

Noblemen's apparel

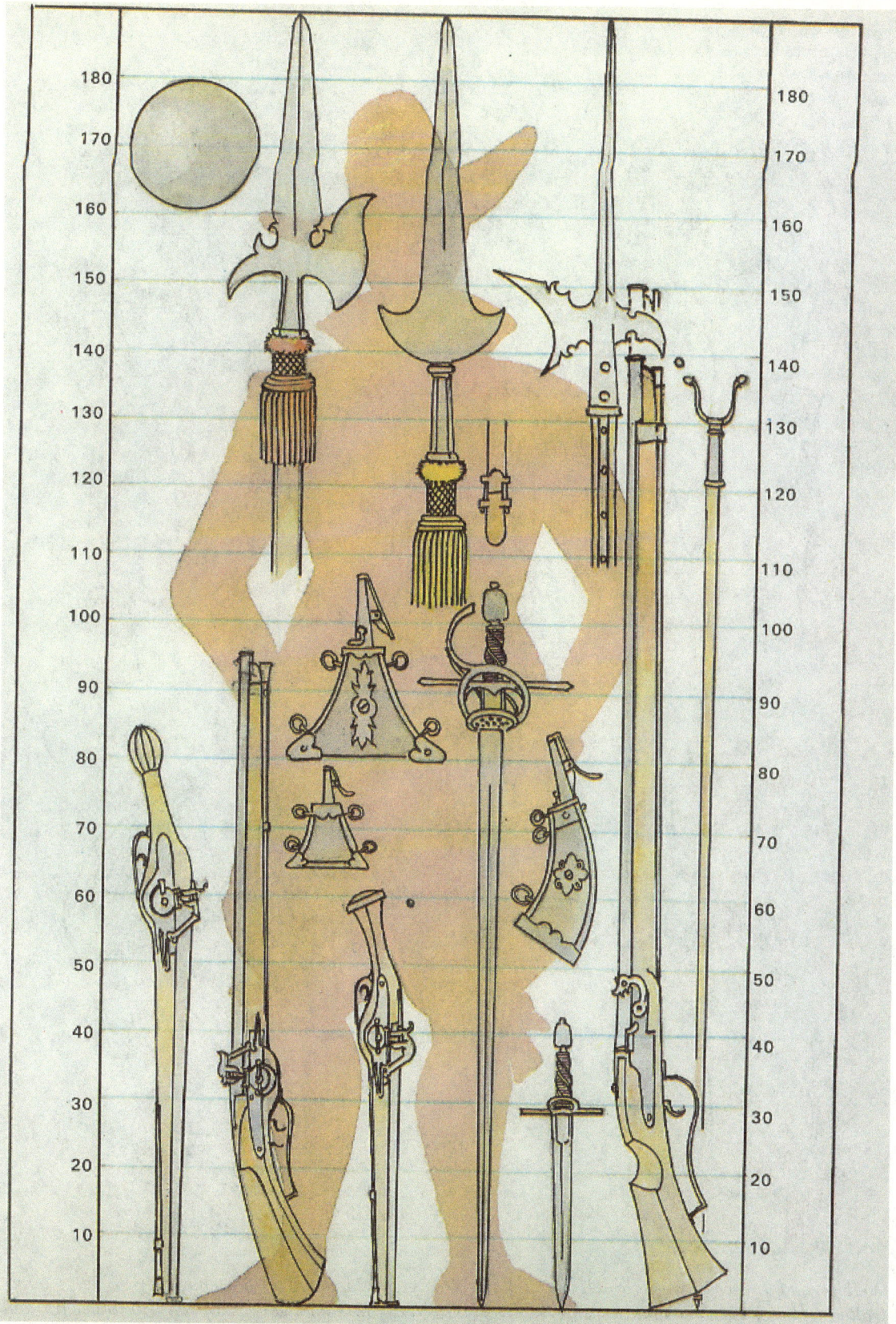

Weapon dimensions compared to height of the soldier

a) Doublet and breeches worn by elector Johann George, with detail of fastening, 1618 b) Collar worn by Wallenstein c) Doublet and breeches worn by Gustavus II Adolphus of Sweden d) Breeches and doublet which has false sleeves and lace-trimmed collar and cuffs e) Doublet with slashed body and sleeves, Zwinger, Dresden, collections f) Shoe, from Van Eyck's portrait of Robert Rich, Earl of Warwick (1635)

Riding boots with spurs, early 17th century

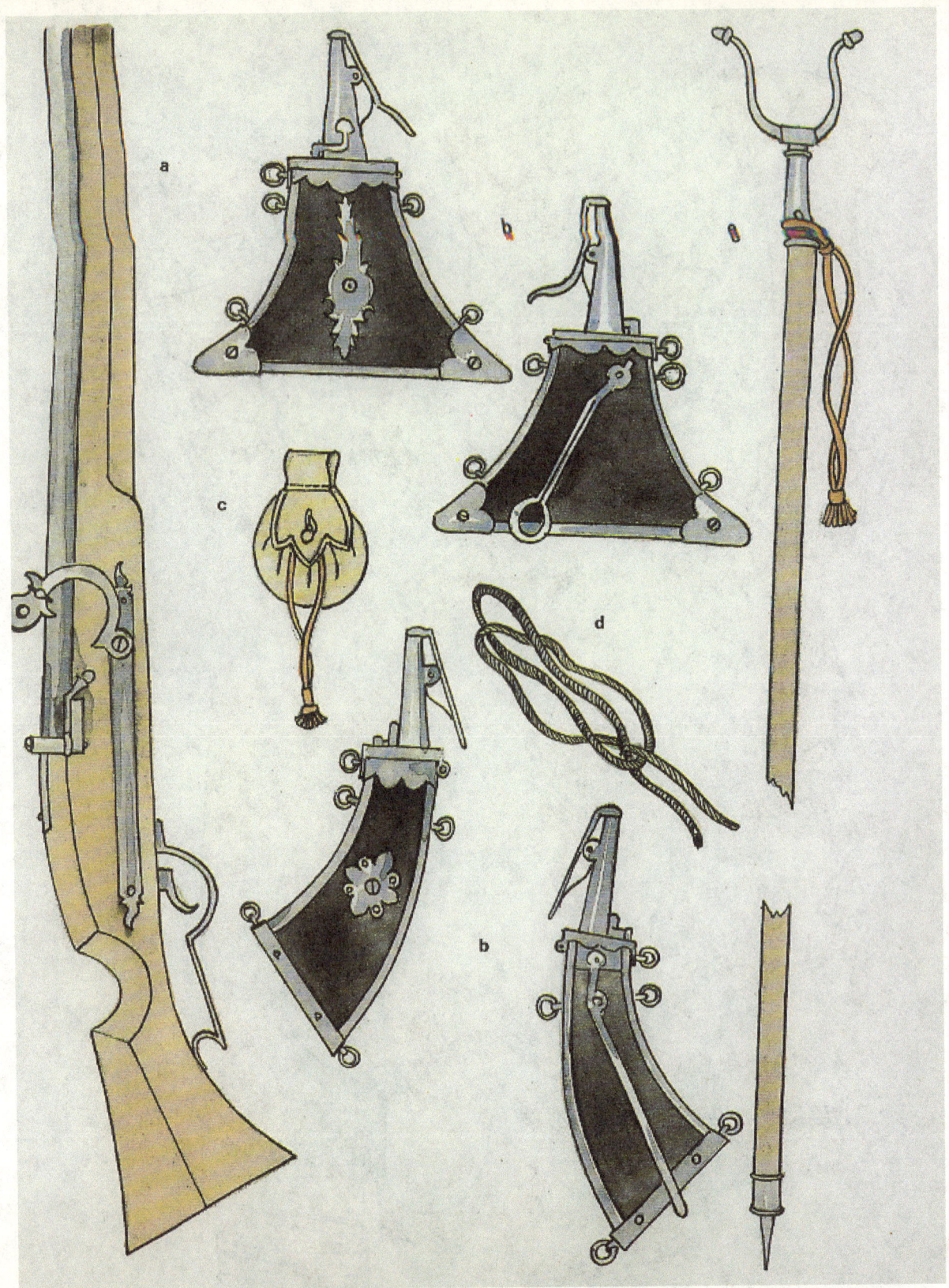

Matchlock musket with accessories
a) Matchlock musket b) Powderhorns c) Shot bag d) Match e) Musket fork

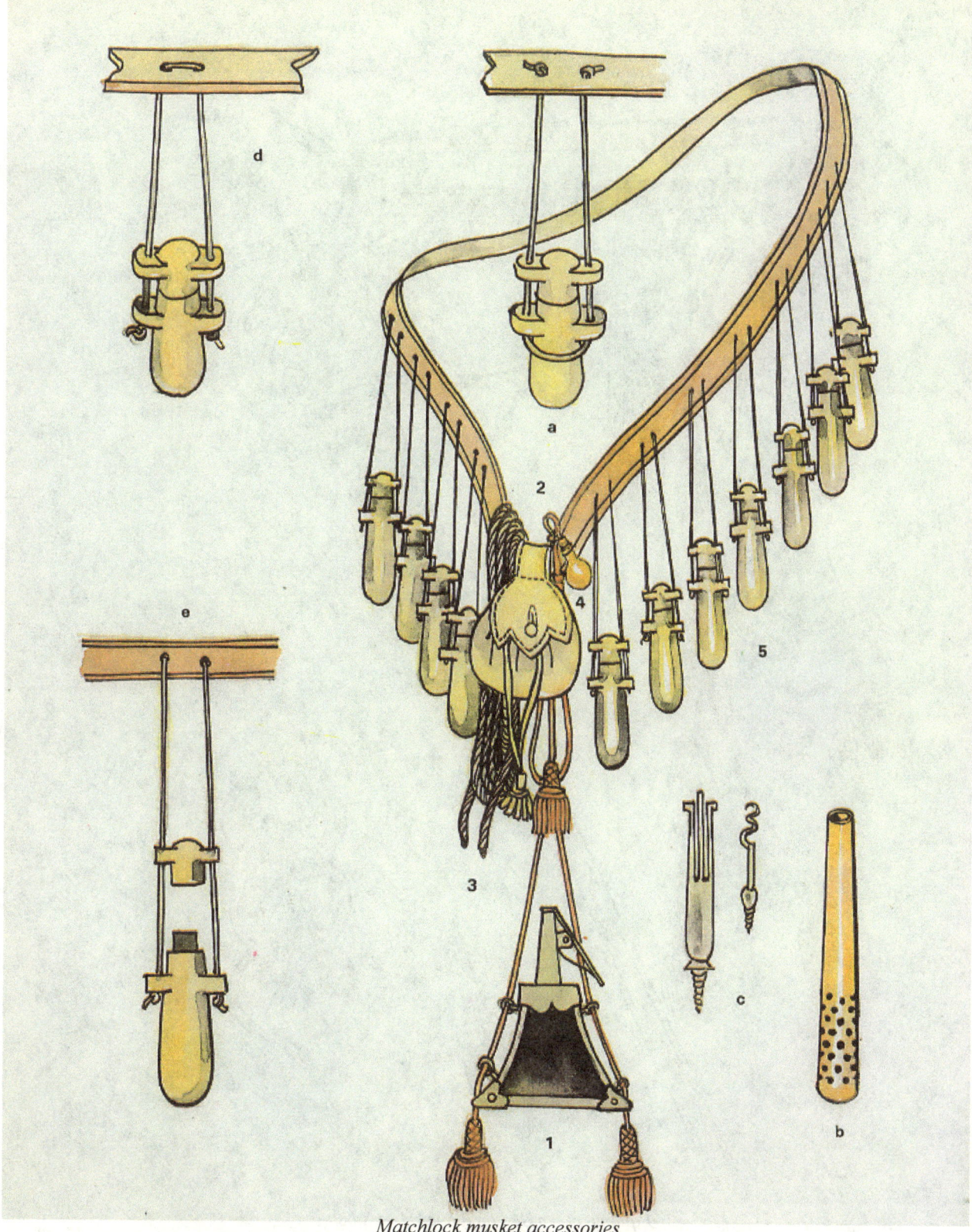

Matchlock musket accessories
a)Bandolier with single round powder, receptacles 1-powderhorn 2- shot bag 3 – match
4- round oil can 5- powder measures b) Brass match-tip cap c) Cleaning rod and ball extractor
d) Suspension of single round receptacles from bandolier e) Open single round powder receptacle

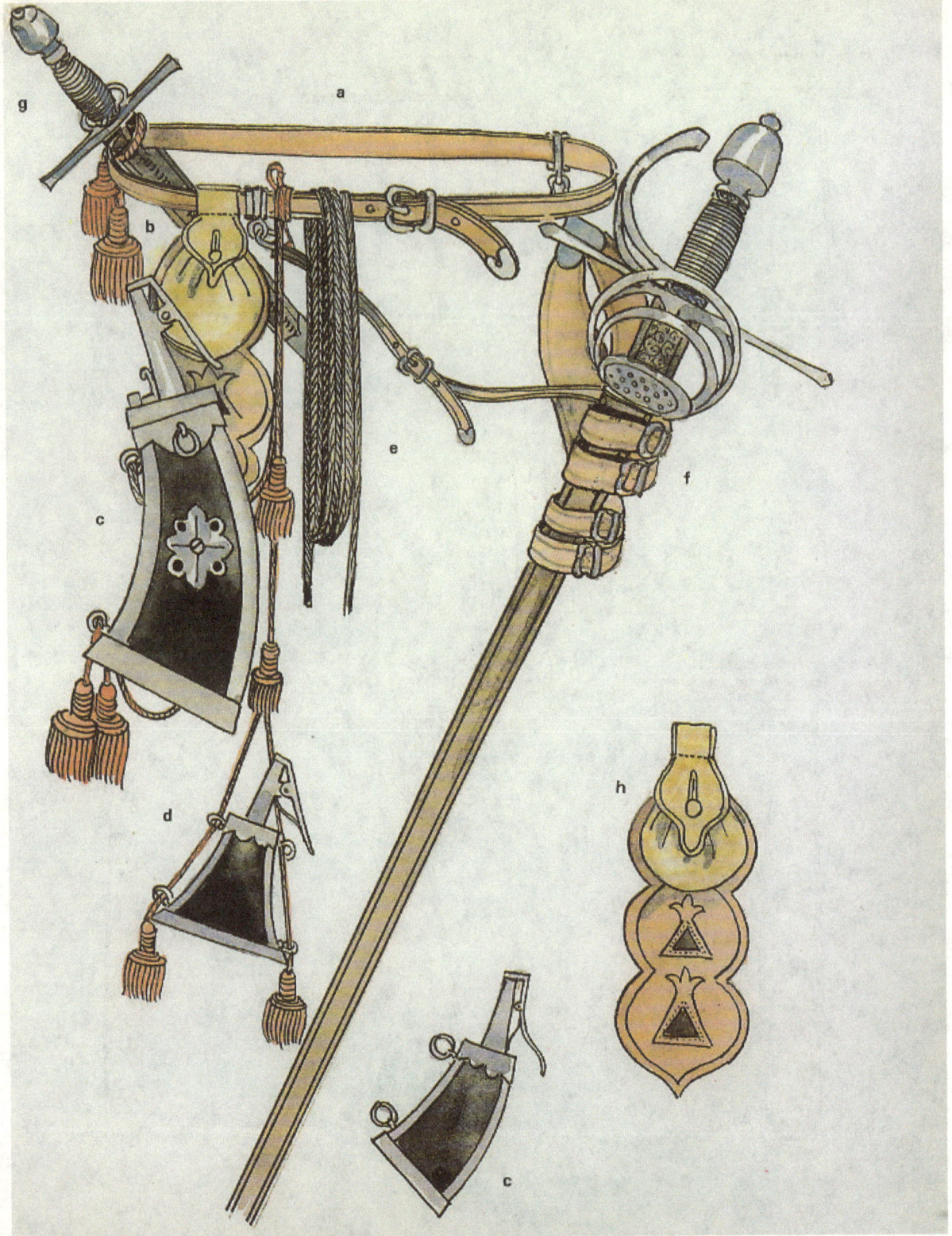

Equipment carried on a musketeer's belt
a) Musketeer's girding b) Leather powderhorn hanger, with shot bag c) Powderhorn
d) Primer powderhorn e) Match f) Rapier g) Dagger h) Detail of leather hanger with shot bag

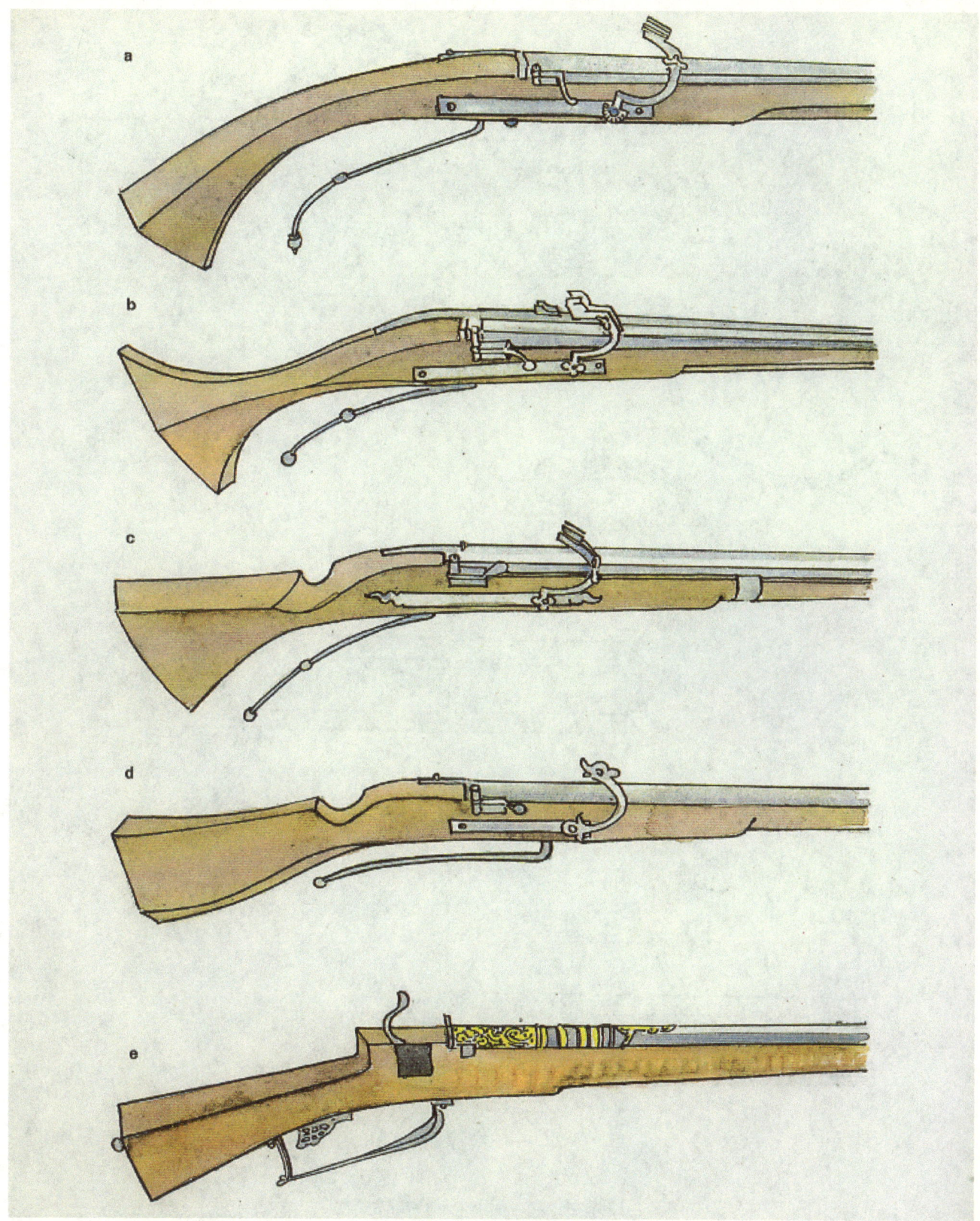

Musket types
a) And b) English muskets c) German musket d) French musket e) Turkish musket

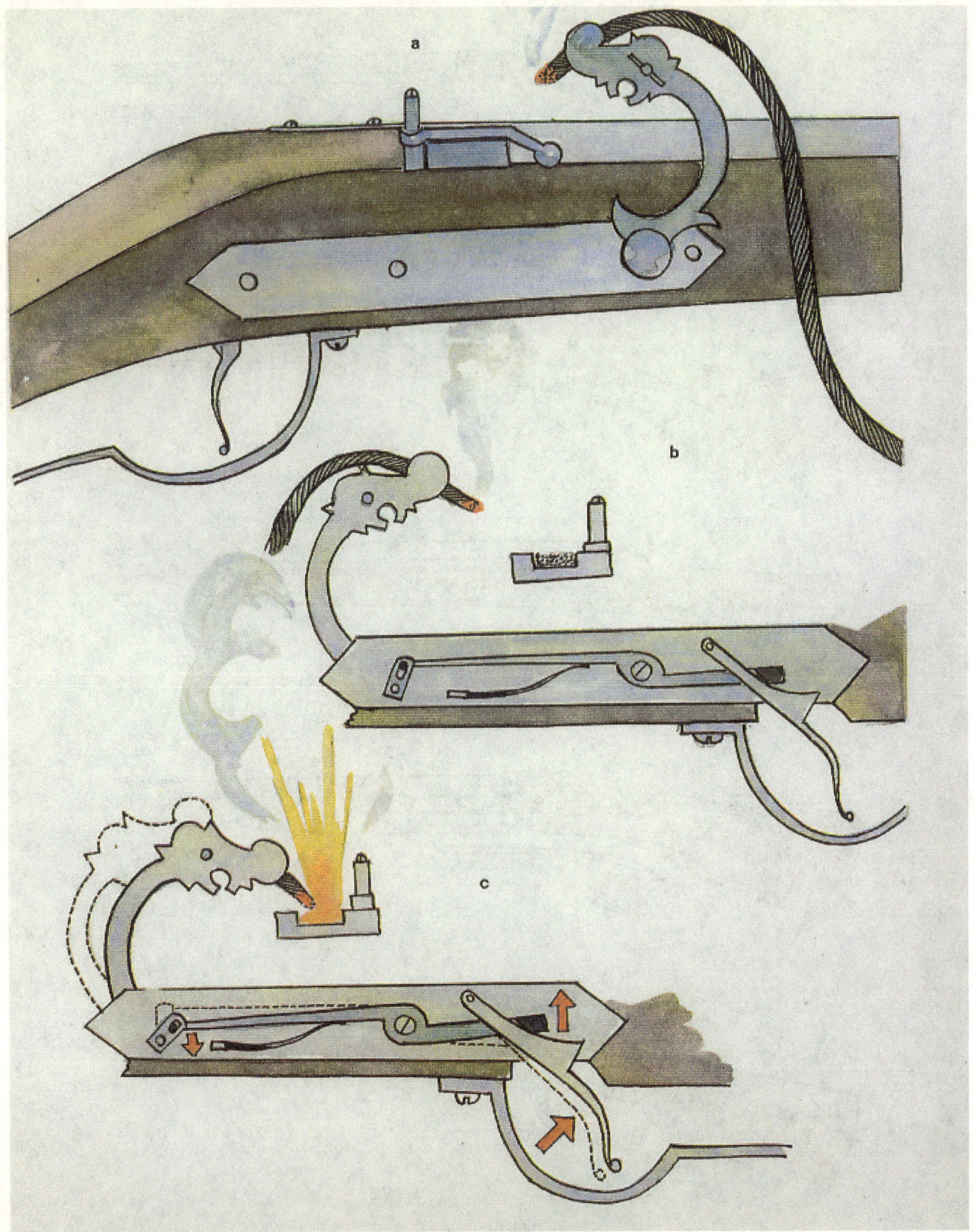

Matchlock action
a) Outer view b) Inner view c) Matchlock after firing

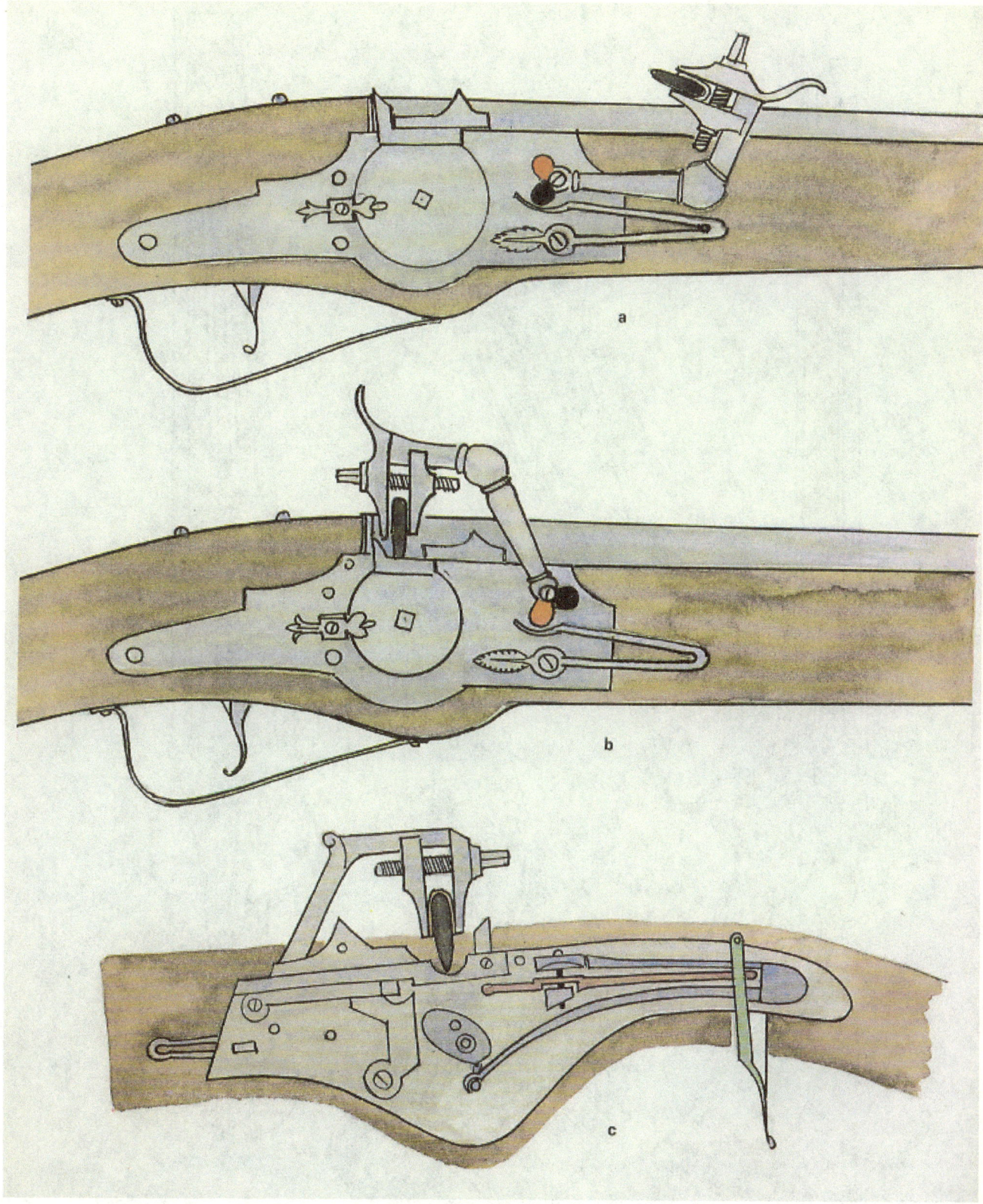

Wheellock
a)Doghead down, flashpan cover shut b) Doghead down, flashpan cover slid open, weapon ready to fire
c) Wheellock, in section

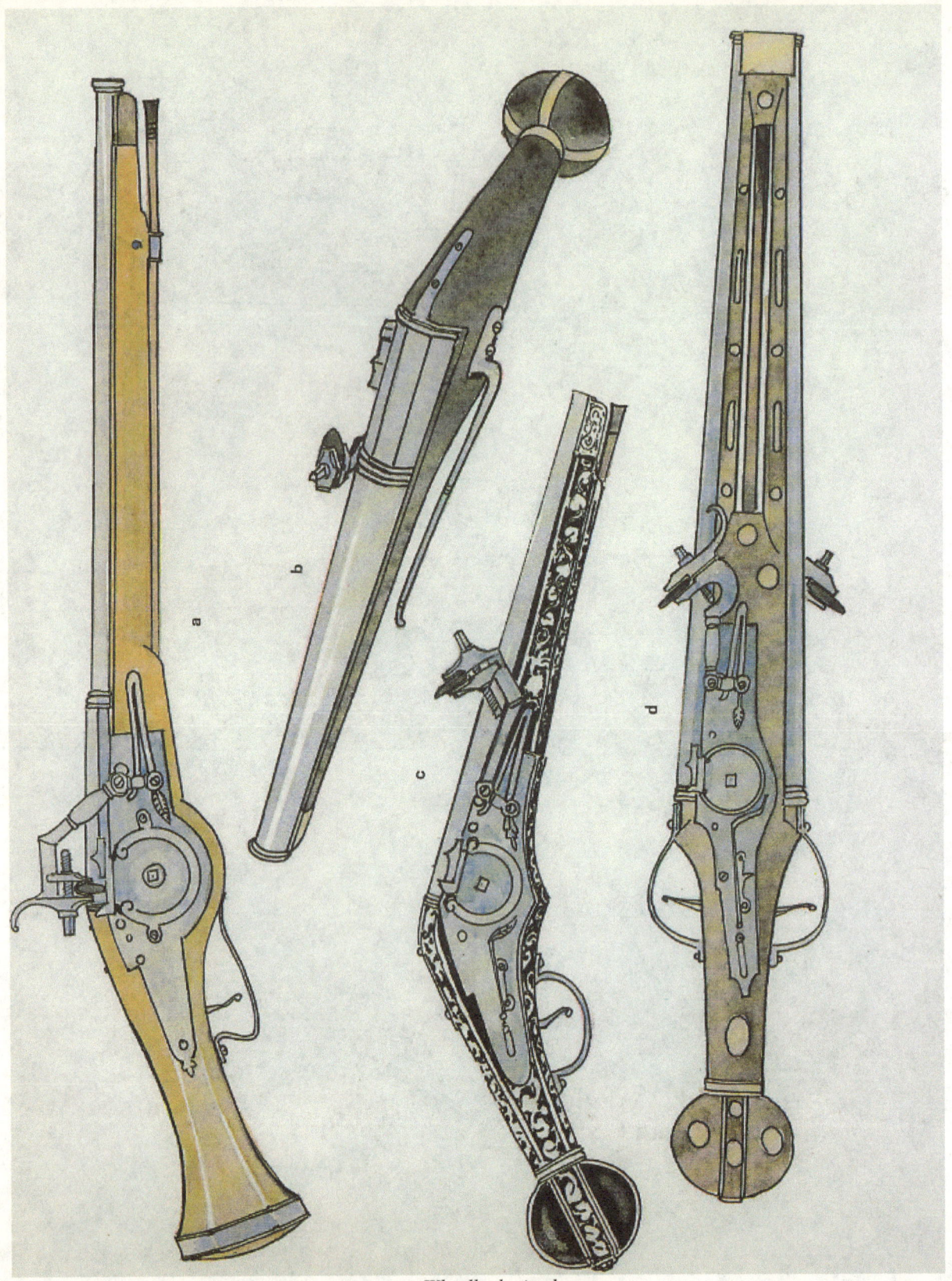

Wheellock pistol
a) Wheellock pistol b) Pistol with a hook, to be worn in belt c) Pistol with ivory inlay d) Double-barrelled pistol

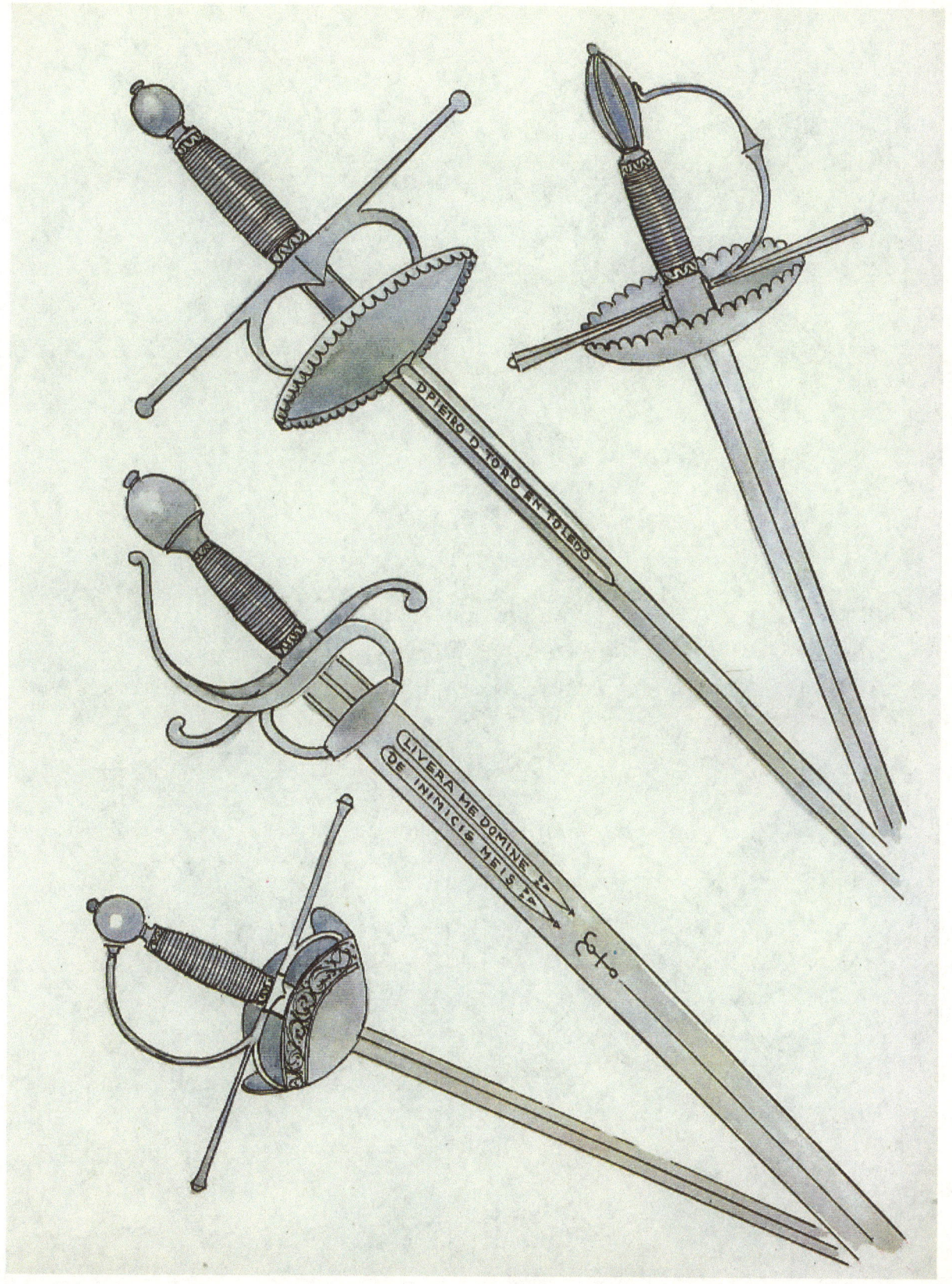

Early 17th century rapiers

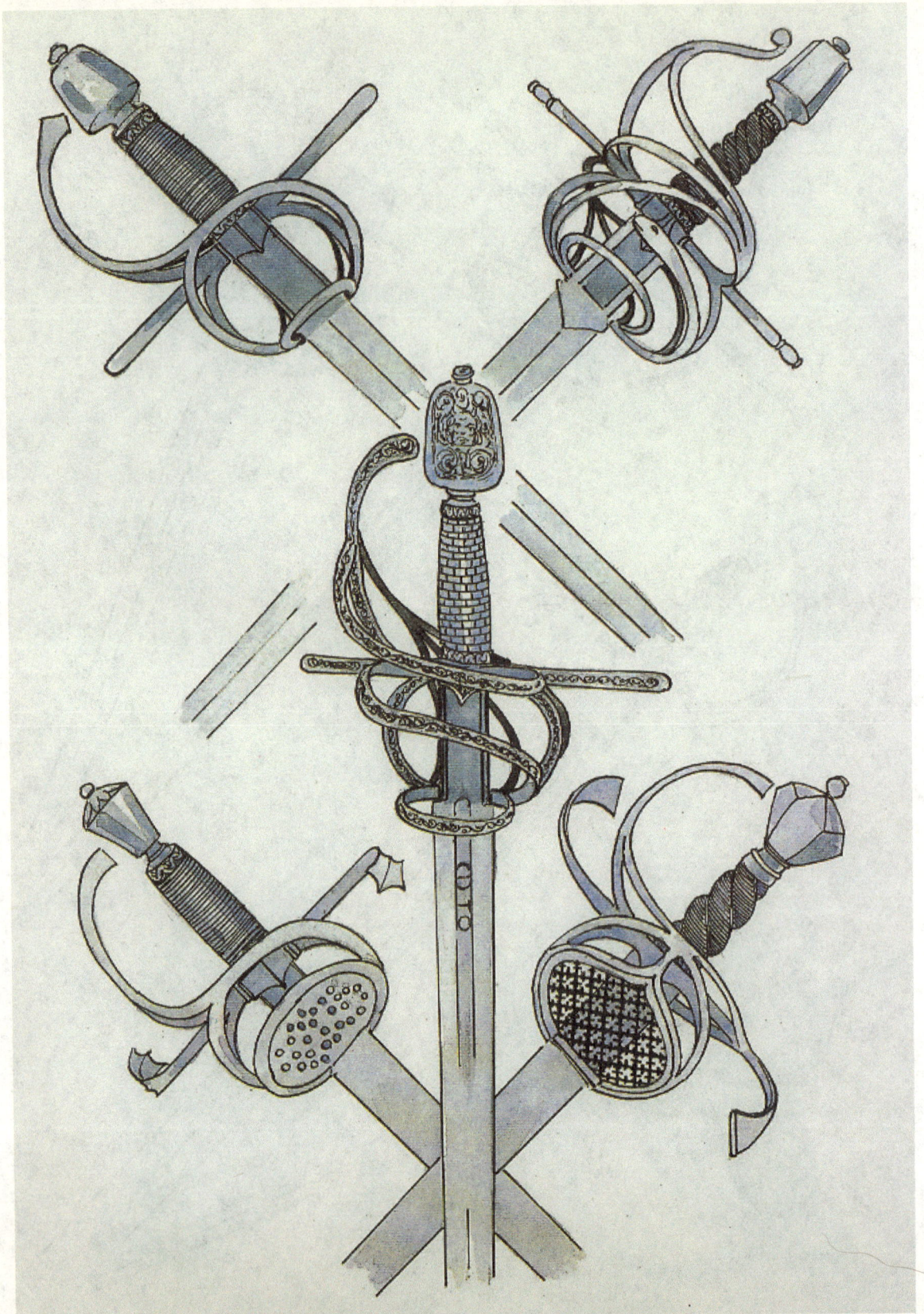

Swept hilt rapiers, first half of 17th century

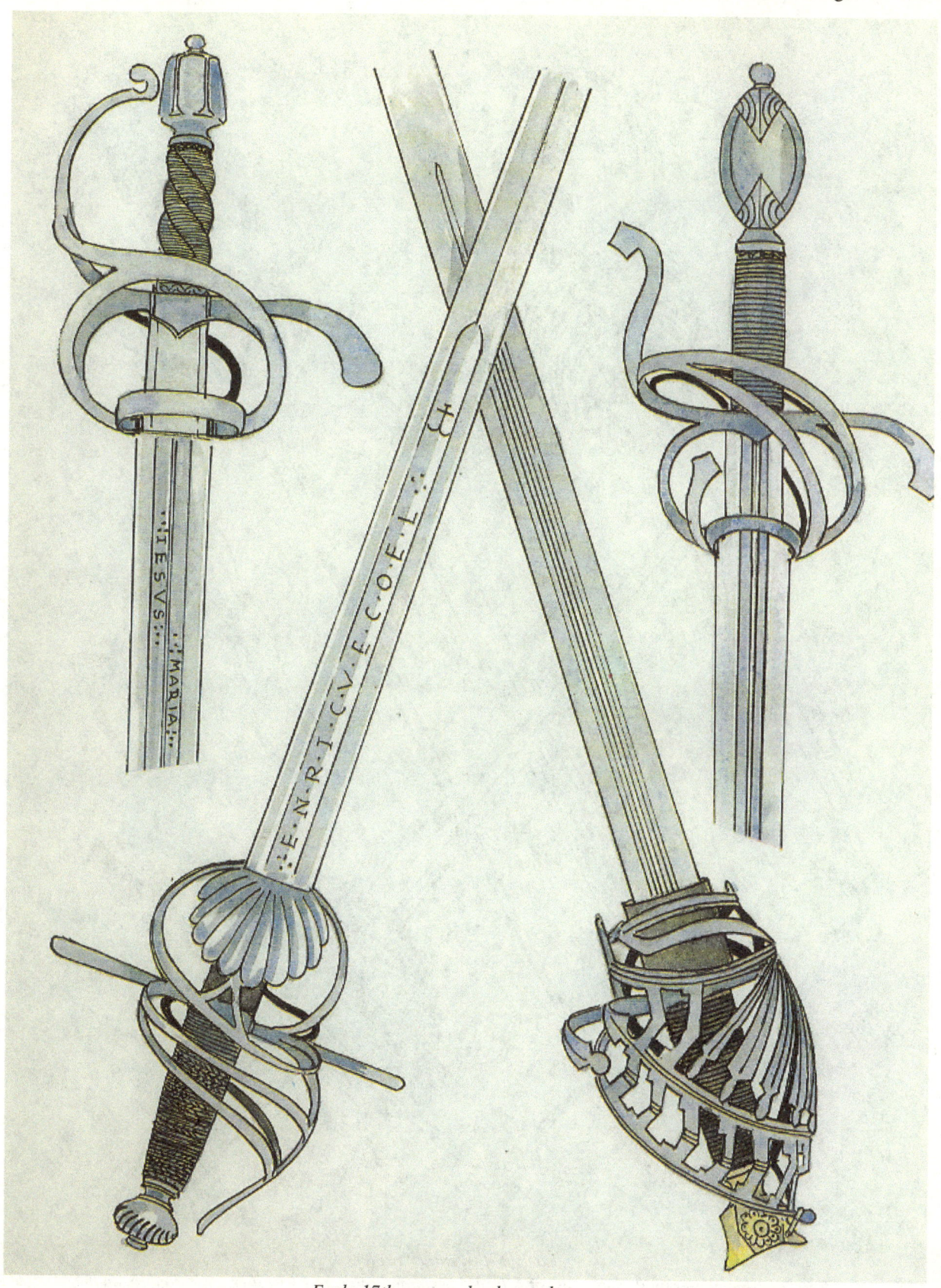

Early 17th-century backswords

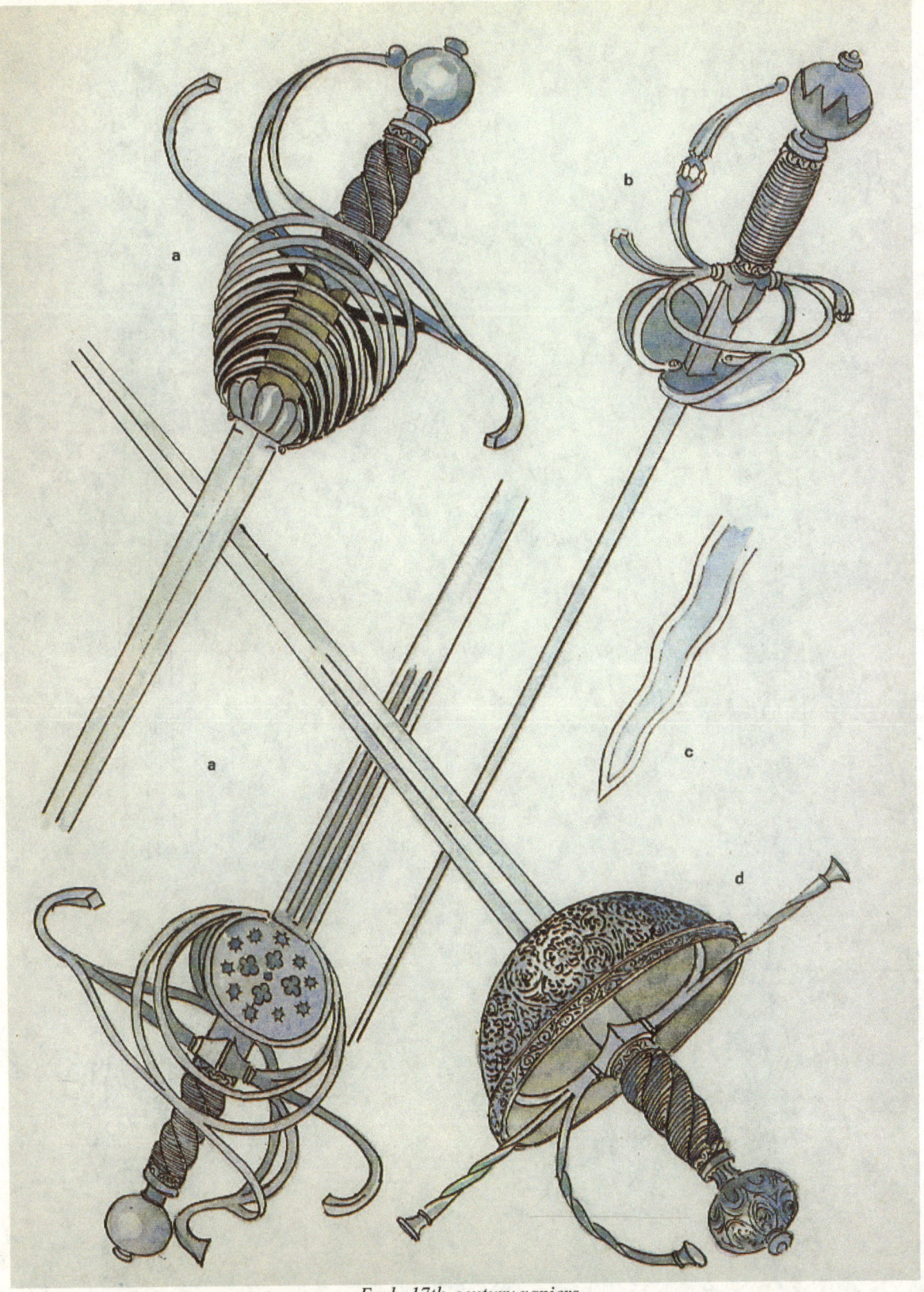

Early 17th-century rapiers
a) Duelling rapier, with dense swept hilt and S-shaped quillon b) Rapier with double shell-shaped guard c) Point of the so-called flame blade d) Rapier with deep cup guard

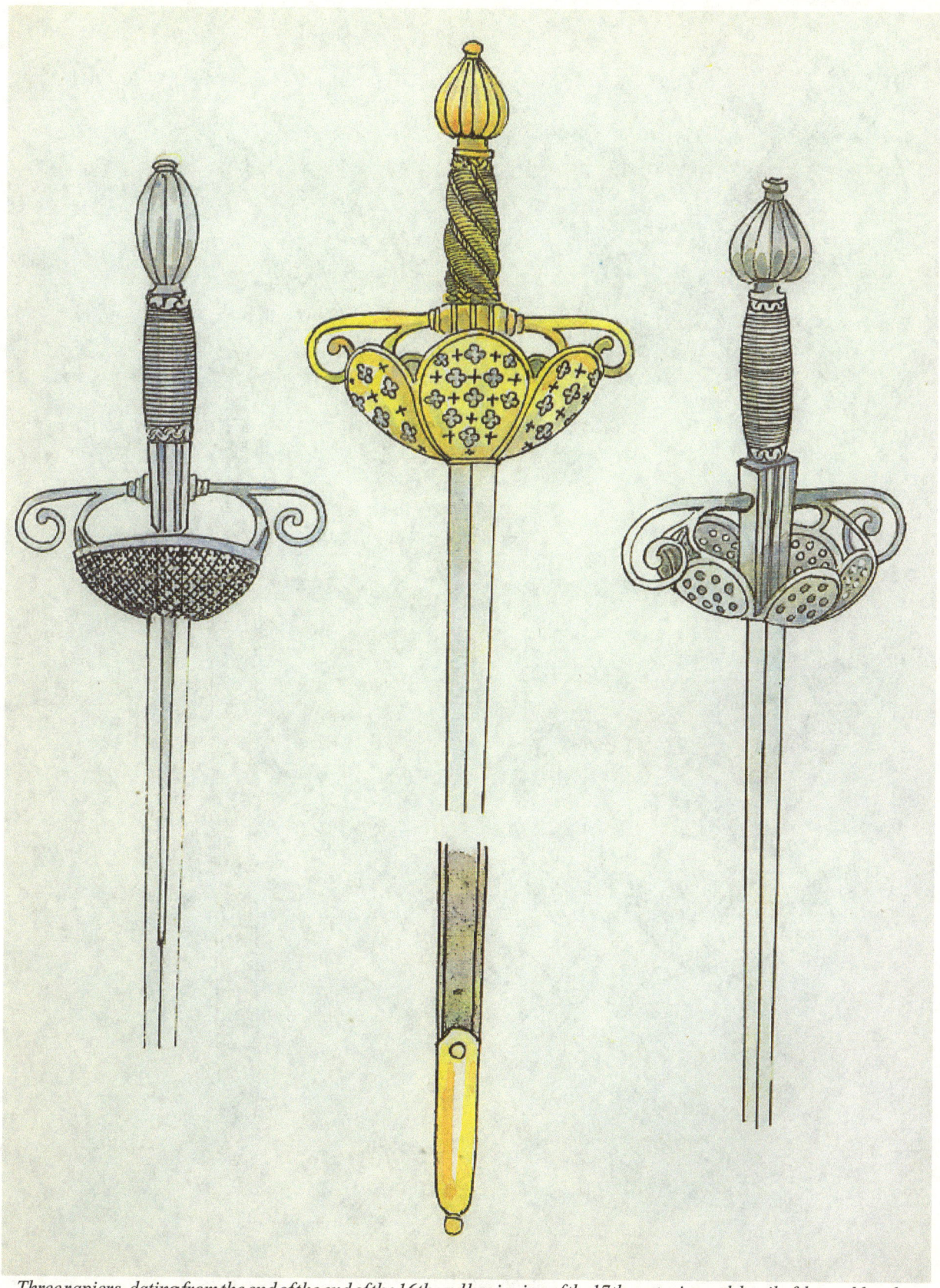

Three rapiers, dating from the end of the end of the 16th and beginning of the 17th centuries and detail of the scabbard

Rapier and dagger sets
Rapier and dagger sets of the same manufacturer bear characteristic features of the warsmith

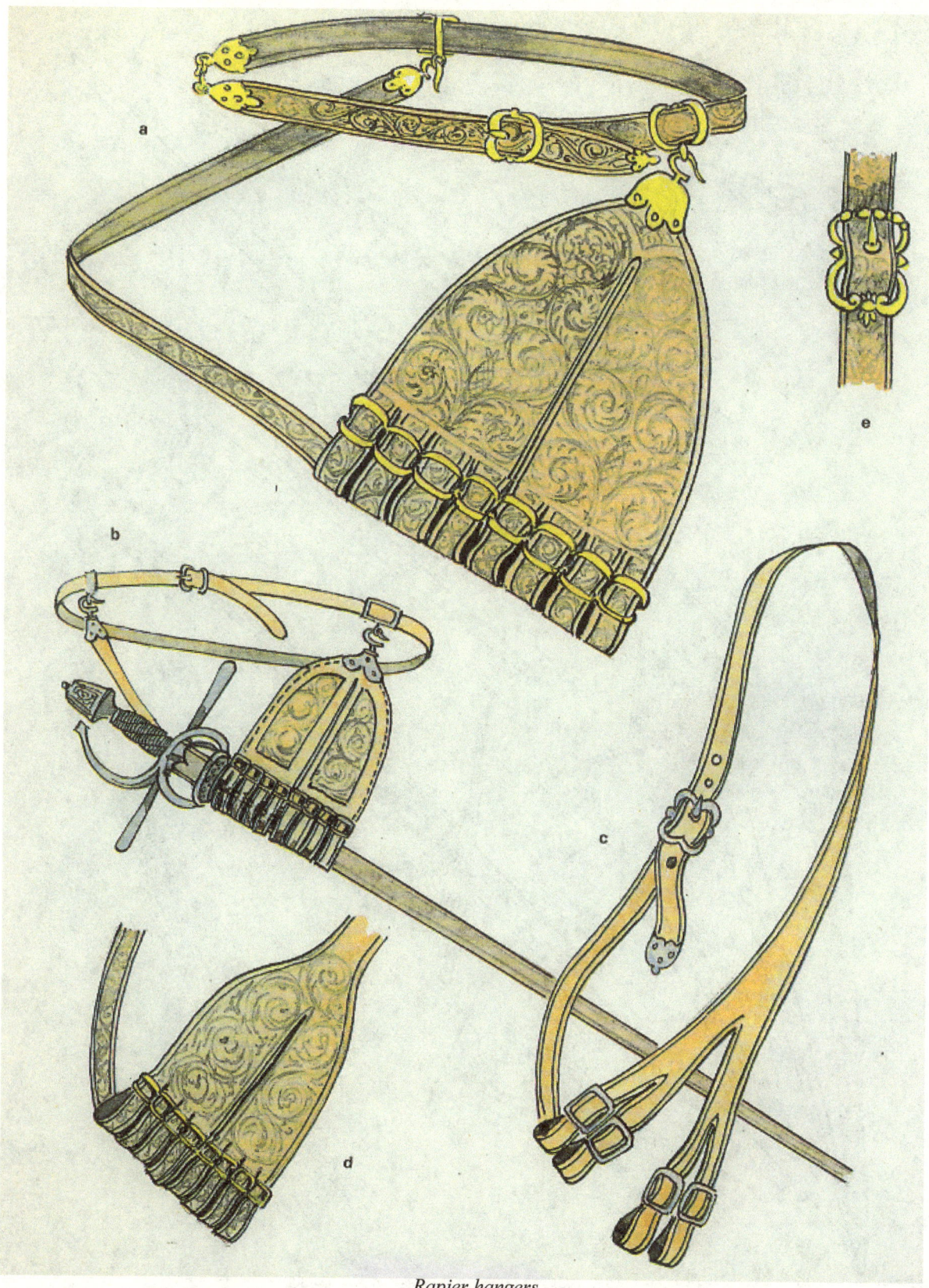

Rapier hangers
a) *Rapier hanger attached to belt* b) *Rapier hanger of the same type, with inserted rapier* c) *Rapier bandolier worn over the right shoulder and on the left hip* d) *Detail of bandolier lower end* e) *Ornate bandolier buckle*

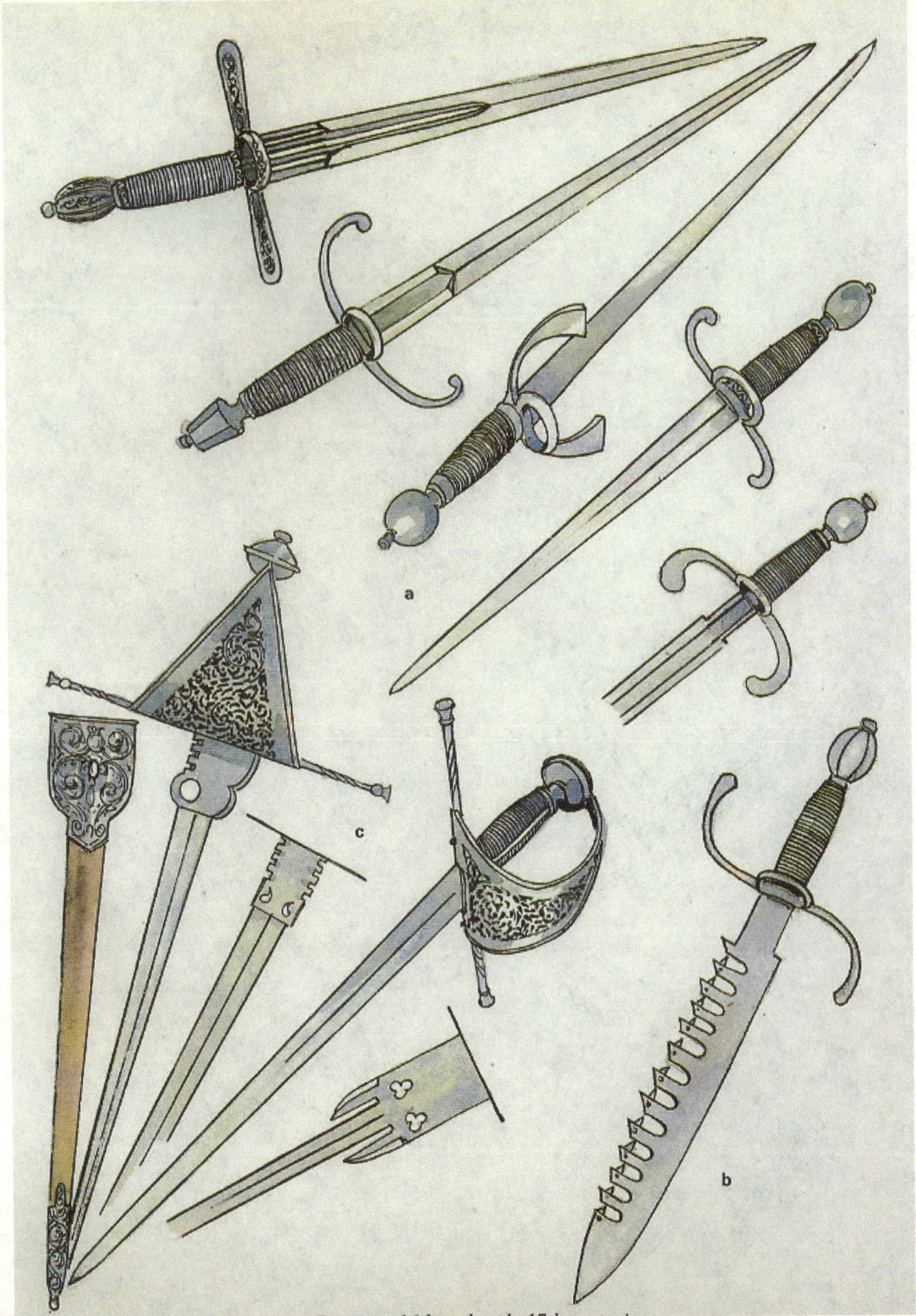

Daggers, 16th and early 17th centuries
a) Common dagger types b) Broad bladed dagger; the blade is equipped with teeth and spring-loaded catches in the latter. The teeth and catches could retain and break the attacker's blade c) Spanish daggers for left hand use

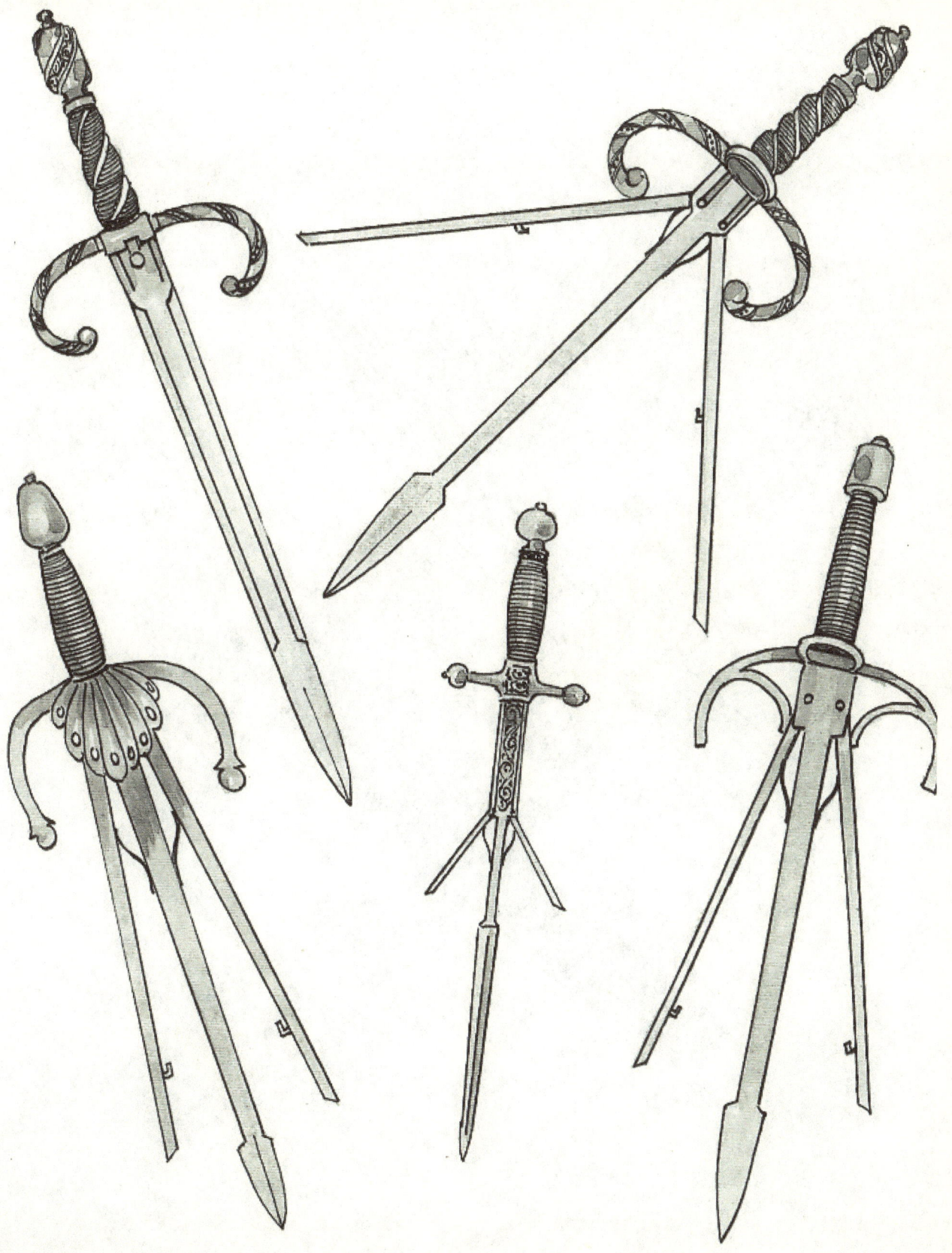

Various types of three-bladed daggers

Sabres
a) Polish sabre b) Hungarian sabre c) Polish karabela sabre d) Turkish sabre with bone hilt and silverwork

Stave weapons
a) Halberds b) Partisan – a weapon as well as insignia of higher officer rank

Weapons of personal guards
a) Halberd of the Saxon personal guards b) Scythe of personal guards,
late 16th century c) Halberds of personal rank-and-file guardsmen

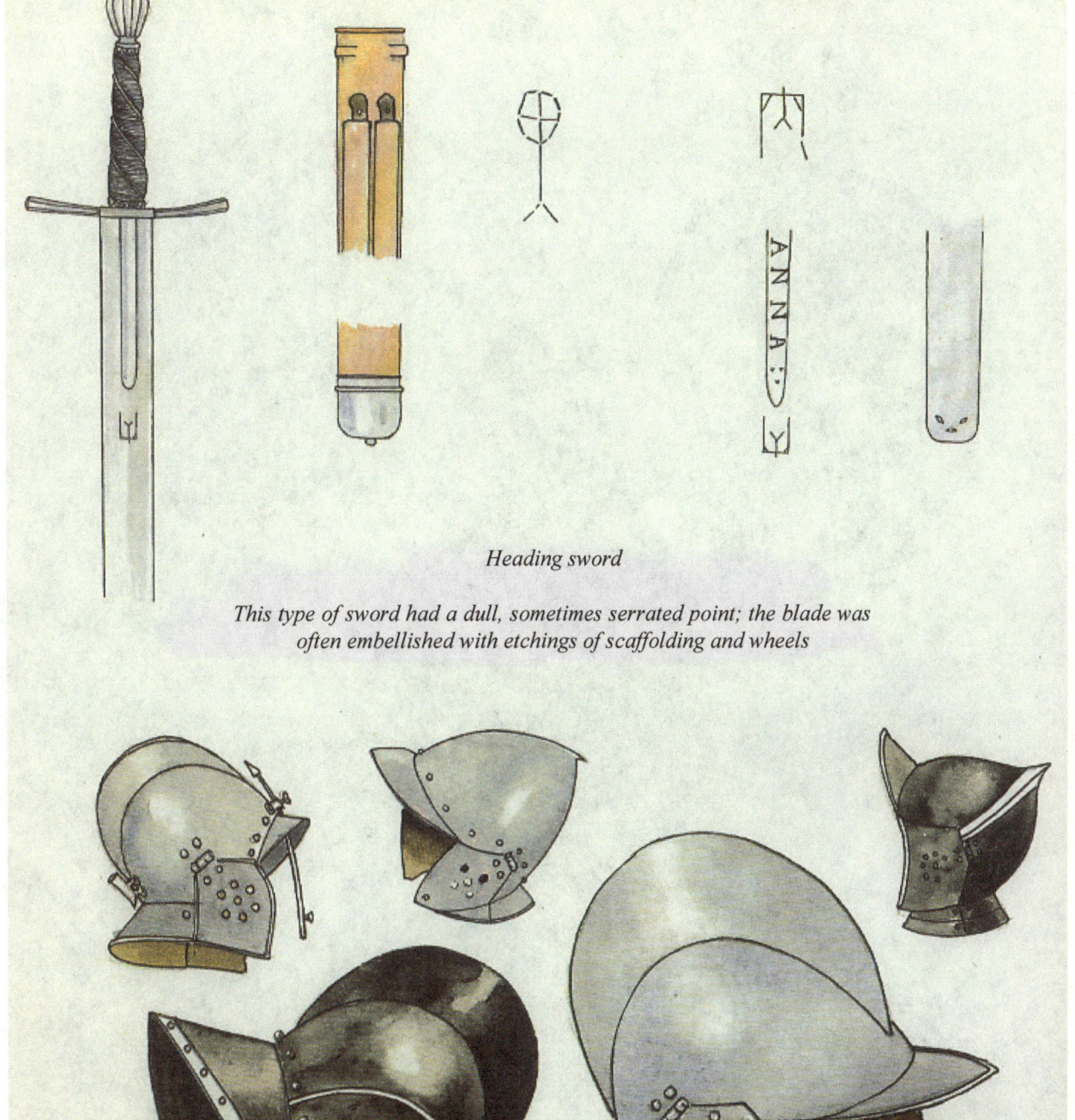

Heading sword

This type of sword had a dull, sometimes serrated point; the blade was often embellished with etchings of scaffolding and wheels

Infantry helmets with cheek pieces

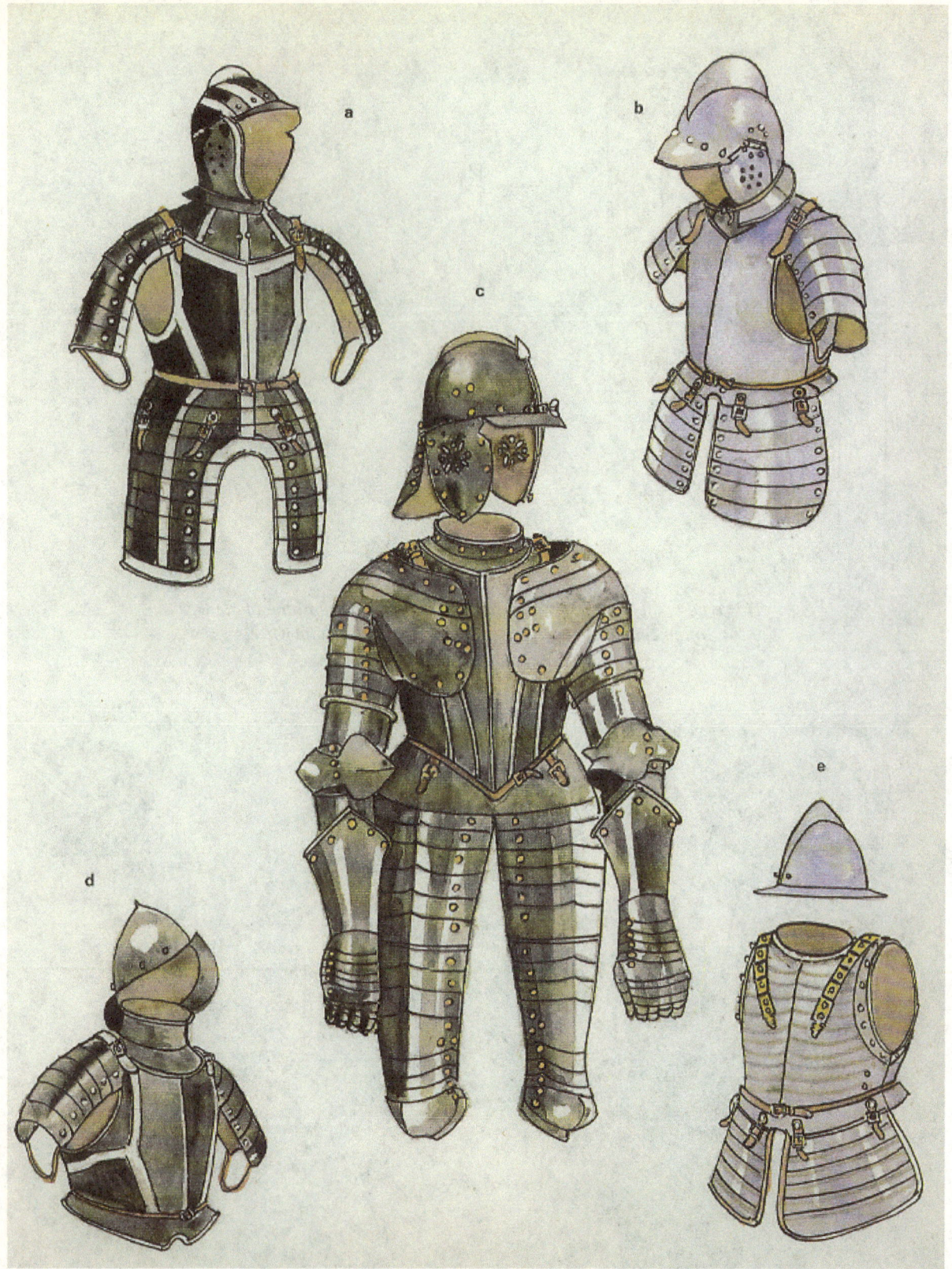

Plate armor

a) Cavalry plate half-armor, late 16th century b) Burnished plate half-armor c) Dark cuirassier half-armor embellished with brass rivets d) Plate half-armor, Germany, circa 1630 d) Infantry officer plate half-armor, early 17th century

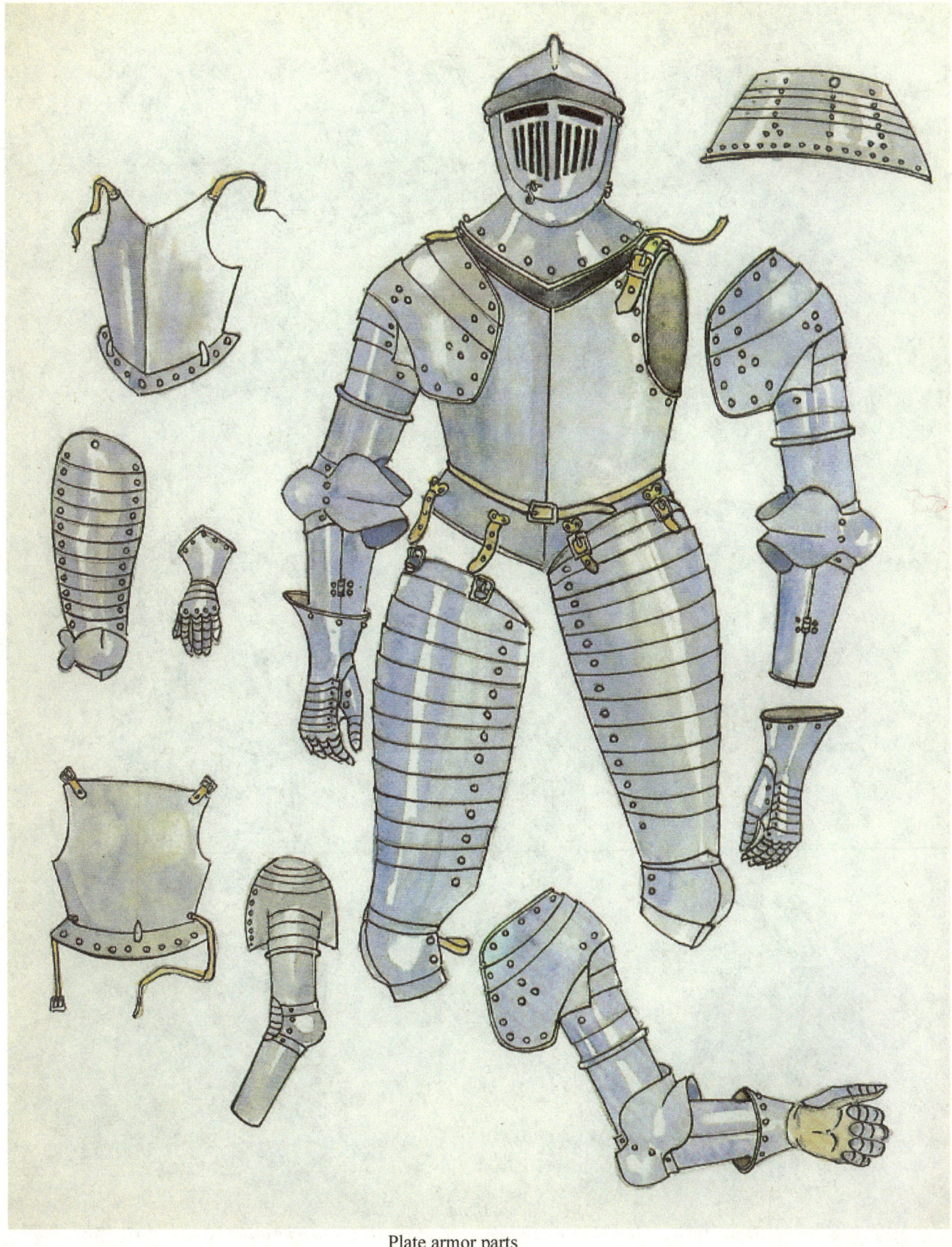

Plate armor parts

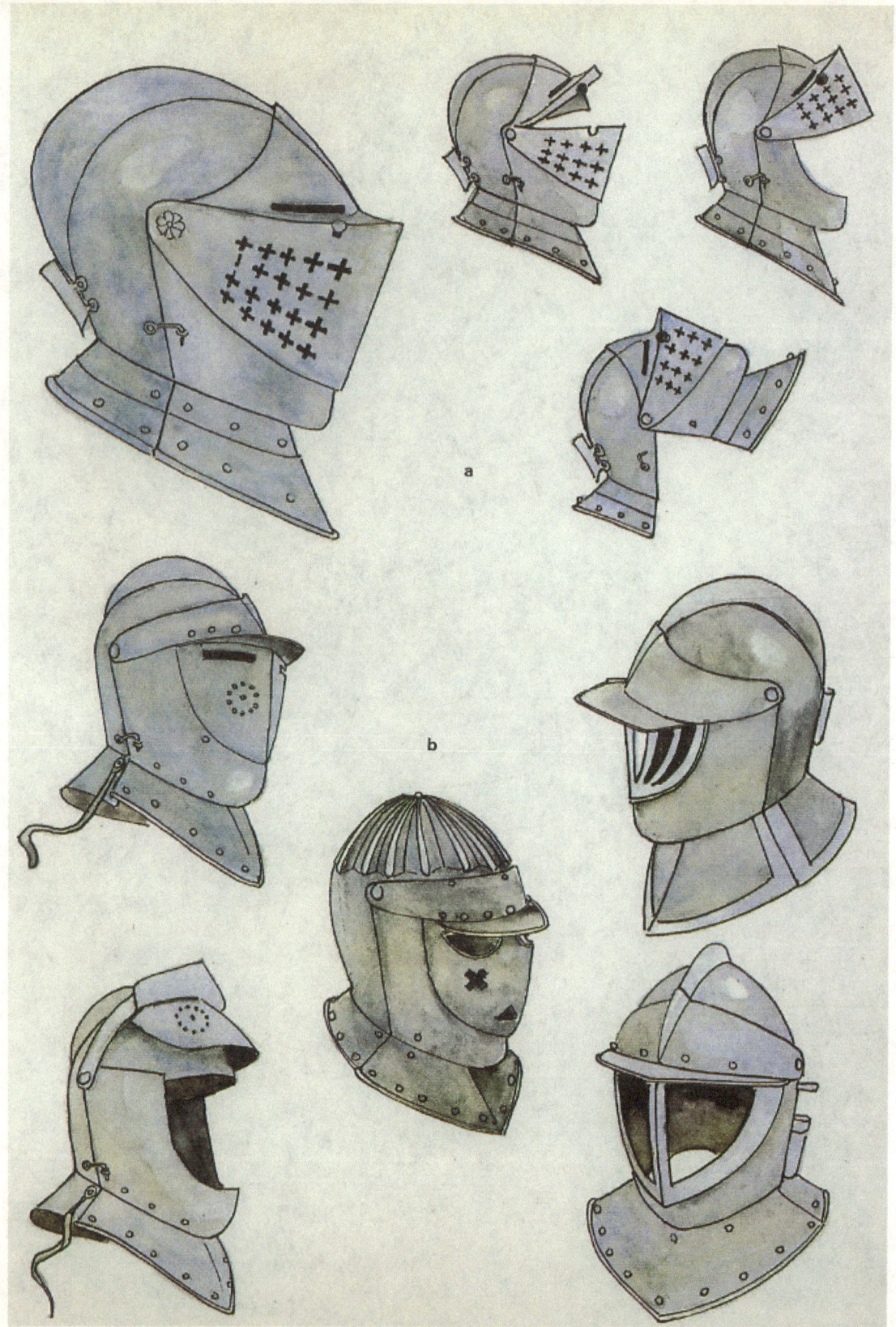

Helmets
a) Closed helmet showing movement of the visor and hinge for removal b) Closed cuirassier helmets, early 17th century

Cavalry lobster-tail burgonets with sliding nasals
a) European types b) Hungarian types c) Polish Hussar type

Infantry helmets, end of the 16th and beginning of the 17th centuries
a) Morion helmet b) Birnhelm helmet

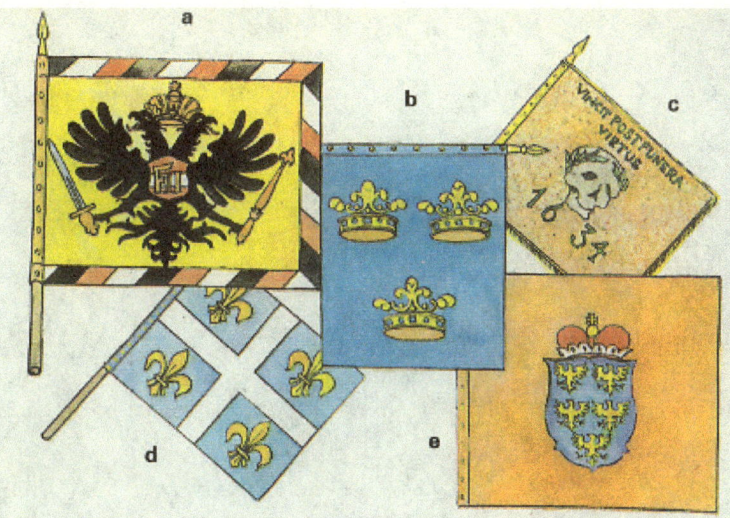

Colors

a) Colors of the Imperial Infantry during the reign of Ferdinand II (1619 – 1637)
b) Swedish colors c) Colors of the Hessian Green Regiment d) Colors of a French regiment,
early 17th century e) Colors of an unidentified Lower Austrian regiment, early 17th century

Colors of an unidentified Imperial regiment
(reconstructed from a painting)

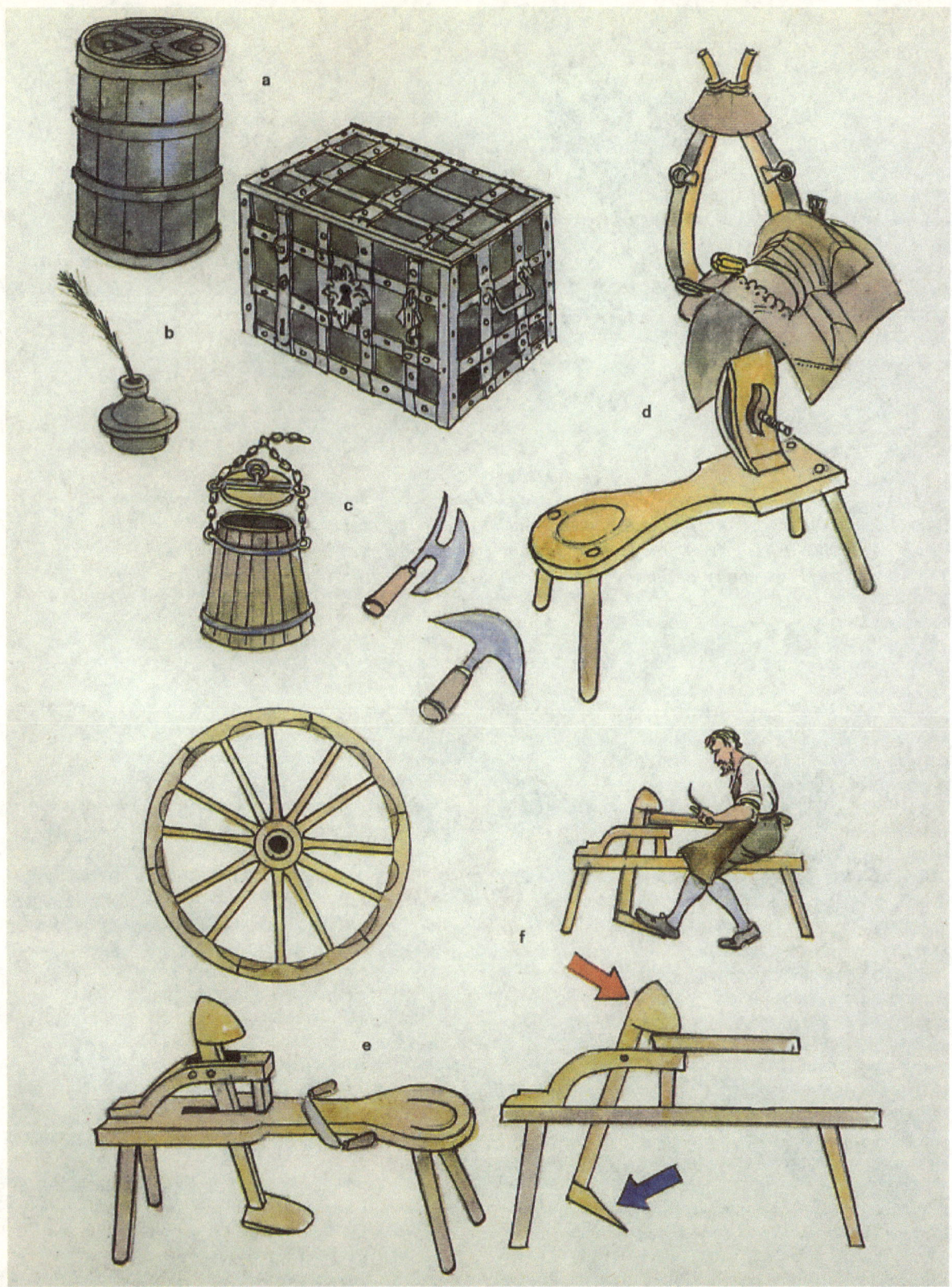

Various equipment used by troops in the Thirty Year's War period a) Iron clad military pay chests b) Inkwell with a quill c) Axle grease pot, with cap, on a chain d) Saddler's stitching horse with block and round leatherworking knives e) Saddler's and wheelwright's benches f) Working on a wheelwright's bench

PROVISIONS FOR THE TROOPS

An army on march during the Thirty Years' War was a threat to the population of friendly as well as enemy territory. Since the soldiers often had no regular pay to speak of and the organization of their provisions left much to be desired, the soldiers solved their plight by taking to a sort of self-help provisioning from local sources, in short by looting, plunder and extortion. The common folk were thankful just to survive and army passage through their countryside, since whenever an army passed through, it left the fields and villages stripped bare.

According to the regulations of the period a provision store was to be set up in every military encampment, located in a safe place, protected against enemy fire and guarded against pilfering by its own troops. In overnight or short-term camps built along the route of the march the provisions were kept store on special wagons guarded by thoroughly dependable sentries. Regulations recommended that sentries should be given enough to eat before going on duty, to be able to devote their full attention to protecting the victuals from their hungry comrades.

Commanders and their deputies in charge of supplying the troops were to issue meat on 16 days in a month. Fish was to be issued on six days; eight days were to be butter-and-cheese days. Out of the 16 meat days eight were allotted to beef, four to mutton and four to bacon and pork. As a side dish to the meat the troops had peas, barley, semolina and sauerkraut. Beans, gruel, dried apples, plums, cherries and pears were also common. As an important and healthy condiment, garlic was recommended.

The meat issued to the troops was fresh or cured – salted or smoked. Butter was either fresh or processed. There were also processed meats such as sausage and Westphalian ham.

In lean time's fish was the staple food, mainly cod but also dried plaice, kippers, pickled herring, fried lamprey, smoked salmon and perch. It was recommended that fish should, if possible, be issued only on fasting days, such as Fridays, and the troops should not be fed on fish daily.

Daily troop rations were also prescribed by the regulations, the exact amount depending on the soldier's rank. Officers' rations were naturally the largest; the smallest rations were issued to rank-and-file troopers who had to deed from them their wives and children as well as themselves. An example of an ordinary trooper's ration was 14 lbs bread, four lbs meat, three lbs cheese, one lb butter, half lb salt and one qt beer. A single infantry or cavalry regiment of 3,864 men are daily 10,592 loaves.

In 1623, General Tilly, Supreme Commander of the Catholic League armies, provided his troops with the following rations: Rittmaster, daily: 8 maass beer; 12 maass wine, 20 lbs bread, 12 lbs meat, two hens, one half or calf. Lieutenant daily: four maass wine, six maass beer, 10 lbs bread, six lbs meat, one quarter sheep or calf. A low non-commissioned officer of corporeal rank was given two maass wine, two maass beer, four lbs bread and three lbs meat daily.

In 1627, when the fighting against the troops of the Danish king reached its culmination, Wallenstein ordered the following rations to be issued daily per head: three lbs bread, two lbs meat and three maass beer. A corporal's ration was doubled and those of the officer were proportionately higher according to rank.

When Wallenstein had been discharged from service and was returning home to Jicin in the autumn of 1630, his enormous entourage consumed weekly no less than six oxen, 57 sheep, 150 hens, 40 lbs bacon, 1,800 eggs and huge amounts of other foods.

The commanding officer of the Imperial troops at the very end of the Thirty Years' War in the country of Schaumburg required for himself 300 guilder in cash weekly and 450 guilder between the men of each of his companies. Apart from this, each company was weekly supplied with 300 scheffel of oats, 10 fuder of hay, 10 fuder of straw, six scheffel of rye, four scheffel of wheat, five scheffel of barley, one head beef, two well-fed head of pork, two calf, four sheep, 15 geese, 20 capons, one half cwt fish, the same amount of butter and 200 eggs.

Food for the army was requisitioned by compulsory food dues which were levied from the people of the district where the army was laying in camp or through which it marched. The war lasting for thirty years, with its permanent and temporary camps and endless marches, was enormous drain mainly on the countries of Central Europe. Never-ceasing campaigns and innumerable battle destroyed the crops before they could even be harvested and army requisitions dramatically diminished the number of cattle, sheep and poultry. Even if a crop of sorts survived, there was not enough labor to harvest and process it.

The problems of army supply gradually became worse and worse during the period. Food prices were growing sky high and the mercenary's pay could buy less and less from the sutlers. All this constantly undermined the troops' morale. An account of the Gallas cavalry's retreat from Holstein to Bohemia may serve as an illustration. The troops passed through deserted and desolate areas where nothing to eat was to be found. Whenever possible, they fed on horse meat. In the end they were so weakened that even when they reached the towns, where at least some food could be scraped together, many troops never recovered, and died in throngs of diseases caused by starvation. According to a chronicler's record, perhaps a single man out of fifty sick survived the ordeal of the famine.

The mercenaries cooked simple dishes in a cauldron. Quite often several men would pool their food and make a hot pot together, a sort of soup or stew, simply putting everything that was to be had in boiling water. Huge copper cauldrons and other copper utensils of various shapes were heated on different types of open fire. If the troops were accompanied by their womenfolk, the latter also took over the cookhouse duty. But the most common method of preparing meat was roasting it on a spit, to be eaten with bread and liberally washed down with ale or wine.

Senior officers often had personal cooks. On their dining tables, there was a good choice of food and there appeared many a favorite delicacy. Whenever a great victory had been won or rich booty taken, the senior officers would organize a sumptuous feast topped with a wild drinking bout. These occasions also meant food times for the ranks, who would have a whole ox, pig or sheep roasted on a spit so that the ever-hungry mercenary could once again fill up his eternally empty stomach.

Military kitchens
a) Roofed military kitchens, built of nailed boards b) Open air kitchen, with typical spit

Typical military encampment buildings and structures
Sutlers' pothouses, shacks and stalls

Early 17th-century cooking utensils

Beer and wine vessels

Soldiers' food

Early 17th-century tableware
a) Platters with paté, lobster, fruit, soft-boiled egg and a pretzel b) Method of holding goblets
c) Knife, fork and spoon d) Fine glass goblets e) Cooling vessel f) Playing cards and smokers'
requisites: match, plug of tobacco, bundle of kindling, various pipes – fire is held in an earthware tripod

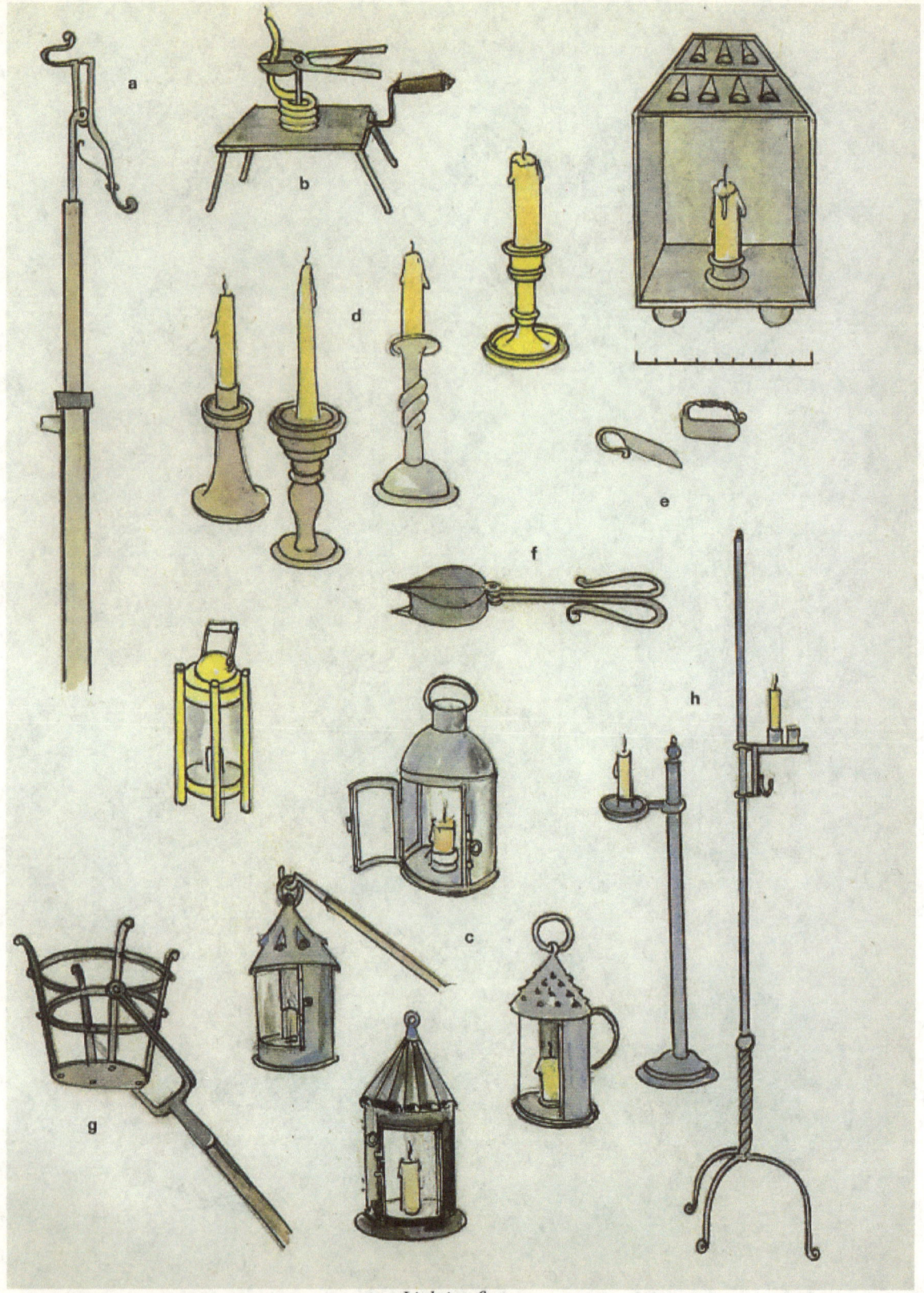

Lighting fixtures
a) Torch holder b) Candlestick with trimming shears c) Lanterns d) Candlesticks e) Flint and steel
strike-a-lights f) Snuffers g) Torch made of iron rods on a wooden handle h) Candelabra

Wooden tubs, piggin, pail, can, wicker baskets, panniers and dossers

SOURCE OF PLATES

ABELINUS, J. Ph.: Theatrum Europaeum (…). Frankfurt-am-Main 1643.

ADAM IF VELESLAVIN, D.: Politica Historica (…). Prague 1606.

ANGER, G.: Illusttrierte Geschichte der k.k. Armee. Vienna 1887.

BENNET, R-ELTON, J.: History of Corn Milling, vol. I. London, Liverpool 1898.

BITAINVIEU DE: L'art universel des fortification francoisses, holandoisses, espagnoles, italiennes, et composees (…) Dubrueil, Jacques – Eschat, Francois, Paris 1685.

BOCHNIAK, A. – BUSZBOWSKI, K.: Rzemioslo artystyczne w Polsce. Warsaw 1971.

BOECKLER, G.A.: Manuale Architecturae Militaris oder Handbuechlein ueber die Fortification und Vestungs, vol. I. Georg Andreas Boeckler, Frankfurt-am-Main 1659/60.

BOCKLER, G.A.: Theatrum Machinarum Novum. Nuremberg 1673.

BOEHN, M. VON: Die Mode XVII. Jahrhunderts. Munich 1925.

BOHATCOVA, M.: Irrgarten der Schucjsale. Einblattdrucke vom Anfang des Dreubigjahrigen Krieges. Artia, Prague 1966.

BREEN, A VAN: Le maniment d'armes de Nassav, avecq Rondelles, Piques, Espees, et Tarques (…). La Haye 1618.

BRY, I.T. VAN: Il Maestro di Campo Generale (…). Iohann Theodorus de Bry, Frankfurt 1617.

CASTLE, E, M.A.F.S.A.: Schools and Masters of Fence. London 1969.

CEDERSTROM, R. – MALMORG, G.: Der alder Livrustkammaren 1634. Stockholm 1930.

CELARIUS, A.: Architectura Militaris (…)

CELARIUS, A.: Amsterodami apud Iodocum Iansonium. 1645.

CSILLAG, F.: Kardok tortenekmunkben. Zrinyi Kiado, Budapest 1971.

CUNNINGTON, P.: Costumes in Pictures. London

DAMASE, J.: Carriages. Weidenfeld and Nicolson, Frankfurt-am-Main 1968.

DEMMIN, A.: Kriegswaffen. Leipzig 1893.

DILICH, J.W.: Peribologia (…) Frankfurt-am-Maine 1640.

DILICH, W.: Kriegsbuch (…) Frankfurt-am-Main 1689.

DILICH, W.: WIlhelmi Dilichii (…) Krieges-Schule (…). Frankfurt-am-Main 1689

DOGEN, M.: L'architecture militaire modern ou Fortification (…). Amsterdam 1648.

DOLLECZEK, A.: Geschuchte der Osterreichischen Artillerie von den fruhsten Zeiten bis zur Gegenwart. Vienna 1887.

ENDRES, F.T.: Deutsche Kunst und Wissenschaft des Mittelalters. Stuttgart.

ENGELHARD, G. VON LOHNEISEN: Hofkrieg- und Reitschule. Nuremberg 1729.

ENGELSHOFEN, V.: Force d'Europe, Staette, Vestungen, Seehafen, Paesse, Camps de Bataille in Europa (…). Gabriel Bodenhauer Kupfferstecher, Augsburg s.a.

ERRARD DE BAR, I., LE DUC: La Fortification. Paris 1622

ESSENWEIN: Quellen zur Geschichte der Feuerwaffen. Leipzig 1877.

FELDHAUS, F.M.: Die Technik der Vorzeit, der geschichtlichen Zeit und der Naturvolker. Leipzig and Berlin 1914.

FER, N. DE: Les Forces de l'Europe (…). Paris 1693-1697.

FER, N. DE – BEAULIEU: Suite des Forces de l'Europe, vol. IV. Pier Mortier, Amsterdam.

FERRARI, E.L.: Velazquez. Skira, Geneva 1960.

FRAUENHOLZ, E. VON: Entwicklungsgeschichte des deutschen Heerwesens. Munich1935-1941.

FROSBENIUS, L.: Weltgeschichte des Krieges. Hannover1903.

FRANSPERGER, L.: Kriegsbuch (…), vol. I. Frankfurt 1596.

FURTENBACH, J.: Halinitro – Pyrobolia (…). Ulm1627.

FURTENBACH, J.: Architectura Militaris (…). Ulm 1630.

FURTENBACH, J.: Architectura Universalis (…). Ulm 1635.

FURTENBACH, J: Mannhafter Kunst Spiehel (…) Augsburg 1663.

GEYN, J. DE: Wappenhandelinge. Amsterdam 1607.

GEYN, J. DE: Die Drillkunst (…) Nuremberg 1664.

GIMBEL, K.: Waffen- und Kunstsammlung (catalogue). Berlin 1904.

GOLDMANN, N.: La Nouvelle Fortification. Elsevier, Leyden 1645.

GRISONIUS, F.: Kuenstlicher Bericht (…) wie die streitbaren Pferde (…) zum Ernst und ritterlicher Kurzweil, geschickt und volkommen zu machen (…). Willer

Georg, Augsburg 1573.

HANZELET, A.J.: La Pyrotechnie (…). Pont Mousson 1630.

HEBERT: Les Fortifications du comte de Pagan (…) Nicolas Langelis, Paris 1689.

HEISTER, L.D.: Chirugye etc. Nuremberg 1779.

HENNE AM RHYN, O.: Kulturgeschichte des Deutschen Volkes. Berlin 1886.

HERGSELL, G.: Die Fechtkunst im XV. Und XVI. Jahrhunderte. Prague 1896.

HIELSCHER, K.: Rumanien Landschaft-Bauten-Volksleben. Leipzig 1933.

HIERSERLE VON CHODAW, H.: Raiβ Buch und Leben (1586-1656). Manuscript in the National Museum in Prague.

HIRTH, G.: Kulturgeschichtliches Bildernuch aus drei Jahrhunderten, vol. IV. IV. Munich s.a.

HIRTH, G.: Kulturgeschichtliches Bildernuch aus vier Jahrhunderten, col. I.G. Hirts Verlag, Munich 1923.

Histoire Générale des Civilisations, XVIe et XVIIe siècles, vol.. IV. Paris 1954.

HONDIUS, H.: Korte beschrijvinge ende afbeeldinge can de generale regelen de Fortificatie, de Artillerie, Munition (…). The Hague 1624.

HUGO, H.: De Militia Equestri Antiqua et Nova (…). Antwerp 1630.

HULSIUS, L.: Tractat der mechanischen Instrumente (…). Frankfurt 1603.

IOAN, H. – SATTLER D.W.: Von Vestungen Schanzen und Gegenschanzen. Basle 1620.

KÄSTNERN, S.: Vestibulum Pyroboliae. Frankfurt 1671.

Katalog zbiorów, wiek XVII, Muzeum Wojska Polskiego w Warszawie. Wydawnictwo Ministerstwa Obrony Narodoqej. Warsaw 1968.

KOMENSKÝ, J.A.: Comenius Joh. Amos: Orbis sensualium pictus. Loutschoviae 1685.

The Kretschmar von Kienbush Collection of Armour and Arms (catalogue). New Jersey 1963.

Kriegsschiff Wasa (exhibition catalogue). Stockholm 1965.

KRÖL VON BEMBERCH, G.G.: Tractatus Geometricus et Fortificationis. Arnheim 1618.

KRUŽICE, J. OF: Koňské lékařství (Horse Healing). Prague 1608.

LANDSTROM, B.: Das Schiff. Saltsjöbaden 1961.

LASSAIGNE, J.: La peinture Espagnolle de Velazquez à Picasso. Skira, Geneva 1925.

LECHUGA, CH.: Descurso del Capitan Christoval Lechuga, en que trata de la Artilleria (…). Malatesta 1611.

LORINI, B.: Delle Fortificationi – Libri cinque. Venice 1597.

LOSTELNAU, C. DE: Le mareschal de bataille contenant le manimant des armes (…) Mignon Estienne, Paris 1647.

MALLET-MANESSON, A.: Kriegsarbeit oder Neuer Festungsbau (…). Amsterdam 1672.

MARTIN, P.: Waffen und Rüstungen. Frankfurt-am-Main 1967.

MEYER, J.: Gründliche Beschreibung der Freyen Ritterlilchen und Adelichen Kunst des Fechtens (…). Joachim Meyer (Frayfechter zu Strassburg), 1570.

MÜLLER, H.: Deutsche Bronzengeschützrohre 1400-1750. Berlin 1968.

MUSCHG, W.: Die Schweizer Bilderchroniken des 15. Und 16. Jahrhunderts. Zurich 1941.

Museo Ameria de D. José Estruch y Cumella (…). Introduction by A. Garcia Llansó. Barcelona 1896.

NADOLSKI, A.: Polish Arms. Side Arms. Wroclaw, Warsaw, Kraków, Gdańsk 1974.

PLUVINEL, A.: Mangeige royal ou l'on peut remarquer le defaut et la perfection du chevalier (…). Paris 1624.

RASTELLI, G.: La Scherma. Milan 1942.

RICKETTS, H.: Fire Arms. London 1956.

ROWSE, A.L.: The Elisabethan Renaissance, The Life of the Society. Macmillan, London 1971.

RUSCELLUS, H.: Kriegs und Archeley Kunst. Frankfurt 1620.

RUSE, H.: Versterckte Vesting Uytgevonden (…) Amsterdam 1654.

SAINT REMY, S. DE.: Memories d'artillerie (…). Paris 1697.

SCHIER, O.: Eine Mährische Wehrverfassung aus dem Jahre 1612. Brno 1914.

SCHULZ, H.: Blut und Eisen (…). Berlin.

SCHWERTFEGER, B.: Die Deutsche Soldatenkunde (…). Leipzig 1937.

SCHILDKNECHT, W.: Harmonia I Fortaliis construendis, defendis & oppugnendis (…). Szczecin 1652.

SPECKLE (SPECKLIN), D.: Architectura von Festungen. (…). 1589.

STRUM, L. CH.: Grundliche und Practische Unterweisung (…). Jeremias Wolfens, Ausburg 1715.

SZENDREI, J.: Ungarische kriegsgeschichtliche Denkmäler. Budapest 1896.

TARR, L.: Karren, Kutsche, Karosse. Budapest 1970.

THETI, C.: Discorsi delle Fortificationi, Espugnationi, et Difese della città, et d'altri Luoghi Vicenza 1617.

THIEL, E.: Geschichte des Kostüms, Berlin 1960.

TOMAN, K.: A Book pg Military Uniforms and Weapons. Artia, Prague 1964.

UFANO, D.: Archeley (…). Frankfurt 1620.

ULLSTEINS WELTGESCHICHTE, Neuzeit I., II. Berlin 1910.

VALENTINE, E.: Rapiers, Arms and Armour Press. London 1968.

VEGETIUS, F.R.: Fl. Vegetius Renantus et alli Scriptores Antiqui de Re Militarii Vesaliae 1670.

VILLE, A. DE: Les Fortifications (…). Lyons 1640.

VIOLET-LE-DUC, E.E.: Dictionaire Raisonné de l'Architecture Francaise du XI. Au XVI. Siècle. Paris 1875.

WAGNER, E.: Hieb-und Stichwaffen. Artia, Prague 1966.

WALLHAUSEN, J.J. VON: Kriegskunst zu Fuss (…). Oppenheim 1615.

WALLHAUSEN, J.J. VON: Ritterkunst (…). Frankfurt 1616.

WALLHAUSEN, J.J. VON: Manuale Militare (…). Frankfurt 1616.

WALLHAUSEN, J.J. VON: Kriegskunst zu Pferde (…). Frankfurt 1616.

WALLHAUSEN, J.J. VON: Romanische Kriegskunst (…). Frankfurt 1616.

WALLHAUSEN, J.J. VON: Archiley Kriegskunst. Hanau 1617.

WEESE, A.: Skuptur und Malerei in Frankreich im XV. Und XVI. Jahrhundert. Potsdam 1927.

WEYGAND: Die Geschichte der Französischen armee. Berlin s.a.

WIKINSON, F.: Militaria. London 1969.

WIKINSON, F.:Arms and Armour. Hamlyn, London, New York, Sydney, Toronto 1971.

WREDE, A VON: Geschichte der k.k. Wehrmacht. Vienna 1901.

ZATOXIL, OF LEVENBURK (LÖWENBRUCK), J.N.: Leto a denopis celého království Starého i Nového měst Pražských léta Páně 1684 (…). (The Chronicle of the Old and New Towns of Prague of Anno Domini 1648). Prague 1685.

ZUBLER, L.: Newe Geometrische Buechsenmeisterey (…). Zurich 1617.

ZYGULSKI Jr, Z.: Broń w dawnej Polsce. Warszaw 1975.

BIBLIOGRAPHY
A SELECTION OF CONTEMPORARY LITERATURE

ABELINUS, J. Ph.: Theatrum Europaeum oder Ausfuehrliche und Wahrhafftige Beschreibung aller und jeder denckwuerdiger Geschichten so sich hin und Teutschlanden (…) zugetragen haben. Frankfurt-am-Main 1643.

BASTA, G.: Il Governo della cavalleria leggier Venice 1612.

BERNEGGERUS, M.: De Fortalitiis. Strasbourg 1616.

BILLON, J. DE: Instructions militaries dividées en six livres. Lyons 1617.

BOGISLAFF VON CHEMNITZ, Ph.: Koeniglichen Schwedischen In Teutschland gefuehrten Kriegs. Szczecin 1652.

DILICH, W.: Kriegsbuch darin die alte und newe Militia allerörther vermehret (…) Baw und Büchsenmeistern au nutz publicirett. Frankfurt-am-Main 1689.

ELERD, F. VON: Newes Kriegs-Büchelein, darinnen tractiret wird, wie anjetzo die Kriege geführet und auch wie dieselben am nüzlichsten zu führen sind. Copenhagen 1647.

FREITAG, A.: Architectura militaris nova et aucta oder Newe Vermehrte Fortification von Regular Vestungen. Leyden 1630, 1631, 1635, 1642, Amsterdam 1654, 1663.

GEYN, J. DE: Wappenhandelinge. Amsterdam 1607.

GUTSCHOWEN, G.: Regula munitiorum. Brussels 1613.

HULSIUS L.: Traktat der mechanischen Instrumente und gründlicher Unterricht des neuen Büchsen-Quadrants. Frankfurt 1603.

KLEIN, D.: Discours, Rathschlag und Bedencken wie und welcher Gestalt das H. Röm. Reich Teutscher Nation wider möchte (…) versöhnt werden. Und wie zu Schutz und Befriedung desselben eine neue Kriegs Wahl unter der jungen Mannschafft anzustellen und solche durch Übung zu Sieg hafften. Soldaten zu machen weren. Stuttgart 1603.

KRÖL VON BEMBERCH, G.G.: Tractatus Geometricus et Fortificationis. Arnheim 1618.

LAURENTIUS À TREUPITZEN: Kriegskunst nach königl. Schwedischer Manier eine Compagny zu richten, in Regiment, Zug und Schlacht Ordnun zu bringen. Frankfurt-am-Main 1633, 1638.

LAVATER, H.C.: Kriegsbüchlein, d.i. Grundliche Anleitung zum Kriegswesen. Zurich 1644.

MAROLOIS, S.: Opera mathematica. Amsterdam 1613-15.

MAROLOIS, S.: Fortification ou architecture militaire tant offensive que defensive. The Hague 1615.

PFAFFEN, F.: Stratiotica antiquanova, von Zustand des alten und neuen Kriegs. Stuttgart 1680.

SCHWACHIUS: Historischer und Theologischer Discurs von der Artigliaria, d.i. von des Geschützes, der Stücke, Mörseln, Feuerwercke, Petarden, und aller darzu gehörigen Kunste. Dresden 1624.

TORSTENII, J.: Secreta munitionum et fortificationum. Stockholm 1614.

TREW, A.M.: Compendium fortificationis oder Kurtzer Mathematischer Underricht von dem Vestung-Baw. Nuremberg 1641, 1652.

UFANO, D.: Tratado de la Artilleria y uso de la platicado. Brussels 1613.

VILLE, A. DE: Traité de Fortification. Lyons 1628.

WALLHAUSEN, J.J.: Kriegskunst zu Fuss. Oppenheim 1615.

WALLHAUSEN, J.J.: Ritterkunst. Frankfurt-am-Main 1616.

WALLHAUSEN, J.J.: Kriegskunst zu Pferde. Frankfurt-am-Main 1616.

WALLHAUSEN, J.J.: Archiley Kriegskunst. Hanau 1617.

WALLHAUSEN, J.J.: Corpus militare, darinnen das heutige Kriegswesen in einer perfecten und absoluten Idea begriffen und vorgestellt wird. Hanau 1617.

WALLHAUSEN, J.J.: Camera militaris oder Kriegskunst – Schatzkammer (…) Frankfurt-am-Main 1621.

ZETTER, J. DE: Kriegs und Archeley Kunst. Frankfurt 1620.

A detailed list of the original prints and manuscripts dealing with the military art of the end of the 16th and the early 17th centuries can be found in:

JÄHNS, M.: Geschichte der Kriegswissenschaften, vornehmlich in Deutschland. Bd. II. (XVII. und XVIII. Jahrhundert bis zum Auftreten Friedrichs des Grossen 1740.) Munich and Leipzig 1890.

Eduard Wagner
SELECTION OF MORE RECENT LITERATURE

ARNOLD, F.: Das Kriegswesen des Hochstiftes Würzburg zur Zeit des Dreissigjährigen Krieges. Würzburg 1934.

BAUSTAEDT, B.: Richelieu und Deutschland. Von der Schlacht bei Breitenfeld bis zum Tode Bernhards von Weimar. Berlin 1936.

BOHATCOVÁ, M.: Irrgarten der Schicksale. Einblattdrucke vom Anfang des Dreissigjährigen Krieges. Prague 1966.

BRANDI, K.: Gegenreformation und Religionskriege. Leipzig 1927.

BUDER, Ch. G.: Geschichte des dreissigjährigen Krieges und des Westphälischen Friedens. Frankfurt 1748.

Documenta Bohemica bellum tricennale illustrata, vol. 1. Prague 1971.

EDWARDS, W.: The Reformation and the Ascendancy of France 1464-1715. London 1965.

ELSTER, O.: Die Piccolomini Regimenter während des 30jährigen Krieges, besonders das Kürassier Regiment Alt Piccolomini. Vienna 1903.

FOGOWITZ, J.: Der Krieg und seine Waffen. Vienna 1915.

FREUENHOLZ, E. VON: Entwicklungsgeschichte des deutschen Heerwesens, 12 volumes. Munich 1935-41.

FRYXEL, A.: Geschichte Gustav Adolf's. Nach der vierten Auflage des schwedischen Originals. Leipzig 1868.

GARDINER, S.R.: The Thirty Years' War 1618-1648 London 1877.

GINDELY, A.: Geschichte des dreissigjährigen Krieges. Prague 1882.

GÜNTHER, W.: Grundzüge der sozialen und wirtschaftlichen Entwicklung in Deutschland im Zeitalter des Dreissigjährigen Krieges. Rostock 1904.

HALLWICH, H.: Gestalten aus Wallenstein's Lager. Leipzig 1885.

HALLWICH, H.: Fünf Bücher Geschichte Wallensteins. Leipzig 1910.

HEXTER, J.H.: Europe since 1500. New York 1971.

HUBATSCH, W.: Das Zeitalter des Absolutismus 1600-1789. Braunschweig 1970.

HUCH, R.: Der Dreissigjährige Krieg. Leipzig 1942. j

JAMES, W.: Habsburg and Bourbon 1494-1789. London 1965.

JANÁČEK, J.: Valdštejnova smrt (The Death of Wallenstein). Prague 1970.

JANSEN, A.: Svenska minnen fran Böhmen och Mähren. Kulturhistoriska skisser fran treorioariga kriger. Lund 1910.

KEYM, F.: Geschichte des 30jährigen Krieges. Freiburg-im-Breisgau 1873.

KLOPP, O.: Der dreissigjährige Krieg bis zum Tode Gustav Adolf's 1632. Paderborn 1891-93.

KOCH, M.: Abrégé de l'Histoire des Traités de Paris entre les Puissances de l'Europe depuis la paix de Westphalie. Basle 1796.

LÍVA, V.: Prameny k dějinám třicetileté války (Sources to the History of the Thirty Years' War). Prague 1955.

MEBOLD, K.A.: Der 30jährige Krieg und die Helden desselben. Stuttgart 1838-40.

MILCH, W.: Gustav Adolf und der 30jährige Krieg. Jena 1926.

MURR, Ch. G.: Bayträge zur Geschichte des 30jährigen Krieges. Nuremberg 1790.

NORDMANN, C.: La montée de la puissance européene 1492-1661. Paris 1974.

PAGES, G.: La guerre de Trente ans 1618-1648. Paris 1939, 1949.

PEKAŘ, J.: Wallenstein 1630-1634. Berlin 1937.

PETRY, W.: Irrwege Europas 1519-1648. Göttingen 1967.

POLIŠENKÝ, J.: Třicetiletá válka a evropská krize 17. Století (The Thirty Years' War and the European Crisis of the 17th century). Prague 1970.

SODEN, F. VON: Gustav Adolf und sein Heer in Süddeutschland von 1631 bis 1635. Erlangen 1865-1869.

SPORSCHIL, J.: Der Dreissigjährige Krieg. Braunschweig 1843, New York 1848.

STEINBERG, S.H.: The Thirty Years' War and the Conflict for European Hegemony 1600-1660. London 1966.

VAYNSTEYN, O.L.: Rossiya I tridtsatiletnyaya voyna 1618-1648. Leningrad 1947.

VILLERMONT, VON: Tilly oder der dreissigjährige Krieg von 1618 bis 1632. Schaffhausen 1860.

WAPLER, R.: Wallensteins letzte Tage. Leipzig 1884.

WATSON, F.: Wallenstein. Soldat unterm Saturn. Berlin 1936.

WEDGEWOOD, C.V.: The Thirty Years' War. London 1938.

WINTER, G.: Geschichte des Dreissigjährigen Krieges. Berlin 1893.

ZANTHIER, F.W. VON: Feldzuege des Vicomte Tuerenne. Leipzig 1779.

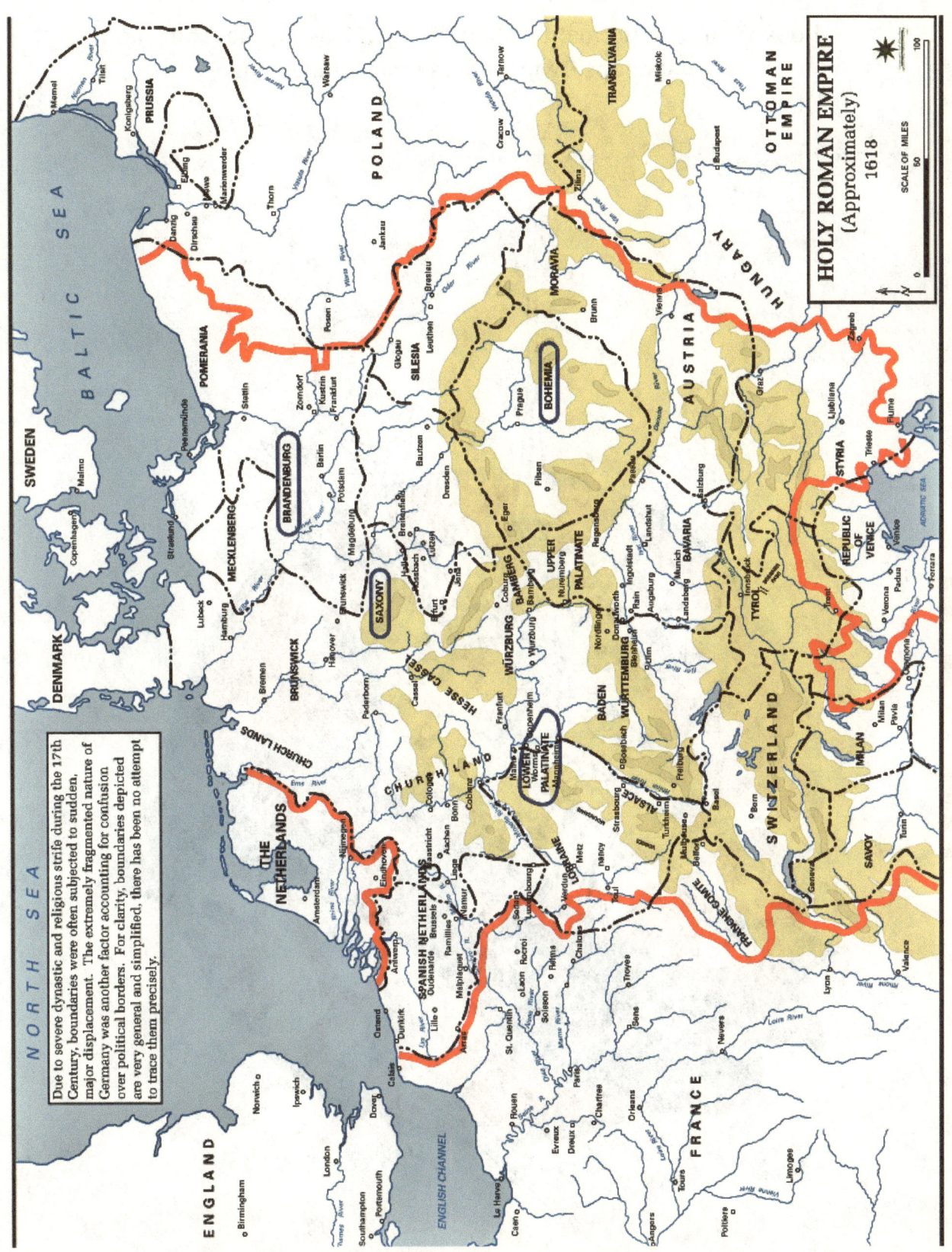

Map courtesy of US Military Academy at West Point

Look for more information about Winged Hussar Publishing at:
www.https://wingedhussarpublishing.com